Organizational Communication

Foundations, Challenges, and Misunderstandings

Daniel P. Modaff

Ohio University

Sue DeWine

Hanover College

Jennifer A. Butler

Ohio University

PEARSON

Boston   New York   San Francisco
Mexico City   Montreal   Toronto   London   Madrid   Munich   Paris
Hong Kong   Singapore   Tokyo   Cape Town   Sydney

Series Editor: *Jeanne Zalesky*
Editorial Assistant: *Brian Mickelson*
Marketing Manager: *Suzan Czajkowski*
Senior Production Administrator: *Donna Simons*
Composition Buyer: *Linda Cox*
Manufacturing Buyer: *JoAnne Sweeney*
Cover Administrator: *Elena Sidorova*
Editorial Production Service: *Modern Graphics, Inc.*
Electronic Composition: *Modern Graphics, Inc.*

For related titles and support materials, visit our online catalog at www.ablongman.com.

Between the time website information is gathered and then published, it is not unusual for some sites to have closed. Also, the transcription of URLs can result in typographical errors. The publisher would appreciate notification where these errors occur so that they may be corrected in subsequent editions.

ISBN-10: 0-205-49349-1
ISBN-13: 978-0-205-49349-4

Library of Congress Cataloging-in-Publication Data

Modaff, Daniel P.
  Organizational communication : foundations, challenges, and misunderstandings / Daniel P. Modaff, Sue DeWine, Jennifer A. Butler.—2nd ed.
    p. cm.
  Includes bibliographical references and index.
  ISBN 0-205-49349-1
1. Communication in organizations. I. DeWine, Sue II. Butler, Jennifer A. III. Title.
HD30.3.M62 2008
658.4'5—dc22

                                                                              2007005780

Printed in the United States of America

10 9 8 7 6 5 4 3 2 1   11 10 09 08 07

This book is dedicated to our families
with gratitude and appreciation
for their love and support.

CONTENTS

Preface   xi

Acknowledgments   xiv

PART ONE   Foundations

1 Introduction   1

Defining the Study and Practice of Organizational
Communication   2

The Prevalence of Misunderstandings   5

The Changing Nature of Organizations   8

The Realities of a Diverse Workforce   9

Ethical Frameworks and Organizational Communication   13

Three Important Constructs   18
Organizational Identification   18
Job Satisfaction   20
Communication Satisfaction   20

Summary   21

2 Classical Theories of Organizations   23

The Metaphor of the Machine   24

Minimizing Misunderstandings   24

Taylor's Theory of Scientific Management   26
Elements of Scientific Management   27
Scientific Management in the Modern Workplace   29

Fayol's Administrative Theory   31
Principles of Management   31
Elements of Management   34
Administrative Theory in the Modern Workplace   35

Weber's Theory of Bureaucracy   37
Tenets of Bureaucracy   38
Bureaucracy in the Modern Workplace   39

Summary   40

3 Humanistic Theories of Organizations 42

Human Relations Theory 42
Misunderstandings and the Emergence of the Worker 43
The Beginning of the Human Relations Movement: The Hawthorne Studies 44
The Emergence of Communication: Chester Barnard 49
Theory X and Theory Y: Douglas McGregor 53

Human Resources Theory 57
Four Systems of Management: Rensis Likert 59
Blake and Mouton's Managerial Grid 63

Summary 66

4 Systems Theory 68

Misunderstandings and the Organization as a System 68

Systems Framework 70

Principles of General Systems Theory 71
Open-Systems Theory Principles 72

Characteristics of Organizations as Systems 74
Input-Throughput-Output 75
Feedback and Dynamic Homeostasis 75
Equivocality and Requisite Variety 76
Role of Communication 77
System, Subsystems, and Supersystems 77
Boundaries 79
The "Closed" System 79

Contingency Theory 81

The Learning Organization 82

Summary 86

5 Organizational Culture Theory and Critical Theory 87

Organizational Culture Theory 88
What Is Organizational Culture? 88
Misunderstandings and Organizational Culture 90
Two Perspectives on Organizational Culture 91
Definitions of Organizational Culture 97
Schein's Model of Organizational Culture 100

Critical Theory   103

Organization as a Site of Domination   103

Power, Hegemony, and Concertive Control   104

Communication and Critical Theory   108

Critical Theory: Issues and Challenges   109

Summary   112

6 The Communicative Organization   114

Talk as Action: Structuration and the Communicative Organization   115

Structuration Theory   117

The Communicative Organization Model   122

Anticipate Misunderstandings   122

Social Interaction   127

Strategic Communication Planning   129

Summary   133

PART TWO   Challenges and Misunderstandings

7 Realistic Recruitment   134

When Applicants and Organizations Misrepresent Themselves   135

Misrepresentation by the Applicant   136

Misrepresentation by the Organization   137

The Costs of Traditional Recruiting   138

The Human Factor   138

The Financial Factor   140

Addressing the Problem: Realistic Recruitment   141

How RJPs Work   142

The Medium of the RJP   142

Time of Administration of the RJP   146

Realistic Recruitment and the Communicative Organization   146

Summary   147

8 Socialization of New Members   149

The Need for Information   150

Organizational Assimilation   154
Anticipatory Socialization   155
Organizational Encounter   156
Metamorphosis   158
Criticisms of the Assimilation Approach   160

Organizational Socialization   160
Factors Affecting Socialization: Loyalty and Congruency   161
Socialization Processes   163

Emotions in Organizational Settings   169
Emotional Labor   171

The Challenges of Work and Family   174

Summary   176

9 Conflict in the Organization   177

Defining Conflict   179

How Does Conflict Start?   180

Consequences of Conflict   182
Negative Consequences of Conflict   182
Positive Consequences of Conflict   184

Individual Conflict Styles   184
Diversity and Gender as Related to Conflict Styles   187

Organizational Responses to Conflict   188
Resolution or Management   188
Alternate Forms of Dispute Resolution   190

**Individual and Organizational Conflict Management
and Resolution Strategies   192**
Individual-Level Strategies   192
Organizational-Level Strategies   193

Summary   194

10 Superior–Subordinate Communication   196

Nature and Importance of the Superior–Subordinate Relationship   198

The Prevalence of Misunderstandings in the Superior–Subordinate Relationship   199

A Dyadic View of the Superior–Subordinate Relationship   203

Communication Activities: Superior to Subordinate   206
Trust   206
Immediacy   208
Feedback   209
Compliance-Gaining   212
Humor   213

Communication Activities: Subordinate to Superior   214
Upward Influence   214

Women and the Superior–Subordinate Relationship   215

Summary   217

11 Peer and Coworker Communication   218

Nature of Relationships in Organizations   218
Proxemics   220
Relational Communication   220
Relational Balance   221
Interpersonal Needs   221
Relational Control   222

Relationship Development in the Workplace   223

Positive Consequences of Workplace Relationships   226

Negative Consequences of Workplace Relationships   228

Romantic Relationships in the Workplace   228
The Organizational Perspective on Workplace Romance   231

Relationship Deterioration   233

Strengthening Workplace Relationships   234
Provide Positive Feedback   234
Mediate Conflict   235
Discuss Communication   235
Help Manage Relationships   235

Summary   237

12 Organizational Teams   238

Characteristics of Teams   239
Relational Communication   239
Decision Making   241
Norms   241
Cohesiveness   242
Diversity   243
Satisfaction   244
Stress   245
Stuckness   246

Teams at Work   246
Types of Organizational Teams   248
Connecting Teams with the Environment   248

Self-Managed Work Teams   250

Virtual Teams   252

Effective Teams   254

Misunderstandings and Organizational Teams   255

Summary   257

13 Leaders and Leadership   258

Overview of Leadership   259

Development of Leadership Theories   261
Trait Approach to Leadership   261
Situational Approach to Leadership   262
Charismatic Leadership   265
Transactional and Transformational Leadership   266
Feminist Perspectives on Leadership   268

Communication Concepts and Effective Leadership   270
Message Delivery: Impression Management and
Communicator Style   270
Impression Management   270
Communicator Style   271
Building Trust   273

Responsibilities of Leadership   274

Power and Ethics in Leadership   277

Passion   279

Summary   280

14   Communication Technology in the Organization   281

Overview of Communication Technology   282
Basic Forms of Communication Technology   284
Criteria for Selection of Mediated Communication   289

Communication Technology and Virtual Ways of Working   292
Telework and Telecommuting   293
Communication Technology and Monitoring Employees   296

Applying Organizational Theory to Communication Technology   297
A Structuration Perspective on Communication Technology   297
A Critical Approach to Communication Technology   298

Summary   299

Bibliography   301

Index   316

PREFACE

In preparation for writing the first edition of this book we conducted more than 60 interviews with leaders and workers in a variety of organizations. For this second edition, we have conducted an additional 40 interviews. We attempt to weave stories from our interviewees throughout the book to breathe life into and illustrate the concepts and theories discussed. These interviews revealed a common theme that organizational life tends to be characterized by what we (broadly) term *misunderstandings*. The concept of misunderstandings, as we use it here, involves more than ineffective communication between members of an organization; it is an umbrella term used to connote the problematic nature of interaction in organizational settings. Misunderstandings seem to characterize communication in organizations. As organizations develop, both productive and unproductive features emerge, such as layers of hierarchy, opposing goals, struggles for power, use of technology, gender and cultural differences, reward systems, and control mechanisms. These features serve to complicate the communication process at almost every moment, such that misunderstanding is at least as prevalent as understanding.

This edition of the book offers many new additions, including:

- The integration of new interview data throughout the book.
- A new chapter on leaders and leadership.
- An additional section on feminist organizations.
- A significantly expanded discussion of structuration theory.
- A revised communicative organization model.
- An expanded description of the metamorphosis phase of assimilation.
- A new section on emotions in organizations, including a discussion of emotional labor.
- A new section on the challenges of work and family.
- A significantly revised chapter on conflict in the organization, which includes additions in the areas of organizational responses to conflict and individual and organizational conflict management strategies.
- A new section on humor in the superior–subordinate relationship.
- A significantly revised chapter on peer and coworker communication that includes additions in the areas of consequences of workplace relationships, romantic relationships in the workplace, and relationship deterioration.
- A significantly revised chapter on organizational teams, with new sections on teams at work, self-managed work teams, virtual teams, and misunderstandings in the team environment.
- A significantly revised chapter on communication technology in organizations, with new sections on instant messaging; videostreaming; the Internet, intranets, and extranets; telecommuting and work-family balance; and the application of current theories to communication technology.

This book is written for an introductory course in organizational communication. In writing this book, we made several assumptions: (1) students will have had some previous course in communication; (2) the purpose of this course is to familiarize students with the basic elements of the field of organizational communication; and (3) students will cover methodological and philosophical orientations of organizational communication more deeply in a subsequent advanced course.

Given these assumptions, we had to make choices regarding content. For example, we have not included chapters on external organizational communication (e.g., public relations) or macro-organizational communication (e.g., organizational memory, lifespan). Our intention is to focus on internal communication and organizing issues that are on the organizational behavior level.

The title of the book describes our twofold intentions—to introduce basic concepts and to deal with misunderstandings. In Part One, we expose students to the foundations of organizational communication. Therefore, in early chapters we offer extensive discussions of the foundations of the discipline. Chapter 1 introduces students to the field of organizational communication and discusses the central organizing feature of the text—*misunderstandings*. It includes introductory material on ethics and diversity; issues in these areas are woven throughout the rest of the book, particularly in Part Two. Chapter 2 lays the foundation for the field by examining the classical management theories. Chapter 3 describes the progression from the classical theories to those based more on concern for individuals. We have chosen to treat the theories of human relations and human resources together in this chapter because they are so closely linked. Chapter 4 covers systems theory and the learning organization, which represents a shift from material dedicated to prescriptive theories of organizational communication and management to theories that provide an analytical framework. Chapter 5 continues with additional analytical frameworks for understanding communication in organizations and focuses on organizational culture and critical theory. Chapter 6 presents a new model for organizational communication, the *communicative organization*. This model is based on the acceptance that misunderstandings will occur and that organizations should be prepared for them. The way to prepare is to determine if these misunderstandings can be resolved or if they are issues with which the organization must learn to live.

In Part Two, we present challenges and misunderstandings, which underscore our particular approach to the field of organizational communication. Throughout Part Two, we have attempted to frame the topics traditionally covered in organizational communication textbooks in terms of misunderstandings and to illustrate the relevant issues with excerpts from the interviews we conducted or from current news stories. Chapter 7 explores the concept of realistic recruitment. We use it as the beginning of Part Two in order to show that organizational communication is a process that begins even before an individual becomes an official member of the organization. Chapter 8 continues with the next step of the process, detailing the socialization of organizational members. Conflict in the organization is the focus of Chapter 9. Chapter 10 explores the relationship and communication between supervisors and subordinates. Chapters 11 and 12 examine communication in other important organizational relationships—among peers and within teams, respectively. Chapter 13 is new to the second edition and provides an overview of communication as it relates to leadership in organizational settings. The final chapter, Chapter 14, offers a discussion of communication technology and its impact on communication in modern organizations.

ACKNOWLEDGMENTS

This book would not have been possible without the help of many people. We would like to thank the staff at Allyn & Bacon, particularly Karon Bowers and Jenny Lupica, for giving us the opportunity to pursue a second edition of this textbook in the way we envisioned it.

Several people served as research assistants for us on the first edition of this book, and their work is still evident in this edition. Carey Noland, Amy Stelzner, and Charney Fitz conducted interviews and gathered research for us in the early stages of the project. Several others conducted interviews for the second edition, and we truly appreciate their assistance: Courtney McAtee, Diana Stolar, Teresa Calanni, Holly Hamman, Trischa Snyder, Tom Ramage, Allison Smith, Bridget Kelly, and Aly Boggs.

Many people contributed helpful insights and stories that have found their way into this book in some fashion. They include Mark Collins, Kelly Crawford, Jeanne Erichson, Leslie Jarmon, Caryn Medved, Phil Modaff, Roberta Modaff, Kristie Luebbe, Vanessa Schaber, and William Moss. We would also like to thank Liane Gray-Starner for her hard work in constructing the instructor's manual for this edition.

Finally, we appreciate the reviewers around the country who took the time to help us improve this textbook from the first edition: Sandy H. Hanson, University of North Carolina, Charlotte; and Calvin Brant Short, Northern Arizona University.

We hope you enjoy reading this book as much as we enjoyed writing it.

Dan Modaff
Sue DeWine
Jennifer Butler

Introduction

Modern organizational life is complex and complicated. Consider the following situation described by Caden, a 49-year-old inside sales/customer service representative for a large manufacturing company:

> The trend in many industries recently has been for large, global organizations to swallow up former competitors, blending them into their corporate culture. As a former employee of one of these smaller companies being absorbed, I can state that these transitions are anything but smooth. One of the first tasks of the new management of the acquiring organization is to reduce the workforce by eliminating unnecessary and redundant positions. The same process must occur with the products. The process of eliminating competing or duplicative products began almost immediately with little concern for customer needs. This resulted in the elimination of various products still in demand by important customers. Our location became the main source for all customer purchases and inquiries. Although offering us some sense of job security, we blindly fumbled our way through a rough transition.
>
> Management offered very little training, and customers who were accustomed to exceptional service now were confused and finding their needs unmet. All of a sudden the "experts" in the field who were familiar with the products were gone, replaced by new management with limited knowledge and experience. It has been three years now since the acquisition, and unfortunately the effects of quick management decisions and poor communication throughout the newly formed company are still being felt in our division. Before we can react to changes within and adjust, more changes are occurring. Our jobs have become more difficult, but more importantly our customers' confidence and commitment to our products and services have suffered.
>
> For example, I now have to deal with multinational customers, but I do not have the appropriate foreign language training. The other day I was dealing with a Spanish-speaking customer, but I do not speak Spanish. Because I did not have the background to communicate effectively, and the customer did not have English language skills either, his order did not go to the right place, and did not even contain the right equipment.

Caden's situation shows the realities of the modern workplace. Mergers and acquisitions, a global economy, disparate organizational cultures, corporate downsizing, lack of attention to training, insufficient customer focus, a profit-driven marketplace, management complacency, and a host of other issues came to bear on this organizational member's life. Any perspectives could be taken (e.g., legal, material, or functional) to help to understand this situation and others like it, but none address the core issue from which the others arise—communication.

How different might this situation have been if communication was the primary concern? The relatively hostile acquisition may have been managed and communicated as a partnership instead of as an instance of marketplace domination. Cultural specialists would have been on staff from the very beginning to help the newly partnered companies bridge cultural differences and assist the employees with the necessary language training and appropriate cultural sensitivities. Managers would have not only communicated to the remaining organizational members about the changes that were occurring, but would have constructed opportunities for them to participate in the planning and implementation of the newly formed organization's goals and mission. Finally, the development of an organizational culture that reflected the needs and expectations of the members of the newly partnered companies could have been fostered through social interaction.

A communication-centered approach to the study of organizations is the basis of the field of organizational communication. It is our intention in this book to provide you with an overview of the field of organizational communication and to demonstrate the critical role communication plays in most every aspect of organizational life.

Defining the Study and Practice of Organizational Communication

Organizational communication as a discipline seeks to help people understand the central nature of communication in all aspects of organizational functioning. As we examine the process of communicating within an organization, we view organizations as instruments created to achieve other ends. It is rare that an organization is established as an end in itself. Rather, an organization may be established to realize some goal, such as selling a product, providing a service, or generating an income. Connie Bullis (2005) helps us understand this idea:

> Organizations accomplish much of what changes history. They get presidents elected, wage war, make laws, create jobs and work experiences, commit crimes, save souls, create cures, engage in research and development, look out for community well being, produce the goods and services people use, and so on. (p. 596)

The English word *organization* comes from the Greek word *organon*, which means "tool" or "instrument." Communication is both the means by which that tool or instrument (the organization) is created and sustained *and* the prime coordinating mechanism for activity designed to attain personal and organizational goals. Hence, communication and organization are intimately interrelated.

The definition of organizational communication that we propose is a slightly modified version of one developed by Fred Jablin (1990a, p. 157). According to our definition, *organizational communication* is the process of creating, exchanging, interpreting (correctly or incorrectly), and storing messages within a system of human interrelationships. Central to this definition is the concept of a message. A *message* is a "nonrandom verbal symbolization" (Stohl & Redding, 1987, p. 452). In other words, a message is a use of language (written or spoken) that the recipient interprets as having been created intentionally. The focus on language use becomes important as a means of differentiating the study of organizational communication from related fields, such as management and industrial psychology, and as we develop the central feature of the text—misunderstandings.

Inherent in the definition of organizational communication are several assumptions and features (we will cover these elements in greater depth in Chapter 6):

- Communication is central to the existence of the organization; it creates and re-creates the structure that constitutes the organization. That structure, in turn, affects the nature and flow of communication within it.
- Organizational communication as "process" indicates its dynamic nature. The concept of process implicates the past, present, and future, such that communication within an organization at a particular moment in time is dependent upon prior conditions as well as expectations for the future. For example, a particular interaction between a superior and a subordinate at a given point in time (the present) is related to their prior interactions and interactions with other superiors and subordinates (the past) and their expectations for how they will interact in the future.
- Communication involves more than the physical act of exchanging messages. Communication is an inherently complex process that also includes the cognitive energy associated with creating, exchanging, interpreting, and storing messages.
- Things can go wrong at any point in the communication process and often do. Throughout this book we will refer to this very broadly as "misunderstandings." The concept of misunderstandings, as used here, involves more than ineffective communication between members of an organization; it is an umbrella term used to connote the problematic nature of interaction in organizational settings.
- Misunderstandings seem to characterize communication in organizations. As organizations ("systems of human interrelationships") develop, both productive and unproductive features emerge, such as layers of hierarchy, opposing goals, struggles for power, use of technology, gender and cultural differences, reward systems, and control mechanisms. These features serve to complicate the communication process to such an extent that misunderstanding is as prevalent as understanding if not more so.

Researchers in organizational communication study the various elements associated with our definition in a variety of ways. All the following research topics have the study of messages as a common theme. Researchers attempt many tasks:

- Examining the flow of messages in the organization to determine how information is disseminated.
- Investigating the role of emotion in organizational decision making and the execution of members' job duties.
- Studying relationships in the organization (e.g., between superiors and subordinates or between peers) and how those relationships are created, maintained, and dissolved through communication.
- Examining the role communication has in the development of organizational spirituality.
- Attempting to understand the process of organizing.
- Identifying how formal and informal policies regarding family medical leave are communicated to workers, and how that communication affects the use and abuse of those policies.
- Describing the interaction between technology and human communication.
- Analyzing the creation and maintenance of democracy in the workplace.
- Analyzing how communication can serve to produce and reproduce power structures that serve to oppress workers.
- Studying control mechanisms in work teams.
- Studying the intricate relationship between communication and organizational culture.

This list is just a sample of the kinds of topics relevant to the study of organizational communication. All of them are important for an effective communication specialist in the organizational environment.

Organizational communication researchers Dennis Mumby and Cynthia Stohl (1996a) point out that a common theme among all of these concepts and research activities is language: "The use of language as a symbolic means of inducing cooperation in beings that by nature respond to symbols, constitutes our disciplinary foundation . . . a concern with collective action, agency, messages, symbols, and discourse" (p. 53). How messages are sent and understood, through the use of language, forms the basis of communication study in general and organizational communication specifically. For this reason, we offer a message-centered definition of organizational communication and integrate issues of the creation, exchange, interpretation, and storage of messages throughout the text.

Mumby and Stohl (1996) suggest that students of organizational communication are:

> well equipped to address contemporary workplace issues (such as the development of a temporary workforce, the implementation of teams, the adoption of new technologies, and multiculturalism) because they are trained to focus on the complex and collaborative nature of communicating, organizing, and knowing. (p. 54)

These skills—communicating, organizing, and knowing—are central to effective membership in any organizational setting. As partial evidence of this, the *Job Outlook 2006* study conducted by the National Association of Colleges and Employers showed that communication skills are considered critical by potential employers. Communication skills, along with honesty/integrity, topped the list of important candidate qualifications. Being articulate about ideas; understanding the task of organizing individuals, teams, projects, and thoughts; and knowing how to learn are the foci of the field of organizational communication.

In this initial chapter, we introduce issues and concepts that provide the foundation for the chapters that follow. We begin by presenting a central feature of this book—the notion of misunderstandings—followed by an outline of the changing nature of organizations. Next, we give an overview of diversity in organizations and then turn to a sketch of ethics. We conclude the chapter with three common processes and outcomes relevant to the study and practice of organizational communication: organizational identification, job satisfaction, and communication satisfaction.

The Prevalence of Misunderstandings

The central idea of this book is that organizational life is inherently problematic and that communication plays a major role in the creation and resolution of this quality. As the number of people in an organization increases, the following phenomena also tend to occur:

- More levels of hierarchy *or* more work teams with more members
- Cultural, age, sex, gender, religious, and value differences
- Struggles for power
- Emergence of sub- and counter-organizational cultures
- Competition among peers for scarce resources
- Increased use of impersonal communication media

As you can see from this much abbreviated list, organizational life, almost by definition, is fraught with problems in human interaction.

We have chosen the term *misunderstandings* to represent the inherently problematic nature of organizational life. In her book on misunderstandings in interpersonal relationships, Julia Wood defines misunderstandings as "instances in which people who are communicating don't share meanings" (1998, p. 8). This book expands on Wood's definition to include situations in which features of organizational life (such as those just listed) serve to impinge upon the efficient and effective functioning of organizational members. We chose the term *misunderstandings* because it highlights the central nature of communication.

Our use of the term *misunderstandings* is in no way meant to oversimplify the complicated nature of organizational functioning. Truly, many organizational problems are caused by a lack of "shared meaning" between organizational members owing to the limits and constraints of language, but just as many are related to deeper organizational characteristics. Consider the following story relayed to the authors from a development manager named Ian Lambert. Although on the surface it may seem to be an instance of a lack of shared meaning between people, the problem is much deeper and is related to many issues, including organizational culture, technology use, relationships between superiors and subordinates, and organizational alliances.

I help resell my company's products to other outlets. I form partnerships between my company and another company that could use our software. The job is part marketing and part sales. We do voice data systems; for example, when you call up a bank or a clothing store and you hear menu choices, that's our software.

Approximately six months ago, I engaged a corporation in discussions toward a strategic alliance between my organization (Company A) and another corporation (Company B). The alliance would involve the reselling of our core product line to Company B's base of existing clients, as well as creating new products based on our technology. Things were progressing quite well and we were in the process of contract negotiations when Company B merged with another organization. Although this presented a host of problems, ranging from support to a new management infrastructure, I was confident that we were still working under our agreed-to timelines for executing the agreement. Company B's president and CEO, my main contact, was now the chief financial officer and VP of strategic technologies in the newly merged company (Company C). Therefore, I thought I had the right individual on my team in order to close the agreement quickly. Also, you should know that if this deal went through, my commission would be close to $20,000. My boss also thought that we needed to execute the agreement quickly so I could spend my time on other pending relationships. Like most organizations, quarterly revenues drive us, and as the end of the quarter approached, I was presented with a communication problem.

On Monday the 29th, I had a very good conference call with executives from the newly merged company (Company C) and felt that we could get the deal executed in due time. On Tuesday the 30th, I spoke with Company C about 9 A.M., which was about noon their time. We spoke briefly on a few issues and agreed to resolve all remaining issues during a noon conference call. As a result, I assembled my president and CEO; my VP of sales; and my boss, the director of channel sales, to speak with the executives from Company C on any concerns they might have had or changes that needed to occur within the body of the agreement. Company C never showed up for the call.

I unsuccessfully attempted to track them down and the afternoon wore on. Hours passed with no response or messages. My executive team grew increasingly impatient and was very disappointed in the lack of communication. Thus, once 5:00 P.M. had passed (8:00 P.M. their time), I assumed that this company had decided not to partner with us and their lack of communication spoke to a lack of interest in moving forward. I left voice mails concerning the termination of our relationship. I was under a lot of pressure and overreacted in the way I presented that message. I said I was personally and profession-ally disappointed in their lack of communication and that we should cease all future conversations. Then, out of the blue, I was paged and Company C wanted to chat on getting the agreement executed. I was amazed and embar-rassed.

Since they had not communicated to me that they could not make our scheduled meeting, I had decided that they must not want to form the part-nership. I had reacted too quickly and without enough information and made assumptions. After I apologized to them, they explained that there had been some situation going on due to restructuring and that had distracted them. Had I received the correct information, I wouldn't have jeopardized the deal, my company's reputation, and my personal reputation.

Although on the surface Ian's account may seem to be a "simple" case of mis-communication, the misunderstandings associated with it were much more com-plicated than that. An examination of the narrative shows that several issues were at play here that led to the problem:

- Company B's merger and the eventual formation of Company C meant a significant change for Company A. Internal organizational functioning is interdependent with changes in the relevant environment of the focal or-ganization.
- The fast pace and profit-driven nature of modern organizational life created a situation where a delay of a few hours caused tremendous concern and the flow of potentially damaging communicative action.
- Reliance on conference call technology meant a removal of important layers of relevant information. A lack of personal presence (i.e., face-to-face meet-ing) caused members of Company A to jump to conclusions regarding the lack of contact with Company C.
- In light of the seemingly broken deal, Ian was confronted with the need to save face in front of his superiors. To do so, he reacted more negatively and sternly than he should have and perhaps would have if his superiors had not been privy to the problem.

Although these were certainly not the only issues relevant to this case, it is obvious that this misunderstanding was not merely a matter of a lack of shared meaning. It was much more complex than that. When we use the term *misunder-standings* in this book, we are referring to situations such as this one.

Now that we have introduced the general topic of misunderstandings and how it relates to life in organizations, in the next section of the chapter we discuss how conceptions of organizations have changed in the past few decades. As you read about these changes, keep in mind how each affords opportunities and advantages for organizational members while at the same time it creates new are-nas for misunderstandings to arise.

The Changing Nature of Organizations

Over the past several decades, the way academics and practitioners have thought about organizations and how they should be structured has changed. Changes in thought have translated to changes in practice in many organizations, often to the benefit of the members and the bottom line. In other ways these changes have created a climate of stress in the work environment. The globalization of corporations today, combined with the competitive pressure and a diverse workforce, has forced organizational members to be highly flexible and responsive to change. Table 1.1 summarizes these changes.

The first major change for many organizations has been the shift from hierarchical, or tall, organizational structures to decentralized, or flat, structures. A tall organization has many layers through which messages and instructions must go before reaching the workers. A flat structure has few reporting levels, and managers have a much larger span of control, meaning that a greater number of individuals report directly to one person. A large span of control may make the job of supervision more complicated and time consuming; however, the advantage is wider participation in decision making. Ellis (2003) provides evidence that organizational structures are indeed flattening by showing that "the managerial levels between the CEO and the lowest-level managers with profit-center responsibility (division heads) have decreased by more than 25 percent" (p. 5).

In a flat organization, decision making is shared among a larger group of individuals. Participative decision making (PDM) is often a key characteristic of flat organizations. To the extent that a manager wants someone to implement and be supportive of a decision, she should allow that individual the opportunity to participate in making the decision.

A second major difference in thought about organizations has been a shift from a climate of authority characteristic of prior decades to a climate of coaching. Many contemporary organizations use the term *coaching* as a password for management. Instead of controlling the behavior of others through authority (e.g., fear of punishment), supervisors are now encouraged to coach individuals to increase productivity. Thomas Crane (1998) attempts to give managers a better understanding of coaching by defining it this way:

TABLE 1.1   Organizational Changes

Feature	1960s–1980s	1990s to Present
Organizational structure	Hierarchical, tall	Decentralized, flat
Climate	Authoritative	Coaching, empowering
Competition	Local, national	Local, national, global
Communication flow	Top down	Multidirectional, complicated

> [Coaching is] a comprehensive communication process in which the coach provides performance feedback to the coachee. Topics include broad, work-related dimensions of performance (personal, interpersonal, or technical) that affect the coachee's ability and willingness to contribute to the meaningful personal and organizational goals. (p. 31)

When a person becomes a coach instead of a supervisor or manager, it means the focus has shifted from control to support, though we suspect that many supervisors still attempt to control employees' behaviors even when they call what they are doing "coaching."

Another term that has entered management vocabulary is *empowerment*. When people are given decision-making responsibility, they are empowered to act on their own. It makes sense that an organization would want thinking individuals who can act on their own with good judgment. In order to empower others, managers have to trust employees to make wise choices.

One of the most significant contributors to stress in the workplace is competition. The third major change is that today an organization's competition is no longer just local or national, but global. Communication information technologies, such as the Internet, that expand the reach of a particular organization have made this a reality. Whereas once an organization's scope of business was constrained by geography, now even a small, local retailer has the chance to enter the global marketplace. The effect of this is that organizations must consider that their competition can come from anywhere around the world, not from just down the block. Consequently, certain skills and knowledge are at a premium. Knowledge of the international marketplace is essential, as is being comfortable in many types of cultural environments.

All these developments have definitely changed communication within organizations. The new coaching style demands the sending of different messages in different ways from those employed under an authority-based system. Competition demands quicker responses, and a variety of cultural environments require a heightened sensitivity in communicating messages. As hierarchies flatten and self-managed work teams dominate organizational structures, communication flows in every direction and, in doing so, becomes quite complicated.

It is important to remember that the changes discussed in this section may not reflect current reality for every organization, but they certainly hold true for many. The next section of this chapter focuses on important changes in the workforce that affect every organization.

The Realities of a Diverse Workforce

One of the most dramatic changes in organizations has been the diversification of the workforce and the need to integrate workers of many cultures, backgrounds, and ideologies. When we talk about diversity in the workplace, we are including people of all kinds of diverse backgrounds. Brenda Allen (1995) suggests that "diversity in the workplace encompasses a variety of personal and social bases of identity, including race-ethnicity, gender, age, socio-economic status, and country of origin" (p. 144). As a way of understanding the breadth and depth of the reality of diversity in the workplace, consider the following statistics. According to the U.S. Department of Labor, in 2003 almost 60 percent of women in the United States worked full time, compared to 41 percent in 1970. In 2004, the Department of Labor reported that women held nearly half of all management and professional occupations. While there were approximately 18 million women in the workforce in 1950, it is projected that there will be 92 million by the year 2050.

The U.S. labor force has also changed in terms of race and ethnicity. According to Toossi, in the 2002 *Monthly Labor Review* published by the Department of Labor, the percentage of white non-Hispanic workers is expected to decrease from 73 percent in 2000 to 53 percent in 2050. This same report also predicted that the Hispanic workforce would double by 2050 to 24 percent, while the African American population will increase by 14 percent. Lien in the 2004 edition of *Occupational Outlook Quarterly* stated that the fastest growing minority segment of the workforce is Asians and predicts that between 2002 and 2012 the labor growth rate for Asians will be 51 percent, compared to only about 3 percent for Caucasians.

Although gender, race, and ethnicity are the most commonly discussed diversity variables, other forms of diversity do exist in the U.S. workforce. As the Baby Boom generation (individuals born between 1946 and 1964) ages, the percentage of older workers has increased in the workforce. While the 55-and-older age group comprised only 13 percent of the workforce in 2000, it is predicted that this group's presence will increase to 19 percent by 2050.

The fastest growing segment of the U.S. population in the workplace though is individuals with a disability. The Americans with Disabilities Act defines an individual with a disability as being a person who has a physical or mental impairment that substantially limits one or more major life activities. Approximately 50 million individuals in the United States have been identified as having a disability; in other words, one out of every five individuals. According to the 2004 *National Organization on Disability/Harris Survey of Americans with Disabilities*, although individuals with disabilities are just as likely to have obtained a college degree as their nondisabled peers, only 35 percent report working full or part time. This same survey also found that 22 percent of those surveyed reported discrimination in either the hiring process or after they began employment.

We have discussed diversity as including gender, race, ethnicity, age, and disability. Diversity can also include sexuality and religion. Statistics for these variables though are often falsely low, because many individuals fear repercussion if they accurately report certain labels as applying to themselves. For this reason, statistics are not particularly useful for describing these individuals, but we must recognize that these variables also contribute to the overall diversity of the workforce.

Diversity can introduce tensions in work-related groups as well as richness of ideas. Organizational members need to be able to turn diversity into a positive characteristic of the work environment. For example, research suggests that members of cultural groups from collectivist traditions, or cultures where group cohesiveness is more important than individual success, tend to engage in more cooperative strategies than persons from individualistic cultural traditions. Asian, African American, and Hispanic cultures tend to be collectivist, whereas Anglo-American culture tends to be individualistic (Allen, 1995). If the goal is a group product, workers from collectivist cultures may be more helpful to the group than those from individualistic cultures. Meanwhile, if the task calls for independent work, those from individualistic cultures may excel. The task of a good manager is to accurately identify which type of skill is needed at any one time and draw upon individuals with that skill to help others acquire it. We return to these issues throughout the text as we discuss topics in organizational communication.

There are, of course, cultures within cultures. Often the greatest discrimination has existed among people living in the same environment: "Persons of color tend to have limited access to social networks, to experience blocked mobility, and often do not have mentors or sponsors [and] have been expected to check their race at the door, to become assimilated" (Allen, 1995, p. 150). Allen is suggesting that in U.S. culture, people of color experience limitations in the organization that are not experienced by others. The following story told by Marilyn, an elementary school teacher, reinforces Allen's point:

When I was 24 years old, my husband, George, was going to be starting a doctoral program in Illinois. So, I had to get a job in Illinois. I had been teaching in New Jersey for two years and it had been a wonderful experience. Here [in Washington, D.C.], there are a ton of schools to work for, but in Illinois the jobs were more spread out. So, my choices of where I wanted to teach were more limited.

I began applying for jobs, and one of the first ones I applied for was in a small town in northern Illinois. I sent all the information they needed. The application did not include a picture because that would have been illegal. I sent the application in and then I left for a trip to Puerto Rico for two weeks to see a friend. When I returned from vacation, there was a telegram under the door. It said that the school had a position for me and they wanted me to call them. There were two other telegrams from the same school underneath the door as well, all saying the same thing. The telegram said to call no matter what time of day or night in order to arrange an interview. They were dying to have me!

I called the school right away and asked when I could set up an interview. They were very excited to hear from me and set up an appointment immediately. They were probably excited because no one wanted to work in that rural area. I went the following week to the elementary school to interview. I walked in and I went to the principal's office. I said, "Hi, I'm Mrs. Gardner. I'm here about the job." The principal looked me up and down and in a nervous voice said, "Oh gee, that job was filled this morning." I said, "You knew I was coming." The principal told me that a more qualified applicant had come in that morning and he was sorry it didn't work out. Then he told me he had to take me to the central office. I had no idea why but I got in his car anyway. He brought me to the head of the school and introduced me. Then he said in a very loud, booming voice, "THIS is Mrs. Gardner." He leaned in and said loudly, "I told her that we filled the job with a more qualified applicant this morning, isn't that right?" Then he leaned over and they began whispering. I knew something strange was going on. I ended up getting a job somewhere else.

It turned out later that one of my friends in the area was hired for that same job after me. She was very inexperienced at the time. She told me that I was crazy to think I could have gotten the job because there were no ethnic people whatsoever in that town.

We introduced this story with the idea that persons of color often experience limitations in organizations that are not experienced by others. In this situation, Marilyn never even had the opportunity to gain entry into the organization, by all accounts, because of her ethnicity. Several features of the story indicate that, prior to knowing her ethnicity, the organization was courting her very seriously. The three telegrams with anxious messages and the enthusiastic scheduling of an interview support this theory. The odd behavior of the principal after seeing Marilyn points to this conclusion as well. As this story illustrates, despite the social advances of the past three decades, members of minority populations still have difficulty gaining entry into certain organizations and positions, regardless of their qualifications.

In addition to problems associated with being hired as a member of a different culture, people are often evaluated less positively if they are perceived to be hired as a result of affirmative action. Three researchers (Heilman, Block, & Stathatos, 1997) conducted a study with 264 male and female managers who were asked to review information about the job performance of persons portrayed as either a man or a woman, and, if a woman, as either an affirmative-action hire or not. The following statement was placed on their performance record: "Hired through women/minority recruiting program." As expected, subjects rated female affirmative-action hires as less competent and recommended smaller salary increases for them than for men and women not associated with affirmative action. This pattern held even when negative performance information was provided for those not identified as affirmative-action hires. Affirmative-action hires are then marginalized, thereby reducing the variety of perspectives that could be available to the group and negating the benefits of diversity. Behavior such as this is often based on entrenched organizational and societal norms, which tend to reinforce the values and status of white males, who are the primary players in the shaping of those norms from the start (Elsass & Graves, 1997).

Discrimination can also result from "simple" misunderstandings. As reported by salary.com, in 1999, 1,400 members of the Society for Human Resources Management were polled to gain an understanding of their attitudes and behaviors toward individuals with a disability in the workforce. Thirty-one percent of these individuals reported lack of knowledge about accommodations, and 22 percent cited supervisor or coworker attitudes and stereotypes as being reasons that individuals with a disability were not hired. In 2002, the John Heldrich Center for Workforce Development published *Misconceptions about Hiring Workers with Disabilities* as a result of a survey of over 500 employers. In this report, 15 percent of employers cited a general reluctance or hesitation to hire workers with disabilities, while 10 percent cited their own discomfort or lack of knowledge about a particular disability. While 5 percent reported fear of discrimination or prejudice by coworkers, 10 percent cited a fear of what the job accommodations would cost their organization. In an attempt to comply with federal antidiscrimination laws, many employers were afraid to discuss the disability with the employee and in turn relied only on their own experience or lack of experience to judge what would be reasonable for the potential employee or the organization. Interestingly, the Job Accommodation Network reports that the majority (over 70 percent) of people with disabilities requires no special job accommodation, and 19 percent of those requiring accommodation require something that will cost the organization nothing. Fifty percent of accommodations cost less than $500, and only 17 percent of accommodations cost more than $1,000.

Ironically, in an attempt to avoid discrimination, lack of communication or miscommunication by the employer often results in discrimination. The misunderstandings may well cause the organization to lose out on an invaluable segment of the work population. According to the U.S. Department of Labor, three multiyear studies conducted by DuPont demonstrated that over 90 percent of employees with disabilities rated average or better on their performance reviews, had no greater absenteeism rates than nondisabled employees, and had virtually identical safety records as nondisabled employees.

As should be becoming clear, organizational life is inherently problematic; hence our focus on misunderstandings in this textbook. Whether those misunderstandings are based on miscommunication, management style, information technology, or cultural diversity, they must be acknowledged and acted upon in an appropriate manner. For appropriate and responsible decisions and actions to be accomplished, organizational members must have a solid foundation from which to operate. In the next section, we discuss an important element of that foundation—ethics.

Ethical Frameworks and Organizational Communication

Organizational ethics is difficult to define outside the unique culture of a particular organizational environment. Organizations that encourage members to give voice to concerns about the organization and increase the choices members can make are establishing an ethical framework. These choices may take the form of actions or rhetorical acts. Many factors operate against such choices. W. Charles Redding (1984), one of the earliest writers on organizational communication, concluded: "There is something inherently present in any modern organization that facilitates unethical or immoral conduct" (p. 1). As organizational members make choices on a day-to-day basis, the "inherent" desire for such things as control, power, information, resources, money, and promotions could promote unethical behavior. Soule (2002) extends this point by noting that two aspects of the commercial world point to the need to attend to moral/ethical standpoints:

> First, business involves a competitive struggle for scarce resources (be they possessions, positions, status, power, and so forth), and as is the case with most human struggles, opportunities abound for harmful wrongdoing and injustice. Second, some of the rewards of commercial competition are so crucial to living a good life that most people are obliged to engage in the struggle. (p. 115)

Given this, attention to the ethics of organizational behavior, particularly communicative behavior, is warranted.

Allowing organizational members to voice their concerns rather than eliminating anyone who speaks against the goals of the organization takes a great deal of trust in the workers on the part of the organization's leadership. Workers will have little reason to act in ethically appropriate ways, however, if management does not set the standard. Richard Johannesen, known for his work in the ethics of human communication, argued this point:

> Top management must set a high ethical tone for the entire organization by demonstrating a firm and clear commitment to ethical behavior for all employees. The personal example of their own daily behavior is one way for the top management to demonstrate such commitment. Also desirable is development of a formal code of ethics or set of written ethical expectations that explain in clear terms the ethical standards demanded by the organization. (1996, p. 176)

It would be nice to think that all organizational members would inherently want to operate in an ethical fashion, but history and human nature tell us differently. The Ethics Resource Center (ERC) released the results of their *2005 National Business Ethics Survey* (NBES), which indicated that unethical behavior is prevalent in the workplace. The following is a summary of some of the relevant findings from the ERC's survey:

- 52 percent of employees observed at least one type of misconduct in the workplace in the past year, with 36 percent of these observing at least two or more violations.
- 21 percent observed abusive or intimidating behavior towards employees.
- 19 percent observed lying to employees, customers, vendors, or the public.
- 18 percent observed a situation that places employee interests over organizational interests.
- 16 percent observed violations of safety regulations.
- 16 percent observed misreporting of actual time worked.

- 12 percent observed discrimination on the basis of race, color, gender, age, or similar categories.
- 11 percent observed stealing or theft.
- 9 percent observed sexual harassment.

As these statistics demonstrate, unethical behavior does not seem to be rare in organizational life. It appears that organizational members need models and guidelines to follow if they are to behave ethically.

For this reason, many organizations have attempted to establish ethics programs. Results of the *2005 NBES* indicated that 69 percent of employees reported that their organizations had implemented ethics training, and that 65 percent of employees indicated that their organizations have a place they can seek ethics advice. As further evidence of this trend, membership in the Ethics Officer Association had risen from 12 in 1992 to over 1,000 in 2006.

Formal corporate ethics programs typically include some or all of the following elements: (1) a formal codes of ethics, which articulate a firm's expectations regarding ethical behavior; (2) ethics committees charged with developing ethics policies evaluating company or employee actions and investigating and adjudicating policy violations; (3) ethics communication systems (e.g., telephone lines) providing a means for employees to report abuses or obtain guidance; (4) ethics officers or ombudspersons charged with coordinating policies, providing ethics education, or investigating allegations; (5) ethics training programs, which are aimed at helping employees to recognize and respond to ethical issues; and (6) disciplinary processes to address unethical behavior.

Some ethics programs embody a coercive orientation toward control that emphasizes adhering to rules, monitoring employee behavior, and disciplining misconduct. Such programs can be called *compliance oriented*. Corporate ethics programs may also, however, aim to standardize behavior by creating commitment to shared values and encouraging ethical aspirations. Such systems emphasize support for employees' ethical aspirations and the development of shared values (Weaver, Trevino, and Cochran, 1999, p. 42). A third type of ethics program, termed *social outreach*, was discussed in a story written by Donaldson on corporate ethics in the November 13, 2000, issue of the *Financial Times* (London). Social outreach is the least common of the three types and emphasizes the role of the organization as a social citizen. Social outreach programs take two forms: social accounting and competency based. Social accounting programs advocate that companies should account for their social activities much as they do their financial activities. Competency-based programs emphasize the social contributions a company undertakes over donating money to various causes.

A sense of ethics must be "institutionalized" into the organization. Ethical concerns must be regarded as being on par with economic and pragmatic concerns in decision making. Procedures must be established so that ethical issues automatically are confronted as part of a decision. Opportunities and mechanisms should be established for employees to express their ethical concerns without fear of blocked promotion or of demotion, firing, or other retribution. Employee "whistle-blowing" on ethical violations by the organization truly should become rare and a last resort. Organizations must consciously act to make ethics a legitimate topic of discussion, not only for those times of crisis when a personal value is challenged or painful competing claims are present, as well as allow employees to examine fully the range of options available, to anticipate pitfalls, and to explore creative ways of resolving their dilemmas (Johannesen, 1996). The ERC referred to this institutionalized concern for ethics as the development of an "ethical culture," and results from the *2005 NBES* pointed to the presence of such a culture as being vital to the ethical behavior of organizational members. An ethical culture involves the formal and informal norms that guide an employee as to what is to be considered ethical and unethical behavior.

Codes of ethics and ethics programs provide structures for ethical behavior, but when attempting to determine whether a particular behavior is ethical it is useful to have more specific guidelines or principles to follow. Gary Kreps (1990), George Cheney and Phillip Tompkins (1987), and Marifran Mattson and Patrice Buzzanell (1999) have developed ethical guidelines that are useful for this purpose.

Kreps proposes three ethical principles that can be applied to communication in organizations. The principles are based on the concepts "do not inflict harm" and "justice" (1990, pp. 250–251):

- **Organization members should not intentionally deceive one another.** While on the surface this seems to be a straightforward and uncomplicated principle, it becomes muddy in the organizational context. A tension exists between the old adage "Honesty is the best policy" and the complicated nature of organizational life. As Kreps notes, some information in organizations cannot be disclosed either fully or partially (e.g., certain personnel information or corporate secrets such as food recipes or technical components of products under development). But outside of these restrictions, organization members should make every attempt to provide realistic and truthful information to one another.
- **Organization members' communication should not purposely harm any other organization member or members of the organization's relevant environment.** For Kreps, this is the notion of "nonmalfeasance" or "refraining from doing harm." The key element of this principle is *intentionality*—to what extent did the member intend to inflict harm? Another important question that arises from this principle is what are the acceptable levels of harm in the organization?
- **Organization members should be treated justly.** This principle does not necessarily imply equality of treatment. Justice, according to Kreps, is a relative construct based on the particular organizational context. In some organizations, for example, high performers may be given preferential treatment. It would seem, however, that full disclosure of what constitutes just treatment is imperative to ethical organizational behavior.

The three principles proposed by Kreps are based on two widely held beliefs regarding humane treatment—avoiding harm and doing justice. Operating from a different foundation, George Cheney and Phillip Tompkins (1987) forwarded four broad ethical guidelines that are based less on general doctrine and more on communication, particularly persuasion. Their four guidelines for ethical behavior are as follows:

- **Guardedness.** Organizational members should use their own persuasive abilities to assess the messages from the organization and should avoid automatically and unthinkingly accepting the conventional viewpoint.
- **Accessibility.** Communicators should be open to the possibility of being persuaded or changed by the messages of others. If people are dogmatic, they are blind to useful information and different views.
- **Nonviolence.** Certainly coercion, overt or subtle, of others is ethically undesirable. Recent workplace violence should make everyone more sensitive to early signs of violent behavior toward others. Individuals should avoid using a persuasive stance that advocates one position as the one and only reasonable position, which often forces others to take more radical stances.
- **Empathy.** The empathic communicator genuinely listens to the arguments, opinions, values, and assumptions of others. The goal is to respect the right of all persons to hold diverse views.

Cheney and Tompkins articulate an ethical framework that is grounded in communication and that recognizes the responsibilities of both the sender and the receiver of messages. Their guidelines are essentially skill based, to some extent equating what are considered basic communication skills with ethical behavior. Although there are a number of other ethical perspectives from which to evaluate organizational communication behavior, space precludes us from covering them all. We would like to conclude this section by providing a brief sketch of a few of the basic elements of an ethical perspective derived from feminist organizational communication theory.

Mattson and Buzzanell (1999) posit that feminist ethics differ from other ethical approaches by focusing on "equitable power sharing and decision making" and insisting that "doing ethics" involves being an active participant in the struggle to maintain an ethical community (p. 62). Although their feminist ethical approach is multifaceted, the following issues help to introduce the perspective:

- **Definition of the situation.** Through examination of organizational members' language choices, behaviors, and various aspects of the context, the ethical or unethical nature of the situation can be determined. Mattson and Buzzanell define *"unethical behavior from a feminist organizational communication approach* as communicative actions and processes that attempt to marginalize, silence, and disempower individuals or groups and that prohibit the development of voice" (p. 62). Unethical behavior from this perspective, then, is that behavior that serves to mute or silence the contributions of those members seeking to deviate from the goals of management.
- **Values and ideals.** In this phase, communicative action that violates the values of *voice, community,* and *fairness* are identified. As stated previously, one important value to this feminist ethical framework is voice, and actions that

suppress the voice of those not in power by those in power are immediately suspect. The value of community involves a positive view of relationships and the mutual pursuit of individual and collective needs. "When organization member communicate without consideration of multiple commitments, caring, and community maintenance, then unethical messages may be exchanged" (p. 65).

- **Fairness.** The third feminist value appropriate for ethical analysis is fairness. The value of fairness implies the equitable balance of power and resources, and any behavior that reduces the resources of marginalized organizational members in favor of those in power should be considered unethical.

- **Ethical principle.** Traditional ethical approaches tend to exclude the role and importance of *emotion* in the communicative behavior of organizational members. From this feminist ethical perspective, organizational behavior that precludes the expression of emotion limits the extent of relational and community development, and therefore should be considered ethically suspect.

- **Development of a solution.** This final phase points to the need to constantly reevaluate options and solutions until an acceptable solution is reached: "If options violate ethical principles or result in harms to vulnerable stakeholders, then these alternatives are eliminated from possible courses of action" (p. 67).

All three of the ethical frameworks examined in this section are excellent tools for analyzing organizational behavior, particularly communicative behavior, and determining the extent to which the communicators acted ethically. We use these ethical principles and guidelines throughout the rest of the book to analyze communicative behaviors in the workplace.

Three Important Constructs

We conclude this chapter with a discussion of three constructs important to the study and practice of organizational communication: identification, job satisfaction, and communication satisfaction. Although there are certainly many more constructs that are relevant in organizational communication practice and research, these three are perhaps the most salient to the concept of *misunderstandings*. As we conducted interviews with organizational members for this text, we found that these three constructs were either explicitly or implicitly relevant to the misunderstandings discussed. As a result, explaining them at this early point in the book should help you to understand the stories as they occur throughout the text and provide a vocabulary for discussing and analyzing them.

Organizational Identification

A particularly useful construct in the study and practice of organizational communication is *organizational identification*. The term is adopted from the writing of rhetorician Kenneth Burke and positioned in the discipline most notably by George Cheney and Phillip Tompkins. Burke (1950) believed that the hierarchies present in society naturally divide humans from one another. To overcome the separation, humans act to establish some sense of commonality—a process termed *identification*: "Identification—with organizations or anything else—is an active process by which individuals link themselves to elements in the social scene" (Cheney, 1983, p. 342). Those elements can include people (e.g., coworkers, supervisors, subordinates), policies, products, services, customers, or values.

Organizational identification involves an individual's sense of membership in and connection with an organization. Bullis and Bach (1989) describe it in the following way: "Individuals identify with their collectives . . . to the extent that they feel similar to other members, they feel a sense of belonging, and they consider themselves to be members" (p. 275). A variety of sources of identification are available for an organizational member, including *intraorganizational sources*, such as the organization as a whole, a work team, a department, a union, a lunch group, a supervisor, etc., and *extraorganizational sources*, such as family, customers, influential public figures, and the media. According to Morgan et al. (2004), "Sources then become places both to draw from and to extend forward attachments to certain groups or organizations" (p. 363). In other parts of the literature (for example, Gossett, 2002), the concept of identification sources is broken down into identification *targets* (those people or entities the member looks to for a connection) and identification *pulls* (those people or groups that seek to make connections with the individual).

Organizational identification is not quite as straightforward as we once thought. For example, the realities of the modern workplace have called into question the desire of organizational members to want to have a high level of organizational identification, and at the same time organizations have questioned the viability of attempting to promote identification with all of its workers. If you recall the story told by Caden at the beginning of this chapter, we had a situation where one company acquired another, and Caden indicated, rightly, that this is a growing trend. It is possible that some members of that newly formed organization may not have wanted to identify with it. Pepper and Larson (2006) refer to this as *disidentification*, which is "a purposely chosen, negotiated response by organizational members facing significant change and upheaval in their actual work lives" (p. 64). Importantly, disidentification is not synonymous with low identification; it is instead a purposeful fostering by the worker of separateness, disconnection, and emotional and social exclusion from the organization.

Another reality of the modern workplace is the use of temporary workers. Research has shown that temporary workers may not want to have high levels of identification with their temporary employer because they prefer a feeling of staying on the margins. However, at the same time organizations employing temporary workers may limit the opportunities for developing organizational identification by temporary workers as a way of making it easier to release them when their services are no longer needed. Gossett (2002) showed that temporary workers were regularly denied access to "symbolic artifacts" that defined the organization, such as not being provided with an e-mail address, physical mail-box, or name plate. In these ways, the possible ways for the temporary worker to feel included or connected to the organization were limited, which necessarily limited opportunities for the development of identification.

Despite it's complex nature, organizational identification has been correlated with several relevant organizational outcomes, including motivation, job satisfaction, job performance, decision making, role orientation and conflict, employee interaction, and length of service, among others (Cheney, 1983, p. 342). High organizational identification has been correlated with increased satisfaction and decreased turnover, whereas low organizational identification is related to communicative isolation, negative attitudes toward the organization, and inappropriate organizational behavior (Gossett, 2002).

As you can tell, organizational identification has been construed as both a *process* and a *product* (Scott, Corman, and Cheney, 1998). Organizational identification as a process encapsulates the notion that people act so as to identify with a certain aspect(s) of their organization. In this manner, organizational identification is fluid, changing, and intimately related to the process of communication (Gossett, 2002). As a product, organizational identification is seen as a result of socialization efforts by the organization, which could in turn lead to further positive outcomes such as increased motivation, and job satisfaction.

Job Satisfaction

Perhaps one of the most studied variables in organizational research is job satisfaction. It is the degree to which employees feel fulfilled by their job and related experiences. One of the most often cited definitions of this construct is offered by Locke (1976): *job satisfaction* is "a pleasurable or positive emotional state from the appraisal of one's job or experiences" (p. 1,297). Job satisfaction is often broken down into relevant factors, such as supervision, work, pay, promotion, and coworkers (Pincus, 1986). An employee's overall job satisfaction would be the sum of his or her satisfaction with those individual factors. Job satisfaction has been linked with a variety of organizational outcomes, including absenteeism and turnover (Downs, Clampitt, & Pfeiffer, 1988).

The challenge for managers is to understand that contributors to job satisfaction vary by individual employee. One individual is not satisfied unless he is doing challenging work, whereas another may not be satisfied unless he is in a collegial environment. One variable that has been linked to job satisfaction is communication satisfaction (Pincus, 1986).

Communication Satisfaction

Communication satisfaction is the degree to which employees feel that communication is appropriate and satisfies their need for information and work relationships. Redding (1978) defines *communication satisfaction* as the "overall degree of satisfaction an employee perceived in his [sic] total communication environment" (p. 429). Inherent in this definition are several dimensions associated with varying individual needs, as well as elements of the communication environment.

Cal Downs (1994), in an explication of the Communication Satisfaction Questionnaire developed by Downs and Hazen (1977), indicates that communication satisfaction can be broken down into eight factors concerned with communication information, relationships, channels, and climate (p. 114). Those dimensions are as follows:

1. **Communication climate.** The overall extent to which communication from the organization is positive, as well as the perceived communication competence of other employees.
2. **Relationship to superiors.** Upward and downward communication, as well as issues of openness and trust.
3. **Organizational integration.** The extent to which the employee feels informed of important organizational information, including policies, procedures, and current events.
4. **Media quality.** Helpfulness and clarity of communication as it relates to the particular media used (e.g., meetings, written, dyadic).
5. **Horizontal and informal communication.** The accuracy and adequacy of communication networks within the organization.
6. **Organizational perspective.** The extent to which the employee feels the organization adequately communicates information regarding organizational goals, organizational performance, and changes in the external environment that affect organizational functioning.
7. **Relationship with subordinates.** The flow of communication between superior and subordinate and the ability of the subordinate (from the supervisor's viewpoint) to receive and send information competently.
8. **Personal feedback.** The extent to which employees perceive supervisors as being in touch with organizational and personal problems and employees' perceptions of the clarity of criteria by which their performance will be judged.

Communication satisfaction is often considered the "sum" of an individual's satisfaction with these dimensions (Pincus, 1986). According to their review of relevant research, Gray and Laidlaw (2004) demonstrated that communication satisfaction has been linked with other important organizational communication outcomes such as job satisfaction, productivity, job performance, and organizational commitment. Research continues on these interconnections, and throughout this textbook communication satisfaction will often be referred to in discussing important organizational processes and issues.

Summary

Organizational communication is the process of creating, exchanging, interpreting (correctly or incorrectly), and storing messages within a system of human interrelationships. The study of organizational communication helps people to understand and appreciate communication as the central process in the organization.

In this chapter, we have attempted to outline some of the basic issues related to the study and practice of organizational communication. We have argued that conceptions of organizations have changed dramatically in the recent past, having moved from organizational structures dominated by hierarchy, authority, and local competition to ones characterized by decentralized decision making, coaching, and global competition. Of particular interest is the increasing diversity of the workforce.

We also advanced the notion that misunderstandings characterize modern organizational life. *Misunderstandings* is an umbrella term used to encapsulate the role communication plays in the creation and resolution of organizational problems. Because organizational life is inherently problematic, it is of utmost importance that organizations and individuals approach situations with an appropriate and agreed upon ethical framework. We concluded the chapter with the introduction of three constructs—organizational identification, job satisfaction, and communication satisfaction.

As a student, no matter what your future area of expertise may be—finance, management, health care, law, medicine, engineering, or the arts—it will be important for you to understand how communication functions in an organization and how you can make it work for you. We hope that after reading this book you will have a greater understanding of all aspects of organizational life. An appreciation of the historical development of organizational communication, a more developed sense of organizational culture, and an understanding of the many human communication processes that are a part of organizational life are the desired outcomes. In addition, knowing that there are a variety of choices you can make about your own communication behavior will help you decide how to complete the tasks of your job successfully.

If you are a communication major, or more specifically an organizational communication major, others will turn to you for assistance in improving communication in the organization. You may have an official position devoted to communication, such as communication trainer, manager of internal communication, or work in the general area of human resources management. Or you may use your communication expertise in sales, management, administration, or project management. As a communication specialist, your goal should be to reduce misunderstandings through communication.

CHAPTER

2 Classical Theories of Organizations

We begin the discussion of the study of organizational communication with a brief sketch of three theorists whose contributions represent the classical approaches to organizations. These three theories of organization emerged in the early part of the twentieth century and still permeate certain sectors of organizational life today.

As the Industrial Revolution changed the nature of Western civilization in the eighteenth and nineteenth centuries, it became necessary for newly emerging organizations to have efficient and effective means of managing their modes of production. Theorists turned to the two principal organizations of the time, the military and the Catholic Church, as models for modern industrial management (McGregor, [1960] 1985). Strict control of workers, absolute chains of command, predictability of behavior, and unidirectional downward influence (among others) were characteristics of these two successful organizations that made their way into modern organizational theory. The resulting organizational theories are referred to here as the classical approaches to organizations and communication within them.

As you read this chapter, keep in mind the following points. First, in order to understand how modern organizations function, and particularly the role that communication plays in effective organizing, it is vital to understand the theories that guided organizational functioning in the preceding decades. Remnants of these theories still exist to greater or lesser extent (depending on the industry) in managerial practices today. Understanding the theoretical bases for these practices will provide you with useful information for performing successfully when you are part of an organization. Second, current organizational theorists offer principles and practices that are in opposition to classical theories. Knowing the elements of classical theories will help you understand why modern organizational theorists recommend what they do. Finally, you will perhaps notice that several principles of classical theories seem to make inherent sense. Unfortunately, these principles may never have been integrated into practice or were manipulated in directions not intended by the theorist. The information in this chapter should provide you with enough knowledge to make those distinctions.

The Metaphor of the Machine

A useful way to introduce the different organizational theories covered in the next several chapters is through metaphor. Each type of theory is based on specific assumptions about the nature of organizations, which can be expressed metaphorically. The classical approach to organizations is characterized by the metaphor of a *machine*. From this perspective, organizations are viewed as if they are machines; managerial principles, modes of operation, treatment of workers, and communication in the organization are considered in light of this metaphor.

Consider for a moment the properties of a machine. A machine is very *predictable* in how it will function. It rarely deviates from the norm (outside of operator error) unless some part of it ceases functioning properly or stops completely. In cases where parts of the machine no longer function or function ineffectively, they can be replaced by another *standard* part. Specific rules exist regarding repair of the machine and the specific role that each part of the machine plays in its functioning. In other words, each part of the machine is highly *specialized*.

When the machine metaphor is applied to organizations, the properties just described hold true for the organization as well and guide management as it attempts to regulate behavior, including communication. If an organization is a machine, then the workers are the parts of the machine. In accordance with the properties of a machine, the workers are to behave predictably so that management and the other workers will know exactly what to expect of each member of the organization at any given moment. If a worker operates outside the boundaries of what is expected, someone who can perform the functions of the job effectively, efficiently, and predictably will replace that worker.

Minimizing Misunderstandings

By promoting the principles of specialization, standardization, and predictability in organizations, classical theorists were essentially attempting to minimize the occurrences of misunderstandings (as characterized in Chapter 1). Classical theorists hypothesized that problems in organizations occurred when tasks were not directed and workers were left relatively unregulated; that is, free to experiment with work styles and procedures and able to communicate with anyone about anything at any time. Strictly regulating how work was accomplished, who could speak to whom and when, and managing through fear are all instruments for reducing misunderstandings in classical theories.

As you will see throughout this chapter, however, attempts to regulate behavior strictly through these means created a whole new class of misunderstandings. Attempts to increase predictability by demanding that everyone follow exact rules for behavior led to workers whose creativity and intelligence were underutilized, which in turn increased their dissatisfaction, lowered motivation, and decreased commitment to the task and the organization. Regulating communication by emphasizing messages that flowed mainly in one direction—from supervisor to subordinate—minimized instances of arguments and increased efficiency, but decreased communication effectiveness by generating more miscommunication and decreasing worker satisfaction.

As you read about the three different classical theories, imagine how the creators of these theories were seeking to minimize misunderstandings. At the same time, think about the new forms of misunderstandings created by these theories as unintended consequences. For example, consider the following story from a 53-year-old special education teacher. Leah Stone found herself in a situation where following the strict rules set out by the new principal led to an ineffective education for her students.

> Last year we got a new principal at our school. He was 26 years old. It was his first principal position, coming straight from the classroom as a teacher. I know he wanted to do his best and follow all the rules and make sure we all followed the rules. Most of the staff was veteran teachers with many years of experience.
>
> One of the things he was pushing was the implementation of a new reading program and that it be done "by the book." He kept insisting that we all teach the program exactly as it was laid out by the administration. I tried to explain to him that I had four grade levels instead of just one in my class (I teach kindergarten, first, second, and third grades). More importantly, this is SPECIAL EDUCATION! That means I cannot teach the same lessons to all the kids. The very nature of my class is that these kids need a variety of techniques and curricula. But he just kept insisting that I teach it just like everyone else. He would not change his mind no matter what I said.

As you will discover in this chapter, a primary feature of one of the classical theories is the establishment of rules for every possible situation a worker will encounter. By establishing written rules, management would be able to regulate the behavior of workers, thereby increasing predictability and decreasing the potential for misunderstandings. What Leah's situation demonstrates, however, is that establishing a rule does not guarantee that the rule will apply in every situation, nor will it lead to an effective outcome. Leah's special education classroom demanded flexibility for the individual student. Following the rule (though she eventually ignored her new principal by mid-year) led to an ineffective learning environment and created a tenuous relationship between Leah and her supervisor. This is a perfect example of how elements of classical theory designed to minimize misunderstandings may contribute to the occurrence of different problems.

The classical approach is represented by three theories: Frederick Taylor's *theory of scientific management*, Henri Fayol's *administrative theory*, and Max Weber's *theory of bureaucracy*. They are described in the following sections.

Taylor's Theory of Scientific Management

Frederick Taylor (1856–1915), who is considered the "father of scientific management," proposed his theory of organizations in *The Principles of Scientific Management* ([1911] 1998). In this work, he outlined his *theory of scientific* (or task) *management* and how managers could maximize profits for both the employer and the employee.

The main problem, according to Taylor, was getting employees to work at their maximum capacity at all times. He noticed that employees rarely worked at this level; in fact, most would expend only enough effort to work at the safest, minimum-output level. He referred to the behavior of deliberately working slowly as to avoid expending more effort than deemed necessary as *systematic soldiering*.

Taylor offered three reasons for the prevalence of systematic soldiering. First, he said that workers believe that if each one works to his full capacity, then the number of workers who need to be employed will be reduced. Taylor argued the opposite: as each employee produces more, the price per unit of the product drops. As prices drop, demand increases, and more workers need to be employed to meet it.

The second reason for systematic soldiering, according to Taylor, is the *piecework system of remuneration*. Under the piecework system, employees are paid a sum of money for producing a certain amount during an average day. If the employer discovers that the worker can produce more than she is actually producing in a day, the employer raises the amount to be produced without raising the amount of pay. This adjustment would lead the fast worker artificially to lower her rate of production to that of the slowest worker in the group so that the employer would not change the rate of pay. Consider this simple example:

- Bricklayers are paid 10 cents for every 100 bricks they lay, because it is expected that they can lay 100 bricks every hour. The employer does not want to pay his workers more than 80 cents per day (an eight-hour workday).
- A worker enters the group who lays 150 bricks per hour, earning 15 cents per hour instead of the 10 cents per hour the other workers are earning.
- The employer notices this level of production and lowers the pay scale to 10 cents for every 150 bricks laid.

Taylor argued that every worker knows the maximum amount the employer is willing to pay for a day's work. Given this figure, the worker artificially lowers his output level so that the rate will not be changed.

The third reason for systematic soldiering, according to Taylor, is the use of *rule-of-thumb methods* of training employees. Taylor observed that workers learn how to do their particular tasks by observing the people around them. This would lead to the same job being done in a variety of ways, most, if not all, of which were inefficient. Taylor devoted much of his time to resolving this cause of systematic soldiering, and his theory of scientific management was the result.

Elements of Scientific Management

The theory of scientific management has four elements:

1. The scientific design of every aspect of every task
2. The careful selection and training of the best workers
3. Proper remuneration for fast and high-quality work
4. Equal division of work and responsibility between worker and manager.

The first element of Taylor's theory is "the scientific design of every aspect of every task." Believing that the rule-of-thumb method of training employees was a major contributor to systematic soldiering, he sought to eliminate it. Through the use of *time and motion studies*, the most efficient and effective means of accomplishing every aspect of every task could be determined. Taylor outlined the procedure to follow when conducting time and motion studies:

> *First.* Find, say 10 or 15 different men (preferably in as many separate establishments and different parts of the country) who are especially skilful [*sic*] in doing the particular work to be analyzed.
> *Second.* Study the exact series of elementary operations or motions which each of these men uses in doing the work which is being investigated, as well as the implements each man uses.
> *Third.* Study with a stop-watch the time required to make each of these elementary movements and then select the quickest way of doing each element of the work.
> *Fourth.* Eliminate all false movements, slow movements, and useless movements.
> *Fifth.* After doing away with all unnecessary movements, collect into one series the quickest and best movements as well as the best implements. ([1911] 1998, p. 61)

Taylor conducted time and motion studies using this procedure in a number of U.S. factories during the early 1900s. For example, he examined the science of shoveling at the Bethlehem Steel Company. He noticed that the 600 workers at the company were operating inefficiently and ineffectively; they were using different types of shovels, taking different sizes of shovel loads, and using different mechanics to shovel. To remedy this problem, he conducted exhaustive time and motion studies and determined that the optimal shovel load for each worker was 21 pounds (regardless of the type of material being shoveled, e.g., coal, ore, or ashes). Gathering 21 pounds per shovel load would yield the maximum productivity for each worker; 18 pounds would be too little, 25 pounds would be too heavy and lead to fatigue. Different shovels for different types of material were developed so that 21 pounds of material would comfortably fit on each shovel. Taking 21 pounds per shovel load and using the motions and timing designated by the managers, workers were able to maximize their output and increase their pay accordingly.

The second element of scientific management is "the careful selection and training of the best workers." Once the most efficient way to perform the task is determined through time and motion studies, managers must select workers who are capable of performing the task as designed and capable of producing at the maximum level. Workers are not expected to understand the science of task design, so it is the job of management to train each worker on how to perform the task. This idea reveals an important aspect about Taylor and his view of workers and managers. Taylor believed that there is an inherent difference between the two groups: managers are intelligent, workers are and should be ignorant:

> Now one of the very first requirements for a man who is fit to handle pig iron as a regular occupation is that he shall be so stupid and so phlegmatic that he more nearly resembles in his mental make-up the ox than any other type. The man who is mentally alert and intelligent is for this very reason entirely unsuited to what would, for him, be the grinding monotony of work of this character. (1911, p. 28)

Perhaps nowhere else in Taylor's writings is his view of the difference between management and workers so clear. Read from today's perspective, this passage would seem to indicate a disdain for workers, an absolute hatred of them. Writing such things in the twenty-first century would surely lead to dismissal from the community of scholars, rejection of the theory, and widespread outrage. At the time it was written, however, Taylor was praised for his insight and for his concern with the worker. Although the above passage indicates that he did not have the highest regard for their mental abilities, his overall theory was designed to provide opportunities for workers to achieve greater financial rewards in a more comfortable fashion. Reading just the last sentence of the quotation shows that Taylor understood the need to challenge people mentally in the workplace. Unfortunately, he only considered those in management positions to be worthy of such challenges.

The third element of scientific management is "proper remuneration for fast and high-quality work." Taylor argued that the worker should be able to increase his wages by 30 to 100 percent under the scientific management system. Given that the individual worker is motivated almost solely by wages, Taylor thought that the best way to maximize their output would be to promise them higher wages *if* they provided maximum effort. Through the scientific design of tasks, the most efficient output level is determined. If the worker meets that output level, he is rewarded with appropriate, good wages. If the worker exceeds that output level, he is rewarded with a bonus. If the worker produces under the appropriate output level, he is immediately informed of the fact and given instructions as to how to perform the task to meet the goal. If the worker cannot meet the goal after sufficient training, he is removed from that task.

The fourth element of scientific management is "equal division of work and responsibility between worker and manager." Under old systems of management, the plan for accomplishing the task was left up to the individual worker. Under Taylor's system, the manager was responsible for planning every detail of the task for every worker, training the worker on how to perform the task, and evaluating the process and product of each worker at regular intervals. This increased role of the manager led Taylor to say that there was now an equal division of work.

Scientific Management in the Modern Workplace

Are Taylor's principles present in the modern workplace? In some respects, absolutely. Although Taylor's less-than-politically-correct language has for the most part disappeared, several of his principles still permeate many modern organizations. Assembly line plants are prototypical examples of the scientific design of tasks. Workers (in conjunction with machines) must perform tasks in regulated ways in order for the system to operate efficiently and effectively. Efficiency is promoted through strict control of the task process. Although this form of work may be in sync with the needs of some employees, it may cause tension for others. Consider the following story from Grier, a 22-year-old college student who worked on an assembly line making sandpaper:

> A few years ago, I had a summer job working in a sand paper factory. The turnover rate was so bad they had to warn interviewees that $100 would be deducted from their last paycheck if they quit before they have worked there for six months. Many of the workers were from a different country and worked hard to package as much as possible, but I did not take to the strict rules and constant scrutiny of the manager looking over my shoulder directing me how to package sandpaper in the most efficient way. The manager did not care about the fact that I had to slave over an assembly line for eight hours doing the exact same thing over and over.
>
> I simply was not as good as the other workers, who were all used to it. I wanted to do a good job and meet new people that I could relate to, but none of them were in school, and for the most part were only there to get paid, which in many respects is understandable. But in my point of view, I would have liked the managers to be nicer and more understanding of new employees. I would have liked to have meetings with the other workers to see how the production was going for the day. Simple statistics and information could be helpful or motivating, rather than being told to get as much done possible before they switched to another task. They rarely said anything positive or let anyone make suggestions or comments. It was the closest thing to slavery that I had ever encountered. The hardest part is realizing that most people in that kind of workplace are expected to be that way.

As Grier's story demonstrates, modern-day organizations do indeed continue to follow Taylor's principles, and the effect of those principles on workers varies depending on the individual.

Although Taylorism was designed with "blue-collar" work as the prototypical form of work, modern applications of Taylor's principles have been used to restructure "white-collar" work as well. Advanced communication technology and computerized information systems have made it possible to structure and monitor interactions between organizational members and customers. The call center, which is a segment of an organization or a separate organization responsible for interactions with customers, typically in the form of customer service or technical support, is one organizational form that has been restructured according to Taylor's principles. Taylor and Bain (1999) show how a typical call center employee's work unfolds:

> In all probability, work consists of an uninterrupted and endless sequence of similar conversations with customers she never meets. She has to concentrate hard on what is being said, jump from page to page on a screen, making sure that the details entered are accurate and that she has said the right things in a pleasant manner. The conversation ends and as she tidies up the loose ends there is another voice in her headset. The pressure is intense because she knows her work is being measured, her speech monitored, and it often leaves her mentally, physically, and emotionally exhausted. (p. 115)

As you can see, Taylor's principles of task design have survived and flourish in the midst of modern technology.

Likewise, the system of remuneration Taylor proposed is still present in various forms for salespeople, customer-support personnel, and even corporate recruiters. The presence of these ideas is not always seen as positive. As Percy Barevik stated in the April 19, 1998, issue of the *Guardian*: "I would say that we in the Western industrialized countries still are 'prisoners of Taylorism.' Workers are regarded as a commodity, seen as some sort of machine specialized in certain functions—maybe using 10 percent of their brain capacity" (p. 1).

Although Taylor's influence in modern organizations may be quite explicit as indicated above, it can also be seen more implicitly—recast in new language. Many people argue that current buzzwords and practices such as "redesign" and "reengineering" are just new, more modern-sounding ways of expressing Taylor's principles of scientific management. For example, in a May 15, 1996, article in the *Financial Times* (London), Richard Donkin argued that "Taylorism took personnel management away from the heart and into the head where it has remained ever since" (p. 30). As an example of this, Donkin contends that "benchmarking," the fashionable term for comparing organizational processes to one another, should be added to the list of modern practices born from Taylor's original ideas. Benchmarking reduces any and nearly every aspect of organizational functioning to statistical analysis, much as people do with sports players. These data are used to refine, improve, change, modify, and eliminate organizational processes—including workers. Obviously, either explicitly or implicitly, Frederick Taylor's principles are still affecting workers nearly a century after they were introduced.

Taylor's system of scientific management is the cornerstone of classical theory. The other two classical theorists, Fayol and Weber, both refer to Taylor in their writing and consider him to be a visionary and pioneer in the management of organizations. They differed from Taylor, though, in their foci. Taylor's main focus was on the task, whereas Fayol and Weber had their sights set more broadly. We now turn to the work of Henri Fayol.

Fayol's Administrative Theory

Henri Fayol (1841–1925), a French citizen, had four careers during his lifetime. He was a mining engineer, a geologist who developed a new theory of coal-bearing strata, an industrial leader, and a philosopher of administration (Urwick & Brech, 1949). It was as a philosopher of administration that he contributed most widely to the theory and practice of organizational management.

In his book *General and Industrial Management* (published in French in 1916, then published in English in 1949), Fayol outlined his theory of general management, which he believed could be applied to the administration of myriad industries. His concern was with the administrative apparatus (or functions of administration), and to that end he presented his *administrative theory*, that is, principles and elements of management.

Principles of Management

Fayol forwarded his principles of management as prescriptions for practical ways that managers should accomplish their managerial duties. Notice as you read these principles that Fayol was attempting to minimize problems before they occurred. What follows is a brief description of the 14 principles of management outlined by Fayol (1949):

1. **Division of work.** Each worker should have a limited set of tasks to accomplish.
2. **Authority and responsibility.** *Authority* is "the right to give orders and the power to exact obedience" (p. 21). It can take the form of official authority (from the position in the organization) or personal authority (from intelligence, experience, moral worth, etc.). Personal authority complements official authority. Responsibility is the corollary of authority.
3. **Discipline.** Acting in accordance with the agreements made between the individual and the organization is absolutely necessary for the proper functioning of the organization. If an employee violates the agreement on any level, the employee should be sanctioned.
4. **Unity of command.** An employee should receive orders from only one supervisor. If this principle is not upheld, "authority is undermined, discipline is in jeopardy, order disturbed and stability threatened" (p. 24).
5. **Unity of direction.** Only one head (i.e., one manager) shall administer a group of activities having the same purpose. In other words, two managers should not have direct authority over the same set of activities.
6. **Subordination of individual interest to general interest.** The interest (e.g., demands, needs, wants, desires) of an individual employee or group of employees should not come before the interest of the entire organization.
7. **Remuneration of personnel.** Employees should be paid a fair price for their services. Interestingly, Fayol believed that remuneration could be more than

just financial reward: "There is no doubt that a business will be better served in proportion as its employees are more energetic, better educated, more conscientious and more permanent" (p. 32).

8. **Centralization.** Centralization occurs when decisions are made at the top of the hierarchy rather than at lower levels (decentralization). Although centralization is often tied most directly to decision-making power, Fayol also conceptualized it as being related to the full use of the employee: "Everything which goes to increase the importance of the subordinate's role is decentralization, everything which goes to reduce it is centralization" (p. 34).

9. **Scalar Chain.** The Scalar Chain is the traditional organizational structure that defines the "chain of superiors ranging from the ultimate authority to the lowest ranks" (p. 34). The Scalar Chain is the communication plan for Fayol's theory (see Figure 2.1).

Communication, according to Fayol, should follow the Scalar Chain. If worker F needed to communicate with worker G, the communication would have to flow up the Scalar Chain through supervisors D, B, and A, and then back down to C, E, and finally G. Fayol recognized that there are times when it is necessary to communicate a message quickly. It is proper at such times to go outside the lines of authority and communicate directly across the Scalar Chain. The "gang plank" (represented by the dotted line from F to G in Figure 2.1), which later became know as *Fayol's bridge*, is what allows two people on the same hierarchical level to communicate with each other directly. The gang plank should be employed when not using it will result in a "detriment to the business" (p. 36). Additionally, if F and G need to communicate using the gang plank, they must inform their respective supervi-

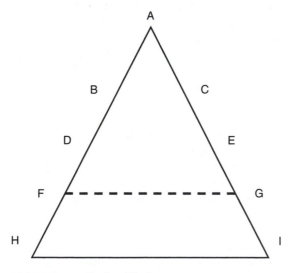

FIGURE 2.1   Scalar Chain

sors immediately and the supervisors must agree that it is necessary. If either of these conditions is violated, the Scalar Chain must be used.

10. **Order.** Fayol believed in the old adage, "A place for everyone and everyone in his place" (p. 36). Without this principle, an organization cannot run effectively or efficiently.

11. **Equity.** Treating all organizational members with a combination of "kindliness and justice" is the essence of equity (p. 38).

12. **Stability of tenure of personnel.** Sufficient time must be provided for the worker to become familiar with a new task and to become successful in completing it. If the worker does not have the proper abilities, though, he must be replaced with someone who does.

13. **Initiative.** Managers and workers should have the ability to think through a plan of action and execute it aptly. Fayol believed that managers should rely on their workers' initiative: "Other things being equal, moreover, a manager able to permit the exercise of initiative on the part of subordinates is infinitely superior to one who cannot do so" (p. 40).

14. **Esprit de corps.** Fayol described the principle of esprit de corps as "Union is strength" (p. 40). Fayol meant that a strong organization is one that has loyal members, who will strive to keep the organization together at the cost of their personal interests.

Fayol's 14 principles plainly tell a manager how she should manage. As opposed to Taylor, who focused mainly on the elements of the task, Fayol believed that managerial practices were the key to predictability and efficiency in organizations. Examining the principles shows that Fayol had a particular interest in minimizing misunderstandings caused by communication. Unity of command, unity of direction, centralization, and the Scalar Chain were all mechanisms intended to simplify the communication process, such that misunderstandings caused by multiple supervisors and free-flowing communication would be eliminated.

From a communication perspective, however, it is readily apparent that such mechanisms can lead to misunderstandings of many forms. The Scalar Chain, for example, with its emphasis on one-way communication (particularly downward), neglects the interactive nature of the phenomenon. We know communication to be a two-way process, where both participants contribute to the process of creating meaning. An example of this was told to us by Isabella, a 43-year-old former employee of a television station:

> When I was working at the TV station, the station manager wanted to change the date we would air a particular program. I think her exact words were that she wanted to "back the program up two weeks." Those were the words she used. What ended up happening was that half of the people at the meeting thought she meant to make it two weeks sooner, while the other half thought that to back it up meant to put it out two weeks later. So half of us, including me, went ahead and contacted TV Guide and changed everything for two weeks ahead. We didn't know we had a problem until we were very close to

the air date and by then it was too late. A lot of the consequences came from the fact that many people thought that it was supposed to air publicly on a particular date, but it didn't. It looked like we didn't know what we were doing.

As Isabella's story demonstrates, one-way communication, though efficient in Fayol's Scalar Chain model, can fail when the message is unclear or open to multiple interpretations. In the end, the message was neither efficient nor effective.

The Scalar Chain also contributes to misunderstandings by minimizing the use of horizontal communication. By relegating horizontal communication to emergency situations as a means of increasing predictability and order, Fayol also removed its positive contributions to communication, such as building collegiality, increasing job and communication satisfaction, and verifying the meanings of messages communicated in other forms.

Elements of Management

Although Fayol's principles of management describe the practices in which managers should engage, his elements of management are the general objectives that management needs to accomplish (1949, p. 7). Through the effective implementation of the principles of management discussed previously, managers should be able to execute the elements of management. Here we discuss briefly the five elements of management (planning, organizing, command, coordination, and control):

1. **Planning.** This first element of management involves creating a plan of action for the future, determining the stages of the plan and the technology necessary to implement it. An effective plan should have the following features: (a) unity—only one plan should be put into action at a time; (b) continuity—the different stages of the plan should progress logically; (c) flexibility—plans should be adjustable to changing environment conditions, and; (d) precision—a specific line of proximate action should be delineated.

2. **Organizing.** Once a plan of action is designed, managers need to provide everything necessary to carry it out, including raw materials, tools, capital, and human resources. To be able to organize effectively, Fayol argued that every high-level manager should have the following qualities and knowledge: (a) health and physical fitness; (b) intelligence and mental vigor; (c) moral qualities; (d) sound general education; (e) managerial ability; (f) general knowledge of all the essential functions of the organization; and (g) the widest possible competence in the central task characterizing the organization.

3. **Command.** With the plan of action in place and the necessary resources secured, managers must begin implementing the plan. To do so effectively, managers must understand the strengths and weaknesses of the personnel, eliminate incompetent workers, audit the organization regularly, and strive to maintain the principles of management as discussed in the prior section (particularly as they relate to personnel).

4. **Coordination.** With the plan of action in place, resources secured, and a system of command implemented, the high-level manager must now work to "harmonize" (Fayol, 1949, p. 103) all of the activities to facilitate organizational success. Communication (particularly information sharing) is the prime coordinating mechanism.

5. **Control.** The final element of management involves the comparison of the activities of the personnel to the plan of action; it is the evaluation component of management. Control procedures must be both timely and strict. Timelines are important because adequate time must be allotted for changes if control procedures indicate that the plan is not being followed. Control must also be strict in that if personnel deviate unnecessarily from the plan of action there must be established penalties until the plan is followed again.

It is perhaps easiest to think of Fayol's five elements as managerial objectives and his 14 principles as tools for accomplishing those objectives. Looked at in this way, it is quite easy to see why Fayol proposed the principles that he did. The five elements are phrased in machinelike terms, with little attention paid to the humanistic side of the organization and its members. The objectives were to keep the machine functioning effectively and efficiently and to replace quickly any part or process that did not contribute to these objectives. The principles were tools for accomplishing exactly that. Downward communication, unity of command, esprit de corps, and subordination of individual interests, for example, seemed to be the best ways to allow for planning, organizing, command, coordination, and control to occur.

Fayol's administrative theory differs noticeably from the theory of scientific management advocated by Taylor. The main difference lies in their foci; Taylor focused on the task, whereas Fayol focused on management. Another difference between the two theorists is important to the study of organizational communication. Fayol appears to have slightly more respect for the worker than Taylor had, as evidenced by Fayol's proclamation that workers may indeed be motivated by more than just money (e.g., opportunity for better education and more job security). Fayol also argued for equity in the treatment of workers, which should include being kind to them and helping to promote justice for them. Perhaps of most importance to the study of organizational communication is the emphasis Fayol placed on communication. Although he believed in a strict Scalar Chain, he did acknowledge the necessity of employing horizontal communication at certain times. While these principles seem overly stringent today, Fayol's positioning of communication as a necessary ingredient to successful management was an important step in the early twentieth century.

Administrative Theory in the Modern Workplace

Fayol's elements and principles of management are still alive in modern organizations in several ways: as accepted practices in some industries; as revamped versions of the original principles or elements; or as remnants of the organization's history to which alternative practices and philosophies are being offered.

TABLE 2.1   Comparison of Managerial Skills

Management Skills—Fayol	Managerial Skills—Modern Managers
Health and physical fitness	Communication skills
Intelligence	Organizational skills
Moral qualities	Team-building skills
Sound general education	Leadership skills
Managerial ability	Coping skills
General organizational knowledge	Technical skills
Central task competence	

Fayol's elements of management, for instance, are recognizable as the main objectives of modern managers, though today they are often expressed in more humanistic and participative terms. In other words, although the labels for the objectives themselves seem to have survived into the new century, the meaning of those objectives has changed. Consider two of the elements in this fashion. As Fayol described the element of "planning," he talked about it as a unidirectional phenomenon where the manager plans the activities, goals, and objectives of the workers. A large part of the modern manager's job is indeed planning, but now the planning is often done in conjunction with the workers in a participatory fashion.

Fayol's element of "organizing" is another example of how the objective remains in the modern workplace but its meaning has changed. As stated earlier, Fayol argued that every high-level manager should have certain qualities and knowledge. Modern managers must be equipped with several of these qualities but are now expected to be much more skilled in the areas of human relationships and communication. Table 2.1 restates Fayol's list and also the skills needed for modern project managers, as summarized by James Taylor in his book *A Survival Guide for Project Managers* (1998).

The two lists certainly have some overlap, but they contain a few very interesting differences. Of particular note is the fact that the majority of the modern manager's skills need to be in the area of communication and relationships, whereas Fayol's managers needed technical mastery and strong personalities. These differences are illustrative of the changes that have occurred in many modern organizations; changes that attempt to move past treating organizational members as parts of a machine.

Several of Fayol's principles of management are also followed today, to a degree that depends on the industry and the particular organization. The U.S. military is a prime example of an organization that has continued to use these principles. Division of work, unity of command, subordination of individual interest to general interest, centralization, and the Scalar Chain, in particular, characterize managerial practice in all branches of the military. Other modern organizations, too, follow Fayol's principles. In particular, organizations that have grown large tend to turn to several of these principles, such as the Scalar Chain and centralization as a means of imposing order.

The final classical theorist discussed in this chapter is Max Weber, whose theory has several features in common with Fayol's administrative theory but is more descriptive than prescriptive. Whereas Fayol was *prescribing* objectives and tools for managers to use in the workplace, Weber set out to *describe* an ideal or pure form of organizational structure that would probably never be attained.

Weber's Theory of Bureaucracy

Max Weber (1864–1920), a German sociologist, developed a theory of organizations that, while having some of the same elements as those by Taylor and Fayol, was born more out of theory than of industrial experimentation. The English translation of Weber's book, *The Theory of Social and Economic Organization* (1947), appeared in the United States about the same time as Fayol's *General and Industrial Management*. In it, Weber theorized about an ideal type of organizational structure, which he called a bureaucracy. Weber's *bureaucracy* was not "ideal" in the sense that it was the perfect structure for every organization but that it was a "pure" organizational form.

For Weber, bureaucracy allows for the optimal form of authority—"rational authority." The exercise of authority is the underlying interest for Weber:

> It is necessary, that is, that there should be a relatively high probability that the action of a definite, supposedly reliable group of persons will be primarily oriented to the execution of the supreme authority's general policy and specific commands. (1947, p. 324)

In other words, Weber believed that for organizations to function effectively and efficiently, there needed to be an assurance that the workers would respect the "right" of managers to direct their activities as dictated by organizational rules and procedures. Without this assurance, the system would be ineffective.

Based on experience, Weber posited three types of legitimate authority:

1. **Traditional authority.** Traditional authority is based on past customs and involves personal loyalty to the person in the leadership position. According to Weber, traditional authority rests "on an established belief in the sanctity of immemorial traditions and the legitimacy of the status of those exercising authority under them" (p. 328). The best example of this type of authority is royalty. Kings and queens of nations and tribes often have authority based on inheritance and tradition. Their subjects are loyal to the tradition of the throne and believe that the person occupying it deserves their loyalty, regardless of ability to lead.
2. **Charismatic authority.** Charismatic authority is based on personal trust in the character or skills of the person to whom authority is attributed.

According to Weber, this form of authority rests "on devotion to the specific and exceptional sanctity, heroism or exemplary character of an individual person and of the normative patterns or order revealed or ordained by him" (p. 328). Charismatic authority differs from traditional authority in that the former is rooted in the characteristics, attributes, or skills of the person in authority while the latter is related more to loyalty based on tradition. Martin Luther King, Jr., is an example of a person to whom charismatic authority was attributed.

3. **Rational authority.** Rational authority is often referred to as *rational-legal authority* or *legal authority* because it is based on the rational application of rules or laws. Weber described this form of authority as "resting on a belief in the 'legality' of patterns of normative rules and the right of those elevated to authority under such rules to issue commands" (p. 328). He preferred this form of authority to traditional or charismatic authority because it is rooted in the rational application of rules instead of personal character or loyalty to tradition. According to Weber, the probability that order (and hence organization) would be upheld using this form of authority was higher.

Tenets of Bureaucracy

The basic tenets of bureaucracy are mechanisms dedicated to preserving and enhancing rational authority. What follows are eight components of Weber's theory (the list is by no means exhaustive):

1. **Rules.** Rules are the essence of bureaucracy and the basis of rational authority. Bureaucracy is based on a system of written rules that cover all possible contingencies within an organization. The rules are both *universalistic*, meaning they should be applied impartially to every member of the organization, and *impersonal*, meaning that people are treated according to the rules. Rational authority is effective only to the extent that there is obedience to the established and agreed upon rules and that there is a consistent rational application of those rules to all members of the organization. With a rule for every possible contingency, members of a bureaucracy are able to act predictably and consistently in any situation with which they are confronted.

2. **Specified sphere of competence.** Although rules spell out guidelines for behavior in any situation an organizational member may encounter, a specified sphere of competence delineates tasks for every member. This component of bureaucracy refers to a division of labor. Every organizational member (a) has an obligation to perform the functions specified by the division of labor and (b) should have the authority to carry out those functions.

3. **Hierarchy.** Weber, like Taylor, believed in a strict chain of command. In a hierarchy, every lower office should be under the strict control and supervision of a higher office. Weber also added that there should be the right of appeal and of grievance if workers in a lower office think they have been mistreated or not treated according to the rules.

4. **Specialized training.** Only those individuals who have demonstrated competence through specialized training should be part of the administrative staff, for it is only through a thorough understanding of the functions and procedures that a rational application of the rules of the bureaucracy is possible.

5. **Workers do not own technology.** In a pure bureaucracy, no worker or member of the administration should own any nonhuman form of production used in the functioning of the organization. Ownership of the technology would lead to a form of protectionism, making a rational application of rules impossible.

6. **No entitlement to "official position" by incumbent.** No worker or member of the administration should have "title" to his or her position (as Supreme Court Justices do). If a member does have such entitlement, the tendency to act as if she is beyond the boundaries of the rules would counteract the need for a rational application of rules to all members of the bureaucracy.

7. **Everything written down.** Perhaps the second most important tenant of bureaucracy is the notion that everything should be in writing. All decisions, meeting minutes, rulings, and especially the guiding rules of the organization must be written down and accessible because they constitute the "central office" of the modern bureaucracy. Without a written record, deviation from and nonrational application of the rules is likely to occur.

8. **Maintenance of "ideal type"—bureaucracy.** One of the main functions of any bureaucracy is to maintain the proper and rational functioning of the bureaucracy itself. Without appropriate monitoring, maintenance, and updating, the bureaucracy will fail.

In summary, Weber's theory of bureaucracy is more closely related to Fayol's administrative theory than to Taylor's theory of scientific management, though differences do exist with the former. Whereas Fayol focused on management, Weber was concerned with describing the ideal structure of an organization. The cornerstone of Weber's theory is the existence of written rules, the rational application of which would ensure the promotion of legitimate authority and the effective and efficient functioning of the organization.

Bureaucracy in the Modern Workplace

The word *bureaucracy* is a common one in use today. People easily point to large organizations guided by countless rules as being "bureaucracies" (whether they really are or not) and readily supply examples of having to cut through the "bureaucratic red tape" when attempting to accomplish something. Unfortunately, the concept of a bureaucracy has been linked in modern society with inefficient, slow-moving organizations, which, ironically, is antithetical to the theory outlined by Weber.

Countless modern organizations have characteristics of bureaucracies. Many government agencies, universities, union shops, and assembly-line plants, just to name a few, tend to operate according to bureaucratic principles. Even smaller organizations implement some of these procedures. For example, recall the story from the beginning of this chapter about Leah, the special education teacher, who was given a rule to follow regarding the implementation of a new reading program for her students. The principal seemed to violate several underlying principles of bureaucracy. First, he was more concerned with his authority than with the establishment of context appropriate rules. Second, there was not a rule for every possible contingency, as Weber had prescribed. Instead, there was a general rule for treating students all the same, which seemed to leave no room for meeting the needs of these special education students. As Taylor (2001) pointed out, in a bureaucracy, "if the rules of the organization cannot be formulated explicitly, they do not count" (p. 129).

Summary

The Industrial Revolution brought many changes to the United States by the beginning of the twentieth century. Whereas individuals and families had once been the primary producers of goods and services, large organizations were now taking over. Organizational theorists Frederick Taylor, Henri Fayol, and Max Weber were the major contributors to thought regarding the most efficient and effective means of running an organization.

Although Taylor, Fayol, and Weber differed in their approaches to organizational theory, they remain linked in that all three were attempting to enhance management's ability to predict and control the behavior of their workers. Table 2.2 summarizes the information presented in this chapter and highlights the role of communication in each theory.

Communication was important to the classical approaches to organizations, though the extent to which the three theorists considered communication in their

TABLE 2.2 Classical Theories of Organizations

	Taylor	Fayol	Weber
Theory	Scientific management	Administrative theory	Rational-legal bureaucracy
Focus	Task	Management	Ideal organizational structure
Central Feature	Scientific reasoning; empirical validation	Scalar Chain	Reliance on hierarchy; rules
Role of Communication	Task-structuring orders; downward; written	Task oriented; downward (horizontal when approved); written	Rule oriented; downward (grievances allowed); written

theories is minimal. All three theorists considered only the task function of communication (ignoring for the most part the relational and maintenance functions of communication). For Taylor, communication was the primary means by which workers were informed as to how they were to perform their jobs. In Taylor's theory, communication was primarily written, generally flowed down the hierarchy, and was used to give orders. Fayol's use of communication was also task oriented, but he proposed the notion that communication may at times have to flow horizontally, instead of following the Scalar Chain. That, however, was to be done only in very limited circumstances. For Weber, communication was also central but was mainly limited to written rules and downward communication.

Classical theories of organizations are still evident today, nearly a century after they were introduced. Many manufacturing plants (particularly those whose primary technology is the assembly line); utility companies; certain factions of the local, state, and federal government; and the military are organized in this way. Even those organizations moving toward a more humanistic approach to management (discussed in Chapter 3) still have elements of these classical management theories. Understanding the origin of these elements, why they are in place, and what their benefits and limitations may be is beneficial as you strive to function competently as a member of an organization.

Ironically, classical approaches to organizational management were designed to help predict and control behavior in organizations. Although the strict hierarchies, rigid Scalar Chains, and rule-oriented structures helped reduce misunderstandings based on role obligations, for example, the same elements helped create misunderstandings based on mistreatment of workers, lack of information regarding an overall mission, lack of attention to human concerns, and myriad other issues. In the next chapter, we discuss the next wave of organizational theory designed to help alleviate some of the pressure caused by the misunderstandings fostered in classically run organizations.

3 Humanistic Theories of Organizations

As the number and types of organizations grew in the early and mid-twentieth century, so too did the desires of theorists and practitioners for a more *humanistic* approach to managing. The traditional approaches to management that emphasized coercion, control, and punishment that had been deemed to be effective and efficient were beginning to be questioned. Competing management theories emerged that were based on very different philosophical orientations regarding the relationship between work and workers.

Human relations theory and human resources theory were developed to promote the concerns of the individual worker in an atmosphere that was mainly focused on production. Human relations theory appeared first, soon followed by human resources theory, which attempted to remedy some of the philosophical and practical issues related to human relations. This chapter discusses the origins and the major theorists associated with both human relations and human resources theories.

Human Relations Theory

As we begin the discussion of *human relations theory*, consider the following story from one of the interviews conducted for this book. Kumiko Ozaki was a department head on a pig farm. Her story is a modern illustration of the situation that led to the development of the human relations approach to organizations.

> I personally would like more control over what gets done and how it gets done on the farm. I also feel as if sometimes people's needs and feelings aren't being met at work. I understand it is a job, but still people have to be comfortable there. I need to know that what I say influences what goes on as a whole, not just with my department and me.
>
> In general, my bosses need to listen to me. They need to listen to me and say, "OK, let's discuss this, let's figure out how this can be done." You know—brainstorm. Let's say I tell them something can be implemented on the farm and that these are going to be the results. Well, they should say,

"Let's try it" or "That's a good idea but here's why it won't work." Don't just tell me "No." Consider what input I'm giving, because it's not just talk.

But they don't listen because they're the bosses. They're going by what they know, what their statistics show, what their bosses say, and that doesn't satisfy me. Say, for example, you are a manager, then you should be able to tell your boss, "Look, this is really what is going on. Let me show what we're doing on our farm." But instead of listening, they say, "Well, they told us to do this so you're going to do this." It's just kind of rigid when it comes to certain things, but it doesn't always have to be. For example, you raise children differently, you can raise a pig differently, and we need to consider sometimes that different could be better.

Kumiko's story demonstrates the feelings that arise in some workers when they are confronted with organizational practices based on classical theory. As you may recall from Chapter 2, in order to maintain predictability and control, classically run organizations concentrate the decision-making power at the top of the hierarchy, minimize input from lower-level employees, and rely on science and rules to guide behavior. By doing so, a whole new class of problems is created. Kumiko shows that in such organizations workers tend to feel as if they do not have any control over their work situation, that management does not care about their opinions, and that their feelings and ideas are unimportant. Kumiko would have been much more satisfied in an organization guided by the principles of human relations theory.

Misunderstandings and the Emergence of the Worker

Human relations theory is characterized by a shift in emphasis from task to worker. Human relations theorists argued that the individual worker was being tapped only for his physical contributions, leaving his creative, cognitive, and emotional aspects unattended. The theories suggested by this movement put a greater emphasis on communication, cooperation, and participation and a celebration of the worker.

This shift of emphasis from the task to the worker can be understood in light of misunderstandings. The previous chapter noted that classical theories recommended strict organizational structures and regulated communication as a means of increasing predictability and decreasing misunderstandings. However, as the stories of Leah (the teacher from Chapter 2) and Kumiko, the pig farm manager, illustrate, those attempts created a whole new class of misunderstandings that served to reduce the effectiveness and satisfaction of the workers. Lower-level workers felt as if their creativity, initiative, and experience were not being used in a system that relied primarily on one-way, downward, and rule-based communication. Therefore, the very system designed to reduce misunderstandings actually served to produce misunderstandings in other forms.

Human relations theory is based on a slightly more dyadic (two-way) conceptualization of communication. Human relations theorists argued that social relationships are at the heart of organizational behavior and to promote effectiveness managers must promote the social well-being of the workers. The prime mechanism for doing so is communication that flows in all directions in the organization. Workers should be allowed to voice their opinions, complaints, suggestions, and feelings; the result should be a reduction in misunderstandings as well as increased satisfaction and production.

Just as classical theory created misunderstandings in an attempt to reduce them, so did human relations theory. As you read, keep the concept of misunderstandings in mind and think of what new forms of misunderstandings may have arisen. In this section, we discuss two precursors to human relations theory: the Hawthorne Studies and the work of Chester Barnard. This section concludes with a summary of the major work on human relations theory, Douglas McGregor's Theory X and Theory Y.

The Beginning of the Human Relations Movement: The Hawthorne Studies

From 1924 to 1932, a series of industrial studies was conducted at the Hawthorne Works of the Western Electric Company in Chicago (Roethlisberger & Dickson, 1939). The *Hawthorne Studies*, as they have become known, eventually led to the development of the human relations school of management, most closely associated with Elton Mayo of Harvard University (Landsberger, 1958).

Officers of the Hawthorne Works conducted the first of the Hawthorne Studies in 1924. The officers (who were essentially following Taylor's scientific management principles) were interested in the "relation of quality and quantity of illumination to efficiency in industry" (Roethlisberger & Dickson, 1939, p. 14). The results of the illumination studies surprised the investigators and served as the impetus for a series of three studies (conducted between 1927 and 1932) by Elton Mayo, in conjunction with F. J. Roethlisberger (also from Harvard) and William Dickson, from Western Electric. The methods used and conclusions drawn from the Hawthorne Studies have been subject to much criticism, but their impact on the theory and practice of management cannot be discounted. In the pages that follow, we briefly summarize each of the four studies.

Illumination Study.   The Illumination Study began in November 1924 and was conducted in conjunction with the National Research Council of the National Academy of Sciences. The study was designed to test the effect of lighting intensity on worker productivity. The prediction of the researchers (following Taylor's principles) was that a certain level of illumination would lead to an optimum level of worker output. To find this level of illumination, the researchers segregated two groups of workers into two separate rooms of equal illumination and measured their output. In one room, the light remained relatively constant (this was the experimental control room). In the other room, the light was increased and decreased. After each change in illumination level, worker output was measured. Output was also measured at regular intervals in the control room.

In both the control room and the test room, productivity increased; there was no significant difference in the production rates of the control group (relatively constant level of illumination) and the test group until the illumination for the test group dropped to a point where they could hardly see. The researchers noted that despite obvious "discomfort and handicap of insufficient illumination" for the test group, they were still efficient in their production, as efficient as the control group (Roethlisberger & Dickson, 1939, p. 17).

Despite the apparent "failure" of the Illumination Study to determine the appropriate level of illumination for optimum output, the researchers found value in the results. The general conclusion was that more investigation into the influence of human relations on work behavior was necessary. The results of the Illumination Study led to the next study, this time headed by Mayo and his Harvard University research team.

Relay Assembly Test Room Study.   The Relay Assembly Test Room Study was conducted from 1927 to 1932. The research team wanted to exercise more control over the research environment than occurred in the Illumination Study. The researchers thought that control was limited in the previous study by the large group size and the multiple factors present on the regular shop floor where the Illumination Study took place. Therefore, the current study was conducted with a smaller group (five experienced female workers who were willing and cooperative) in a separate room, away from the regular shop floor.

The task the five women were to complete was the assembly of telephone relays (consisting of putting together 35 small parts and assembling them with 4 machine screws). As with the Illumination Study, various factors were manipulated to determine their effect on worker output. The number of hours per day and the number of days per week worked were changed throughout the course of the study, as were the number and duration of rest pauses, the method of remuneration, and the extent to which informal talk between the workers was allowed or encouraged. Each worker's output was measured regularly, they were given periodic physical exams, the temperature and humidity of the room were recorded, and the workers' comments and suggestions were shared with an observer.

The results of this study were similar to the results of the Illumination Study. In general, production and satisfaction tended to increase regardless of the changes made in workday length and rest pauses. As Roethlisberger and Dickson noted:

> In many respects these results were puzzling to the investigators, for they were not what they had expected. The general upward trend in output independent of any particular change in rest pauses or shorter working hours was astonishing. The improvement in mental attitude throughout the first two years was also perplexing. (1939, p. 86)

The research team posited five possible explanations for these results, but eventually concluded that the workers' increased output and increased satisfaction were related to changes in supervisory practices (Roethlisberger & Dickson, 1939). The team noticed that the worker–supervisor relationship was different in the test room from that on the regular shop floor, particularly in the following respects:

- In the test room, workers were often consulted regarding proposed changes. In several instances, proposed changes were not implemented because of the workers' displeasure.
- In the test room, workers were asked about their reactions to different working conditions.
- In the test room, workers were allowed to talk to one another while working.
- In the test room, the general well-being (both mental and physical) of the workers was considered.

These facts led the investigators to conclude: "The experimental periods had been essentially carriers of social value. . . . Social factors were the major circumstances limiting output [on the regular shop floor]" (pp. 88–89). In other words, the investigators were beginning to believe that human interrelationships (particularly between worker and supervisor) could be an important contributing factor when considering worker productivity.

Interviewing Program.   The Relay Assembly Test Room Study indicated a connection between supervisory practices and employee morale. The Interviewing Program, conducted from 1928 to 1930, was designed to gather data regarding this possible connection.

The Interviewing Program began in the Inspection Branch in September 1928. When the interviews were finished, a total of 21,126 employees had taken part. The purpose of the interviews was threefold (Mayo, 1933):

- To gather information regarding the employees' likes and dislikes concerning their jobs
- To provide reliable data for use in training supervisors
- To validate the previous studies conducted at the Hawthorne Works

Interviewers were trained to be conversational as they conducted the interviews and to allow the employees to take the discussion down any path they thought appropriate. As a result, employees were provided with a forum for expressing their ideas and feelings regarding whatever they deemed important or relevant to their satisfaction and working conditions.

The actual results of the interviews were perhaps less important than the process itself. As a byproduct of having the opportunity to provide feedback on their personal work situation, many workers indicated a more positive feeling toward the company and a better mental attitude. Although some employees could not see the benefit of the Interviewing Program, Roethlisberger and Dickson indicated that many of them welcomed the chance to talk about their feelings and ideas. The interviews provided them with an opportunity to participate in the effort to improve the workplace. The results of the Interviewing Program led the researchers to the concluding study in the series.

Bank Wiring Room Observation Study.   The final study, conducted between November 1931 and May 1932, resulted from information gathered during the Interview Program. The data indicated that social groups might exercise very strong control over the production of individual work behavior on the shop floor. The primary concern of the research team and company officers was the possibility that there might be a form of informal leadership operating to restrict employee output. The Bank Wiring Room Observation Study was conducted to provide overt behavioral data regarding this supposition, because it was reached using only the statements of workers gathered during the Interview Program. In other words, the research team wanted to see for themselves how the social control they had heard about in the interviews actually manifested itself on the shop floor.

For this study, the researchers put 14 bank wiremen in a separate room and had them complete their individual tasks. They were not informed of the nature of the study, and the researcher present in the room acted like a disinterested spectator.

The investigators concluded, based on observations and output data, that each worker was artificially restricting his output; output was lower than the company-established target. As Roethlisberger and Dickson related, "This standard was not imposed upon them, but apparently had been formulated by the workmen themselves" (p. 445). Informally developed group norms were present in the work group that operated to restrict individual worker output. From the Bank Wiring Room Observation Study, it became clear that an *informal organization* that serves to constrain individual employees' behavior is present within the formal organizational structure.

Implications of the Hawthorne Studies.   The Hawthorne Studies had several implications for management theory. First, the Illumination Study led to the notion that the mere practice of observing people's behavior tends to alter their behavior (a phenomenon that has come to be known as the *Hawthorne Effect*). Management theorists translated this conclusion into a principle for supervisors: Pay attention to your workers to increase their satisfaction and productivity.

Second, the Relay Assembly Test Room Study changed the way *human inter-relationships* were viewed. As a result of these studies, the relationships among workers and between workers and their supervisors were believed to be very powerful. Whereas classical theory treated these relationships only according to task requirements and in a unidirectional form, resulting theory began to view them more personally. This set of studies also demonstrated that this new relationship form would increase the amount and quality of worker participation in decision making.

Third, the Interviewing Program demonstrated for the first time the powerful influence of *upward communication*. The fact that workers were asked for their opinions and told that they mattered was enough to increase their positive attitudes toward the company.

Fourth, the Bank Wiring Room Studies led future theorists to account for the existence of *informal communication*. Classical theories did not acknowledge the usefulness of communication other than that which occurred formally (e.g., supervisor to subordinate). In fact, as you may remember, great pains were taken to ensure that horizontal and upward communication were minimized at all costs.

Although these implications may not seem newsworthy today, it is important to remember that at the time of these studies little was known about the powerful nature of social relations in the workplace. The Hawthorne Studies represented a major turning point in the development of management theory and practice, moving managers more toward the interpersonal aspects of organizing. Despite the humanizing impact of these studies on management theory and practice, however, they have been subject to much criticism over the years.

Criticisms of the Hawthorne Studies. The Hawthorne Studies and the management theory that followed from them have not been fully accepted by everyone; the studies themselves have come under close scrutiny since their publication (e.g., Carey, 1967; Gale, 2004; Jones, 1990; Landsberger, 1958). For example, on the one hand, Carey (1967) suggested that the Hawthorne Studies were not conducted with the appropriate scientific rigor necessary and therefore the results should be dismissed. He objected that the number of subjects studied in the Relay Assembly Test Room Study was too small (five women), that no control groups were used, and that real production did not increase until two of the women workers were replaced with workers who were more "cooperative." Characterizations such as "worthless," "gross errors," and "incompetence in the understanding and use of the scientific method" peppered Carey's analysis of this work.

On the other hand, critiques by Landsberger (1958) and Jones (1990) defend the studies (though Landsberger admits some mistakes were made) and the resultant human relations approach to management. Jones (1990) reexamined the original Hawthorne data using modern statistical procedures and concluded: "The human relations approach to industrial sociology is not controverted by the original Hawthorne data from which it began" (p. 189).

Despite its limitations, the extent to which the Hawthorne Studies affected the trajectory of management theory cannot be denied. As Sonnenfeld (1983) remarked, "Given such unusual breadth of validity and significance, one must question just whose interest is truly served by continuing this tired historical debate" (p. 908). The processes and results of these studies led not only researchers at Hawthorne to reconsider the underlying principles of classical theory, but now other theorists were beginning to propose competing theories based on vastly different views of human nature. In the next section, we discuss the contribution of Chester Barnard to the development of the human relations approach.

The Emergence of Communication: Chester Barnard

Chester Barnard, an executive with American Telephone and Telegraph Company for more than 40 years, can be considered a bridge between classical and human relations theories (Kreps, 1990). Barnard's book, *The Functions of the Executive* (1938), is an executive's analysis of organizational life, written because Barnard found that previous writings on the subject neither mirrored his experience as an executive nor demonstrated an understanding of the leadership practices of successful organizational executives with whom he interacted.

Another impetus for Barnard's book was his disagreement with Max Weber's philosophy of organization:

> [T]hough I early found out how to behave effectively in organizations, not until I had much later relegated economic theory and economic interests to a secondary— though indispensable—place did I begin to understand organizations or human behavior in them. (1938, p. 3)

Although some of Barnard's ideas are rooted in classical theory (e.g., he argues for strict lines of communication), he spends much of his time arguing for a "human-based system of organization" that recognizes the potential of every worker and the centrality of communication to the organizing process. Based on these ideas, Barnard can be considered an important link between classical theory and human relations theory and an important person in the development of the field of organizational communication.

The Functions of the Executive covers a variety of topics related to industrial life. Here, we discuss six issues most relevant to the field of organizational communication: (1) formal vs. informal organization, (2) cooperation, (3) communication, (4) incentives, (5) authority, and (6) zone of indifference.

Formal versus Informal Organization.　Barnard recognized the existence of an informal organization and how it differs from a formal organization. He defined a *formal organization* as "a system of consciously coordinated activities or forces of two or more persons" (1938, p. 73). The formal organizational system comes into being when the following occurs: (1) There are persons able to communicate with each other (2) who are willing to contribute action (3) to accomplish a common purpose (Barnard, 1938, p. 82). The *informal organization*, by contrast, is based on myriad interactions that take place throughout an organization's history. The informal organization has the following characteristics: (1) it is indefinite; (2) it is structureless; and (3) there are no definite subdivisions of personnel.

The informal organization differs from the formal organization in two main ways. First, the formal organization is a definite, structured entity, whereas the informal organization is not bound by structure or function. Second, the concept of a common purpose is not present in the definition of an informal organization as it is with a formal organization. This is not to say, though, that the informal organization does not have definite effects. According to Barnard, the informal organization has the following consequences (1938, p. 116):

1. The most general direct effects of informal organization are customs, mores, folklore, institutions, social norms, and ideals.
2. The informal organization creates the conditions under which a formal organization may arise.

Barnard believed that most executives were unaware of the existence of the informal organization and its relationship to the formal organization. According to him, the informal organization must be recognized and understood so that the formal organization may operate effectively. One of the keys to successful organization for Barnard is the concept of cooperation.

Cooperation.   *Cooperation* is a central term in *The Functions of the Executive*. Barnard's arguments concerning human behavior and how it can best be promulgated revolve around this concept. Although he uses the term in a variety of ways, cooperation should be considered a precursor to and necessary component of a formal organization.

Whereas Weber and other classical theorists argued that the way of inducing workers to work was through threat, fear of punishment, and remuneration, Barnard proposed the notion that cooperation was the key. To cooperate, the individual worker must find something more beneficial to himself in cooperating than in doing otherwise:

> Willingness to cooperate, positive or negative, is the expression of the net satisfactions or dissatisfactions experienced or anticipated by each individual in comparison with those experienced or anticipated through alternative opportunities. (Barnard, 1938, p. 85)

If we return to Kumiko's situation at the pig farm, this discussion of cooperation comes to life. Kumiko was expressing her dissatisfaction with the current situation at the pig farm (e.g., she had no control and was not allowed to participate in decisions) and was comparing that to an anticipated situation where management did value her input. According to Barnard's principle, her willingness to cooperate was probably not very high because she could imagine another situation in which she would be more satisfied.

Communication.   *Communication* is critical to cooperation. As Barnard wrote, "The most universal form of human cooperation, and perhaps the most complex, is speech" (1938, p. 46). He considered communication to be both the most likely reason for the success of cooperation and the reason for its failure. Given this, he argued that the primary function of the organizational executive is to serve as a channel for communication. To aid the executive in serving this function, Barnard outlined a system of communication, summarized as follows (Barnard, 1938, pp. 175–180):

1. **Channels of communication should be definitely known.** Every member of an organization should have an assigned position, be aware of every other member's assigned position (through an organizational chart), and respect

lines of authority. Authority rests with both the position and the person (though more importantly with the position).

2. **Objective authority requires a definite formal channel of communication to every member.** Every member of the organization must report to someone (communication in one direction) and must be subordinate to someone (communication in the other direction).

3. **The line of communication must be as direct or short as possible.** Barnard recognized that misunderstanding is inherent in communication. Therefore, he proposed that the fewer channels communication must pass through, the higher the probability that the message will not become distorted.

4. **The complete line of communication should be used.** Every communication should pass through all levels of authority in order to minimize misunderstanding due to conflicting messages and multiple interpretations.

5. **The competence of the persons serving as communication centers, that is, officers and supervisory heads, must be adequate.** The more central the organizational member is to the communication flow in and out of the organizational system, the more competent that person must be in understanding operations at all levels of the organization.

6. **The line of communication should not be interrupted during the time when the organization is to function.** This component of the communication system is a bit repetitive of the fourth component but emphasizes the importance of the position (not the person) to the flow of communication in a properly functioning organization.

7. **Every communication should be authenticated.** It must be known that the person communicating has the authority to communicate regarding a particular issue and that the communication can be verified as coming from that particular person.

Barnard's system of communication is an interesting mix of classical theory and something more humanistic. As opposed to classical theorists, Barnard seemed to understand the centrality of communication to the functioning of the organization and to the manager's job. But his understanding of communication is still quite limited. His system appears to be aimed directly at reducing misunderstandings, but it lacks in the areas of relationship formation and maintenance, which are the essence of organizational life. Although communication is central to cooperation for Barnard, a cursory review of the system of communication just outlined reveals it to be tied to the concept of authority.

Authority.   Authority is associated with securing cooperation from organizational members and is intimately tied with communication. As Barnard defined it, *authority* is

> the character of a communication (order) in a formal organization by virtue of which it is accepted by a contributor to or "member" of the organization as governing the action he [sic] contributes; that is, as governing or determining what he [sic] does or is not to do so far as the organization is concerned. (1938, p. 163)

Authority, then, is an interrelationship among at least three elements: the originator of the communication, the communication itself, and the receiver.

Barnard privileged authority based on position over authority based on an individual (much as the classical theorists did). *Authority of position* is authority ascribed to a communication based on the fact that it originates from a superior position in the organizational structure, regardless of the relative ability of the person occupying the position. *Authority of leadership* is authority ascribed to a communication based on the knowledge and ability of the person communicating the message, regardless of the position she occupies. Combining authority of position with authority of leadership creates a situation where those receiving the communication will tend to obey a given order with little question.

Zone of Indifference.   The final concept we will discuss from Barnard integrates communication, authority, and human behavior. According to Barnard, if you were to line up all the possible orders for action that could be given, some would be clearly unacceptable (outside the boundaries of what the individual anticipated was necessary as a member of the organization) and would not be followed. Other orders would be either mildly unacceptable or mildly acceptable and might or might not be followed. The remaining orders would be acceptable and would be followed. The *zone of indifference* is that set of orders for action "that in a general way was anticipated at time of undertaking the connection with the organization" (1938, p. 169) (see Figure 3.1). In other words, an individual's zone of indifference marks the boundaries of what that person will consider doing without question, based on expectations developed on entering the organization.

The best interest of the executive is to broaden the zone of indifference for each worker, such that orders for action are carried out with little questioning of authority or appropriateness. The zone of indifference narrows or broadens depending on the extent to which the perceived benefits of following the order outweigh the costs.

As is evident from Figure 3.1, though, a large portion of orders for action may fall outside of a worker's zone of indifference. How, then, do organizational executives induce workers to follow such orders? Barnard posited that the answer to this question lies in the combination of position and leadership authority:

Orders not followed	Orders sometimes not followed	Orders sometimes followed	**Zone of Indifference** Orders followed

Unacceptable	**Neutral**	**Acceptable**

FIGURE 3.1   **Zone of Indifference**

> When the authority of leadership is combined with the authority of position, men [sic] who have an established connection with an organization generally will grant authority, accepting orders far outside the zone of indifference. (p. 174)

In other words, an executive who has authority based on both formal position and personal knowledge can create a situation in which organizational members will follow orders they might not otherwise have obeyed.

Although authority of position is an element of the formal organization, authority of leadership is more a property of the informal organization and arises through interaction. It is for this reason that Barnard can be considered an organizational communication theorist. The principles discussed here, drawn from *The Functions of the Executive*, represent an important contribution to the development of a theory of organizations based on communication.

Barnard's work represents an important link between classical theory and human relations theory because he began to draw attention away from formal organizational structures toward such things as communication, cooperation, and the informal organization. His work introduced important concepts that were then integrated by other theorists in the human relations movement. In the next section, we discuss the prime example of a human relations theory that developed based on the work of Mayo, Roethlisberger, Dickson, Barnard, and others.

Theory X and Theory Y: Douglas McGregor

Douglas McGregor (1906–1964), a Sloan Professor of Management at Massachusetts Institute of Technology, articulated the basic principles of human relations theory. In *The Human Side of Enterprise* ([1960] 1985) he argued that to understand human behavior one must discover the theoretical assumptions upon which behavior is based. Of particular interest to him was the behavior of managers toward workers. McGregor believed that the best way to understand managerial behavior in practice was to examine the theory that guides it:

> Every managerial act rests on assumptions, generalizations, and hypotheses—that is to say, on theory. Our assumptions are frequently implicit, sometimes quite unconscious, often conflicting; nevertheless, they determine our predictions that if we do a, b will occur. Theory and practice are inseparable. ([1960] 1985, p. 6)

In other words, McGregor believed that managers are guided in their treatment of workers by beliefs about how the workers collectively think, act, and feel.

McGregor understood that managers wanted to accomplish two interrelated objectives with regard to workers: (1) predict and control their behavior and (2) tap their unrealized potential. The problem for him was that existing managerial theory, classical theory in particular, was inadequate in this regard. The theoretical assumptions of classical theory are unable to assist managers in accomplishing these objectives for three reasons ([1960] 1985, pp. 16–17):

1. The principles of classical theory were developed primarily from the study of models, such as the Catholic Church and the military, which differ significantly from modern industrial and service organizations.
2. Classical theory does not acknowledge the changes that occurred in the political, social, and economic milieus that shape organizations and influence managerial behavior.
3. The assumptions regarding human behavior that underlie classical theory are misguided and, at best, only partially true.

It is this third issue, misguided or wrong assumptions of classical theory, to which McGregor turned his attention in *The Human Side of Enterprise*.

He took the most exception to the assumption of "authority [as] the central, indispensable means of organizational control" (p. 18). Overreliance on authority as a means of control meant that other, perhaps more productive, forms of control were ignored, particularly those that acknowledge and foster the individual skills and abilities of the worker. If a manager is seeking collaboration, authority "is at best a weak crutch" (p. 30).

Because McGregor rejected the basic assumptions of classical theory, he put forward a competing theory of management based on vastly different assumptions; assumptions that he argued were more firmly rooted in the reality of human nature. He termed classical theory and its assumptions Theory X and human relations theory and its assumptions Theory Y.

Theory X.   *Theory X*, or classical theory, consists of three assumptions that managers hold regarding workers ([1960] 1985, pp. 33–34):

1. The average human being has an inherent dislike of work and will avoid it if he [*sic*] can.
2. Because of this human characteristic of dislike of work, most people must be coerced, controlled, directed, threatened with punishment to get them to put forth adequate effort toward the achievement of organizational objectives.
3. The average human being prefers to be directed, wishes to avoid responsibility, has relatively little ambition, wants security above all.

Based on these assumptions, managers naturally treat workers with little respect, motivate them mainly through punishment and financial reward, and spend the majority of their time monitoring and coercing them into behaving appropriately. McGregor disagreed with these assumptions and the resulting practices: "Theory X explains the consequences of a particular managerial strategy; it neither explains nor describes human nature although it purports to" (p. 42). In other words, while McGregor understood that managers could coerce and control people into working, it is against their nature to be treated in this way. What is needed is a theory of management that more soundly resonates with human nature.

Theory Y. McGregor argued that while management was becoming more concerned with the human aspects of organizational life, managers' basic assumptions about human nature had not changed; they were still firmly rooted in Theory X. In contrast to Theory X, McGregor proposed *Theory Y* and its competing assumptions about human nature ([1960] 1985, pp. 47–48), which are as follows:

1. The expenditure of physical and mental effort in work is as natural as play or rest.
2. External control and the threat of punishment are not the only means for bringing about effort toward objectives. Man [*sic*] will exercise self-direction and self-control in the service of objectives to which he is committed.
3. Commitment to objectives is a function of the rewards associated with their achievement.
4. The average human being learns, under proper conditions, not only to accept but to seek responsibility.
5. The capacity to exercise a relatively high degree of imagination, ingenuity, and creativity in the solution of organizational problems is widely, not narrowly distributed in the population.
6. Under the conditions of modern industrial life, the intellectual potentialities of the average human being are only partially utilized.

The assumptions of Theory Y are vastly different from those of Theory X and paint a more positive picture of human nature. When managers operate from the assumptions of Theory X, the potential ways in which they can interact with their employees is limited. If they operate from the assumptions of Theory Y, though, the range of possibilities for new managerial practices expands.

Perhaps the greatest implication of Theory Y rests in the matter of control. If work is as natural as play or rest, the average human seeks responsibility, and most people are inherently more creative and driven than Theory X would lead one to believe. How do managers control their behavior such that they achieve quality production? For McGregor, the answer was commitment to objectives. If workers could be committed to the organizational and task objectives, they would naturally respond with high-level production. It was important, he noted, that commitment to objectives would come not from punishment or financial reward (necessarily), but from the promise that the individual's goals are best achieved by the success of the organization (a principle McGregor termed *integration*): "Theory Y assumes that people will exercise self-direction and self-control in the achievement of organizational objectives *to the degree that they are committed to those objectives*" (p. 54). Commitment, then, is the key to control and production.

Although the assumptions of Theory Y are attractive in principle, what does Theory Y look like in practice? McGregor suggested the Scanlon Plan, a philosophy of management based on the assumptions of Theory Y, as a prototypical example. The Scanlon Plan (named for its creator, Joseph Scanlon) has two central features: (1) cost-reduction sharing and (2) effective participation.

A few words about the first feature may be useful for the present discussion. The Scanlon Plan advocates cost-reduction sharing for organizational members or, in other words, "sharing the economic gains from improvements in organizational performance" (McGregor, [1960] 1985, p. 111). As organizational members contribute to the overall performance of the organization, they should be rewarded financially (in addition to the personal satisfactions they are already receiving from increased participation) when the organization increases its profitability.

More important to the study of organizational communication is the second feature of the Scanlon Plan—effective participation. Effective participation is a formal means of providing opportunities to every member of the organization to contribute ideas for improving organizational effectiveness. Effective participation is based on the Theory Y assumption that workers are generally underutilized:

> Even the repetitive worker at the bottom of the hierarchy is potentially more than a pair of hands. He is a human resource. His know-how and ingenuity, properly utilized, may make a far greater difference to the success of the enterprise than any improvement in his physical effort, although of course his effort is not unimportant. Moreover, he achieves recognition and other important social and ego satisfactions from this utilization of his capacities. (pp. 113–114)

This particular quotation forwards terminology that changed the way workers were thought of. In a January 2002 article in *Workforce*, Steve Brzezinski, former director of management programs at Antioch College, argued that McGregor "is the reason we use the term 'human resources' instead of personal department . . . The idea that people are assets was unheard of before McGregor."

Although participation seems to be the key to member satisfaction and productivity as well as overall organizational effectiveness, McGregor warned that it must be implemented appropriately. Groups of managers, consultants, and academics have divergent views regarding participation. Some believe it to be the magic formula for every organizational problem, whereas others see it as a form of "managerial abdication" that wastes time and undermines the manager's power. Those who understand participation, however, know how to use it successfully. They recognize that it is useful, but that it is not the solution to every problem. This group would never use participation in a manipulative way. McGregor aligned with the latter group and argued for a sincere but realistic implementation and vision of what effective participation could produce for an organization.

What the adoption of Theory Y assumptions and practices means for an organization and its members is very complicated. Perhaps the most important change that occurs is that there is a concern for relationships in the organization. As the need to increase commitment increases, so does the need to develop strong, communication-based relationships among organizational members, particularly between supervisor and subordinate. Supervisors must have genuine concern for the attitudes, needs, and potential contributions of their subordinates and must recognize the interdependent nature of their relationships. Cahn

(1971) stated this point simply by saying, "embracing this philosophy does not remove the fact that one does not easily solve the problems of people working with people" (p. 23).

Human relations theory, originating from the Hawthorne Studies and perhaps best exemplified by McGregor's Theory Y, attempted to reverse the treatment of workers as it occurred under classical theory. Although human relations theorists posited new ways of managing organizations, organizational practitioners were less enthusiastic about the full-scale implementation of the "participative management" principles. In the next section, we discuss the emergence of human resources theory as a remedy to the misapplications of and misunderstandings caused by human relations theory.

Human Resources Theory

Managers and workers of the time (and today) often found it difficult to adopt the principles of human relations theory. The following story from one of our interviews illustrates the problems that occur when making the transition from classical theory to human relations theory.

Kevin was a 35-year-old Marine Corps noncommissioned officer who had been in the USMC for 18 years.

> It was July 4th last year and it was time for the Pikeville parade, which is the big town outside the gates of Camp Maybrey. When we got committed to do this parade, every single commander was supposed to write a letter of instruction saying how the troops were going to execute their duties. Well, I was in charge of putting that together. I wrote the letter of instruction that told everybody when the parade rehearsals are going to be, what gear to wear, what time to be there, and where to be for the practices and the parade. It was signed-off by the commanding officer.
>
> Well, at the first practice, one of our company first sergeants, who is one grade higher than I am, brought his company out at 6:00 A.M., not 8:00 A.M., as I had instructed. So he was all upset and mad and when I showed up at 8:00 A.M., he said, "How come you were not out here at 6?" I told him, "Because I am the one who wrote the letter of instruction and I told everybody to be out here at 5 minutes to 8:00 so we can practice."
>
> He was trying to tell me that he is the first sergeant of my company and when he says to be out there at 6:00, then I am supposed to be there with him. I disagreed with him. I told him, "No. I may be in your company, but I work for the battalion commander who is above you." He just walks away and says, "This discussion is over." I say, "No it's not over." We kept going at it.
>
> Later on that day I went and talked to the senior enlisted, who is called the sergeant major; he was out there during the argument. The sergeant major told me that I was flat out wrong for arguing and trying to stress my point, whether I was right or wrong. That is the way the Marine Corps operates; if

> the individual is senior to you, he is always right regardless. We ought to never question it.
>
> But here is what really gets me. A few years back, probably about five years ago, I was *forced* by the Marine Corps (as were all staff NCOs and officers) to take a course called total quality leadership, known in the civilian sector as TQM and the Deming principles. In that class I learned about empowerment. Empowerment means that if somebody junior is right about something or has an idea they should be allowed to voice it without being told to shut up. Unfortunately, the Marine Corps is just not like that. It's like . . . a dictatorship.

Kevin's story illustrates what happens when classically trained managers are told to change their ways, to care more about their workers. In this case, the structure of the Marine Corps and years of being inculcated with the traditional ways of doing things did not allow for the implementation of TQM or participative management on a day-to-day basis. What sounded good in principle was seemingly impossible in practice.

This, too, was the fate of human relations theory. Managers, trained according to traditional principles, were instructed to start "caring" for their workers and to allow them to participate in the decision-making process. In many cases, managers were not equipped with the new skills or the supporting organizational structure or culture to make this rather dramatic change.

Miles, writing in the *Harvard Business Review* (1965), argued that the key element of human relations theory, participation, was used only to make workers *feel* as if they were a part of the organizational decision-making processes:

> Participation, in this model, is a lubricant which oils away resistance to formal authority. . . . In sum, the human relations approach does not bring out the fact that participation may be useful for its own sake. The possibility that subordinates will, in fact, bring to light points which the manager may have overlooked, if considered at all, tends to be mentioned only in passing. . . . The ultimate goal sought in both the traditional and the human relations model is compliance with managerial authority. (pp. 149–150)

Kevin's story comes to mind at this point. He was trained to participate in the decision-making process, but when the situation arose regarding a dispute with his superior, his superior was unwilling to adhere to the new participative system, reverting instead to the compliance model of authority.

This situation also returns us to the notion of misunderstandings. As mentioned earlier in the chapter, elements of human relations theory served to reduce the misunderstandings created under a classical management system, but new forms developed. In particular, misunderstandings arose when workers were told they were important but were not treated as such. This contradiction led to suspicion on the part of the workers and unwillingness to trust management. Misunderstandings also occurred because managers lacked the communication skills necessary to interact with workers on a humane level. Managers knew how to communicate using fear, orders, threats, and one-way communication, but were seemingly lost when they were supposed to show concern for their workers, solicit their input, and engage them personally. The good intentions of the theory led to a whole host of misunderstandings.

Given the apparent failure of human relations to improve the general state of affairs for workers in organizations, Miles proposed the *theory of human resources* as an alternative. Human resources theory differs from human relations theory in three main ways. First, human resources theory is based on an assumption that all people (not just managers) are "reservoirs of untapped resources" (p. 150). Given this assumption, it is the obligation of the manager to tap these resources, whether they are physical or creative.

Second, human relations theory (as practiced) often led to managers retaining decision-making power for all but the most routine decisions. Human resources theory prescribes that many decisions can be made more effectively and efficiently by those workers who are most directly involved with their consequences. That is what Kumiko, the pig farm manager, was advocating. Miles argued that "the more important the decision, the greater is [the manager's] *obligation* to encourage ideas and suggestions from his subordinates" (p. 152). In other words, participation in decision making and actual decision-making power cannot be relegated to either false or perfunctory status.

Finally, Miles suggested that the greatest difference between human relations and human resources is the relationship between employee satisfaction and performance. In human relations theory, increased satisfaction is a direct result of increased participation in the decision-making process. The eventual outcome of increased satisfaction in this model is greater compliance with authority. Human resources, by contrast, suggests that satisfaction is not necessarily a direct result of participation but is instead a derivative of the improved decision making and self-control that results from effective, genuine participation. With this gain, the cycle feeds itself again, and improved satisfaction and morale contribute back to improved decision making and control.

In essence, the human resources theory of satisfaction and morale says that workers are not satisfied with merely being given a voice in the decision-making process; far too often their voice is not heard. Instead, increased satisfaction is related to the improved decision making and self-control that occurs due to participation that is genuinely solicited and heard.

Interestingly, Miles noted that most managers in his day subscribed to the human relations model for their workers, but when it came time to being viewed by their own superiors they subscribed to the human resources model. In the next section, we discuss two prevalent human resources theories: those of Rensis Likert and Robert Blake and Jane Mouton.

Four Systems of Management: Rensis Likert

In his book *New Patterns of Management* (1961), Rensis Likert proposed a theory of management that exemplifies the basic tenets of human resources theory outlined

TABLE 3.1   Summary of Likert's Systems of Management

	System I	System II	System III	System IV
Type	Exploitative, authoritative	Benevolent, authoritative	Consultative	Participative
Basis for motivation	Fear, threats, reward	Potential of both reward and punishment	Rewards and some punishment	Economic and participation
Level for decision making	Top	Top for policy; constrained at lower levels	Top for general decision; specific decisions at low	Spread throughout
Communication	Downward	Downward with limited upward	Downward; upward with some constraints	Free flowing

Source: Adapted with permission of McGraw-Hill Companies: Likert, R. (1961). *New Patterns of Management*. New York: McGraw-Hill.

by Miles. Likert maintained that a new system of management was necessary because of the changes occurring in U.S. society at the time. As a result of increased education, Likert argued, people are less likely to accept direct orders and close supervision. Society, in general, was promoting greater freedom and individual initiative.

He suggested a series of four management systems that range from a more classically oriented system to one based on human resources theory (see Table 3.1). The four systems appear to be separate, but Likert regarded them as blending into one another, making a "continuum with many different patterns" (1961, p. 234). He focused on management systems for his theory because he believed management to be critical to all organizational activities and outcomes:

> Every aspect of a firm's activities is determined by the competence, motivation, and general effectiveness of its human organization. Of all the tasks of management, managing the human component is the central and most important task, because all else depends upon how well it is done. (Likert, 1967, p. 1)

According to Likert, high-producing departments and organizations tend toward System IV, or the participative system, whereas low-producing units favor System I, the exploitative authoritative system.

System I: Exploitative Authoritative.   The first system of management, the *exploitative authoritative system*, is rooted in classical theory. In this system, managers tend to motivate their workers through fear, threats, punishment, and occasional reward. Decision making under this system occurs at the top of the organizational hierarchy, and the decision makers are rarely aware of problems at lower levels of the organization. Goal setting takes the form of orders being issued from the top. As a result, workers are generally hostile toward the goals of the organization and may engage in behavior that is counter to those goals. Upper-level management generally feels highly responsible for the organizational goals; lower-level managers feel less responsible; and workers feel little or no responsibility.

Communication in an exploitative authoritative management system is mainly downward. Subordinates tend to be very suspicious of their superiors and rarely initiate any communication upward. In general, a high level of distortion characterizes communication. The distorted communication and hierarchical structure result in rampant distrust in the organization. Subordinates feel subservient to supervisors, who in turn have contempt for their subordinates, while peers are generally hostile toward one another.

Under this system, relevant outcomes such as satisfaction and productivity are not very positive. Employees are generally dissatisfied with the organization, their supervisors, and their own achievements. Productivity is mediocre and there is high turnover throughout the organization.

System II: Benevolent Authoritative. The second of Likert's systems of management, *benevolent authoritative system*, is only a bit less controlling than the exploitative authoritative system. Motivation under the benevolent authoritative system is based partially on rewards and also on the potential for punishment. The decision-making arena is expanded a bit. Policy decisions are made at the top of the hierarchy. Lower levels are granted some decision-making power but within a framework prescribed by upper management. Decision makers at top levels have some awareness of the problems that occur on the lower levels. Managers tend to feel a high level of responsibility for organizational goals, while workers show relatively little responsibility. The resulting attitude toward the goals of the organization is split; sometimes it is hostile and sometimes it is favorable.

Communication in the benevolent authoritative system is mostly downward, though there is a limited amount of upward communication. Upward communication, however, tends to be distorted so as to avoid the communication of bad news. Subordinates are sometimes suspicious of the communication coming from their superiors. Subordinates are still subservient to their superiors and tend to have some hostility toward their peers owing to the competition inspired by this system; supervisors remain condescending toward their subordinates. Relevant outcomes are only slightly more positive than under the exploitative authoritative system. Employees tend to be dissatisfied to moderately satisfied. Productivity is fair to good, while turnover and absenteeism remain moderately high.

System III: Consultative. The *consultative system* of management is perhaps most closely aligned with the way human relations theory is traditionally practiced (as outlined by Miles). Workers are motivated through rewards, occasional punishment, and limited involvement in decision making and goal setting. Although policy decisions and general decisions are made at the top of the hierarchy, more-specific decisions are made at lower levels where the effects are most consequential. Higher-level managers are moderately aware of the problems at the lower levels of the organization. Goal setting occurs after managers discuss the problems and plan actions with their subordinates. It is of importance that subordinates do not play an integral role in this process; they act more as semi-active consultants to the real decision makers. This process spurs overt acceptance of the organizational goals, though many of the workers may covertly not accept them because of their lack of full involvement in the goal-setting process.

Communication in the consultative management system flows both up and down the hierarchy, though upward communication is not as free flowing as downward. The increase in communication tends to create an atmosphere where employees are cooperative and their relationships are generally positive. Competition with peers and condescension toward subordinates still exists but at a much lower level than in the benevolent authoritative system.

Satisfaction, productivity, and turnover all improve in the consultative system. Although there may be some dissatisfaction in the ranks, there tends to be moderate to high satisfaction throughout the organization. Productivity also tends to be good; turnover and absenteeism are moderate.

System IV: Participative.   Likert argued for the *participative system* of management as the most effective form. This system underscores the basic elements of human resources theory: genuine participation in decision making and goal setting, free-flowing communication, full use of every worker's skills and creative energy, and a high level of responsibility and accountability for the goals of the organization.

Under participative management, a comprehensive compensation system is developed from which employees gain economic rewards. This is but one form of motivation in the participative system. Other forms include participation in group decision making and goal setting, as well as the opportunity to evaluate and improve the methods of operations leading to the accomplishment of organizational goals. Decision making occurs widely throughout the organization, and management is well aware of the problems that occur at the lower levels. Organizational goals are fully accepted by members because in all situations except for emergencies goals are determined through group participation.

Communication in a participative management system is critical to its success. Communication flows in all directions and can be initiated at any level within the organization. Subordinates have the opportunity to question communication from superiors. Given the open nature of this management system, distortion is minimal. As a result, attitudes toward others in the organization tend to be favorable, with cooperation being the norm. Employees and managers alike tend to have a high level of trust and confidence in one another. As stated earlier, Likert asserted that productivity is at its highest level under the participative system. Satisfaction tends to be relatively high, production is excellent, and turnover and absenteeism are low.

Likert's participative system of management addresses Miles' concerns about the genuine versus surface use of participation in organizations subscribing to the human relations approach. Another problem associated with the human relations approach was the notion that the theory attended too much to the needs of the workers, to the disadvantage of advancing the task of the organization. Blake and Mouton's Managerial Grid® is another human resources theory that was designed to alleviate this difficulty with human relations theory. We now turn to an abbreviated discussion of this work.

Blake and Mouton's Managerial Grid

Robert Blake and Jane Mouton, in their book *The Managerial Grid: Key Orientations for Achieving Production through People* (1964), proposed a human resources theory of management that stresses the interrelationship between production and people. Management's main purpose, according to Blake and Mouton, is to promote a culture in the organization that allows for high production at the same time that employees are fostered in their professional and personal development.

As a framework for promoting such a culture, Blake and Mouton recommended the Managerial Grid (later termed the Leadership Grid; see Figure 3.2). The Managerial Grid provides managers with a useful way of diagnosing their

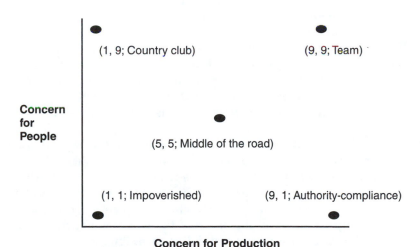

FIGURE 3.2 The Managerial Grid

Source: The Leadership Grid figure for *Leadership Dilemmas—Grid Solutions,* by Robert R. Blake and Anne Adams McCanse. (Formerly the Managerial Grid figure by Robert R. Blake and Jane S. Mouton). Houston, TX: Gulf Publishing Company, p. 29. Copyright © 1991 by Scientific Methods, Inc. Reprinted by Permission of the owners.

personal orientation toward people and production within the organization; it can be used at all levels of the organizational hierarchy.

Much like McGregor, Blake and Mouton argued that the assumptions managers hold affect their behavior and managerial style. But Blake and Mouton differ from McGregor in what those assumptions concern. Whereas McGregor focused attention mainly on a manager's assumptions about human nature, Blake and Mouton argued that it is important to uncover a manager's assumptions about concern for people and concern for production. Concern for people involves the "productive unit" (p. 7) of the organization and can involve a number of things:

- Concern for the degree of personal commitment to one's job
- Trust-based rather than obedience-based accountability
- Self-esteem of the individual
- Interpersonal relationships with coworkers

Concern for production is the "emphasis supervision places on production" or the basic tasks of the organization (p. 7) and involves the use of people and technology to accomplish organizational tasks. "Concern for" in these cases does not refer to issues of quantity or even quality, but instead indicates the degree to which the manager has consideration for these matters. In other words, to what extent do the manager's basic attitudes toward people and production (and their interrelationships) affect actual supervisory behavior?

Blake and Mouton offer an extensive survey that attempts to measure a manager's concern for people and for production. The results of the survey are compiled and the individual manager is assigned a value on the Managerial Grid that indicates his managerial style related to these two concerns. Five points on the Grid have been assigned descriptive titles and will be discussed below. It is important to realize, according to Blake and Mouton, that the points on the Grid do not represent personality traits of the manager, but instead indicate a specific orientation toward production and people. This distinction is important, because, they argue, a manager (based on the situation) has the ability to acquire skills and hence change her managerial style.

In view of the similarities between Blake and Mouton's styles to Likert's four systems of management, this section will provide a snapshot of the styles rather than an extensive discussion. The *authority-compliance management style* is rooted in classical theory, in which there is high concern for production and low concern for people. This manager feels a contradiction between meeting the production needs of the organization and the needs of the workers. In order to accomplish production, the manager minimizes attention to feelings and attitudes. Communication in the authority-compliance management style is unidirectional, downward through the hierarchy.

The *country club management style* puts concern for people above concern for production; employees are "valuable in their own right" (p. 57). This manager avoids direct pressure to perform with the hope of gaining acceptance from the workers. The manager tends to lead by example rather than goad employees into working hard for the organization. Communication under this management style is heightened, with particular emphasis on the informal communication systems of the organization, such as the "grapevine" (gossip).

The *impoverished management style* can be characterized as being laissez-faire, that is, hiring workers for particular jobs and then leaving them alone to do their work. The manager is not concerned with the well-being of the workers and exercises no power, opting instead merely to pass down orders that come from higher levels. The impoverished-style manager uses the communication system minimally.

The *middle-of-the-road management style*, indicated by a medium concern for both people and production, is best characterized as a compromise or balance-seeking position. The manager uses the carrot-and-stick approach to supervision, prodding the workers when necessary to increase their production but also offering adequate social and personal rewards to maintain adequate worker satisfaction. Communication in this approach can also be characterized by balance. Formal and informal communication systems are used equally.

The *team management style* is the prototypical human resources approach to management and is the one Blake and Mouton advocated. It is characterized by a high concern for people and a high concern for production with no inherent conflict between them. The intent of the team style is to "promote the conditions that integrate creativity, high productivity, and high morale through concerted team action" (p. 142). It may seem on the surface that the team and middle-of-the-road orientations are very similar in that both are concerned for people and production. The essential difference between the two approaches is an important one. The team style does not seek a compromise between people and production (thereby reducing the eventual effectiveness of both). Instead, it seeks the highest level of production through a commitment to the creativity, skill, and energy of the workers. The goals of the organization and the goals of the individual can be achieved simultaneously if the satisfaction of one leads to the satisfaction of the other (or if they correlate with each other).

The team orientation promotes self-direction and self-control through genuine participation in planning, decision making, and goal setting. It differs significantly from the fear-of-punishment system present in the authority-compliance style. The theory is that organizational members attempt to reach maximum production when they have a stake in the process and the outcome. In order to accomplish this goal, communication must flow in all directions and must be "authentic and candid" (p. 150).

Particularly interesting about this approach is its position regarding misunderstandings, one that we advocate in a different form in Chapter 6:

> Mistakes occur because of misunderstandings, not because of deliberate intent. . . . Mistakes frequently can be traced to misunderstandings, assumptions based on faulty information and facts or differences in expectations between a boss and a subordinate. [T]he aim here is to discover the cause of the problem, not just to identify and punish the person associated with its occurrence. Through problem

identification, critique and follow-up action, the work situation becomes a learning situation, par excellence. (Blake and Mouton, 1964, pp. 148–149)

The team style recognizes the natural existence of misunderstandings in organizations and proposes the notion that they should be used as learning situations for all involved. This perspective on misunderstandings demonstrates a significant move forward in organizational theory and practice, one that is more humanistic in nature and grounded in the realities of human communication.

Summary

The middle of the twentieth century saw a flurry of activity regarding organizational management theory. With the Hawthorne Studies pointing to the need to focus on the relational aspects of management and organizational behavior, emerging theories emphasized the worker over the task. Chester Barnard and Douglas McGregor offered theories of management and organizations that replaced ideas of strict control and authority with improved social relations, cooperation, communication, and the informal organization. The human relations movement sought to improve organizational life by reversing the attitudes of managers toward workers. Workers were no longer to be considered lazy, deceitful, and in need of coercion, but energetic, creative, underutilized, and eager to participate in decision making at all levels.

Human resources theory (as exemplified by Likert's systems of management and Blake and Mouton's Leadership Grid) was developed to remedy the problems associated with the misapplications or misguided applications of human relations theory in organizations. Theorists realized that participative management strategies were not being used appropriately; workers were being told overtly that they were important but were not being treated accordingly. Human resources theory emphasized genuine participation in organizational processes and advanced the idea that both production and personal satisfaction could be maximized if they were interrelated.

It would be hard to deny the impact that human relations and human resources theories have had on modern organizational life. "Human resources" departments are now commonplace in organizations. Total quality management, quality circles, management by objective, project teams, and decentralized structures are all outgrowths of these theories. As management theory has changed, so too has our understanding of a manager. According to a November 21, 1999, article in the *Los Angeles Times*, since the beginning of the twentieth century (the time of Taylor) the manager has gone from "measurer" to "thinker." It seems that our understanding of a worker must also change, as more and more labor shifts from physical to mental. As a January 21, 2006, article in the *Economist* claimed, a growing percentage of the workforce can now be classified as "knowledge workers," those people who are paid to "think for a living." A *knowledge worker* is one who generates ideas and innovations for other employees to use.

A September 27, 2005, article in the *Financial Times* (Asia/Africa) went so far as to say:

> Since knowledge is an invisible asset that is more metaphysical than physical or empirical, management can no longer be done or defined as a function of control and overview of employees. Further, because knowledge work can and is being done by both managers and workers, the line of distinction between the two has blurred, becoming almost extinct.

Although their final point may be a bit overstated, particularly for the breadth of organizational situations, it is a point well taken—as the management theory has changed, so too has the nature of work and the nature of organizational structures, and vice versa.

However, it would be shortsighted to believe that all organizations in all industries operate according to the principles of human resources theory. A brief article by Collins about tapping the human potential in organizations in the December 1996 issue of *Inc.* magazine lamented:

> Theory X management still dominates most organizations. Many managers and entrepreneurs still hold hidden assumptions that people cannot be fully trusted, need to be "checked up on," need "motivation," or don't really like to work all that hard. And it's not just limited to big old companies; many entrepreneurs rule with a Theory X iron fist, too. (p. 55)

Human relations and human resources theory will continue to do battle with the tenets of classical theory, particularly as organizations feel the pressure of globalization, increased competition, and mega-mergers. The tendency for management to revert back to traditional control mechanisms in times of uncertainty is typical, but we must remember that the easy way is not always the most effective way. The principles of human resources theory attempt to integrate the concern for production from classical theory with the concern for the worker from human relations theory. This mix, though more taxing at times owing to the emotional energy involved, is more congruent with human nature and more effective and satisfying in the long run.

4 Systems Theory

In Chapters 2 and 3, we discussed various classical and humanistic theories of organizations, each of which proposed principles or prescriptions for organizational structure or managerial practice. Each theory contained fairly specific elements or characteristics that could be implemented in day-to-day practice, either at the interpersonal or organizational level, depending on the theory.

In this chapter, we present a theory that has less to do with prescribing organizational behavior or structure and more with providing an analytical framework or perspective for viewing an organization in general. Systems theory and its derivatives provide new and varied lenses for analyzing and understanding organizations and the behavior within them. Management practices have emerged from these theories and, where appropriate, will be discussed. We begin this chapter with a discussion of the systems framework, and then outline the perspective of an organization as a system. We conclude by highlighting one modern instance of systems theory—the learning organization.

Misunderstandings and the Organization as a System

When organizational life is viewed from a systems perspective, new areas for potential misunderstandings come into focus. Consider the following story told to us by Adam, a 25-year-old software consultant.

My specialty is Lotus Notes, and the company I work for is supposed to go out, market my skills, and buy me the assignment. Then I go to the assignment and fix its database. Then what the company would like to happen is that the project keeps on rolling into other things. But that hasn't happened, so I have been back and forth to the "bench," as they call it when you are off assignment.

A major problem was that my company only had one person to go out and generate new sales. When the vice president was fired, his girlfriend, who was an account manager for sales, quit too. I guess it was just a good example of relationships in the workplace. Anyway, obviously they needed to hire more salespeople to get out there and market our services.

The company made a bad strategic plan because it kept hiring people with specific mainframe skills, and now that the year 2000 dilemma is over, all the big projects are coming to an end—all these people are coming off the projects and there is no more work for them. What is happening is, since we don't have the resources to market these people, the company is just saying we have to fire them and cut our losses.

Another thing that the company has done that has really made me angry is that out of the blue it made an announcement that our division is up for sale. The reason it wanted to sell us is to boost the price of the overall company because its stock was dropping. There are 5,000 people employed in this one section that I'm employed with and it is disregarding 5,000 people just to boost its stock so it can make money. The consultants like me are the ones that make money for the company anyway. So there is really not any kind of loyalty shown to the employees.

If they don't show loyalty to me, I don't show any loyalty towards them. It has made me go out and seek other employment. Every time I go back to the bench, I have no faith that they will find me an assignment. What I have had to do is go out and find other opportunities on my own.

They do recognize the problem, but in this industry it is tough for them to find a salesperson because usually the salesperson would have a noncompete clause. Anybody who is going to know the industry and what is going on with all the different companies here in the area is going to be coming from another company with a noncompete clause that will keep them from working for us. The only kind of people they can get for the job are young people right out of college, and they don't have the experience to sell, so it is kind of a catch-22.

The situation Adam described is complex. From a classical theory perspective, one would probably approach it by examining the task functions of the sales staff and the software consultants to determine exactly what needs to be accomplished and how in order to maintain optimal productivity. Rules would be instituted for the number of sales calls to be made every day, and quotas would be established to determine acceptable levels of production. From a human resources perspective, one would explore the impact of interpersonal relationships and loyalty on productivity. Management would have to be instructed to pay more attention to the needs of the employees and to seek their input to help redirect the efforts of the division.

The approach from a systems theory perspective would be a bit different. Systems theory, as you will discover in this chapter, demands that a broader picture be drawn of the situation, a picture that includes the environment within which the organization exists and how changes in the environment affect the organization. A systems approach also looks at the interconnections between the different parts of the organization to determine how well it is functioning.

What does systems theory have to offer the study of misunderstandings? Several things. First, the organization must realize the interdependence of personnel. In this example, the firing of one individual led to another person quitting, which affected the productivity of the sales department, which in turn affected the software consultants. Second, the organization must realize changes in the environment outside of the organization affect the structure and function of the organization. In this case, the company structured itself around the need to make other organizations' computer systems compliant with the year 2000. As that problem passed, so did the need for the thousands of workers employed by the software consulting division. Third, the organization must recognize that outside stakeholders can affect the internal functioning of an organization and even the morale of its employees. Adam revealed the fact that the company was going to sell the consulting division in order to raise profits for the stockholders. This fact sent shockwaves through the division and made the members seriously question the organization's loyalty to them. As noted in Chapter 1, such behavior can lead to dissatisfied workers and lower productivity. Finally, managers must recognize that industry norms and standards can lead to a restriction in the types of people entering the system. Because many software-consulting firms have a "noncompete clause" (which means that if you leave one software firm, you cannot go to work for a competitor for a specified length of time), the potential applicant pool was seriously depleted of candidates with experience. The organization was forced to hire recent college graduates with little experience.

Clearly, then, the systems approach broadens the lens through which we view organizational behavior, particularly misunderstandings. Systems theory reminds organizational members to view interconnections within the organization and between the organization and the environment as possible sources of misunderstandings. Keep Adam's situation in mind as you read this chapter, and think about how you would analyze it using the concepts and approaches you encounter.

Systems Framework

The movement from classical theory to human relations and human resources theories marked the recognition of the role the individual plays in organizational functioning. The focus on workers and their interrelationships, however, was myopic according to some theorists, who argued that a more comprehensive view of organizations was necessary, one that situated the organization within its relevant environment. Organizational theorists turned to *general system theory* for guidance, particularly to the work of the biologist Ludwig von Bertalanffy.

Systems theory replaces the "machine" metaphor of classical theory with the metaphor of an "organism." Viewed as an organism, an organization is a living entity in an environment that can provide it with energy and to which it can return an output. The organism is surrounded by a permeable boundary (much like skin or cell walls) that allows for the exchange of inputs and outputs with the environment. These organisms must be structured such that they can efficiently and effectively turn inputs into outputs and adapt to changes in the environment. If inputs are restricted or the internal processes of the organism are not functioning properly, the organism begins to deteriorate.

Although systems theory itself is not a theory of management, such as those offered by classical, human relations, and human resources theorists, it does provide us with a new way of conceptualizing organizations and studying them. According to organizational communication scholar M. Scott Poole (1997), systems theory can be very useful for the field of organizational communication. Poole outlined four "promises" of systems theory (1997, p. 49):

1. **It is designed to deal with complexity.** The complexity comes from a model with many interdependent elements and an understanding of the multiple levels of associations (e.g., organization with a group, organization with the environment, individual with the organization). For evidence of the number and types of interdependencies, recall the complexities of the situation Adam described earlier in the chapter.
2. **It attempts to do so with precision.** Despite the complexities, systems theory seeks to specify relationships between elements and levels. To understand how the organization functions, it must be determined exactly how the parts interrelate.
3. **It takes a holistic view.** Systems theory forces us to look outside the organizational or departmental boundaries to see the bigger picture of how all aspects are interrelated. Adam's situation is a perfect example, because interpersonal relationships, computer technology, and industry norms all affected the functioning of the organization and the satisfaction of its members.
4. **It is a theory of emergents.** Systems theory demonstrates how actions and outcomes at the collective (department or organization) level emerge from the actions and interactions of the individuals who make up the collective. In this way, systems theory combines individual-level behavior with broader organizational- and environmental-level issues, a perspective unique to this point in this discussion of organizational theories.

As you can see, systems theory offers significant insight into the realm of communication in organizations. In the next section, we discuss several basic principles of general system theory proffered by von Bertalanffy, outline the characteristics of organizational systems theory, and conclude with a discussion of a current application of systems theory—the learning organization.

Principles of General Systems Theory

Ludwig von Bertalanffy, in his landmark book *General System Theory* (1968), proposed that the laws that govern biological open systems (living organisms) could be applied to systems of any form (such as an organization):

Thus, there exists models, principles, and laws that apply to generalized systems or their subclasses, irrespective of their particular kind, the nature of their component elements, and the relations or "forces" between them. It seems legitimate to ask for a theory, not of systems of a more or less special kind, but of universal principles applying to systems in general. . . . There are correspondences in the principles that govern the behavior of entities that are, intrinsically, widely different. (pp. 32–33)

The leap from organisms-as-systems to organizations-as-systems is not that large: "An atom, a crystal, or a molecule are organizations. . . . In biology, organisms are, by definition, organized things" (von Bertalanffy, 1968, p. 47). If organizations are systems, then what are the "universal principles" applicable to both living organisms and organized human activity? Several principles from von Bertalanffy's theory are relevant for our purposes, and we discuss them below.

Open-Systems Theory Principles

A *system* is "a set of elements standing in inter-relations" (von Bertalanffy, 1968, p. 55). This is a rather simple explanation of a rather complex concept, but it is sufficient for beginning our discussion. Perhaps the most important aspect of this definition is the notion that the parts that make up the system (which can be referred to as *subsystems*) are *interrelated*; the existence and proper functioning of one part is dependent on the existence and proper functioning of the other parts. If we consider the human body to be a system, then it is defined by its subsystems (e.g., the respiratory system, nervous system, reproductive system) and their interrelationships. The relative "health" of the overall system is determined by the extent to which the subsystems coordinate their functions effectively and efficiently. The same holds true for an organization when conceptualized as a system. The interrelated parts (e.g., marketing, engineering, sales, accounting) must function well together for the overall strength of the organizational system to be maintained.

But the news of general system theory is that biological systems do not exist in a vacuum; they are situated within an environment within which there is a regulated flow of energy. To capture this notion, von Bertalanffy argued that biological systems are open systems. *Open systems* are those that import and export material from and to the environment. *Closed systems* are those that have no exchange of material with the environment:

The organism is not a static system closed to the outside and always containing the identical components; it is an open system in a (quasi-) steady state, maintained constant in its mass relations in a continuous change of component material and energies, in which material continually enters from, and leaves into, the outside environment. (von Bertalanffy, 1968, p. 121)

The environment, often referred to as the *relevant environment* by organizational systems theorists, consists of those entities outside of the system that are relevant to the survival of the system. Returning to our example of the human body, the system (body) constantly adapts to changes in the environment. When nourishment is diminished, for instance, the body slows down its metabolism to conserve energy and use what energy it has stored up more efficiently. Or, when the external temperature decreases to an uncomfortable level, the body often goes into involuntary shakes to produce heat. The body, as a system, does not remain unchanged in the face of changing environmental conditions; it self-regulates in an attempt to function effectively and efficiently and promote its own survival.

Systems should be considered open in nature because they have permeable boundaries. A *boundary* is that part of the system that separates it from its environment. A boundary is *permeable* in that it is capable of having material pass through it, to and from the environment.

The concept of "openness" is particularly useful in the study of organizations. Past theories of organizations (particularly Weber's theory of bureaucracy) virtually ignored the fact that organizations exist within an environment. Viewing the organization as an open system, however, demands that the organizational theorist understand the complex interactions the system has with its environment *in addition to* the means by which the subsystems of the organization import and export material from and to the environment. This point is made very clear in Adam's example from the beginning of the chapter. The environment of the software consulting organization was integral to the internal structure of the organization, and the specialties within the organization existed primarily in response to the changing demands of the environment.

One further point about openness in organizational systems theory is necessary. The permeable nature of a system's boundaries is often under the control of the organization itself. At certain times, the system can restrict the amount and type of material imported and exported, while at other times it can maximize these efforts. In other words, the system has some ability to regulate permeability. This notion is referred to as *relative openness*. We will discuss this concept in more depth later in the chapter.

In a closed system (where material neither enters nor exits), the tendency is for the system to become disorganized. This essential property of organized systems is referred to as *entropy*. The debilitating effect of entropy on a system is presupposed by what von Bertalanffy refers to as the *second principle of thermodynamics*, which states that entropy must increase to a maximum (1968, p. 39). In other words, this principle asserts that, unless checked, entropy will continue to increase until the system weakens and eventually ceases to exist. In order to combat these effects, systems seek to enhance *negative entropy* (also termed *negentropy*), or a state of survival and growth.

To foster negative entropy, the parts of the system must function well together. When the subsystems work in conjunction with one another they produce extra energy, or *synergy*. The synergy produced allows for an attractive feature of systems known as *nonsummativity*, or "the whole is more than the sum of [its] parts" (von Bertalanffy, 1968, p. 55). In other words, when operating efficiently and effectively, the subsystems working together are able to produce more than if they were working alone and their outputs were added together.

One final principle from von Bertalanffy is important because it differentiates potential management strategies based in systems theory from those based in classical theory. Classical theory is characterized by the "one best way" to do every job. From a closed system point of view this makes sense; because conditions rarely change, the "best way" to accomplish the task can be established and performed every time. But if a system is considered open, there will inevitably be changes in the system making the "one best way" quite unlikely. The concept of equifinality illuminates this situation. *Equifinality* indicates that "the same final state may be reached from different initial conditions and in different ways" (p. 40). In other words, if the desired final state for a biological organism is to secure enough food to stay alive, it can do so by eating a variety of harmless food gathered in a variety of ways. It does not have to eat the same thing garnered in the same fashion. The same lesson holds true for organizations. Organizations have the capacity to reach the same final state (e.g., product or service) in a variety of ways; the "one best way" does not have to guide organizational functioning, and in many instances may be counterproductive.

Now that we have introduced some of the basic elements of systems as presented by von Bertalanffy and offered some initial implications of them for organizational theory, we move on to the characteristics of systems theory applied to organizations based on the work of later scholars.

Characteristics of Organizations as Systems

In their book, *The Social Psychology of Organizations* (1978), Daniel Katz and Robert Kahn put forward a theory of organizations based on systems constructs, though the impetus for the book is rooted in the work of Rensis Likert. Their work signals a shift away from the psychological, interpersonal-relationship bases of human resources theory toward what they argue is a more comprehensive view of organizational reality. Katz and Kahn advocated systems theory as a way to approach organizations because it is able to encapsulate both micro- and macroconcepts (human relationships and organization-environment relationships, respectively), something that human relations theory and human resources theory (both micro-oriented theories) were unable to do:

> Open-system theory emphasizes the close relationship between a structure and its supporting environment. It begins with the concept of entropy, the assumption that without continued inputs any system soon runs down. One critical basis for identifying social systems is therefore their relationship with energic sources for their maintenance. For almost all social structures, the most important source is human effort and motivation. If we wish to understand the maintenance of social systems, we are at the social-psychological level. (Katz & Kahn, 1978, p. 3)

This theory differs from psychology-based theories of organizations in that the central focus is less the thoughts and behaviors of organizational leadership and more the input-processing-output relationship the system has with its environment. To this end, Katz and Kahn offered a theory of organizations built on systems characteristics derived from the work of von Bertalanffy and others. What follows are selected characteristics of organizational systems theory that are most relevant to the study of organizational communication.

Input-Throughput-Output

When an organization is viewed as an open system, the emphasis shifts from managerial behavior to the relationship between the system and its environment. This relationship is characterized by three interrelated processes: input, throughput, and output, which form the basic model of systems functioning. The model is simple. An open system imports some form of energy or material through its boundaries from the environment. This importation is referred to as *input*. Inputs are of two general types: *maintenance inputs*, or energic imports that help sustain the system, and *production inputs*, or "energic imports which are processed to yield a productive outcome" (Katz & Kahn, 1978, p. 40). Once inside the system, *throughput* occurs, where the parts of the system (or subsystems) transform the material or energy in some fashion. Finally, the system returns some product to the environment; that product is termed the *output*. Because the input undergoes some form of a change when processed by the subsystems, the systems model is often referred to as the *transformation model* (Kreps, 1990).

Any organization can be examined using the transformation model. For example, Harley Davidson, a major motorcycle manufacturer, must import a variety of material and energy from its relevant environment. Inputs for Harley Davidson include such things as steel, rubber, wire, aluminum, electricity, gas, bank loans, customer demand, information on competitors, and so on. Once the inputs enter the system, the subsystems must coordinate their efforts such that the material and energy are transformed into an appropriate output, in this case, motorcycles.

The transformation model provides a wider-angle lens through which we can view organizational behavior and functioning. From this perspective, it is impossible to consider the internal functioning of the system without considering the relationship of the system to its relevant environment. What systems theory teaches us is the need to coordinate internal functioning with changes in the environment. It is through the process of feedback that this coordination happens.

Feedback and Dynamic Homeostasis

System inputs carry with them information that is useful in both regulating the relative openness of the system itself and coordinating the efforts of the subsystems. This information is often referred to as *feedback* and can take two primary forms. *Positive feedback* is information that alerts the subsystems to move from status quo behavior to a specified state of behavior. For example, if Toyota's salespeople double the sales of their latest hybrid car, the manufacturing division will need to move from its normal state of behavior to one that allows it to produce twice as many cars. *Negative feedback* is information that indicates to the subsystems that they should return to the status quo. Returning to our example, if Toyota's salespeople were unable to secure the same number of sales during the next sales period, the manufacturing division would need to stop producing at the doubled rate and return to its normal level of production.

Feedback is necessary to promote a balance of inputs and outputs between the subsystems and between the system and the environment. The balance, in turn, is important to help stave off entropy (or, to promote negative entropy). *Dynamic homeostasis* is the term used to describe this balance. Katz and Kahn described dynamic homeostasis in the following manner:

> The importation of energy to arrest entropy operates to maintain some constancy in energy exchange, so that open systems that survive are characterized by a steady state. . . . The ratio of energy exchanges and the relations between parts, remains the same. (1978, p. 26)

Dynamic homeostasis, then, represents a balance of energy exchange. An imbalance would lead to an excess or debit of energy or material, causing the system undue strain, thereby enhancing the potential for entropy. One example of this comes from an interview with the manager of a fast food restaurant:

> There was one time that we had coupons that were going to be advertised in the paper. The advertising agency sent out the wrong date that they were going to be dropped in. We ran out of a lot of product because these coupons were in the paper, and we didn't know they were going to be in there. The promotion was something like "buy one hamburger get another one free." So we were running out of hamburger buns, and running out of meat. We had to have a special delivery made, which was expensive because you pay a big price for special delivery.

As this example shows us, due to a problem in the relevant environment, there was a debit of material (not enough hamburger buns or meat), which leads to strains on personnel and finances.

Equivocality and Requisite Variety

Karl Weick, a well-known organizational psychologist, offered a systems approach to organizational behavior in his influential book *The Social Psychology of Organizing* (1979). He contended that any input into a system carries with it some level of uncertainty, ambiguity, or what he referred to as *equivocality*. Whether the input is raw material, energy, customer orders or complaints, or federal legislation, it will carry with it the potential for several different outcomes. To deal with this fact, Weick argued that the main function of organizing is to reduce equivocality to a manageable level.

Dealing with equivocality is not a simple matter. Weick proposed that the concept of requisite variety be employed when attempting to manage equivocal information inputs. *Requisite variety* is the notion that complex inputs must be addressed with complex processes, and vice versa. In other words, the old adage applies: "There are no simple answers to difficult problems." If a simple process is applied to a complex input, the chances are high that only a portion of the input will be attended to, leaving the remainder unaddressed and potentially damaging the system and its components.

Role of Communication

In systems theory, communication acts as a "system binder" (Almaney, 1974). Communication binds the parts of the system together and binds the system to the environment. To say this a different way, the role of communication in systems theory is twofold. First, communication mechanisms must be in place for the organizational system to exchange relevant information with its environment. This is referred to as an *adaptive mechanism* (Almaney, 1974). People who perform this function are often referred to as *boundary spanners* because they move information across the boundaries of the organization. Boundary spanners have contact with the relevant environment through the course of their jobs. Individuals who work in such areas as sales, customer service, advertising, and public relations are typical boundary spanners and should be considered important communication links with the environment. In addition to boundary spanners, media outlets also serve as an important communication link between the system and the environment. Publications such as the *Wall Street Journal, Advertising Age*, and *Radio & Records*, and broadcast outlets such as CNBC serve as important sources of receiving and distributing information.

The second role of communication in systems theory is to provide for flow of information among the subsystems. This role of communication is also known as a *maintenance function* (Almaney, 1974). In order to maintain homeostasis, the subsystems need to coordinate their inputs and outputs; this is a matter of information exchange. Meetings, memos, retreats, intraorganizational websites, and electronic mail are all examples of the mechanisms used to provide for the necessary communication among subsystems. Given their interdependent nature, subsystems are reliant upon efficient and effective communication to promote homeostasis and negative entropy.

Systems, Subsystems, and Supersystems

As discussed earlier, a system is a set of interrelated elements. In light of the transformation model, a *system* can be considered to be a set of interrelated parts that turns inputs into outputs through processing. The interrelated parts of the system that do the processing are the *subsystems*. Every system is part of a larger system, or *supersystem*, which consists of other systems in the relevant environment important to the survival of the focal system.

Whether an organized unit is considered a system, subsystem, or supersystem to some extent depends on the level of analysis. Consider university life for a moment. If the university is the focal system, then the different colleges in the university would be subsystems; the supersystem could be the conference to which the focal system belongs (e.g., Big 10, MAC). If the College of Business is the focal system, then the subsystems may be the different departments within the college (e.g., Marketing, Finance, Management). The supersystem would be the university. Finally, the Marketing Department itself may be the focal system, making the College of Business the supersystem and the professors, staff, and students within Marketing the subsystems.

As you can tell, level of analysis is a critical factor when analyzing organizations using systems theory. Also important is distinguishing among the different types of subsystems involved in the transformation process. According to Katz and Kahn, there are five main types of subsystems (1978, p. 39). *Production or technical subsystems* are concerned with the throughput aspects of the system, such as the assembly line, custom crafting, and production inspection. *Supportive subsystems* ensure that production inputs are available at all times. Subsystems that import raw material (such as wood, coal, metal, plastic, conduit, etc.) and energy into the system are examples of supportive structures. *Maintenance subsystems* are focused on the social relations in the system. Human resources, training, and personnel departments as well as communication experts are typical members of these subsystems. Adaptive subsystems monitor the environment and the system and generate appropriate external responses. Public relations departments communicate with the relevant publics regarding the concerns of internal or external systems. Research and development teams are responsible for understanding the demands of the changing environment and generating appropriate internal changes in procedures and products. *Managerial subsystems* coordinate, adjust, control, and direct the subsystems. Typically, management teams are in place to ensure proper coordination among the subsystems. The prototypical mechanism for doing so is communication.

All five types of subsystems are vital to the system and its attempts to promote negative entropy. Without effective and efficient coordination among the subsystems leading to dynamic homeostasis, the system will eventually become strained and die. This is not to say, however, that the different elements in a system are tightly linked, highly responsive to one another, and have indistinguishable identities. It may be that systems (or subsystems or supersystems) could instead be loosely coupled (Orton & Weick, 1990; Weick, 1976) *Loosely coupled systems* contain elements that "are responsive, *but* that each also preserves its own identity and some evidence of its physical or logical separateness" (Weick, 1976, p. 3). This way of thinking about relationships between systems, subsystems, and supersystems is important because it provides a more realistic picture of the nature of structural and interpersonal relations in organizations. Without it, there may be a tendency to expect very logical, rational, and seamless connections between organizational elements. For example, one might expect that in a city fire department the fire chief and deputy fire chief, whose offices are right next to each other, would be tightly connected and willingly supporting the same mission. However, in reality, although these two officers are connected and responsive to each other's changing situations, they still retain their own identities and may pursue goals or objectives that are divergent or even competing. These two elements of the system would be considered to be loosely coupled.

Boundaries

With all this talk about systems, subsystems, and supersystems, not to mention the system's relevant environment, the question becomes: How do you know where one stops and the other begins? As mentioned earlier in this chapter, the concept of *boundaries* is designed to make this a bit clearer. In social systems, however, a boundary is not a distinguishable entity as it is in physical systems. The boundary of the human body, for example, is the skin, but in social systems there is no such tangible feature that marks the end of one level from the beginning of another. Yet, organizational members are quite readily able to distinguish system and subsystem boundaries.

Becker (1997) offered four types of boundaries that may help provide a bit more meaning to the term as it relates to social systems (p. 133). A *physical* boundary is the most concrete and can be something such as a security system that prevents unauthorized personnel from entering the actual organizational location. A *linguistic* boundary involves the use of jargon, or specialized language, to separate members from nonmembers. *Systemic* boundaries are rules that regulate how members interact or how members interact with nonmembers. For example, organizational members may be allowed to address one another by first names but are required to address all outsiders using last names and titles. Finally, *psychological* boundaries are stereotypes, prejudices, or biases that members hold toward others that serve to restrict communication. For example, members of a sales department may believe that the members of the manufacturing division are not as "refined" as they are, and as a result they treat them with contempt.

Thus, different systems and subsystems can be distinguished in ways that do not involve concrete, physical boundaries. It is important for organizational members to recognize the existence of the different boundary types, particularly those that may be causing unintended misunderstandings. Linguistic boundaries may cause computer customers, for example, not to understand what computer technicians and salespeople are telling them. Psychological boundaries may lead to barriers among parts of an organizational system that truly need to interact with one another for the overall success of the organization.

The "Closed" System

One of the central features of systems theory is that a healthy organization is an open system that is able to exchange information and resources with its environment and adapt its structure as dictated by environmental change. In reality, however, not all organizations are "healthy," and they vary regarding the extent to which they are open to the environment. McMillan and Northern (1995) charge that many modern organizations can be considered "neurotic," "addictive," or even "dysfunctional" because they tend to be closed systems rather than open systems.

Closed systems differ from open systems in a variety of ways (McMillan & Northern, 1995, p. 10). First, they do not recognize that they are embedded in a relevant environment. Second, they are overly focused on internal functions and behavior. Third, they do not recognize or implement the concept of equifinality (more than one way to accomplish a goal). Finally, they have an inability to use feedback appropriately. McMillan and Northern argued that individual organizational members serve as "codependents" for the dysfunctional closed system. This happens easily because (1) members bring codependent "survival" skills with them from other organizations and (2) as organizational life seems to breed "unhealthy" behavior, members feed off and model the codependent actions of other members.

Codependency as a means of maintaining a closed (unhealthy) system is an interesting use of systems theory because it combines micro-oriented, individual-level practices and communication behaviors with macro-oriented, organizational-level issues and problems. McMillan and Northern posited four "master premises" for enabling codependency in closed systems that are useful in illustrating this point (1995, pp. 21–31):

- **Asymmetrical communication status of the hierarchy.** Codependency often involves levels of authority, where the lower-status individual is left to "please" or "appease" the other, thereby enabling the bad behavior. Fear of punishment in the organization often leads to appeasing, covering up bad news, and avoiding conflict, thereby recreating a dysfunctional situation.
- **The socially acceptable addiction.** Workaholics are commonplace and seemingly acceptable in the organizational setting. There is always something to be done and never enough time to do it. This "addiction" serves to drive members to engage in deeper and deeper codependent behavior.
- **The organization's selective attention.** Money and power provide a means of distraction from the organization's unhealthy behavior. As a result, there is a focus on the ends instead of the means, a focus that inevitably will lead to negative consequences.
- **Skilled communication incompetence.** This phrase refers to the old adage, "If you can't say anything nice then don't say anything at all!" In organizations, this practice leads to an unhealthy atmosphere as the organization is deprived of useful feedback, which is a central concept in systems theory. This incompetence at communication involves such things as the masking of emotion, use of indirect language, and "reactive" (versus confrontational) communication.

The research by McMillan and Northern provides a fascinating look into the depths of organizational life that was really only possible through the lens of systems theory. In the next section, we discuss one of the first extensions of systems theory into management practice—contingency theory.

Contingency Theory

The first applications of systems concepts to organizations are now referred to under the umbrella term *contingency theory*. Contingency theory posits the notion that there is no one best way to structure and manage organizations. Instead, structure and management are contingent on the nature of the environment in which the organization is situated. This approach extends to communication in the organization as well; contingency theory "argues for finding the best communication structure under a given set of environmental circumstances" (Barnett, 1997, p. 21). In the interest of space, we will briefly discuss only two of the better-known contingency theories (see Woodward [1965] for another contingency theory not covered here).

Burns and Stalker provided a contingency theory based on environmental stability in their book *The Management of Innovation* (1968). There they described how they set out to study workers in a factory, but that "was never realized, because it soon became evident that the social structure of the factory interlocked with, and often mirrored, that of the small isolated town in which it was situated" (p. 1). What followed was a theory that showed how organizational systems should vary based on the level of stability in the environment.

Through their research in a variety of organizations, Burns and Stalker noticed that there were two different types of management systems: mechanistic and organic. *Mechanistic systems* are appropriate for a stable environment, where there is little change or the change is predictable. They are characterized by specialization, centralization, clearly defined roles, and vertical communication (particularly downward instructions). *Organic systems* are required in changing environments with unstable conditions. Such systems have several characteristics. First, specialized tasks are performed in light of interdependence with other specialized tasks. Second, jobs and tasks are continually redefined through interaction among organizational members. Third, communication is both horizontal and vertical and tends to be in the form of consultation rather than orders. Finally, information is a commodity used in decision making, where "the limits of feasible action are set more widely" (p. 11). Mechanistic and organic systems represent two ends of a continuum, not two parts of a dichotomy.

In this theory, management is considered to be a "dependent variable" (p. 96) that changes to conform to variations in environmental factors. According to Burns and Stalker, "the beginning of administrative wisdom is awareness that there is no optimum type of management system" (p. 125). Although there are many more details and nuances to this theory, the essence is that an organizational system and management practices are intimately related to the environment within which the system is situated. Stable environments provide for mechanistic systems, whereas unstable environments demand an organic system capable of adapting quickly to the novelties of the shifting environment.

In their book *Developing Organizations: Diagnosis and Action* (1969), Lawrence and Lorsch offered another contingency theory similar to the one offered by Burns and Stalker. Whereas Burns and Stalker focused on the stability of the environment, Lawrence and Lorsch pointed to *environmental uncertainty* as the key issue. They began with the premise that more attention had been paid to improving internal relations in organizations than to exploring and improving the organization's relationship with the environment. This focus, they contended, was at least partly owing to the fact that it is easier to attach blame or cause to an internal organizational member (e.g., a corporate leader) than to an external entity. It is also quite difficult to gather information about boundary spanning because the information sources are outside of the control of the organization.

Lawrence and Lorsch theorized that the organization would have to match certain characteristics with the demands and nature of the environment. In particular, they postulated that an environment could be characterized along a certainty–uncertainty continuum. Environments that were fairly stable or certain would require less and less complex information for the organization than would environments that were more uncertain (changing).

The focus of this theory then was on *information flow*. Organizations that have a stable environment can operate more easily from predetermined rules; any changes in the environment can be handled through the hierarchy, because time is not a critical factor. It follows that the managerial style should be primarily task oriented. In essence, this is a *centralized organizational structure*.

Organizations in a more uncertain, changing environment must have more complex systems for adapting to the information gathered from that environment. To increase contact with the environment, they should use a *decentralized structure*. Rules would be too constricting, so free-flowing communication is necessary. Given this situation, strong interpersonal relationships are needed, as is a person-centered managerial style.

Both contingency theories covered here posit a direct relationship between the internal structure of the organization and the type of environment in which it is situated. Burns and Stalker started with the notion that it is the stability of the environment that is important, whereas Lawrence and Lorsch, developing that thesis, focused on the level of uncertainty present in the environment. Both theories treated organizations as systems, inextricably tied to their environment, which must attend to the changes (or lack thereof) in the environment to survive.

Among several pragmatic applications of systems theory, perhaps the most recent is the concept of the learning organization, which we discuss in the concluding section.

The Learning Organization

Perhaps the most prolific use of systems theory concepts in current organizational theory and practice involves the learning organization. With the publication of Peter Senge's book *The Fifth Discipline: The Art and Practice of the Learning Organization* (1990), systems theory gained widespread attention. Senge argued that a new model of organizational behavior was necessary, one that emphasized the interconnectedness of individual organizational members with one another and with their environment. If organizations are to survive, Senge contended, they must provide an atmosphere "where new and expansive patterns of thinking are nurtured, where collective aspiration is set free, and where people are continually learning how to learn together" (1990, p. 3). This new atmosphere is a *learning organization*, which Senge defined as "an organization that is continually expanding its capacity to create its future" (1990, p. 14). Organizational learning and the learning organization are therefore inextricably linked. As Amy (2005) tells us: "Fundamentally, organizational learning refers to learning processes and activities that occur within the organization whereas learning organization refers to a particular organizational form" (p. 13).

While Senge brought mass exposure to the learning organization and organizational learning in 1990, the concepts were alluded to several decades prior by Chapman, Kennedy, Newell, and Biel (1959) and by Cangelosi and Dill (1965). Chapman et al. (1959) were particularly interested in the patterns of behavior that would contribute to the organization's ability to increase their adaptive potential. They argued that there are several "conditions necessary to promote organizational learning: clarify the goal, give the organization as a whole experiences with tasks of increasing difficulty, and provide immediate knowledge of results" (p. 267).

Cangelosi and Dill (1965) offered a multilevel perspective on adaptation and learning, arguing:

> The basic concept of the model of organizational learning must be viewed as a series of interactions between adaptation at the individual or subgroup level and adaptation at the organizational level. Adaptation occurs as a result of three kinds of stress, one of which stimulates subsystem learning, one total-system learning, and one both subsystem and total-system learning. (p. 200)

The three kinds of stress to which they alluded are discomfort, performance, and disjunctive. *Discomfort* stress is related to complexity and uncertainty of the environment in relation to time and resource constraints. In other words, this is stress caused by the difficulty in securing appropriate money, materials, workers, and time to meet the changing needs of the environment. *Performance* stress involves expectations for success or failure related to past experience, incentives, or changes in preferences of leaders. Both of these kinds of stress are felt by individuals and therefore tend to lead to subsystem and individual adaptation.

Organizational learning comes from performance stress and disjunctive stress. *Disjunctive* stress results from the violation of norms regarding the need for coordination and tolerance for conflict between and among individuals and subgroups. Organizational learning takes place when disjunctive stress surpasses tolerance.

According to organizational learning researcher Chris Argyris (1999), organizational learning occurs under two conditions. First, it occurs when the design for organizational action matches the intended outcome. For example, if a computer hardware company planned to increase sales by 10 percent by promising delivery of an order within 48 hours of its being placed, learning would occur if that plan matched reality. The organization *learned* because it validated a theory and the actions that supported it. Second, learning occurs when an initial mismatch between intentions and outcomes is corrected, resulting in a match. The move from a mismatch to a match is another condition under which learning occurs. Returning to our computer hardware company, let's say that their plan to increase sales by 10 percent by reducing delivery time to 48 hours did not work. In fact, sales declined by 5 percent. In order for learning to occur, managers must diagnose why that mismatch occurred and correct the situation to provide for a match. What they may have discovered is that, in the rush to decrease delivery time, both hardware quality and customer service were compromised, thereby decreasing sales.

The key attribute of the learning organization is increased adaptability (Senge, 1998). Adaptability can be increased by advancing from adaptive to generative learning. *Adaptive (single-loop) learning* involves coping with a situation and is limited by the scope of current organizational assumptions (Garavan, 1997; Senge, 1998). In other words, when an organization is involved in adaptive learning, it does not "think outside the box"; no attempts are made to draw upon thoughts, ideas, or resources outside of the normal procedures the organization employs. Put in another way, single-loop learning occurs when a mismatch between action and outcome is corrected without changing the underlying values of the system that enabled the mismatch (Argyris, 1999).

Generative (double-loop) learning occurs when the basic assumptions and processes of the organization are challenged and novel ways of seeing problems and possibilities are fostered. Generative learning moves past "coping" with the current organizational situation to "creating" an improved organizational reality (Garavan, 1997; Senge, 1998). Only through generative learning does the possibility for adaptability increase because new ways of thinking and behaving can be generated that are outside the bounds of current organizational assumptions and practices.

Argyris made the point, however, that both single-loop and double-loop learning are necessary in an organization. Single-loop learning is necessary as problems are encountered in real time on a day-to-day basis. Double-loop learning is necessary, though, for the eventual survival of the organization. The concepts of single-loop and double-loop learning and their importance to organizational communication are central features of the model of the communicative organization offered in Chapter 6.

Essential to the learning organization are the interrelated concepts of increased communication and teams. Barge and Little (2002) contend that it is through dialogue that learning happens. Dialogue, which connotes authenticity, examination of assumptions, and deep understanding, is often considered "special" and "out of the ordinary," but instead should be instilled in everyday organizational life. Through dialogue, members can articulate patterns of organizational practice that may be non- or counterproductive and can "generate new patterns that foster learning, innovation, and change" (Barge & Little, 2002, p. 375).

Although learning can occur on an individual basis, Senge argued that the essence of the learning organization is the promotion of team learning that occurs through communication:

> When teams are truly learning, not only are they producing extraordinary results but the individual members are growing more rapidly than could have occurred otherwise.... [T]eam learning starts with dialogue, the capacity of members of the team to suspend assumptions and enter into a genuine "thinking together." (Senge, 1990, p. 10)

The concepts of synergy and nonsummativity are apparent in the Senge's description; through communication, teams are able to learn more than individuals operating alone. Not all critics are convinced, though, that team learning is essential to the learning organization. Some argue that teams may actually inhibit learning because team learning is a skill that needs to be practiced but rarely is (Garavan, 1997). In other words, team members might not know how to interact with one another on a level necessary for in-depth thought and processing to occur. As a result, they may wind up belaboring the process more than improving it.

Leadership is a key element in creating and sustaining a learning organization. Senge (1998) contended that leaders are responsible for promoting an atmosphere conducive to learning. To do so, leaders must understand the notion of *creative tension*, which represents the difference between the "vision" of where the organization could be and the reality of the current organizational situation. The gap created by the difference between the vision and reality creates a natural tension that can be resolved through learning, particularly generative learning. If generative learning is to take place, though, all organizational members (not just the leaders or managers) must have a role in the process (Dixon, 1998).

Several factors may serve as impediments to organizational learning (see Senge et al., 1999, and Weick & Ashford, 2001, for reviews). Two are *complexity of the environment* and *internal conflicts* (Weick & Ashford, 2001). First, when an organization is faced with a complex environment, it is often difficult to determine cause and effect, which is useful for learning to occur. This difficulty arises from the fact that there are multiple contributing elements in complex environments that may serve to act and interact to cause organizational problems. Targeting the relevant variables and their combinations is often a difficult if not impossible task in a complex environment. Second, internal conflicts in the organization inhibit organizational learning. Individuals, teams, departments, and subcultures are often so at odds with one another that they are unable to concentrate long enough to engage in learning. Energy is drained by the conflict, energy that is needed to examine actions and processes that may promote learning. Therefore, organization members must be trained in communication and conflict-negotiation skills so that the processes contributing to learning can be unencumbered by misunderstanding and dissent.

Critics have noted that much of the literature concerning the learning organization talks only of managers learning, not all organizational members, as Senge proposed. From this perspective, organizational learning is but another management tool used to achieve managerial goals. Senge et al. attempted to answer this criticism by addressing a follow-up book, *The Dance of Change* (1999), to leaders of all types in organizations, including informal network leaders, low-level managers, and top executives.

Summary

In this chapter we have offered an overview of a framework of viewing organizations that is different from those presented in prior chapters. Systems theory is not the typical prescriptive management theory, such as the theories of classical management or human relations. Instead, systems theory principles were adopted from the natural sciences in an attempt to widen the lens through which we examine and understand organizational behavior. This chapter presented the various elements of systems theory, the way those elements have been adapted by organizational theorists, and a tour through the initial and more recent practical applications of systems theory.

The learning organization, based on systems theory, highlights the principles of synergy, nonsummativity, interdependence, equifinality, and requisite variety and emphasizes communication in the learning process. You will recognize many of the principles from the learning organization in the model of the Communicative Organization we present in Chapter 6. In that model, we attempt to integrate the concepts of misunderstandings and learning into one model that can serve as a guide for organizational members as they confront the challenges and opportunities of their positions.

Given the extent to which we have integrated systems and learning concepts in our own model of organizational communication, we obviously believe that there is merit in this approach to organizational life. It is shortsighted to believe that organizations are separate from their environment, that organizational teams or subsystems can operate in isolation from one another, or that the same misunderstandings and problems can continue to occur without eventually causing fatal damage to the system.

5 Organizational Culture Theory and Critical Theory

Over the last 30 years, changes in the global marketplace and society have affected the way we conceive of, practice, and evaluate organizational life. In the 1980s, the United States was experiencing intense competition from Japan in many industries, particularly the automotive and electronics industries. Japanese products and services were outselling and outperforming those from the United States, which led practitioners to ask why. Concurrently, organizational theorists began to reconsider the basic assumptions of traditional management theories and found that they were unable to explain adequately the behavior and practices occurring in modern organizations. Both of these issues led to interest in the concept of organizational culture. Organizational practitioners examined their values and rituals and attempted to change them to meet the demands of the new marketplace. Organizational theorists embraced the concept, because it provided a philosophical shift from traditional, highly rational theories to one that was more fluid and capable of explaining behavior that seemed to be irrational, yet deeply rooted.

During this same time period, Americans started to experience a form of societal consciousness-raising with regard to the oppressive atmosphere in organizations for workers, particularly women and minorities. Both theorists and practitioners of all types (including corporate and government leaders) began to discuss the inequities and oppressive circumstances present in the workplace. Organizations started examining their hiring practices, treatment of employees, and promotion standards in light of the disparity between members of the majority and the minority. Also, organizational theorists with roots in the work of Karl Marx turned their attention to the structure of organizational life to show how accepted management practices and "agreed upon" values were serving to advance the interests of management while restricting those of the workers.

In this chapter, we discuss organizational culture theory and critical theory as they have developed and gained prominence over the past 30 years. Both areas are incredibly rich, and therefore can receive only brief attention here. We begin with a discussion of organizational culture theory.

Organizational Culture Theory

To begin the discussion of *organizational culture theory*, consider the following story:

> Dr. Collins, a professor specializing in organizational communication, accepted a job with a new university. The move was exciting for him because, although the state university, where he had taught for five years was well respected, the reputation of the department he would be joining at Southern University was hard to beat.
>
> As Dr. Collins settled into his new office, he noticed several things that seemed different. There were very few other professors visible in the hallway and in the faculty lounge. No one had offered to help him move into his house, and only a few people (mostly graduate students) asked how he was getting along. Dr. Collins also noticed that people rarely did more than greet each other in the hallway, professors almost never kept their doors open, and there was no socializing among faculty outside of the office.
>
> As the academic term began, Dr. Collins was involved in faculty and committee meetings where faculty members consistently argued with one another, criticized one another's research and teaching styles, and made it excessively difficult for even the best of graduate students to complete their academic requirements.
>
> Dr. Collins was astounded, but even worse, he was miserable. His experience at Southern University was the complete opposite of his experience at State University. There, people would greet each other warmly and genuinely in the hallway. They had helped him move in when he first arrived on campus, and they had even thrown him a welcome party. Professors at State University always had their office doors open when they were available, and meetings rarely erupted to the level of shouting he had experienced at Southern University.

Why were these two departments so vastly different? They were both well respected, had similar numbers of students and faculty, and had very similar course offerings. They differed, though, in their organizational cultures. The behaviors and atmosphere of State University indicated an underlying cultural value of cooperation, whereas the underlying cultural value of Southern University was competition. These very different values affected the way people interacted with one another in the hallway, in meetings, and in the classroom. Dr. Collins was upset with himself, having been lured by prestige without investigating the culture of the organization to see if it fit with his personal values and beliefs.

What Is Organizational Culture?

Scholars have been studying culture since the end of the eighteenth century (Sackmann, 1991), but in the 1970s and 1980s organizational theorists turned to such study to help explain the behavior they were observing in organizations. Traditional explanations of organizational behavior (classical theories and humanistic theories) were too limiting in scope; they were unable to explain satisfactorily all forms of behavior *within* organizations, and certainly were not able to account for vast differences *among* organizations. The logical, rational explanations offered by classical and humanistic theories were no longer sufficient for many scholars, who were beginning to believe that unspoken (often nonrational) norms, values, and beliefs of organizational members may guide their behavior on a day-to-day basis.

The concept of culture is derived from the field of anthropology. Anthropologists study groups of people (such as tribes and nations) and attempt to understand their culture. To do so, they immerse themselves in all aspects of the group's life, examining (and where possible, living) their customs, rituals, rites, language, dress, food, values, beliefs, and attitudes. Through an in-depth examination of these (and many more) dimensions of culture, anthropologists are able to provide a rich description of the people, including *how* they tend to behave and *why* they behave as they do.

The word *culture* is used regularly in conversation when describing groups of people or geographic regions. For example, you hear people talk about Appalachian culture, Third World cultures, Hispanic culture, African American culture, the culture of the inner city, American culture, Western culture, and so on. When the term is used in this way, it is meant to encapsulate the dress, language, customs, acceptable behavior, values, and so on, for a certain group of people. The culture of a group is a description of how members of that group live and make sense of their world together.

Perhaps most important, a culture provides a lens through which its members interpret, interact with, and make sense of reality (Louis, 1980). As a member of a culture, you may have become enculturated with the values and assumptions of the group. As you go through your daily life, those values and assumptions help you to make sense of what is going on around you. They provide you with meanings for routine events so that you do not have to be cognitively involved in every aspect of your life. Although culture does not *determine* how you will think and behave in every situation, it may help explain patterns of behavior and thought that characterize you and the group with which you are associated. These ideas regarding organizational culture led Alvesson (2002) to argue that:

> the culture dimension is central in all aspects of organizational life. Even in those organizations where cultural issues receive little explicit attention, how people in a company think, feel, value, and act are guided by ideas, meanings and beliefs of a cultural (socially shared) nature. Whether managers that the culture is too soft or too complicated to bother about or whether there is no unique corporate culture does not reduce the significance of culture. (p. 1)

In summary, managers and researchers interested in organizational culture believe that organizations have the same characteristics as societies and therefore can be understood through a cultural lens. The cultural lens also provides a new way of looking at misunderstandings in organizations, one that focuses less on systemic and structural issues and more on the values, attitudes, and beliefs of members.

Misunderstandings and Organizational Culture

Perhaps one of the most intriguing aspects of anthropological research is how it has shown that groups of people, who are essentially the same biologically and physically, develop cultures that are so vastly different. As a result, differences in attitudes, values, and beliefs, not to mention language, dress, and appropriate social behavior, are far ranging. These variations are often the cause of major and minor misunderstandings as the groups come into contact with one another. Israel and Palestine, African Americans and Caucasians, Native Americans and government bureaucrats, environmentalists and land developers, Christians and atheists are but a few well-known examples of groups with different cultures that seem to clash on a daily basis in the modern world. Bridging the differences between them often seems like trying to bridge the Great Divide.

Consider the realm of organizations instead of anthropology, and for "environmentalists and land developers" substitute Microsoft and Apple Computers or United Airlines and Southwest Airlines. These paired organizations, although in the same industry, are known to have vastly different cultures that espouse different values, have different assumptions about how to treat employees and customers, and have even developed different specialized languages to facilitate their day-to-day operations. Apple Computer and Southwest Airlines are two organizations that have positioned themselves as being "different" from their competition (i.e., Microsoft and United Airlines, respectively). The differences are not only reflected in business practices, products, and services, but also in their cultures. These organizations embody different core values, attitudes, and beliefs that make them appear quite distinct from each another.

But the value of the organizational culture perspective is not in illustrating the misunderstandings that occur *between* organizations due to cultural differences, though that can be enlightening. The true value of this perspective is the insight it provides into the basic underpinnings of organizational behavior *within* an organization. The culture perspective sheds light on why things are happening in organizations that seem to have no logical explanation. As you read this chapter, you will discover that these same issues serve as the basis for many misunderstandings in organizations.

Misunderstandings based in organizational culture issues take many forms, and as you read this chapter you will quickly recognize the breadth of this reality. They are readily apparent, for example, when a newcomer enters an organization and has not yet learned its culture. The newcomer struggles to understand the language that is used, the relationships that people have and how they may differ based on level in the hierarchy or function, the appropriate ways to act in meetings, or even how late to stay at the end of the workday, among many other things.

As stated earlier, organizational culture provides meanings for routine organizational events, thereby reducing the amount of cognitive processing and energy members need to expend throughout the day. Although culture can be beneficial, it may also be the root of misunderstandings. Organizational culture provides a certain way of viewing reality that may have proven to be successful in the past, but that same culture may hinder the organization from progress in the future. In a marketplace characterized as fast-paced, multidimensional, and evolutionary, it is likely that deeply entrenched values could make change and adaptation difficult. This likelihood holds true both on the organizational level regarding such things as market strategy and customer relations and on the individual level in terms of how individual workers approach organizational problems.

As we will discuss later in this chapter, organizations consist of many *subcultures*. Subcultures may be based on proximity, function, level in the hierarchy, or a variety of other possibilities. Subcultures differ slightly from one another with regard to the cultural elements discussed to this point. As a result, as members from these different subcultures interact on a daily basis in the organization, they may encounter misunderstandings based on differing values, practices, and meanings for events and language. It is common to hear people on the account executive side of an advertising agency, for example, say that they "just don't understand those people in the creative department." These subcultures, though part of the same organization, often seem worlds apart.

A last general area of misunderstandings as related to organizational culture involves the merging of organizations. Mergers have always been a part of organizational life, but now with increased communication technology and practical intercontinental travel, mergers between international companies are becoming more common. Whenever organizations merge, misunderstandings caused by the clash of cultures are inevitable. When the organizations are based in different societal cultures, however, the difficulties are increased. For example, when KLM Royal Dutch Airlines and Alitalia, Italy's national carrier, announced a joint venture in 1999, they had to consider more than the merging of business practices and strategies; they had to agree to work with each other's cultural demands. In an August 11, 1999, article in the *Journal of Commerce*, it was reported that KLM executives agreed to eating dinner later in the evening as dictated by Italian custom, while Alitalia management promised to restrict cellular phone use during meetings. Although these issues may seem trivial, they represent serious breaks from organizational and societal norms. When energy is not devoted to the cultural aspects of organizational mergers, misunderstandings abound.

There are certainly many more areas in which misunderstandings are related to organizational culture. As you read this chapter, continue to think of ways in which the issues discussed may shed light on organizational misunderstandings. In the next section, we offer two alternative ways of viewing organizational culture as a phenomenon—culture as variable versus culture as root metaphor.

Two Perspectives on Organizational Culture

Linda Smircich (1983) provided useful terminology for explaining two competing perspectives on organizational culture: (1) culture as variable and (2) culture as root metaphor. The two perspectives are fairly separate and distinct belief systems regarding the nature of organizational culture.

Culture as Variable.   From the *culture-as-variable perspective*, organizational culture is something the organization *has* (Smircich, 1983). Organizational culture is a byproduct of organizational activities; as organizations produce goods and services, they also produce cultural artifacts, such as stories, rites and rituals, and heroes. Organizational culture, from this perspective, is likened to other influential elements in the organization, such as the organizational structure, the performance-appraisal system, or the formal organizational policies.

Consider the term *variable* for a moment. A variable, in research terms, is something that does or can be changed. From the culture-as-variable perspective, then, culture is something that is considered changeable, particularly by the management of the organization. Because culture resides mainly in the artifacts, behaviors, and practices of the organization, it follows that it can be manipulated and changed by those with the power to do so. Those who subscribe to this perspective treat culture as a management tool to enhance organizational effectiveness and productivity.

Two successful popular press books from the 1980s typify the culture-as-variable perspective: *In Search of Excellence* by Tom Peters and Robert Waterman (1982) and *Corporate Cultures: The Rites and Rituals of Corporate Life* by Terrence Deal and Allen Kennedy (1982). These two books were bestsellers and influenced much of the managerial thinking about organizational culture in the decade that followed. The authors prescribed methods for creating ideal organizational cultures.

Peters and Waterman argued that excellent companies (those that continually respond to changes in their environment) tend to have similar cultures guided by a limited set of shared values (or themes). The authors attempted to convince managers that the "soft side" of organizations (shared values), once thought to be beyond the scope of management, could and should be managed. In essence, they consider organizational culture to be a "tool" for enhancing organizational effectiveness. With the appropriate awareness, managers can develop the "skill" to use the tool to improve their organization's productivity and performance.

Deal and Kennedy argued that effective, high-performing organizations have *strong cultures*, or "powerful lever[s] for guiding behavior" (Deal & Kennedy, 1982, p. 15). They described four key components to a strong culture:

1. **Values.** *Values* are the basic beliefs and concepts of an organization and comprise the core of corporate culture. They define the fundamental character of the organization and provide concrete guidelines to members for achieving success.
2. **Heroes.** *Heroes* are people who best represent or personify the cultural values. Heroes provide organizational members with a concrete role model for behavior. Although heroes may be extraordinary individuals with legendary abilities, they demonstrate what is achievable in the organization. Heroes are often founders of the organization, who despite great difficulty persevered

and succeeded through hard work (e.g., Michael Dell, founder of Dell Computers). Other heroes are designated by the organization through awards, such as salesperson-of-the-year.

3. **Rites and rituals.** *Rites and rituals* are public performances that display and enact the values of the organization. Rituals are mundane, day-to-day activities that give direction to an otherwise chaotic world. They include such communication issues as how superiors and subordinates address each other, who may call a meeting, where and when meetings are held, and so on. Rites, or ceremonies, as Deal and Kennedy came to call them, are larger, more public events such as lavish retirement celebrations or annual banquets to honor top performers. Rites and rituals provide expectations for members' behavior and reiterate the connection between corporate values and success.

4. **Cultural network.** The *cultural network* consists of the informal communication network in the organization and is the primary carrier of cultural information between management and workers. Stories, myths, legends, jokes, and gossip all carry culturally relevant information and serve to promote the values of the organization.

In Search of Excellence and *Corporate Cultures* are prototypical examples of the culture-as-variable perspective. Although these popular books were on the reading list of most corporate managers in the early 1980s, many critics were less enthusiastic. They gave three main criticisms of the perspective embodied in these two books. First, they stated that the idea that certain cultural values or beliefs are "strong" and will lead to "strong" or "excellent" organizations is shortsighted. Several of the attributes discussed by Peters and Waterman (such as "autonomy and entrepreneurship" and "productivity through people") are viable principles worthy of emulation, but to prescribe these attributes as the key attributes for every organizational culture ignores both the unique nature of the organization's situation and the true essence of culture as a construct. Second, they maintained that although values certainly represent the core of organizational culture, they are equal to more than business strategy and managerial goals. Third, they declared that culture is not simply a tool, skill, or lever to be used by management to improve organizational productivity. Culture is a complex, communicative phenomenon, rooted in the history of the organization's events. The culture-as-root-metaphor perspective acknowledges these aspects of culture.

Culture as Root Metaphor. The *culture-as-root-metaphor perspective* treats culture as something the organization *is*. This perspective "promotes a view of organizations as expressive forms, manifestations of human consciousness" (Smircich, 1983, p. 347), as opposed to treating the organization as a material entity, such as a machine or organism. Treating the organization in this way yields a complexity and human nature that is missing when an organization is considered to be a material entity.

Whereas the culture-as-variable perspective considers culture to be a managerial tool, and rituals, stories, legends, gossip, and other symbols as "culture itself," the root-metaphor perspective treats culture as the process of sense-making created and sustained through communication and interaction. Rituals, stories, and so on are very important to this perspective, but they are considered "generative processes that yield and shape meanings and . . . are fundamental to the very existence of organization" (p. 353).

The root metaphor perspective on organizational culture is more difficult to delineate than the variable approach, which is one reason many organizational practitioners have not embraced it. It does not offer any quick-fix tools or methods for managers, nor does it offer generalizable knowledge useful for every organization. What it does do is provide a deep understanding of the way members of a particular organization make sense of the world around them.

Consider the label *root metaphor* for a moment. When we say that something is a root metaphor, we mean that it is more than just a way of using one concept to help us understand another. Instead, we mean that it is the *essence* of that concept, that the two constructs are essentially inseparable. In other words, the essence of an organization is culture from this perspective (see Smith and Eisenberg [1987] for an extended discussion). One cannot consider the organization without considering culture, for the organization *is* a culture. The root metaphor perspective is composed of many elements; three are described below.

The first is that *organizational culture is complex*. Edgar Schein (1985) put forward the notion that "culture is a *deep* phenomenon . . . *complex* and difficult to understand" (p. 5). Contrary to the culture-as-variable perspective, the root-metaphor perspective treats organizational culture as a multilevel construction with surface and deep levels. The surface level of culture consists of fairly tangible and concrete elements, such as rites, rituals, ceremonies, architecture, clothing, decorations, logos, slogans, stories, and language use. The culture-as-variable perspective often considers culture only at this surface level; if a leader can change the surface level, then he has changed the culture. However, that perspective often overlooks the deeper levels of organizational culture.

Below the surface-level manifestations of organizational culture are its basic elements. Values, beliefs, attitudes, sense-making logics, and basic assumptions are the essence of organizational culture. They reside not in the surface-level artifacts but in the minds and bodies of individuals and groups. Some researchers argue that this is why organizational culture is such a powerful force; its connections to the deeply seeded emotional needs of the organizational members makes it so (Pizer & Härtel, 2005).

Researchers who espouse the root-metaphor perspective often begin their examinations of organizational culture by studying one or many surface-level forms in an attempt to help them understand the deep levels. For example, Trice and Beyer (1984) advocated examining rites and ceremonials in organizations such as induction ceremonies, hiring and firing practices, and office parties to understand the underlying values of the organization. Boje (1991) recorded and analyzed stories told during executive meetings, training sessions, and hallway conversations. Friedman (1989), in an attempt to understand the culture of International Harvester, examined labor negotiations during a 1979 strike.

It is important to remember that an organization's culture cannot be understood by examining one or a few surface-level forms of culture in isolation. Researchers using the root-metaphor perspective integrate their observations of surface-level forms with in-depth interviews, long-term observation, and any other available forms of data they can gather before they attempt to describe an organization's culture. This process takes a tremendous amount of time and energy, but the result is often an understanding of not only the surface but also the deep nature of organizational culture (Martin, 2002).

The second element of organizational culture is that it is a *communicative construction*. From the root metaphor perspective, organizational culture is not something that is dictated by the management of the organization (as some in the variable camp would argue); it is, instead, constructed and reconstructed as members of the organization interact together and confront their environment. This perspective assumes that organizational culture is a sociohistorical construction (Deetz, 1982). In other words, organizational culture is created and recreated as people interact (communicate) over time.

In attempting to explain the concept of culture, Clifford Geertz likens culture to a web. Michael Pacanowsky and Nick O'Donnell-Trujillo (1990) articulate Geertz's metaphor, which connects culture and communication:

> [T]he web not only exists, it is spun. It is spun when people go about the business of construing their world as sensible—that is, when they communicate. When they talk, write a play, sing, dance, fake an illness, they are communicating, and they are constructing their culture. The web is the residue of the communication process. (p. 147)

The metaphor of a web is an interesting choice, in that webs represent strength, life, and cohesion, but they are also things that need constant maintenance, vary to meet the conditions, and are the direct result of the energy supplied by those who spin and inhabit them. By using the web metaphor, Pacanowsky and O'Donnell-Trujillo argued for the centrality of communication to culture; the two, in fact cannot be separated (see Eisenberg and Riley [2001] for an extended discussion of the connection between communication and culture).

The third element of organizational culture is that it *consists of subcultures and countercultures*. The culture-as-variable perspective proposes the idea that there is one overarching culture shared by all members of the organization. The root-metaphor perspective acknowledges that although many members may share certain organizational values, organizational culture is not monolithic; instead it is appropriate to consider that the culture of an organization may consist (naturally) of subcultures and countercultures.

According to culture researchers Trice and Beyer, organizational subcultures (smaller groups of organizational members sharing values that may differ slightly from the whole) arise from one of three social conditions (1993, pp. 176–177):

- **Differential interaction.** Interacting with certain people more regularly than others provides an opportunity for a subculture to develop. Separation by geographic location (e.g., Midwest branch vs. Southern branch of an organization), department (marketing vs. distribution), hierarchical level (vice president vs. regional manager), or union affiliation (union vs. nonunion) leads to differential interaction between groups and, hence, the possible development of subcultures.

- **Shared experiences.** As people live and work with one another, they experience a common reality and the problems associated with it. Over time, they develop shared meanings for events, common solutions to regular problems, and similar mind-sets regarding their environment. As the meanings, solutions, and mind-sets prove to be useful in dealing with everyday life, a subculture develops.

- **Similar personal characteristics.** Just as shared experiences may lead to the development of a subculture, so may the sharing of personal characteristics such as age, race, sex, gender, religion, social class, or education. According to Trice and Beyer, "Such similarities encourage the formation of subcultural ideologies because members do not need to displace their old beliefs and values very much to find common ground with one another" (p. 176).

One research study that demonstrated the existence of subcultures and how they converge and diverge was conducted by Kramer and Berman (2001) as they sought to understand a university's culture through undergraduate stories. They argued that an organization's subgroups view culture differently and that past studies of university culture tended to emphasize the stories and perspectives of employees (faculty, staff, and administration) while ignoring the student perspective. What they found was that stories do indeed contribute to the constitution of a university's culture, but students and employees tell different stories that do not necessarily lead to a unified culture. Students told stories that helped to maintain the culture as espoused by officials when they told stories about famous people or buildings or monuments. However, students also told stories that indicated a divergence from the dominant culture when they told stories about pranks, partying, or the supernatural or stories about officials demanding that espoused values be followed.

Although a subculture may diverge only minimally from the values and practices of the organizational culture, a counterculture may develop that is in opposition to the accepted culture. As Trice and Beyer define it, a *counterculture* is a subculture "whose basic understandings question and oppose the overall culture in some way" (1993, p. 244). Countercultures may develop as a result of corporate mergers, disgruntled employees, or highly differential group missions. Although countercultures certainly have the potential to be destructive to organizational cohesiveness, they may also be productive. Countercultures, by nature, oppose the values of the dominant culture. If values and assumptions go unchecked in any organization for too long, they may become so deeply entrenched that change, even change necessary to survival, becomes difficult if not improbable.

TABLE 5.1 Comparison of Variable versus Root Metaphor Perspectives

Issue	Variable	Root Metaphor
Nature of culture	Something the organization "has"; a tool, skill, or lever	Something the organization "is"; expressive form
Role of communication	Inform workforce of values	Create, sustain, and influence culture
Culture change	Through management directive and intervention	Through natural evolution; all members influence culture

In summary, the root-metaphor perspective offers a view of organizational culture that is complex, is communicatively based, and rejects the notion of a homogeneous culture. Table 5.1 outlines the differences between the variable and root-metaphor perspectives.

The variable and root-metaphor perspectives are not the only ways to characterize the research and thinking about organizational culture. For example, Martin (1992) offered three perspectives on organizational culture that differ in the extent to which there is one core culture in an organization and the extent to which culture is a stable entity. More recently, Eisenberg and Riley (2001) put forward seven theoretical frameworks regarding organizational culture, each with a different philosophical starting point. Given the variety of ways in which culture has been approached, it should be no surprise that it is difficult to find agreement on how to define the concept. In the next section, we discuss existing definitions of organizational culture and offer our own working definition.

Definitions of Organizational Culture

Definitions of organizational culture abound. Table 5.2 presents definitions offered by researchers from a variety of fields.

Table 5.2 is certainly not an exhaustive list of definitions (there are literally hundreds), but it does provide an understanding of the differences and similarities among them. These definitions of organizational culture appear to share three characteristics: (1) some aspect of culture is shared, (2) culture is intangible, and (3) culture affects human behavior.

The first common characteristic is that organizational culture involves something that is *shared*. Authors differ regarding the terms they use to describe what members of an organizational culture share, but they are all essentially saying the same thing: The members of the culture share common ways of understanding and interpreting organizational phenomena. This statement does not mean that all

TABLE 5.2   Definitions of Organizational Culture

Author(s)	Definition of Organizational Culture
Pettigrew (1979, p. 574)	Culture is the system of such publicly and collectively accepted meanings operating for a given group at a given time.
Schwartz & Davis (1981, p. 33)	Culture . . . is a pattern of beliefs and expectations shared by the organization's members.
Deal & Kennedy (1982)	The way we do things around here.
Sathe (1983, p. 523)	Culture is the set of important understandings (often unstated) that members of a community share in common.
Schein (1990, p. 111)	Culture is (a) a pattern of basic assumptions, (b) invented, discovered, or developed by a given group, (c) as it learns to cope with its problems of external adaptation and internal integration, (d) that has worked well enough to be considered valid, and therefore, (e) is to be taught to new members as the (f) correct way to perceive, think, and feel in relation to those problems.
Pinnington (2004, p. 206)	A collective . . . interpreted for its sense of social integration, differentiation, and fragmentation.
Pizer & Härtel (2005, p. 335)	Shared assumptions, values, and beliefs of a social group . . .
Keyton (2005, p. 1)	Organizational culture is the set of artifacts, values, and assumptions that emerge from the interactions of organizational members.

members of the culture think the same way, believe the same things, or act in the same way. It simply means that an organizational culture provides its members with frameworks for understanding and interpreting events, but the extent to which a member is enculturated with them is a matter of socialization (see Chapter 8) and individual differences.

The second common characteristic is that organizational culture is *intangible*. Organizational culture is a construction formed through human interaction, but it is not concrete at its core. Organizational culture, as described previously, consists of values, assumptions, norms, and frameworks for understanding, none of which are tangible objects.

Organizational culture is often confused with the tangible objects or observable activities that occur within an organization. The dress code of an organization, the stories that are told in it, the daily rituals and ceremonial rites, are all elements of organizational culture that serve to create, maintain, change, and reflect it, but they are not in and of themselves the organization's culture. A mistake often made by managers is to consider a change in one or more of these elements as a change in culture; this mistake reflects the culture-as-variable perspective. Given that culture is complex and intangible, the change made is not in the culture itself (values and assumptions), but on the surface.

The third common characteristic is that organizational culture affects *human behavior*. This is perhaps the most important, though it may not seem so. Organizational culture is not merely another way of attempting to run organizations more profitably; it is a construction of human interaction that affects and is affected by the behavior of all members of the organization. Organizational culture provides frameworks (or logics) for interpreting organizational events as the members experience them on a day-to-day basis. If we are to understand how and why organizational members behave as they do, we must understand the organizational culture that guides and constrains them.

In defining organizational culture, Charles Conrad, in his textbook *Strategic Organizational Communication* (1990), makes two important points that are relevant to the content as it applies to the communicative organization. Organizational cultures are (1) communicative creations and (2) historical. We feel that these two issues are not adequately addressed in previous definitions of organizational culture (Table 5.2) and therefore warrant discussion.

First, organizational cultures are *communicative creations*. They do not exist separate from organizational members; cultures are created, sustained, and influenced by and through human interaction. In telling stories, writing memos, having meetings, conducting rites and rituals, and other communicative actions, members develop and articulate (to themselves, as well as to other members and nonmembers) the central values of the culture.

At the same time, the culture of the organization influences the communication of its members. Organizational members communicate based on the values and interpretive frameworks of the culture, thereby legitimizing use of specialized language, appropriate media for communication, and the conventions of who talks to whom about what. In other words, the relationship between communication and organizational culture is reciprocal; communication influences organizational culture and organizational culture influences communication (see Figure 5.1).

Figure 5.1 and the preceding discussion should not be interpreted as advocating a direct causal relationship between organizational culture and human behavior. Although organizational culture certainly may *influence* human behavior in organizations, it does not *cause* members to act predictably in every situation. Because individuals are, by nature, unique and have freedom of choice, human behavior will always be unpredictable. Nevertheless, organizational culture provides frameworks for what is acceptable and expected; it is the members' choice to behave within that framework.

Conrad's second important point is that organizational cultures are *historical*. "[Cultures] emerge and develop over time, adapting to changes in their member-

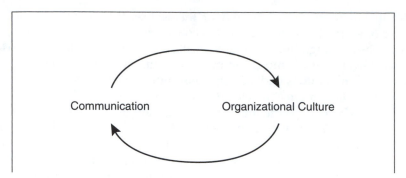

FIGURE 5.1   **Relationship between Communication and Organizational Culture**

ship, functions, problems, and purposes" (p. 17). Organizational cultures are rooted in the history of events and actions (particularly the communicative actions) as they have unfolded in and around the organization.

In light of Conrad's two important points, we feel a definition of organizational culture that emphasizes communication and history is necessary. Therefore, the following definition is offered: *Organizational culture is a communicatively constructed, historically based system of assumptions, values, and interpretive frameworks that guide and constrain organizational members as they perform their organizational roles and confront the challenges of their environment.*

In the final section of the discussion of organizational culture, we offer one model of organizational culture from the vast literature on the subject, that of Edgar Schein. It offers a multilevel perspective on culture that acknowledges both its surface and its deep aspects.

Schein's Model of Organizational Culture

In his book *Organizational Culture and Leadership* (1985), Edgar Schein outlined a model of organizational culture that articulates three interrelated levels of culture: (1) artifacts and creations, (2) values, and (3) basic assumptions. Although they are conceptually distinct, it is important to understand how they are related to one another.

Level 1: Artifacts and Creations.   The first level of Schein's model of organizational culture, *artifacts and creations*, consists of the tangible, physical, or hearable things in the environment of the organization. Schein argued that, despite the fact that this level is the most "visible," its elements are quite difficult to decipher.

Researchers often begin their study of an organization's culture by familiarizing themselves with its artifacts. Much as anthropologists study the artifacts of a tribe to understand how they live, organizational culture researchers examine the physical creations (whether they be tangible objects or communicative events) to help them understand the culture. For example, as mentioned earlier, Trice and Beyer (1984) examine rites and ceremonials. They argue that certain rites, such as training programs, seminars, and holiday parties, may be reflections or manifestations of the values of the organization. Stephen Barley (1983), in an analysis of the culture of the funeral home industry, studied the physical artifacts of the funeral home, the behaviors associated with removal of the body from a home after a death, and the practices associated with preparation of the corpse for disposal. Barley found that these physical manifestations were important in creating a sense of "normalcy" and "naturalness" for the loved ones of the deceased.

Although artifacts and creations are observable elements of organizational culture, they should not be confused with the culture itself. Schein argued that it is important to understand the connection of the artifacts of the first level to the values of the second level.

Level 2: Values. Schein defined values as an individual's or group's "sense of what 'ought' to be, as distinct from what is" (1985, p. 15). As individuals come together to form a collective (e.g., work group, research team, organization), they are soon confronted with the need to have a common basis for operating together. Schein argued that someone in the group, typically the leader or the founder, has particular thoughts and feelings (or convictions) about the nature of reality and will articulate ideas about the problems the group faces on the basis of those convictions. If the actions proposed by that person are adequate in addressing the problems, the convictions that underlie those actions may evolve into preferences as to how situations should be handled in the future. In other words, the convictions of one or a few become useful enough and strong enough to become a basis for what "ought to be" in the future. Members of the culture are often aware of and can articulate the values of the organization, but they do not always recognize the extent to which they are present in the conduct of their actions on a day-to-day basis.

What is the relationship between level 1 and level 2? Values are inherently intangible, cognitive constructions, but many are expressly articulated or codified by the organizational members. In this way, the values may be "visible" in artifacts, behaviors, and creations. At other times, however, organizational members (particularly leaders) may articulate a value that contradicts the artifacts and behaviors of level 1. In this case, the value may not be a "real" value at all, but simply an "espoused value" or a "fantasy value."

Two examples will help with this distinction. In Company A, leadership says that there is a value of "equality" in the organization. An examination of the artifacts of the organization reveals the following: parking spaces are not assigned, office space is equally distributed and furnishings are similar, anyone can speak freely at an office meeting, and pay raises are based purely on performance. For Company A, it would appear as if the articulated value of "equality" is congruent with the artifacts of the organization.

In Company B, the organization articulates a value of "equality," but an examination of the artifacts reveals something different. Pay raises are often based on nepotism and personal associations, corporate officers have the best parking spaces, and office space and furnishings are highly differentiated between management and workers. In this case, the espoused value of "equality" does not reconcile with the artifacts of the organization. The lesson is an important one: Just because a value is articulated by the leadership of an organization does not mean that it is a "real" value of the culture.

Level 3: Basic Assumptions.   Basic assumptions represent the essence of culture for Schein. He argued that once a solution to a problem has shown itself to work time and time again it becomes "taken for granted." That being so, members holding the basic assumptions find behavior that deviates from them to be incomprehensible.

Schein put forward five basic assumptions around which organizational cultures may form and the questions that arise from them (adapted from Schein, 1985, p. 86):

1. **Humanity's relationship to nature.** At the organizational level, do the key members view the relationship of the organization to its environment as one of dominance, submission, harmonizing, finding an appropriate niche, or what?
2. **The nature of reality and truth.** Linguistic and behavioral rules that define what is real and what is not, what is a "fact," how truth is ultimately to be determined, and whether truth is "revealed" or "discovered"; basic concepts of time and space.
3. **The nature of human nature.** What does it mean to be "human" and what attributes are considered intrinsic or ultimate? Is human nature good, evil, or neutral? Are human beings perfectible or not?
4. **The nature of human activity.** What is the "right" thing for human beings to do, on the basis of the above assumptions about reality, the environment, and human nature: to be active, passive, self-developmental, fatalistic, or what? What is work and what is play?
5. **The nature of human relationships.** What is considered to be the "right" way for people to relate to each other, to distribute power and love? Is life cooperative or competitive, individualistic, group collaborative, or communal; based on traditional lineal authority, law, charisma, or what?

As you can see, basic assumptions involve the deepest levels of culture and often pose very difficult questions. Cultures, though, over time and through interaction develop "theories-in-use," as Schein calls them, which are reflected in values and guide behavior. Without assumptions, organizational groups lack guiding principles or baselines to which they can refer for making sense of organizational reality.

Schein's model offers a useful means for both the researcher and the organizational member to comprehend the culture of an organization. It is a tool for digging into the deep layers of organizational culture so that one does not mistake surface elements for the heart of the culture.

In this section, the study of organizational culture has been approached from two perspectives, culture-as-variable and culture-as-root-metaphor. The two perspectives differ in regard to the depth of culture, the role of communication, and whether culture can and should be changed. A definition of organizational culture highlighted the centrality of communication and history to the development of culture. Finally, Schein's model presented one means of examining organizational culture.

In the final section of this chapter, we offer a brief discussion of critical perspectives of organizations. Critical perspectives reject the notion that organizations are value-free sites, as prior theories have implicitly or explicitly advocated. Instead, organizations are viewed as sites of struggle between management and workers resulting in domination and oppression of the powerless by the powerful.

Critical Theory

Critical theory, which is based in the work of Karl Marx, was integrated into the study of organizations in the 1970s (Alvesson & Deetz, 1996). As a field of inquiry, critical theory has its roots in the Institute for Social Research in Frankfurt (now commonly known as the Frankfurt School) founded in the 1920s (Foss, Foss, & Trapp, 1985). The Frankfurt School philosophy was twofold. First, knowledge in society is not objective; it is indelibly tied to the participants and tainted by their interests and the power structure. Second, the plight of the theorist is to involve herself in the inner workings of society, reveal the contradictions associated with the imbalance of power, and provide critique that will allow for the reversal of those conditions in the future (Foss et al., 1985).

Organizational communication scholars operating from a critical theory standpoint attempt to reveal how social and technological structures within organizations serve to oppress workers. Moreover, researchers attempt to educate workers about these oppressive forces and provide means for workers' emancipation. For critical theorists, insight (such as that provided by systems theory or organizational culture) into organizational functioning and problems is insufficient (Deetz, 1982); researchers must also engage in consciousness-raising among members (Redding & Tompkins, 1988).

In this section of the chapter, we offer a brief overview of critical theory as it applies to the study of organizations. Critical theory is complex and multifaceted. Rather than a thorough description, an introduction to the central concepts of critical theory in organizations is presented. The section continues with the contribution of Jurgen Habermas to the role of communication in critical theory and concludes with issues and challenges raised by critical theory.

Organization as a Site of Domination

Critical theorists view an organization as a site of domination where the interests of the dominant group (typically owners and management) are elevated above the

interests of subordinate groups (typically the workers). This framework is substantially different from prior theories (e.g., classical theory or systems theory),
which offered no critique of the negative and harmful results of their prescriptions. Aktouf (1992) articulated this exact point when he wrote, "For almost a century, functional-consensus theories have been masking the welter of conflicts and
contradictions undermining both the discipline and practice of management"
(p. 410). In other words, theories such as those found in classical theory and
human relations and human resources movements often propose visions of management that are far more clear-cut and value free than reality shows them to be.

Traditional organizational structures that rely on bureaucratic procedures,
centralized decision making, and hierarchical control favor the interests of those
in management while the interests of the workers are subordinated. Managers are
able to frame the interests of the workers in relation to their own interests
(Mumby, 1988). For example, management may offer a somewhat lucrative commission plan for its sales force that, on the surface, appears to reward hard work.
Upon further critique, though, the commission plan may lead to an overwhelm-
ing pressure on the sales force to work longer hours, travel more frequently, and
subsequently ignore their personal and family lives in favor of increasing profits
for the organization. In other words, a practice that appears to be in the interest of
one group (workers) is, in actuality, a form of domination and control serving the
interests of the dominant group (management).

Power, Hegemony, and Concertive Control

Management in organizations is based on the control of resources, workers,
and/or consumers (Alvesson & Deetz, 1996). Control is created and maintained in
a variety of ways: through the outright, explicit exercise of power; through the
unknowing adoption of a dominant group's values and beliefs (hegemony); or
through adherence to a work team's socially constructed norms (concertive control). In the following section, we provide an overview of these concepts that are
central to critical theory.

Power.   Classical writers from Aristotle to Hobbes to Machiavelli have offered
conceptualizations of *power*. Modern theories of power have their roots in Marx,
Weber, and Parsons (Hickson, Astley, Butler, & Wilson, 1981). Weber's definition
of power as "the possibility of imposing one's will upon the behavior of other persons" (1947, p. 323) is visible in the conceptualizations of power presented in the
current review. The theories of power offered by Dahl (1957), Bachrach and Baratz
(1970), and Lukes (1974) are cited here because they provide an overview of power
in organizations that documents the evolution of thought about the linkages
between power and two closely related variables: conflict and decision making.
Research on power has progressed from conceptualizing it as intrinsically tied to
moments of decision making and overt conflict (Dahl, 1957), to finding traces of
power in other times that could include overt or latent conflict or both (Bachrach
& Baratz, 1970; Lukes, 1974).

Dahl (1957) advanced a behavioral theory of power that has become known as the *one-dimensional view of power*. His definition reads: *A* has power over *B* to the extent that *A* can get *B* to do something *B* would not otherwise do. Central to this view is the exercise of power. This approach to power is focused on identifying observable, decision-making behavior that, in turn, involves conflict: "Conflict, according to that view, is assumed to be crucial in providing an experimental test of power attributions: without it the exercise of power will, it seems to be thought, fails to show up" (Lukes, 1974, p. 14). Researchers from this perspective monitor overt conflicts, observe members' positions on important issues, and detail the outcomes of the conflicts (Conrad, 1983, p. 175). This conceptualization of power concentrates on behavior in decision-making situations where conflict is present.

Bachrach and Baratz (1970), in their book *Power and Poverty*, responded to Dahl's one-dimensional view of power with a *two-dimensional view* of power. They criticized Dahl for his focus on overt decision making:

> [T]he model takes no account of the fact that power may be, and often is, exercised by confining the scope of the decision-making to relatively "safe" issues. . . . [T]he model provides no *objective* criteria for distinguishing between "important" and "unimportant" issues arising in the political arena. (p. 6)

They argued that a theory of power must consider both decision making and nondecision making, where the latter is "a decision that results in suppression or thwarting of a latent or manifest challenge to the values or interests of the decision-maker" (p. 44). Despite Bachrach and Baratz's addition of nondecision making to the arena of power, they still remain connected with Dahl on the crucial factor of conflict: If "there is no conflict, overt or covert, the presumption must be that there is consensus on the prevailing allocation of values, in which case nondecision making is impossible" (p. 49). The two-dimensional view of power, while still focusing on conflict and decision making, emphasizes that power may be present when conflict is covert as well as overt.

Lukes, in his book *Power: A Radical View* (1974), praised Bachrach and Baratz for their criticisms of Dahl, but argued that their two-dimensional view of power remains inadequate. In response, Lukes offered a *three-dimensional view of power*, which focuses on three main issues: (1) decision making and control over the political agenda (not necessarily through decisions); (2) issues and potential issues; and (3) observable (overt or covert) and latent conflict, where latent conflict is "a contradiction between the interests of those exercising power and the 'real interests' of those they exclude" (pp. 24–25). This view of power introduces the idea that power may be present in situations where there is no conflict on the surface and at times other than those when decisions are made. From this perspective, power has both a surface and deep structure (Conrad, 1983; Frost, 1987). The *surface structure* is a dimension of power "that guides and restricts the strategies adopted by employees during overt, open negotiations about practical decisions" (Conrad, 1983, p. 186); the *deep structure* is a "hidden dimension that influences employees' decisions about which battles to fight, which adversaries to oppose, and which issues to raise" (p. 186). Similarly, Mumby (2000) posits that the two levels of concern with power in critical theory involve (1) individual and group social relations and (2) the interests and values upon which knowledge claims are made.

Hegemony.   Although critical theorists are certainly interested in the exercise of power in all forms and at all levels, they are particularly interested in the ways in which power or control manifests itself implicitly. Therefore, they often attend to latent conflicts and the deep-structure dimension of power. Both these topics are included in the concept of *hegemony*:

> Hegemony does not refer simply to the domination of one group by another, but indicates the process by which one group actively supports the goals and aspirations of another, dominant group, even though those goals may not be in the subordinate group's best interest. (Mumby, 1988, p. 55)

The key to the concept of hegemony is the idea that the subordinated group actively supports the interests of the dominant group, often unknowingly, which results in oppression.

The subordinated group is actively participating in the maintenance of the dominant group's *ideology*. Ideology refers to the "integrated set of values, ideals, and understandings about a particular part of social reality that justifies certain commitment and actions" (Alvesson, 1993, p. 8). According to Gibson and Papa (2000), ideology represents social reality by telling organizational members what is good, what is normal, and what acceptable behavior within the organization is. The relationship between ideology and hegemony is strong. If ideology is the values and beliefs held by the dominant group, then hegemony is the enactment of these values and beliefs by the subordinate group.

For example, consider a midsize steel manufacturing company that purports to uphold the organizational value of "family." In this organization, the metaphor of family is used regularly in newsletters, meetings, and informal conversations in and out of the workplace to describe the relationship between organizational members at all hierarchical levels. Most members seem satisfied with their work life and often talk about making sacrifices for their organizational family; they work late, pick up the slack for other "family members" who are having trouble, and generally feel a sense of dedication to the organization.

A critical theorist, after extensive research in the organization, may consider this situation to be an example of hegemony. The use of the family metaphor may be considered a way for management to create a situation in which the workers actively support organizational interests while working against their own. Despite the fact that many workers may feel comforted by the family metaphor and the atmosphere created by it, they are subtly being forced to work harder, keep longer hours, and sacrifice their own family lives for their organizational "family." The metaphor is representative of the behaviors and attitudes, in other words, the ideology, that management desires workers to hold. What seems on the surface to serve the interests of the workers, in actuality serves the interests of management and may even be oppressive to the workers.

Concertive Control.   As some organizations made the move to more participative, decentralized, self-managing work-team structures, as discussed in Chapter 3, managers feared that they would lose the explicit control built into the traditional structures (e.g., bureaucracy and scientific management). Recent research, however, has shown how a form of member-based control is present that is often considered to be stricter than that in traditional structures (Barker 1998; Larson & Tompkins, 2005; Papa, Auwal, & Singhal, 1997; Wright & Barker, 2000). Tompkins and Cheney (1985) term this form of control *concertive control*. Concertive control is based on adherence to socially constructed norms and values developed by organizational members themselves as they attempt to structure their environment.

When an organization adopts a truly participative system, which usually encompasses the notion of self-managing work teams, organizational members are responsible for structuring the work environment and processes, tasks once assigned to managers in traditional structures and in which workers had little participation. As workers engage in the structuring process, they reach "a negotiated consensus on how to shape their behavior according to a set of core values" (Barker, 1998, p. 130). The consensus to adhere to these values and the pressure to adhere to them is strong because the workers themselves develop them.

In some situations, management establishes a set of core values for the organization but does not provide direct control mechanisms or structured activities for achieving organizational goals. Barker (1998) conducted research in a manufacturing organization where the structure was changed from a traditional one to that of self-managing work teams. As the change occurred, the head of the organization articulated a set of core values he wished to guide the organization in the future. Workers were trained to perform in self-managing work teams and were cross-trained on all necessary organizational tasks. Barker found that workers exerted control over one another as they developed norms for behavior that were congruent with the stated core values. If a team member violated a norm, the other team members immediately confronted the team member. Each member strictly adhered to the norms in order not to have to face the disappointment of other team members. Many workers reported this form of control, concertive control, to be stricter than that they experienced under the traditional structure.

Although concertive control can result from socially constructed norms based on an overall vision provided by management, it can also occur when the members themselves initially develop the values and norms. Papa et al. (1997) describe this form of concertive control in their research on the Grameen Bank in Bangladesh. The Grameen Bank organizes loans for micro-enterprise endeavors in the poorest regions of the country. Despite not requiring collateral at the time of the loan, the bank has a 99 percent loan recovery rate. Papa et al. found that concertive control, based in part on high levels of identification, was operating in this organization. In motivational programs that all field workers and low-level managers attended, a "team" metaphor was proposed. The mutual development of this guiding metaphor resulted in the value of laboring together and constant peer pressure to maintain the high loan-recovery rate. As the workers strove to help their team members, they often sacrificed their personal lives. Of importance, it was the workers themselves, not management, who provided the pressure to recover the loans.

Concertive control in the team environment can have positive and negative consequences. According to Wright and Barker (2000), the positive consequences of concertive control can include role clarity, guidance for team members, and increased discipline within the team. However, if the control mechanisms are either too strict or too loose, negative consequences can occur. If the system is too constraining, then innovation will be restricted, which will result in lower motivation and dissatisfaction. If the system is too loose, team members will not have enough guidance or role clarity to adequately meet the team or individual goals.

In this section, we have discussed a core feature of critical theory—how control manifests itself in a variety of forms, which in turn may serve to oppress workers. In the next section, we continue this thread by focusing on how communication at the interactional level serves to contribute to an imbalance of interests in organizational life.

Communication and Critical Theory

Communication scholars partial to critical theory have found the work of the German philosopher and sociologist Jurgen Habermas (a member of the Frankfurt School) to be particularly useful (e.g., Mumby, 1988). Habermas took as his primary goal "to develop a theory of society that aims at the self-emancipation of people from domination." At the center of his theory was communication (Foss et al., 1985, p. 216).

One of the most influential aspects of Habermas' work as it pertains to critical theory and communication is the notion of the *ideal speech situation*. When the ideal speech situation is embodied, the participants in the interaction are in balance; the interests of some are not privileged over the interests of others. For the ideal speech situation to be realized, the interaction must be characterized by four *validity claims* (Foss et al., 1985; Mumby, 1988):

1. The utterances are truthful.
2. A legitimate relationship has been established between the participants.
3. The utterances are sincere.
4. The utterances are comprehensible.

When any element of the ideal speech situation is compromised, *systematically distorted communication* occurs. The result is interactional asymmetry (an imbalance in power) and false consensus (Mumby, 1988).

The concepts of the ideal speech situation and systematically distorted communication bring the often difficult-to-grasp precepts of critical theory into reach of students of communication. Any interaction can be subjected to the four validity claims of the ideal speech situation; violation of any of the claims leads to a situation where one participant or party is at a disadvantage, creating a situation of imbalance. This imbalance, repeated, propagated, and possibly endorsed by the organizational structure, leads to a situation where the interests and needs of the dominant group are given preference to those of the subordinate group.

Critical organizational communication theorists attempt to uncover the communication practices, whether interpersonal, team-based, or organization-wide, that promote an unhealthy imbalance in organizations. In the final section of this chapter, we discuss some of the issues and challenges raised by critical theory that any member of the workforce will benefit from understanding.

Critical Theory: Issues and Challenges

We realize that the critical framework may be a bit difficult to grasp and the implications of the core concepts and research seemingly unrelated to the other theorists covered so far in this book. But, as with systems theory and organizational culture, critical theory is another way of understanding behavior in organizations that can help make sense of why people behave and feel the way they do. It can also educate them as to how to improve their organizational situations. We close this chapter with two examples of how critical theory is used both to unearth taken-for-granted assumptions that lead to oppression and to offer solutions for change.

Creating a More "Human(e)" Workplace.   Perhaps the greatest contribution the critical framework has to offer is that the oppressive reality of organizational life does not have to continue. Critical organizational theorists are dedicated to uncovering oppressive structural, technological, and communicative practices in organizations that most people accept as a natural part of work life. The reality is that the oppression and oppressive circumstances exist often as a byproduct of the manner in which organizations have classically been run. Workers tend to believe that this is just the nature of the beast; they must sacrifice their selves and their interests so that the organization may run according to plan.

Critical theorists are interested in showing that oppression is not an inherent part of organizational life; that there are perhaps more "human" or "humane" ways to structure it (Aktouf, 1992; Cheney, 1995; Collins, 1998). Of particular note is George Cheney's research and writing on "democracy" in the workplace (Cheney, 1995; see also Deetz, 1992; Hoffman, 2002; Russell, 1997).

Cheney suggests that democracy, the political cornerstone of the United States, seldom extends to the workplace. He envisions a workplace that embraces the principles of democracy held so reverently at the political level. Workplace democracy may be characterized as follows:

> [A] system of governance which truly values individual goals and feelings (e.g., equitable remuneration, the pursuit of enriching work and the right to express oneself) as well as typically organizational objectives (e.g., effectiveness and efficiency,

reflectively conceived), which actively fosters the connection between those two sets of concerns by encouraging individual contributions to important organizational choices, and which allows for the ongoing modification of the organization's activities and policies by the group. (Cheney, 1995, p. 170)

According to Cheney, the process of promoting workplace democracy involves the encouragement of (1) self-reflection, (2) collective development, and (3) individual opportunity. Democracy in the workplace should lead to organizational situations where oppressive circumstances are less likely to take hold. As organizational members are afforded absolute voice in organizational processes and both individual and team-oriented reflection is encouraged, the likelihood of oppression will be minimized.

Critical theory offers you, as future organizational members and workers, both a means of identifying elements of constraint and oppression in your organization and prescriptions for improving the situation. Another area in which critical theorists offer insight for organizational members is the situation of women in organizations.

The Plight of Women: Feminist Organizational Communication Theorizing.

Feminist organizational theory is a form of critical theory that is dedicated to examining the oppressive circumstances experienced by women in the workplace. Although there are many forms of feminism, all share the common assumption that the workplace is dominated by male-oriented social structures and that this situation can and must be changed (Calas & Smircich, 1996). Feminist theorizing raises our collective consciousness regarding the unequal treatment and oppressive circumstances women face in the workplace, attempts to uncover the assumptions upon which those circumstances are based, and offers a variety of means by which the oppression can be alleviated.

As an example of the type of circumstances just described, consider the situation described by Marla, a woman attorney with a large law firm. During a consulting session with one of the authors, Marla told the story of walking into the break room late one Friday afternoon, where she found several of her male counterparts drinking liquor from a cabinet that she did not even know existed. When she asked about it, one of the male lawyers told her that only the "kings" have keys to the cabinet, not the "queens." By "kings" he meant "men," and by "queens," women. Marla realized with that comment the extremely different circumstances that existed for women and men in that organization. Digging deep into her memory (as well as the organizational chart), she recalled many more instances where men were the ones in power situations in the organization and that women were rarely, if ever, afforded such opportunities. Because of the male-dominated structures in this organization, Marla would have a very difficult time advancing professionally or even receiving treatment equal to that of the male attorneys.

Different feminist perspectives offer different reasons for and solutions to the problems women face in the workplace. Natalle, Papa, and Graham (1994) outlined three varied feminist perspectives. *Liberal feminists* believe that people are differentiated on the basis of sex and exist in a patriarchal (male-dominated) structure in which women are oppressed. To resolve this oppression, liberal feminists advocate working within the existing structure, particularly the legal system, to gain equal opportunity for women in the workplace and to promote an equal valuing (financial and social) for equal work done by men and women. *Radical feminists* argue for a separation of men and women as a means of resolving the imbalance between the sexes. This feminist perspective embraces the idea that women have superior cultural and biological qualities that allow them to exist outside the patriarchal system. In other words, women can and should separate themselves from men because they can operate at a higher level without them. Finally, *materialist feminists* advance the idea that gender differences are socially constructed. To alleviate oppression, the existing patriarchal power structure must be uprooted and eliminated so that resources may be equally distributed. For radical feminists (as distinct from liberal feminists), there is no way that women will be emancipated under the current social, political, and capitalist-based structure of society.

Feminist organization theory has drawn significant attention to the association between rationality and masculinity (Ferguson, 1984; Kanter, 1977; Morgan, 1997). Martin (2000) argues that masculinity is at the heart of many seemingly neutral topics such as the Hawthorne studies, Weber's bureaucracy, bounded rationality and emotionality, and prevailing institutional and managerial theory. Historically, rationality has been linked with reason, logic, and objective judgment (stereotypically masculine qualities), whereas subjectivity, intuition, and emotions have been associated with more feminine qualities (Ross-Smith & Kornberger, 2004). Feminists vary on their stances, though, on these issues depending on the framework from which they are operating. Let's consider the example of Weber's bureaucracy.

Liberal feminists argue that bureaucracy can be in line with feminist principles. The principles behind bureaucracy are such as to prevent favoritism and discrimination and ensure that individuals are treated consistently and equitably in all interactions. Liberal feminists argue that bureaucracy only becomes problematic when the individuals enacting it rely on sexist or gendered practices. This liberal feminist critique embodies their tradition of maintaining organizational structure while modifying individual practices and behaviors that occur within the structure.

Radical feminists, however, might argue that Weber's bureaucracy highlights, enforces, and normalizes conditions of subordination, dependence, and powerlessness. Acker (1990) extends this position by arguing that bureaucracies privilege men's status in society and reproduce gender inequality in the workplace. This critique is in line with radical feminist thought that seeks to question dominant organizational forms and expose their gendered bases (i.e., Calas & Smircich, 1996; Mayer, 1995; Natalle et al., 1994).

Organizational communication scholars operating from a feminist perspective are seeking to show the centrality of language and interaction to the circumstances women face in the gendered workplace (Buzzanell, 1994). On the basis of this research, members of organizations are able to understand how their communicative actions and interactions contribute to either the perpetuation or the reversal of the current oppressive situation. Armed with this knowledge, they can seek to change their behavior, affect the behavior of others, and help promote a more equitable and equal workplace for the sexes.

Scholars have also spent time debating the notion of feminist organizing. Morgan (1994) identified several characteristics that typically define feminist organizing. These characteristics include frequent self-disclosure and collective discussions of feelings. Members may experience higher levels of identification with the organization as well as increased commitment to the organization's mission and values. Feminist organizing may also include a degree of bounded emotionality. *Bounded emotionality* refers to bringing elements of nurturance, caring, community, supportiveness, and interrelatedness into the workforce although for task effectiveness the emotionality is bound by feeling rules that emphasize individual and relational needs along side organizational limits (Ashcraft, 2000).

The feminist framework one assumes greatly influences what one views as feminist organizing. Communication scholars argue that feminist organizations may be conceptualized as "alternative discourse communities that develop counterdiscourses of gender, power, and organizing amid cultural and material constraints" (Ashcraft, 2000, p. 352). This definition enables us to conceptualize organizations as sites where workers, through their interactions, continually negotiate and renegotiate organizational structure. The emphasis is on action and the decisions that organizational members make in their daily interactions. This perspective focuses on the interplay between feminist theory and daily practice (i.e., Hatch, 1997; Putnam, 1986; Trethewey, 1999).

To review, critical theory, which is based on Marxist philosophy, assumes that traditionally organized activity inherently places the interests of the dominant group over those of the subordinate group. This section noted the organization as a site of domination; described and illustrated the principles of power, hegemony, and concertive control; outlined the ideal speech situation and the way systematically distorted communication can contribute to asymmetry; and concluded with issues and challenges posed by critical theory.

Summary

This chapter has been a long journey through the basic elements of both organizational theory and critical theory. On the surface, these two theories may not seem to belong in the same chapter, but they have several things in common that dictate their joint treatment. First, both theories call into question the theories and practices of the past and view organizations as more than the sum of management practices and task allocation. Second, communication is central to both of these theories. Organizational culture is intricately and inextricably tied to the communication process in organizations. Most critical approaches to organizations recognize that it is through communication that oppressive structures come into being and that those structures, in turn, serve to restrict the communication of certain groups. Communication, from this perspective, is also the way to freedom from those same oppressive structures. Finally, the intention of these two theories is not to increase profits realized from their implementation, but to excavate the underlying values and assumptions that guide organizational life and may serve to oppress certain members.

The topic of organizational culture among practitioners is not as hot as it was in the early and mid-1980s when popular-press books on the subject were on the desks of many managers. That is not to say, however, that organizational culture is not considered to be important among practitioners today; a cursory look through business magazines and popular-press books shows that such culture is still on people's minds. Culture has, it seems, assumed a secondary role—something to be considered as hiring decisions are made and as organizational change is plotted and executed. Research continues to grow in this area, however, and as new findings emerge and the centrality of communication to the concept becomes even more evident, a resurgence in organizational culture theory should occur. Alvesson (2002) cautions us, however, as we proceed with inquiry in this area: "Culture is, however, a tricky concept as it is easily used to cover everything and consequently nothing" (p. 3).

Critical theory has never enjoyed the popular (pragmatic) success that organizational culture theory has. The most evident of the many reasons is that it asks organizations to examine their own structures and behaviors to reveal instances of domination and oppression. Most organizational representatives are unwilling to make themselves this vulnerable to disapproval. But critical theorists have enjoyed some success; their work has influenced the mindsets of various workers and policymakers throughout the country and the world. Although the work of critical theorists may not yet have been translated directly into theories of practical management, the situations faced by women and minorities in the workplace have been brought out of the shadows, and society has been made aware of the oppressive circumstances fostered in many modern organizations. In the next decade, critical theory will play a vital role in the development of organizational communication.

In the next chapter, we offer an integrative framework that attempts to combine elements of most of the theories covered to this point. The framework highlights the prevalence of misunderstandings and situates communication at the center of organizational functioning. This framework may be called the *communicative organization.*

CHAPTER

6

The Communicative Organization

In this chapter, we present a model of core principles to guide and influence the way people function in organizations. We call this model the *communicative organization* (CO). Although the CO model is influenced by prior organizational theories—particularly the learning organization, organizational culture, and human resources theory—the purposes of this model differ. It is not our intention that the CO model provide a prescriptive theory of managerial behavior (such as administrative theory or Theory Y) or offer an all-encompassing theory of organizational functioning that integrates structure, behavior, competition, and capital. Instead, the CO model is aimed at *all* organizational members (not just management) and accomplishes two interrelated purposes: (1) It highlights the prevalence of misunderstandings in organizational activity and (2) it illustrates how the communication behaviors of organizational members create and re-create organizational structures that can assist in promoting or combating misunderstandings.

The communicative organization has several things in common with a learning organization. As discussed in Chapter 4, a learning organization is one that has an enhanced capacity to learn, adapt, and change. Since Peter Senge's *The Fifth Discipline* (1990) and Gordon Dryden and Jeannette Vos's *The Learning Revolution* (1997), organizations around the world have embraced the concept of an enhanced knowledge base from which to make decisions. Learning organizations are characterized by continuous learning at the systems level, generation and sharing of knowledge, critical and systemic thinking, a culture of learning, a spirit of flexibility and experimentation, and a people-centered focus. Certainly, we would agree that open systems, accessibility of knowledge at all levels of the organization, and a focus on people are important. Of particular relevance to the communicative organization, however, is the concept of flexibility and experimentation. An organization that can allow employees to experiment without unreasonable risk is an organization more likely to be innovative. Additionally, a learning organization is one that is talk oriented (Marshak, 1998), which is a central theme of the CO model.

In Chapter 1, we offered a definition of organizational communication based on several assumptions. Three of those assumptions are particularly relevant to the CO model, so we present them again here:

- Communication is central to the existence of the organization; it creates and re-creates the structure that constitutes the organization. That structure, in turn, affects the nature and flow of communication within it.
- Things can go wrong at any (and every) point in the communication process. Throughout this book we will refer to this very broadly as *misunderstandings*. The concept of misunderstandings, as we use it here, involves more than ineffective communication between members of an organization. It is an umbrella term used to connote the problematic nature of interaction in organizational settings.
- Misunderstandings seem to characterize communication in organizations. As organizations develop, both productive and unproductive features accompany that development, such as layers of hierarchy, opposing goals, struggles for power, use of technology, gender and cultural differences, reward systems, and control mechanisms. These features serve to complicate the communication process at almost every moment, such that misunderstanding is as prevalent as, if not more prevalent than, understanding.

Throughout this chapter we explore these assumptions as they relate to the foundation and elements of the CO model. We begin with a discussion of the first assumption, particularly the theory of structuration and the notion of talk as action. We then present the CO model and explain its elements, at that point involving the second and third assumptions.

Talk as Action: Structuration and the Communicative Organization

You have probably heard the saying "Stop talking and do something!" This adage presupposes that talk and action are not connected, that talk is not related to action. According to this idea, which we can refer to as the *action-over-talk model*, if any progress is to be made, if anything substantial is to be accomplished, the talk must stop so action can begin. The first assumption of our definition of organizational communication, though, argues a different perspective on the talk–action connection. Talk, as it produces and reproduces structure, is action itself. Talk and action should not be considered "disjoint entities" (Marshak, 1998).

The action-over-talk model is not only shortsighted with regard to the structure-producing-and-reproducing function of communication, but it might also promote a potential gender bias. According to Robert Marshak (1998), the action-over-talk model might devalue the contributions of women in the process of organizational functioning:

[This model] implicitly favors strong, silent, linearly oriented action to reciprocal, relationship, and emotionally oriented conversation. When talk is demeaned as relatively worthless, and, if, as it is for some, "talk is women's work," then the consequences are obvious for women in the workplace. (p. 28)

To combat this and other negative implications of the action-over-talk model, Marshak proposes the idea that talk *is* action. Or, put another way, "SPEECH ACTS . . . to talk is to do something" (Modaff & Hopper, 1984, p. 37). This is not to say, of course, that there are times when organizational members *talk* more than they *do*, as that is certainly the case. Most of us have been in situations where we have wanted to say "Enough talking already! Let's stop discussing this and just do it!" These situations, however, are specific instances where talk gets in the way of accomplishing a task. Marshak is using the term *talk* more globally than that; he is asking us to think about talk as communication or interaction from a deeper perspective. From this perspective, talk (or people interacting through time) creates structures that guide how we think, feel, and behave, and these structures in turn affect how we communicate.

To promote the thesis that talk is action, Marshak identified three types of talk and proffered labels that show their relationship to action:

- **Tool-talk.** *Tool-talk* is talk that is necessary for the generation, implementation, and evaluation of outcomes. It is instrumental in nature and is considered literal and objective. It may involve talk such as goal-setting discussions, giving of task directions (i.e., what to accomplish and when), and feedback about task performance.
- **Frame-talk.** *Frame-talk* provides an interpretive context (for tool-talk) and the necessary symbols for deciphering the meaning of events. Frame-talk tends to be connotative and interpretive in nature. This type of talk "frames" or evaluates tool-talk in relationship to the basic assumptions and values of the organization. For example, socialization of newcomers may involve frame-talk as new members are told the underlying reasons for the way things are done in the organization.
- **Mythopoetic talk.** *Mythopoetic talk* "conveys the ideogenic ideas and images . . . that create and communicate the nature of reality within which frameworks and symbols are applied" (1998, p. 22). It tends to be mythic and metaphorical and creates the fundamental ideals of the collective. Mythopoetic talk may occur, for example, when important organizational figures communicate their vision for the organization and use language that establishes dominant metaphors and guiding principles to which everyone should subscribe.

Marshak argued that the three types of talk are interconnected such that tool-talk is contained by frame-talk, which is contained by mythopoetic talk. An example should help clarify the connection.

In Organization X, the basic assumption is that the needs of the organization come before the needs of the individual. The talk that generated and instantiated this reality is mythopoetic talk. As members of the organization attempt to make sense of events, they might talk about being a "team player," being a "good family member," or "giving your all for the company." Talk of this type is frame-talk in that it relates to the nature of organizational reality established in mythopoetic talk. Tool-talk occurs throughout the day as members go about accomplishing their tasks and attempting to generate objective information. So, for example, when a worker says that he wants to go home early today to watch his daughter's soccer game (tool-talk), other members may respond to that with, "That's not being a very good team player. You are hurting the rest of us by doing that" (frame-talk). The frame-talk relates to the basic assumption of "organization before individual" established through mythopoetic talk. As the three types of talk interrelate, they serve to produce and reproduce the structure of the organization. As members use frame-talk to respond to and provide context for tool-talk, they reify the structure established through prior talk. In this and other ways, talk is action.

Marshak's typology of language use is certainly not the only one available or necessarily the most inclusive (e.g., see Austin, 1962), but it does provide two important precepts to use in an introduction of the CO model. First, the typology indicates the complexity of interaction and the extent to which misunderstandings (broadly conceived) can arise because of the different types of talk. Second, the typology shows how talk is action and, subsequently, how structure and interaction are intricately related. As interactions occur over time and structures are produced and reproduced, problems mount. In the next section, we discuss the theoretical basis for how structures are produced and reproduced through interaction—structuration theory.

Structuration Theory

As theory and research in organizational communication have progressed over the past 25 years, thoughts on the relationship between organization and communication have changed. Many theorists have eschewed the idea that an organization is simply a "container" in which communication occurs and have opted instead for the idea that communication and organization "produce" each other (Putnam, Phillips, & Chapman, 1996; Taylor, 1995). Karl Weick (1987) confirms this idea: "Interpersonal communication is the essence of organization because it creates structures that then affect what else gets said and done and by whom" (p. 97).

The coproduction relationship between organization and communication has its roots in the *theory of structuration* proposed by sociologist Anthony Giddens in his book *Central Problems in Social Theory* (1979). Giddens argues that the macro-level structure (organization) is both a medium and an outcome of micro-level social practices (interaction), something he referred to as the "duality of structure" (p. 5). The theory of structuration considers "structure as non-temporal and non-spatial, as *a virtual order of differences* produced and reproduced in social interaction as its medium and outcome" (p. 3). In other words, organizational structure is not a concrete entity, but is produced as people interact on a daily basis, attempting to accomplish their individual and collective purposes (structure as outcome). That structure, in turn, serves to mediate and constrain future interaction (structure as medium).

Structuration theory in part revolves around several principles. These principles include the recognition of agency, differing levels of awareness, routinized rules and practices, power, and unintended consequences. Claiming that structure is created through individuals' daily actions assumes that individuals are knowledgeable agents. In other words, individuals know that their interactions are either helping to maintain or change the existing organizational structure (Goodier & Eisenberg, 2006). Giddens (1979) argues that while individuals are knowledgeable agents, they have both a *practical consciousness* as well as a *discursive* one: "The practical consciousness is the tacit knowledge that is skillfully applied in the enactment of conduct but which the actor is not able to formulate discursively" (p. 57). The individual is, on the other hand, able to verbalize her discursive consciousness. In other words, some activities and/or feelings are easily explained by individuals (discursive consciousness), while other experiences, behaviors, and feelings are not as easily put into words (practical consciousness). Because the practical consciousness is not easily talked about or recognized by individuals, it is easiest to see its role in the organization through the daily routines that individuals use to get through their day. Frequently, when someone is asked how they spent their day at work, they reply that they really didn't do anything but yet managed to somehow remain busy in an eight-hour period. If you were to observe that individual though, you would see a number of activities and behaviors in which they engaged without really being aware that they were doing so. This is what Giddens refers to as rules and *routinized practices* (Goodier & Eisenberg, 2006). Now consider the duality of structure or relationship between structure and interaction as well as the role of the knowledgeable agent.

As a knowledgeable agent, individuals "know a great deal about the conditions and consequences of what they do in their day-to-day lives" (Giddens, 1984, p. 281). With this knowledge, regardless whether individuals can express in words why they participate in the activities that they do, individuals possess a degree of *agency*, which according to Giddens (1979) refers to the "[f]eature of action that, at any point in time, the agent could have acted otherwise: either positively in terms of attempted intervention in the process of events, or negatively in terms of forbearance" (p. 56). What the individual chooses to do (either participate in the existing structure or try to change it through their interactions) is irrelevant. The fact that the individual could chose to act one way or another implies some degree of agency within the structure. In other words, the medium and outcome are very much dictated by the communication choices of the individuals involved.

Another interesting component of structuration theory is Giddens' conceptualization of power. Recall that there is a strong relationship in structuration theory between agency (interaction) and structure (organization). This relationship extends to power within the organization. In the theory, power and action (in other words agency) are inextricably linked. Giddens (1979) conceptualized *power* in a dual sense, "as involved institutionally in processes of interaction, and as used to accomplish outcomes in strategic conduct" (p. 88). In the first sense, power becomes synonymous with domination and structural control, whereas in the latter case the focus becomes the action (McPhee, 2004). If an individual could have chosen to act otherwise (agency), then she is able to produce outcomes based on strategic communication choices. In other words, for Giddens individual power occurs within the larger structural power and occurs through an agent's actions. This is very different from other theorists who claim that power is only held by those in positions of management or ownership within an organization. This is also why the CO model we forward in this chapter is aimed at *all* members of the organization, not just those in management.

In structuration theory, every individual through his own actions possesses a degree of power and influence on how the organizational structure operates. Power relations between coworkers or superior-subordinates then become a reciprocal interaction regardless of how asymmetrically the resources are distributed. According to Giddens (1979), an individual only possesses power if another person is willing to a more or less degree to give that power. If power is a structural component and structure is produced and reproduced through action or interaction, then in the duality of structure both individuals most participate in the give and take of power if power is to exist. For example, a professor in the classroom only has power if students are willing to grant that power. They would grant power by following course procedures and policies, reading the assigned readings, and coming to class. If no one attends class, then the professor has very little power in the classroom, although the larger organizational structure may grant him the power to assign a failing grade. The professor, in turn, participates in the granting of university power by choosing to follow university procedures for assigning grades. According to McPhee (2004), "We typically exercise power by drawing on structural rules and/or resources, and in drawing on them, we (exercise power to) reproduce them as features of the social order" (p. 130). In other words, there is a strong relationship between agency (action), rules and practices, and organizational structure.

We have discussed the various ways that knowledgeable agents enact structure through their interactions. We have also discussed the impact that agent's choices have on the organization. It is important to realize, though, that Giddens (1979) does believe that actions can result in *unintended consequences*. Intentional conduct (i.e., choice) can have unintended consequences for agents during the course of the production and reproduction of social structure. Although we can control the ways that we interact with others, we cannot necessarily control nor predict the ways that others will respond to us. In the example, we stated that students have the ability to extend power to professors in the classroom. Students may choose to behave in a variety of ways in the classroom to demonstrate their ability to show pleasure or displeasure with the professor. In that regard, students have a great deal of power granting ability, but they cannot however predict or control how the professor will react. The unintended consequence of the attempt to produce or reproduce a particular structure could result in consequences ranging from dismissal from the class, a failing grade, or a judicial review at the university level. Actions tend to have consequences and, regardless if an individual is knowledgeable or not, all actions have the potential for unintended consequences.

Kirby and Krone (2002) conducted research examining work–family policies in organizations. They were specifically interested in how talk about these policies influenced individuals to either utilize or not utilize such policies. They found that "the way organizational members talk about work–family programs helps to construct reality as to the meaning of such programs in the organization, which in turn shapes the attitudes and behaviors of organizational members" (p. 55). This is a great example of the duality of structure. In other words, work–family policies exist within the structure of the organization. However, individuals through their actions influence (i.e., exhibit power) how other organizational members perceive work–family policies. If individuals choose to ignore an existing organizational policy as demonstrated by their daily talk and practices, then the policy has very little implication for the operation of the organization.

Consider the following scenario based on interviews with in-home daycare providers:

> Margaret, an in-home daycare provider for three years, receives a phone call from a parent asking if she can watch the kids this weekend because the parent needs to go into the office for a few hours. Margaret has supplied all of her parents with a handbook that details her policies, and it very clearly states that she does not provide daycare services on weekends. Margaret knows, however, that the parent has been struggling financially and is going through a tough divorce and decides to make an exception to her policy. A few weeks later, though, the parent makes the same request and Margaret, due to personal plans, has to decline the request. The parent becomes very upset and they argue before the parent storms out of Margaret's home on Friday afternoon.

This story demonstrates a number of Giddens' structuration concepts. Through her discursive consciousness, Margaret is able to explain that she created her handbook to make clear to parents how she intended to run her business. Through her actions, she is communicating to parents the type of structure that she is intending to create, and she maintains this structure through her interactions with parents. The rules and practices have meaning to both Margaret and the parents, as long as they are followed. However, when Margaret, through her own agency, chooses to make an exception to the rule, she is producing a new organizational structure, and this structure impacts the future interactions that she has with a particular parent. The impact, or unintended consequence, is that the parent expects the exception to be made again and becomes very upset when Margaret is unable or unwilling to do so.

Dierdre Boden, in her book *The Business of Talk* (1994), offers an extended discussion as well as interaction-based research that help connect the theory of structuration with communication. She attempts to answer the question of how talk in organizations is shaped by and shapes organizational structure:

> As people talk organizations into being, they simultaneously pick out the particular strands of abstract order that can relevantly instantiate the moment. In doing so, they significantly support, shape and occasionally subvert the organization, which will then move forward into next moments through other actions with other actors. . . . Simultaneously the myths, languages, cultures, and conditions of past social structural arrangements come alive again in the choices of the moment. If organizations *are* the people who comprise them, then it is rather clear that struc-

ture is dynamic and shaped from within, rather than static or moving independently of action. Action, in turn, is only meaningful through language. (p. 202)

In other words, what people typically think of as "organization" is not something that is concrete and separate from organizational members. Instead, organization or "structure" is something that is constantly constructed and reconstructed as members communicate and interact with one another and the relevant environment.

Diane Witmer conducted research on the culture of Alcoholics Anonymous and used the theory of structuration to explain what she found. In essence, she concluded that the structure of the particular sect of Alcoholics Anonymous that she was studying had no true "reality" except for that created as the members interacted with one another on a daily basis. While the members may interact with one another at a particular time and place, they constantly re-create the "organization" as they draw upon the rituals, values, and norms of the past. As Witmer (1997) concluded, "This places communication squarely at the center of the organization" (p. 327).

The theory of structuration as proposed by Giddens and illustrated by Boden and Witmer (among others) offers three tenets upon which the CO model is based. First, an organization cannot be considered as separate from the members that constitute it. Giddens (1979) articulates this point when he says, "Social systems have no purposes, reasons or needs whatsoever; only human individuals do so" (p. 7). For this reason, the CO model is based on the actions of the individual as he contributes to and is constrained by the structure of the organization. Second, talk is action. If structure is truly produced through interaction, then communication is more than just a precursor to action; it is action.

Finally, the theory of structuration makes relevant our claim that misunderstandings are a natural part of organizational life. The connection between structuration and misunderstandings is most clear in three ways. First, the theory of structuration highlights the centrality of communication and interaction to organizational life. Communication theorists and everyday practitioners know that communication is inherently messy, and that as people muddle through their days using language and symbols to express their feelings and ideas, misunderstandings (linguistic, pragmatic, cultural, and otherwise) are prevalent. Acknowledging the central role of communication in the production and reproduction of organizational structures is also an acknowledgement that misunderstandings will occur as well. Second, if organizational members do indeed have agency in organizational life, then the possibilities of individual member's choices and actions being in sync with each other are low. This reality will necessarily lead to situations where members are at odds with one another, either philosophically or pragmatically, which causes misunderstandings. Third, as members enact their agency, they will produce unintended consequences. These unintended consequences are almost by definition misunderstandings, because the consequences of their actions were neither intended nor could be controlled. Importantly, misunderstandings are not always debilitating or negative, and that will be clear as you explore the CO model.

The Communicative Organization Model

In the communicative organization, (1) members are cognizant of the fact that misunderstandings occur as a natural part of organized activity and should be anticipated; (2) certain characteristics of social interaction are encouraged and supported; and (3) strategic communication planning is commonplace (see Figure 6.1).

Anticipate Misunderstandings

As indicated in Chapter 3, one of the first writers to locate communication at the center of the organization was Chester Barnard. He also addressed the notion of misunderstandings being expected, rather than unexpected, in the organization: "Successful cooperation in or by formal organizations is the abnormal, not the normal, condition.... Failure to cooperate, failure of cooperation, failure of organization, disorganization, disintegration, destruction of organization—and reorganization—are characteristic of facts of human history" (1938, p. 5). I. A. Richards (1936) indicated the need to attend to this problem: "We struggle all our days with misunderstandings, and no apology is required for any study which

FIGURE 6.1   The Communicative Organization

can prevent or remove them" (p. 3). In the communicative organization, misunderstandings are not "removed," but instead are anticipated.

In the communicative organization, misunderstandings are expected and considered to be normal. No one is surprised by them; instead, people assume that misunderstandings can lead to alternative task structures and roles, help them consider new ways of acting, and aid in creative problem solving.

In the most basic sense, misunderstandings occur in "instances in which people who are communicating don't share meaning" (Wood, 1998, p. 8). They also occur when there are differences or uncertainty or ambiguity in values, goals, or courses of action. Julia Wood, author of the text *But I Thought You Meant . . . . Misunderstandings in Human Communication,* points out that too often we hear the claim that communication can solve all problems or that what is needed is better communication: "Some of the tensions that plague human interaction do not result from lack of understanding in communication" (p. 8). We agree. However, we also believe that in communicative organizations certain communication behaviors can help people cope with situations that are difficult, if not impossible, to change. Effective communication behaviors may not change someone's core values, but they can help contain the conflict over different values, or help a person to move on, not necessarily resolving matters, but learning to cope with an irresolvable issue (see Foss & Griffin, 1995, for a useful discussion of invitational rhetoric and its contribution to this situation). In that sense, we explore all forms of misunderstandings that prevent people from functioning effectively in the organization or that simply serve to make people miserable. In order to do that, we need to look at misunderstandings from a different point of view.

First, misunderstandings can lead to new ways of structuring tasks and roles. Recently, one of the authors worked with an organizational team that experienced a series of misunderstandings about the role of each member in the decision-making process. Realization that they had these misunderstandings caused the group to assess how they could best use the human resources available to them. What emerged was a two-step process in which some individuals would be involved in the early stages of developing a new policy and others would be involved later, once the procedures had been partially worked out. In this way, the misunderstandings about their respective roles actually caused the group to move in an entirely new, more effective, direction that probably would not have happened without the misunderstanding being so obvious. The new task structure and work roles emerged from the interactions caused by the misunderstanding. These structures and roles then served to define communication and other task-related behavior as the group encountered new challenges and issues.

Second, misunderstandings can also help people to consider alternative ways of acting. The authors have a colleague who has "open" office hours—times when he is in his office and expects students to drop in. Early in the term not many students stop by, so he usually spends that time working on the computer until someone shows up. Repeatedly, one particular student stopped by, saw him working at the computer, and assumed he did not want to be disturbed. Later, when the instructor confronted the student about why he had not sought help earlier in the quarter, he discovered the student had misunderstood the nonverbal message the instructor intended to send. Because of this misunderstanding, the instructor has changed his behavior. He specifically tells students they should walk into the office even if he is on the computer and he places a sign on the door that says, "Come on in. Please get my attention away from the computer." This misunderstanding changed his behavior. Had he continued to be unaware of the misunderstanding, his behavior would have continued unchanged.

Finally, misunderstandings can lead to creative problem solving. For example, two students, out of a group of 15, were given the wrong times for a special recruitment interview. They had been carefully selected and had prepared for several weeks. When they arrived, they discovered the recruiters had already left. They were devastated. A misunderstanding had occurred between the students and the individuals scheduling the interviews. The first decision the advisors of the group made was to take ownership of the problem. They wanted the recruiters to know that these were responsible students and they did not want to take the time to "blame" a staff member for the misunderstanding. They just assumed guilt for giving the students the wrong time. Because the recruiters had left, there was no way to reach them after office hours, so the advisors arrived at 7 A.M. the next morning to catch them before they began their last round of interviews. This arrival gave them a chance to talk directly with the recruiters, not only about these two students, but about their entire program. The misunderstanding between the students and the schedulers caused the advisors to develop a creative approach to solving a problem and gave them an opportunity they would not have had otherwise. The recruiters agreed to extend their visit so these two students could be interviewed. The advisors gained some valuable information about the organization and were able to market their program more successfully to it.

We would also like to examine the reasons that misunderstandings occur so that we can identify how they could be handled more successfully in the communicative organization. We have identified three reasons that are uniquely addressed in the CO model: (1) conflict in values, (2) lack of information, and (3) strategic misinterpretations.

Conflict in Values. Misunderstandings may result from a conflict in values. Such conflict may involve (1) a disparity between individual and organizational values regarding organizational mission or (2) the suppression of a minority member's contributions. Misunderstandings arising from a conflict in values most likely involve frame-talk and mythopoetic talk because these forms of talk are rooted in the underlying values of the organization.

Misunderstandings that occur because of a disparity between individual and organizational values are not likely to be resolved easily, if at all. For example, there was a graduating college senior who was getting desperate for a job. She was very bright and motivated, but was having difficulty finding a position that utilized her skills. A job came open with an organization in her hometown that endorsed social and religious values that were quite different from her own values; however, the position for which they wanted her was perfect. She took the job, but regularly found she was uneasy with the nature of the events that she was responsible for planning. She talked to her boss, but her boss would only tell her, "That's what we do here." More conversation will not necessarily resolve this situation for the new employee.

Communication strategies can, however, help people cope with an inability to change the situation. Although communication is not likely to dramatically change a person's basic values, the communicative organization accepts the fact that these differences will be present. It can also use these opportunities to push members into creative problem-solving frameworks to contain the differences and limit their negative impact.

Misunderstandings based on a conflict of values also occur when particular "voices" are not valued within an organization. Women and minorities in particular are faced with situations in which their contributions are not given due consideration, either intentionally or unintentionally. As members of these traditionally underrepresented groups begin to occupy more and varied positions within organizations, members are confronted with the reality of interacting with people different from themselves. Some organizational cultures explicitly value the contributions of dominant groups while devaluing those of minority members. Other organizational cultures, although willing and open to change their deeply entrenched values to include the contributions of minority members, might unintentionally suppress the contributions of these members by relying on standard modes of operation. Either way, problems or misunderstandings arise.

Lack of Information. Misunderstandings may also be caused by a lack of information. This is a broad category that encompasses many situations. Some of the most common are (1) intentional and unintentional suppression of information to newcomers; (2) interruption of the chain of communication owing to geographic separation; (3) information gaps resulting from hierarchical or functional differences; and (4) removal of information cues with the use of communication technology. Misunderstandings related to a lack of information will most likely be correlated with tool-talk because of the objective, task-related nature of this form of talk.

First, misunderstandings may result from intentional or unintentional suppression of information to newcomers. As we discuss in Chapter 8, when a person enters an organization for the first time or begins a new role in her present organization, she often experiences a sense of information deprivation (Miller & Jablin, 1991). This information deficit can be the result of either unintentional or intentional circumstances. At times, established members in the organization may simply forget what it was like to be a newcomer and, as a result, not remember everything a newcomer doesn't know but should be told. This unintentional circumstance may lead to a lack of information for the newcomer and subsequent misunderstandings. For example, we have a colleague who started work and was never told where the mailboxes were; he figured someone would tell him soon. After several days, he still did not know and at that point was afraid to ask for fear of looking dumb. In the meantime, several important documents were put in his box that needed immediate attention. Phone calls started coming in from his new boss and colleagues asking why he had not replied. Misunderstandings arose because of a lack of information caused by unintentional circumstances.

At other times, a lack of information may be the result of intentional circumstances. As we discuss in Chapter 7, organizational representatives often neglect potentially negative information and overstate positive information about a job or position when recruiting potential organizational members. As the newcomer begins work, the reality of organizational life sets in and the newcomer senses the lack of information. For example, we know a person who was heavily recruited for a sales position. During recruitment, he was told of the wonderful people with whom he would be working, the great potential for financial gain, and the travel opportunities. The recruiter failed to tell him that he would be working six days a week at least 12 hours a day. The newcomer assumed that he would be working a traditional nine-to-five, five-day work week and behaved in that manner for the first few days. He was eventually called into his boss' office and told that if he did not shape up, he would be fired. The newcomer was shocked to hear that he had done something wrong and quickly changed his behavior.

Although a lack of information can result from recruiting practices, it can also occur after the newcomer begins work. Organizational incumbents often test newcomers by intentionally not supplying them with the information they need or by communicating ambiguous messages (Jablin, 2001). This is often a matter of trust. Incumbents are often unwilling to share pertinent information with a person whom they do not yet trust.

Second, misunderstandings can result from an interruption of the chain of communication owing to physical location, a situation that appears to be quite prevalent. As organizations grow larger, not all members can reside in the same physical location. Indeed, as technology advances and organizations become more global, members are often literally separated by oceans. Whether separated by floors, miles, or continents, members often experience misunderstandings because the chain of communication is broken and important information is not uniformly distributed. For example, we were told of an instance in which the majority of a particular organization resided on one floor of a building, but there was one small department in the basement. Important information often did not reach this out-of-the-way department. On one occasion a meeting was called for 10 A.M. The department in the basement received that information. What they failed to receive was the informal communication about a preliminary meeting to take place at 9 A.M. When no one from the department showed up at 9 A.M., the other members considered it an affront. A simple lack of information caused by physical location resulted in bad feelings between organizational members.

Third, misunderstandings can be caused by information gaps resulting from hierarchical or functional differences. As we discuss in Chapter 10, there is often a gap in information between supervisor and subordinate caused by differing levels of responsibility. Supervisors are often privy to the "bigger picture" in organizations, because they are responsible for more aspects of organizational functioning than are the subordinates. This gap in information can lead to negative feelings, because the supervisor may forget that the subordinate does not have access to the same information and the overall picture.

Finally, misunderstandings may occur as information cues are removed with the use of communication technology. As communication media other than face-to-face are employed, important elements of the communication process are muted or absent. For instance, when telephones, e-mail, and fax machines are used, nonverbal and physical aspects such as eye movement, facial expressions, and gestures are minimized or absent. As a result, the participants are left to fill in the blanks, so to speak, and this lack of information may lead to misunderstandings. The story in Chapter 1 about the strained relationships that were caused by the misinterpretation of a missed conference call is a perfect example of this situation. As the use of communication technology increases, misunderstandings caused by the lack of information inherent in their use will also mount. We discuss communication technology more fully in Chapter 14.

Strategic Misinterpretations.   We have observed individuals who want to misunderstand the message purposely because it benefits them in some way. For instance, we know of a student worker who was stuffing envelopes at her desk while reading a magazine. Her supervisor stopped by the desk and said, "You need to pay attention to your work." Later the supervisor observed this young woman stuffing envelopes faster, still reading the magazine. The next day her supervisor discovered that she had been putting the wrong letter in the envelopes. When she provided feedback to the young worker, the student's response was, "You never told me to put away the magazine." This student strategically misunderstood the message from the supervisor the previous day so she could go on doing what she really wanted to do all along, which was to read her magazine.

The above sources of misunderstandings in organizations are in no way exhaustive. We invite you to consider additional sources of misunderstandings as you read the following chapters. Our intention in this section was to illustrate the prevalence of misunderstandings in organizations and their sources. The purpose of the CO model is to illustrate the fact that misunderstandings are a natural component of organizational life and as such should be expected and planned for. In addition to expecting and being prepared for misunderstandings, we believe a number of particular communication behaviors support the CO model.

Social Interaction

In the communicative organization, certain characteristics of social interaction are encouraged and supported. These include psychological immediacy, timely response, exchange assessment, and behavioral flexibility.

Psychological immediacy is being involved psychologically with another person's message. You are intently aware of the issues they are discussing and your responses indicate not only that you have heard what they have said, but that you appreciate the extent to which this topic or issue is important to them. Many basic communication textbooks detail the kinds of skills used to communicate immediacy. For example, Sue DeWine, Melissa Gibson, and Matt Smith (2000) summarized extant research regarding ways to reduce confusion with verbal messages: interpret and send messages nonverbally, develop specific listening skills, and use confirming and disconfirming messages.

One of the most important characteristics of immediacy is active listening. Tom Peters, an internationally known business consultant, described how important he thinks listening is:

> My correspondence occupies many a file cabinet after years of dealing with managers in turbulent conditions. The most moving letters by far are the hundreds about "simple listening." In fact, if I had a file labeled "religious conversion"—that is, correspondence from those whose management practices have truly been transformed—I suspect that 50 percent of its contents would deal with just one narrow topic: going out anew, with a "naïve" mind-set, and listening to customers. (1988, p. 16)

Timely response is feedback that is proffered at the appropriate time; not too soon, nor too late. People often need a response at exactly the right time if the message is to have the desired impact. Not every situation calls for immediate action. Organizations should be able to identify those occasions when immediate feedback is needed and when a situation is best left alone for a period of time. Nevertheless, when individuals let their frustrations build without providing feedback, it can cause disruption across the organization.

Members of a team we have been working with were depending on one another to finish a task within a short time frame. One of the team members missed three different meetings with the team, and the other team members complained to one another about his lack of commitment. The fourth time he missed a meeting they "unloaded" on him the next day: "Where have you been? We're depending on you. Are you on this team or not?" He then proceeded to tell them he had missed the meeting the day before because he had been in a minor car accident and had trouble getting transportation that morning. The group sheepishly turned their attention to his difficulties and dropped their complaints, recognizing that this was not the time to get a commitment from him. Unfortunately, because they had not brought up the subject sooner, they felt unable to pursue it even at a later time. The problem never was resolved. It is important to give people feedback immediately in "real time" so they can do something about it before resentment builds to such a high level that the hard feelings they have created cannot be overcome.

Exchange assessment is the conscious analysis of any impending message exchange and the conscious choice of the media to be used. Thinking about how you want to say something to someone is an example of this technique. Do you remember your first date with someone special? Did you rehearse in your mind what you might say to that person beforehand? This concept also refers to an assessment of one's own psychological readiness to enter into an interpersonal conversation. If you are having a bad day and things are not going right for you, it is probably not a good day to be an effective listener for anyone else. You would be better off being truthful with the person and planning another time to talk.

Behavioral flexibility is an essential characteristic of the communicative organization. Each person must be prepared to adapt to changes in the environment or context of their communicative activity, changes in the relationship itself, patterns of interaction, and the dialectical tensions in those relationships.

One example of the kind of flexibility required is in your relationship with your boss. In the work environment, most boss–employee relationships are task-oriented. There may be occasional informal banter and discussion about family and outside interests, but for the most part conversations focus on the work. One way behaviors change is when the boss and employee move to a social context, at a party for example, where they should be more informal and relaxed. In fact, it may be quite inappropriate to "talk business" during a social occasion. Both individuals must learn the boundaries of a more relaxed relationship. Another way behaviors may change is when the relationship itself changes, for example, to one of friendship. Between friends it is difficult if one person has control over the other. How you negotiate both aspects of your relationship can be quite delicate.

The third way in which behavioral flexibility is relevant is when the boss–employee interaction patterns change. For example, one may initiate conversations as the boss but as friends both may be equally comfortable initiating contact and conversations. The way conversations begin and end may change as well. The fourth way behaviors may change is to meet the requirements of the dialectical tensions present in any relationship. *Dialectical tensions* are those feelings of opposition one may experience during dialogues with others (see Baxter, 1988, and Montgomery and Baxter, 1998, for further discussion of dialectical tensions in personal relationships). For example, you may appreciate the guidance your boss gives you and at the same time want to make independent decisions. The tension there is between dependence and independence. You can experience both feelings at the same time, and your behaviors will vary based on the strength of one tension, or "pull," over the other.

In short, one of your greatest competencies as a successful communicator in an organization is the ability to recognize when certain behaviors are more appropriate than others and to be flexible enough to respond to the demands of the changes in the environment, in the relationship itself, in the patterns of interaction, or to respond to the changes in dialectical tensions present in every relationship. On a larger scale, flexibility must be present in the company as a whole as well. In the CO model, the organization and its employees are in constant motion, ready for change. Along with flexibility comes strategic planning, the final characteristic of the CO model.

Strategic Communication Planning

Strategic communication planning embraces the notion of planning strategies to address the misunderstandings that the organization knows will occur. Strategic communication planning consists of one overarching principle (recognize) and three separate strategies, or practices: contain, cope, and construct.

The overarching principal of strategic communication planning is to *recognize* that organizational life is inherently problematic and characterized by misunderstandings. It is the obligation of every organizational member to recognize misunderstandings as they occur and acknowledge their impact. If organizational members can recognize that misunderstandings will naturally occur in any organizational situation, then their occurrence will not be paralyzing. Instead, depending on the strategy used to address them, they can be either easily managed or they can lead to individual and/or organizational learning.

The first practice for addressing misunderstandings is to *contain* the problem or misunderstanding so that its negative impact is minimal. No energy is put into dealing with the emotional or pragmatic needs of those involved in the misunderstanding. When time or resources are limited, organizations may choose this strategy. Additionally, if the organization does not want to draw attention to itself or to the misunderstanding, it may choose this strategy because it stops the problem and then continues with status quo operations. For example, when one of our interviewee's employees was caught stealing from the cash register, he chose to contain the situation by firing the employee in question, immediately hiring a new employee, and not discussing the situation with the rest of the workers.

The second practice is to *cope* with the communication problem or misunderstanding, which means dealing with the present situation and allowing all affected members to express their concerns and have their problems addressed. This strategy takes more time and resources to address the human resources involved in the situation. For example, when a beloved assistant pastor of a large Southern church was discovered to be addicted to drugs and had been stealing from the church to support his habit, the church used the coping strategy. They relieved the assistant pastor of his duties, but also paid for him to go to drug rehabilitation. The pastor took time out of a regular Sunday service to address the issue and hear the concerns and emotions of the congregation. This strategy allowed those affected to cope with their feelings regarding this very difficult situation.

The final practice is to *construct* a new interpretation of the misunderstanding so learning can occur; in particular, new attitudes, values, behaviors, or practices should emerge. The use of this strategy requires that the misunderstanding be addressed; that the affected organizational and environmental members are allowed to express their concerns, emotions, and ideas; and that the individuals and organization somehow change as a result of the process. For example, in 1982, seven people in the Chicago area were killed when they unknowingly ingested Tylenol Extra Strength capsules laced with cyanide. Once it became clear that the cyanide-laced capsules were the issue, the maker of Tylenol, Johnson & Johnson, immediately alerted the public throughout the nation via the media not to consume Tylenol until further notice. They also stopped production of all Tylenol products and suspended advertising. In addition, they recalled all Tylenol products from the market. If Johnson & Johnson would have stopped there they would have engaged in the coping strategy because they addressed the problem and allowed the affected public and employees to express their concerns. However, over the next several months, Johnson & Johnson rethought their product packaging and as a result changed the way they and the industry packaged many goods. Later that year, Tylenol was back on the shelves, but this time with tamper-resistant packaging that would make attempts to alter the product evident. In response to this tragedy, Johnson & Johnson engaged in the construct strategy, which allowed the company to rebound and the consumers to have safer products.

As we developed this portion of the CO model, we conceptualized strategic communication planning in terms of a continuum, with contain, cope, and construct as different strategies for dealing with misunderstandings (see Figure 6.2). The basic premise is that organizational members must recognize that misunderstandings can occur in any situation and that they can arise from many different catalysts (as described in an earlier section of this chapter). With recognition as a baseline practice, the remaining three practices are arranged on a continuum with *no learning* and *learning* as the two poles. The argument is that for any particular misunderstanding, one strategy may be more appropriate than the others. Associated with the particular strategy use is a certain level of learning; the least amount is learned with containment, whereas constructing allows for the most learning.

Saliency of the issue, time availability, and willingness to engage in constructive dialogue are three factors that affect the choice of practice. If one or more of the factors are limited, containment is the most likely choice. As saliency, time, and willingness to communicate increase, coping and constructing, further along the continuum, may be chosen.

One of the interviews we conducted for this book provides a good example of how strategic planning might help uncover ways to deal with misunderstandings in organizations. Susan is a secretary in a small insurance office, and her coworker, Audrey, is the senior secretary and office manager. Susan tells their story:

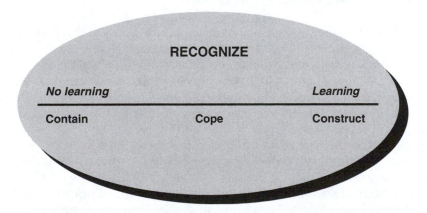

FIGURE 6.2   Strategic Communication Planning Continuum

There are two secretaries here, and it's really important that we are able to get along and communicate well and tell each other if something is bothering us or if we don't think something is right. Normally, that happens but we had an incident last spring where I had told the senior secretary, Audrey, that I might need some time off in late April. I had indicated to her that I might take two days off, but I was real "iffy" and not sure of my plans. I still had to work out the exact plans with my sister.

So as time passed I told the senior secretary that I would be taking those days off. Audrey said that she didn't realize I'd be taking the time off. She said to me that I should just go ahead and take the day off. Well, then I found out that she couldn't come in that day either because she had a babysitter conflict. And she was just planning to turn on the voice mail that day. I found this out through all these other people that she didn't get her babysitter conflict resolved and instead of telling me that I needed to come in, she was just going to turn on the voice mail. Being me, I got upset, because all along I said that I didn't mind coming in, I just needed to know. I didn't feel it was right just to turn on the voice mail and leave the office wide open. It just wouldn't be right to do that. It was a working day and I felt someone should be there. I just gave up and took the day off. I tried not to worry about it but I just wished that she had told me I needed to come in, instead of dragging other people into it and telling other people she couldn't find a babysitter.

Audrey's solution to the problem was to turn on the voice mail, but I don't know what in her head said that would be okay, since there wouldn't be anyone here to greet people coming into the office. That's never been okay. The rule is that when one of us is gone, the other has to be here. I was upset because I was willing to come in. My sister and I just wanted to do something fun, but it wasn't concrete. I think Audrey just didn't want to say no that I couldn't take the day off or do what I wanted to do. That's how she is. She doesn't like conflict or like to complain. She doesn't want anyone to be upset. But her behavior had the opposite effect.

How does the strategic planning continuum apply to this problematic situation? First, both Susan and Audrey must "recognize" that there is a misunderstanding about who will cover the office and how they will decide who can take time off. As Susan points out, Audrey does not like conflict and hopes that if she ignores it, it will go away. The solution Audrey chose was a solution to "contain" the misunderstanding by turning on the voice mail. This was a short-term solution that prevented the problem from getting worse (i.e., no one answered the phone for the day). Susan needed to decide if she wanted to "cope" with the problem in a different way, perhaps by creating a master schedule for the office. Or she could have decided that the problem was big enough, and the relationship important enough, to spend time "constructing" a new list of priorities and solutions. That would have taken a good deal of discussion with Audrey and being clear about the frustration Susan experienced. Any of these practices—contain, cope, or construct—could have worked, with different results for the interpersonal relationship between Susan and Audrey and the level of learning that would occur. These four practices are the keys to the CO model.

Summary

In this chapter, we presented a model of core principles to guide the way we function in organizations called the *communicative organization model*. The CO model is based on the assumption that organizational structure is created and re-created through social interaction (theory of structuration) and that talk is a form of action.

The CO model assumes that misunderstandings are a central feature of organizational life and that certain communication behaviors and practices can assist members as they encounter them. In their daily activities, members are confronted with misunderstandings resulting from a variety of sources, including a conflict in values, a lack of information, or strategic misrepresentations. As these misunderstandings are addressed through communication, members create and re-create the organizational structure that encompasses them.

The CO model is a practical model of communication in organizations as well as a theoretical guide. It is theoretical in that it proposes that the essence of organizational life is communication and, as such, is fraught with misunderstandings. It is practical in that it offers specific communication skills as being central to effective organizational involvement and provides alternatives for addressing unavoidable misunderstandings. Our intention was that the CO model provide a practical and analytical tool for confronting life in organizations, both as a member and as a critic. Approaching your future organizational life with the CO model in mind will allow you to understand the types of organizational problems you may encounter and know how to approach them from a communication perspective.

As you read the following chapters, please keep the CO model in mind, particularly the concept of misunderstandings. Through the lens of the CO model, you should be able to visualize the types of misunderstandings that might occur in organizational relationships, processes, and outcomes and anticipate solutions to them. In the next chapter of this book, we discuss the recruitment process, which you will see is fraught with potential misunderstandings.

7

Realistic Recruitment

The study of organizational behavior, particularly communication, does not begin when the new employee begins work. Understanding the process of how organizational members are recruited and selected (or *not* selected) is important. The communication during this time by both the applicant and the employer affects vital individual and organizational outcomes if and when the applicant becomes a member of the organization.

The hiring process is a stressful time for both the applicant and the employer. The applicant is attempting to find the best position that matches his or her needs and wants, as well as abilities. The employer is searching for the best employee who matches the requirements of the position as well as the intangible aspects of the organization, such as the culture of the workplace. The desire for both parties to find the "best" often results in each exaggerating strengths and positive qualities, while downplaying negative or weaker ones.

Applicants might intentionally invent or exaggerate their skills in order to meet the demands of a particular job. At the same time, employers might intentionally mislead applicants on important factors such as working conditions and hours in an attempt to recruit the best employees. Although this situation could seem like the status quo for the employment process, such behavior can have negative short- and long-term consequences for both the individual and the organization. Consider the following stories. The first story reflects the misrepresentations of a 20-year-old intern, Danielle, who was hired by a social services organization. The second story details what happened to Jacque when he was misled by the organization for which he was working. We begin with Danielle's situation:

> When I first got the job, my resume said that I was proficient in Microsoft tools such as PowerPoint and Excel, and I thought I knew what I was doing with them. However, there was a time when I was asked to import data with Excel and I didn't know how to do that. I tried a number of times. It took a full day of work to import the data and figure out that application in the program.
>
> So the next day I called my boss to ask him how to use the program. He was a little surprised that I didn't call him sooner. Ironically enough, he did

not know how to do it either, so he directed me to his secretary, who instructed me how to correctly import data into Microsoft Excel.

There was another time that he wanted me to use the fax machine, and I had no clue how to do that. I got to a point that I was calling him all the time. I sometimes thought my questions weren't important, but they needed to be answered for me to do my job. He was at work earning a salary, and I was calling him asking him step-by-step questions during the day. Overall, I guess he had expectations of me that were attainable, but the misrepresentations made me look bad because I could not complete the tasks.

Now consider Jacque's situation:

I had worked at the bank for many years as a teller before I decided to work towards becoming a financial planner. My bosses had strongly encouraged me to do this, and it was not easy. This is something that is a huge conflict with me right now.

With becoming a financial planner, so many better things were supposed to happen to me and my job—more money and more satisfaction. I have picked up a huge amount of responsibilities, most of them I was not expecting or I thought didn't come with the job. When my bosses were pushing this for me I really felt that they needed me to do it for the company, but they left out important information that would have definitely affected my decision.

They told me the good things about the new job, but omitted the bad. I feel that they purposely left out the negative of the job so they could convince me to become the financial planner for the company. It is so bad right now that I'm considering leaving the company.

As you can see, providing information that is exaggerated or false can lead to negative consequences for both the organization and the individual. In this chapter, we discuss the recruitment and selection process from the perspectives of both the individual and the organization. We contrast the traditional recruitment process with a process called *realistic recruitment*.

When Applicants and Organizations Misrepresent Themselves

If most organizations and applicants engage in misleading communication during the recruitment process, what is the harm? In fact, if most applicants exaggerate their skills and abilities, won't people who do not do so be at a disadvantage? If most organizations provide only positive or misleading information about the job and organization, won't the ones that do not engage in such practices lose the most qualified employees to the organizations that do?

The concerns cited are short-term concerns. In the long run, exchanging realistic, truthful information during the recruitment and selection process will benefit both the individual and the organization, affecting such important outcomes as job satisfaction, organizational commitment, job performance, and turnover. Let's begin a discussion of the problem by focusing on the applicant.

Misrepresentation by the Applicant

The lure of exaggerating one's qualifications, skills, work history, and so on, is strong when searching for a job. Applicants often believe, especially during times when the job market is tight, that the only way they will get their foot in the door of a good company is to "stretch the truth" on their application and resume, making themselves more attractive to the potential employer. Resume fraud, perhaps better termed "misrepresentation," takes many forms, including overstating qualifications, providing altered or nonexistent academic credentials, offering phony references, misreporting previous work history, and a variety of other exaggerations and lies. As reported by the Society for Human Resource Management (SHRM) in an October 2003 article online, 25 to 40 percent of applicants provide misleading information during the application process. SHRM also reported that 95 percent of college students in one study said that they would lie to get a job, and 41 percent of those same respondents admitted to doing so previously.

When the applicant misrepresents herself and is subsequently hired by the organization, any number of problems can develop. If the misrepresentation was in the area of skills and qualifications, the newcomer might not be able to perform the duties of the job to the extent necessary (if at all), as happened to Danielle in our earlier example. If the misrepresentation concerned the type of organizational culture the applicant preferred, the newcomer could find herself in a situation where her values, attitudes, and communication style are not in sync with the reality of the organization. The potential consequences of applicant misrepresentation can be represented as a logical chain of events (see Figures 7.1 and 7.2).

Figure 7.1 represents a proposed chain of events when an applicant misrepresents his qualifications. When the applicant is hired based on misrepresented qualifications, he must confront the reality of the job requirements. Chances are if the misrepresentation was great enough, the newcomer will be unable to perform the duties as the organization expects. Dissatisfaction on the part of the organization with the newcomer's performance will ensue, resulting in low performance evaluations. If performance does not increase to an expected, satisfactory level, the newcomer might be fired.

Figure 7.2 illustrates what could happen when an applicant misrepresents her cultural preferences (shorthand here for attitudes, values, beliefs, communication style, etc.). The top line follows the chain of events from the organization's

---

Misrepresentation ➝ Unmet Expectations ➝ Dissatisfaction with Newcomer ➝ Involuntary Turnover
(of qualifications)   (for organization)   (low performance ratings, . . .)   (i.e., firing)

FIGURE 7.1   Applicant Misrepresents Qualifications

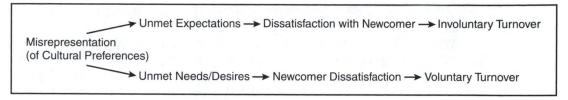

FIGURE 7.2   **Applicant Misrepresents Cultural Preferences**

perspective. When the applicant misrepresents her cultural preferences and is subsequently hired partly on the basis of these preferences, she will ultimately have to perform within the constraints of that organization's culture. If there are significant discrepancies between the newcomer's attitudes, values, beliefs, and communication style and the culture of the organization, the other members of the organization will become dissatisfied with the newcomer for not fitting into the culture. If this dissatisfaction is strong enough, she might be fired for reasons of incompatibility.

The bottom line of Figure 7.2 illustrates the possible chain of events from the individual's perspective. In this situation, when the newcomer enters the organization and finds that her attitudes, values, beliefs, and communication style differ from the organizational culture, she will experience unmet needs and desires. When they go unresolved, dissatisfaction tends to follow. Given the availability of other employment opportunities, the newcomer might leave voluntarily.

Misrepresentation by the Organization

Just as applicants might misrepresent themselves in an attempt to secure the best job opportunities, organizations might also misrepresent the nature of the job and the organization to attract the most qualified employees, as the bank did in Jacque's story. Wanous (1992) refers to this practice of "selling" the organization to the potential employee as *traditional recruitment*. According to Wanous (1992, p. 41), traditional recruitment involves two actions:

- Positive characteristics, rather than those things insiders find dissatisfying about the organization, are communicated to outsiders.
- Those features that are advertised may be distorted to make them seem even more positive.

In other words, traditional recruitment involves painting a picture of organizational reality that includes only information that can be construed as attractive. Any information (regarding details of the job or aspects of the organizational culture) that might seem unattractive to a potential employee is not communicated.

When the organization engages in traditional recruitment, any applicant hired might experience difficulty. Upon entering the organization, the newcomer will confront a reality that could be substantially different from the one portrayed during the recruiting process. As a result, a logical chain of events might ensue, as detailed in Figure 7.3.

When an applicant is subjected to traditional recruitment methods, he will have "inflated expectations," or expectations of the organization and job that are hyperpositive, based on inaccurate and overly positive information. When the newcomer encounters reality, these inflated expectations will not match reality, resulting in "unmet expectations," or expectations that have not been fulfilled. When expectations are unmet, job dissatisfaction tends to follow.

At this point, the potential chain of events splits into two directions. These directions should not be considered mutually exclusive, because events in one could be related to events in the other. One direction (the upper line in Figure 7.3) involves unmet expectations of the requirements of the job. Wanous (1992) noted that a mismatch regarding actual job requirements and the newcomer's expectations of them can result in lower job performance and eventual involuntary turnover.

The other direction (the lower line in Figure 7.3) involves unmet expectations of the characteristics of the organizational culture. Wanous proposed that this mismatch between the individuals and the culture can create unmet expectations, which can result in lower organizational commitment and eventual voluntary turnover.

You might be asking yourself, "So what? So what if the newcomer is dissatisfied? So what if there is turnover, voluntary or otherwise; can't the organization just hire someone else? Can't the newcomer just find another job? What does it matter?" In the next section, we address the potential costs, human and financial, of the traditional method of recruitment.

The Costs of Traditional Recruiting

Recruitment methods that lead to a high rate of turnover are expensive in both human and financial terms.

The Human Factor

When applicants and organizations misrepresent themselves during the recruitment and selection process, the potential exists for low satisfaction, low commit-

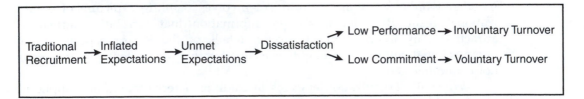

FIGURE 7.3   Potential Ramifications of Traditional Recruitment

ment, low performance, and increased turnover. What begins as an attempt to secure the best job or hire the best employee can result in negative consequences for the people involved. Issues of satisfaction, commitment, and turnover are not merely organizational outcomes devoid of life; they are human factors affecting the lives of real people.

Turnover, whether voluntary or involuntary, is a dramatic event. People's lives are often greatly changed, and the stress and difficulty of the situation affects the lives of their family and friends. This is true not only for the person leaving the organization, but for those with whom that person has worked; relationships have been formed (positive or otherwise), energy has been invested, and time has been spent.

Even if turnover does not occur, satisfaction and commitment can be affected negatively. The possible impact on important characteristics such as self-esteem and self-efficacy should be of concern at a human level.

Traditional recruitment practices (by both the individual and the organization) need to be examined from an ethical perspective. Kreps' three principles to evaluate ethics of organizational communication, discussed in Chapter 1, are useful here (1990, pp. 250–251):

1. Organization members should not intentionally deceive one another.
2. Organization members' communication should not purposely harm any other organization member or members of the organization's relevant environment.
3. Organization members should be treated justly.

Traditional recruitment methods (from the organizational perspective) can be evaluated according to these principles.

First, do traditional recruitment methods intentionally deceive applicants? In some cases, the answer must be yes. In Jacque's experience with the bank, described earlier, his company did not talk to him about the negative aspects of the job; they only emphasized (and overemphasized) the positive aspects. Organizations often intentionally misrepresent the reality of the job or the organization in an attempt to attract a potentially productive employee. The question becomes, to what extent was the deception *intentional*? Given the ambiguous nature of language and reality, one person's opinion of organizational reality can be quite different from another person's opinion. That being so, in some instances the situation is simply a matter of differing opinions of reality. But in other instances, organizational members intentionally deceive the applicant in an attempt to lure him or her into the organization. This behavior is ethically suspect.

Second, do traditional recruitment methods harm the applicant or other members of the organization? As stated earlier, such methods can harm both the applicant and current organizational members. When a newcomer experiences unmet expectations, low satisfaction, and perhaps even turnover, harm has indeed been inflicted.

Third, do traditional recruitment practices allow for just treatment of the applicant? Some might argue that the only way to "win" in the "recruitment game" is for each party to make itself as attractive as possible to the other party because the nature of the game is so competitive. From this perspective, any practices that help either party "win" the game are justified; the means justify the ends.

But is this really true? Can you, as an applicant, only obtain a great job in a strong organization if you misrepresent yourself to one degree or another? Can you, as an employer, only attract the best applicants if you misrepresent your organization by exaggerating or inventing positive aspects and downplaying or not informing the applicants about the relevant negative aspects?

In light of these three principles, traditional recruitment practices can be considered ethically suspect; nevertheless, for some people human costs are not enough to justify a change in behavior. In the next section, we discuss the financial factor involved in traditional recruitment.

The Financial Factor

In addition to the human costs associated with the potential outcomes of traditional recruitment practices, there are financial costs as well. The dollar amount attributed to hiring a new employee is referred to as *cost-per-hire*. In an online report in February 2006, Dooney calculated that the average cost-per-hire is $7,123. This figure represents the average across professions, industries, and areas of the country. Some cost-per-hire statistics are much higher, whereas others are lower. For example, www.selection.com summarized research by AON Consulting that indicated cost-per-hire ranges between $550 and $20,000, depending on the job category.

Perhaps even more revealing is another metric used by human resource managers to measure the financial impact of turnover. *Turnover cost* refers to the amount of money that can be attributed to losing one employee and replacing that employee with another. In 2005, SHRM reported that the cost of turnover involves several categories of expenses. A summary of these expenses follows:

- **Separation costs.** Exit interviewers' time and departing employee's time for the interview, separation pay, unemployment pay
- **Replacement hiring costs.** Attracting new applicants, advertising, travel, recruiter salary or fee, entrance interviews, testing (physical, psychological, drug, health, etc.), hiring decision meetings
- **Training new hire.** Information literature, general orientation training, job orientation training
- **Lost productivity and business costs.** Overtime for remaining employees, temporary workers, performance differential, cost of low morale, lost customers/clients

As you can see, turnover is costly for organizations. An incredible amount of time, energy, and money is invested in the process of hiring a new employee. When turnover occurs, particularly with a new employee, the organization suffers financially. In the next section, we offer an alternative to traditional recruitment practices, which might help reduce instances and costs of unmet expectations, low job satisfaction, and turnover.

Addressing the Problem: Realistic Recruitment

One way to address the problems caused by traditional recruitment practices is for the organization to engage in *realistic recruitment* practices. The genesis of the theory of realistic recruitment can be attributed to Weitz (1956), but modern research and practice regarding the topic is based mostly on the work of John Wanous.

In his book *Organizational Entry: Recruitment, Selection, Orientation, and Socialization of Newcomers* (1992), Wanous outlines the pitfalls of traditional recruitment practices and introduces the reader to the theory of realistic recruitment. According to Wanous, *realistic recruitment* "presents outsiders with *all pertinent* information *without distortion*" (p. 43). Realistic recruitment is designed to increase job satisfaction, thereby decreasing unnecessary turnover caused by unmet expectations.

Central to realistic recruitment is the creation and use of a *realistic job preview* (RJP). An RJP is any attempt by the organization to provide an accurate (both positive and negative) view of the relevant aspects of the job and the organization. The RJP should serve to lower the newcomer's initial expectations and provide a better match with reality, thereby decreasing the possibility of unmet expectations. This decrease, in turn, should lead to positive levels of job satisfaction and strong job performance, and the eventual lowering of unnecessary turnover. Figure 7.4 illustrates the logical chain of events attributed to the use of an RJP.

In the story of Jacque and his job with the bank, we can see how an RJP might have affected the situation. His company's misrepresentation of the financial planning job to Jacque caused his expectations to be significantly different from reality. As he encountered the job as it really was, he became dissatisfied and is considering leaving. His company would probably benefit by portraying the job more realistically, so that newcomers' expectations would be more in line with reality. Many people are attracted to financial planning positions because they match their needs and personalities. If the bank searched for the type of individual who would thrive under the pressure, hours, and demands of this type of job, it would most likely reduce turnover.

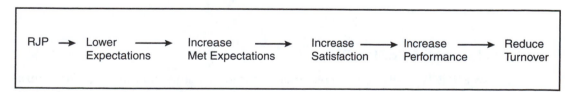

FIGURE 7.4   RJP Chain of Events

How RJPs Work

How do RJPs work? Two theories explain how an RJP accomplishes what it is intended to accomplish: self-selection and vaccination (Phillips, 1998). From the *self-selection* perspective, RJPs function by providing the applicant an opportunity to self-select out of the recruitment process on the basis of a mismatch of needs and/or abilities. The remaining applicant pool should consist of people who think there is a good match between their needs and abilities and the demands of the job and the organizational culture. Self-selection works only if the RJP is given very early in the recruitment process and if the information provided is realistic.

From the vaccination perspective, RJPs act just as a medical vaccination does. A medical vaccination introduces a weak dose of a disease (or the virus that causes it) into the body to give the immune system the opportunity to build up resistance to the disease and prevent an onset of it in the future. Similarly, an RJP can provide an opportunity for applicants to develop coping mechanisms for negative aspects of organizational life. If the vaccination effect is what truly occurs, then self-selection is rendered unnecessary.

Jean Phillips (1998), based on a review of RJP research, contended that RJPs may function more as a result of vaccination than self-selection. She argued this because RJP research shows that attrition from the recruitment process is either slightly negatively related or unrelated to the use of RJPs. In other words, one would expect that if an RJP were given early in the recruitment process, a significant number of applicants would self-select out of the process, leaving a smaller applicant pool (attrition). Her review, however, shows that RJPs do not significantly reduce the number of applicants. Therefore, self-selection most likely does not adequately explain why RJPs function as they do; the most viable explanation for Phillips is vaccination.

It is possible, though, that RJPs given at the very beginning of the recruitment process might serve a self-selection function. RJPs can take the form of job advertisements or informal word of mouth and can serve to preclude a person from ever becoming a formal applicant. When an RJP functions in this way, self-selection is the most reasonable explanation. Present research cannot account for people who self-select out at this point in the recruitment process because they were never formal applicants. For this reason, self-selection should not be dismissed as an explanatory mechanism for how RJPs function.

Two issues are important when constructing and implementing RJPs: medium of communication and time of administration. We discuss each in the following sections.

The Medium of the RJP

An RJP is typically constructed after a thorough analysis of the job and organization is performed. An analysis is conducted following the gathering of information regarding the specifics of the job, including working conditions, hours, opportunity for advancement, managerial style, job freedom, pay and benefits, and organizational values. This data is often gathered via observation of work procedures; surveys of workers, managers, and customers; and interviews with members at all levels of the organization.

Once the data is collected and synthesized, the organization must decide on the appropriate medium or media for presenting the RJP. Typically, RJPs have been presented using video, written, or verbal media. Table 7.1 illustrates the three broad categories of media available, as well as the different manifestations of each, the potential sources from which the RJPs could originate, and the outcomes related to each medium as demonstrated through research (Phillips, 1998).

Video.   *Video* is one medium available for administering an RJP. RJPs using this medium can take the form of job and organizational orientation videos and training videos. One recent development is the incorporation of video RJPs into company websites. Given the fact that potential employees use company websites as a primary source for company information, some organizations have begun to use their site to distribute video RJPs. For example, BellSouth (www .bellsouth.com/employment/preview) streams several different RJPs depending on the position in which a potential job candidate is interested (i.e., network technician, operator services, or sales associate). They also stream a video they titled, "Expectations," which is designed to provide the potential job candidate with general organizational expectations. If companies do not feel adequately equipped to create the RJPs for their websites, there are now companies designed to do just that.

TABLE 7.1   RJP Media

	Video	Written	Verbal
Manifestations	Organizational orientation; job orientation; training video	Job advertisement; aptitude test; informational pamphlet; handbook; training manual	Conversation with insiders; employment interview; on-site visit; prehire orientation; posthire orientation
Source	Actors vs. incumbents Managers vs. workers	Human resources management	Insiders Interviewers Human resources Supervisor/coworker
Related outcomes	Strongest positive relationship with performance	Least effective of the three forms	Greatest reduction in both types of turnover; only medium with positive relationship to job satisfaction

For example, FurstPerson, a company that helps recruit for and staff call centers, has created a product called CC Preview that guides a potential applicant through a multimedia, web-based RJP, and then asks the applicant to decide if they feel they are a good fit for the position and company.

Video RJPs have several advantages. First, they are consistent. The organization can be confident that each time the video is played, the same message will be sent to the audience in the same way. Second, video RJPs are multimedia, reflecting the prevalence of multimedia messages in today's society. Professionally created, video RJPs communicate a message using sight, sound, and music—a multimedia presentation that may be necessary to capture the attention of today's workforce. Unfortunately, RJPs that are unprofessional or of poor quality can have the opposite effect.

However, video RJPs also have several disadvantages. First, professional video production is expensive and can be time consuming. Second, video RJPs can quickly become dated. Organizations and jobs change quickly in today's world; what might have been true yesterday about a particular position can change tomorrow. Third, video RJPs are not interactive. Indeed, they are often considered a form of persuasive communication (Phillips, 1998), and as such can be understood from that perspective. We know, from the body of work in persuasion, that people are more willing to be persuaded when they are actively involved in the process. Video, although it engages many senses, is limited in its interactive capacity.

When producing video RJPs, the organization must decide whom they will use in the video as the source of information. Should the people be actors or real organizational members? Should they be managers? Coworkers? A combination of managers and coworkers? Research has yet to explore adequately the answers to these questions.

Video RJPs have been shown to have the strongest positive relationship with job performance (Phillips, 1998). In other words, the studies that have been conducted to this point have shown that video RJPs have the strongest connection to increased job performance. If increasing job performance is the outcome of interest for an organization, then a video RJP appears to be the most reliable medium.

Written.   RJPs may also be written. These are perhaps the most typical and take several forms, including job advertisements, aptitude tests, informational pamphlets, handbooks, and training manuals. Written RJPs have several advantages. First, just as with video RJPs, written RJPs are consistent. Second, they are relatively inexpensive to produce in comparison to video RJPs. Considering that handbooks and training manuals are common in most organizations, incorporating realistic job information in the preexisting texts can be done with little additional expense. Finally, written RJPs are slightly less difficult to change as conditions within the organization change. A set of addenda can be added to handbooks, job posting ads can be changed, or informational pamphlets can be updated to reflect the current organizational climate.

Written RJPs also have several disadvantages. First, newcomers are presented with so much written information that they might not pay as strict attention to it as they might because of information overload. Second, as with video RJPs, written RJPs are not interactive and are even less engaging than video, which is multimedia.

When constructing a written RJP, the organization is faced with many questions of presentation. For example, in what style is the RJP to be written? Should an informational pamphlet be written in a narrative style or should it be written in a detached, third-person style? Should the RJP be written by the human resources department or by management? Should it contain quotes from organizational members? Is a four-color, glossy publication necessary, or would a traditional black-and-white piece be satisfactory?

Written RJPs have been shown to be the least effective of the three forms of RJPs and to be altogether unrelated to job performance. Perhaps because of the disadvantages mentioned, they appear to be the least productive form, although they are probably the most prevalent because of their lower production cost.

Verbal. Spoken words are the final medium available for RJPs. Verbal RJPs have many manifestations, including conversations with insiders, employment interviews, on-site visits, prehire orientations, posthire orientations, and even discussions with competitors and former employees of the organization (though these last two are more informal RJPs). Verbal RJPs have several advantages. First, given that RJPs are a form of persuasive communication, a verbal medium is perhaps the most appropriate for enhancing the persuasive appeal of the message. If the person giving the RJP is a credible source, the verbal RJP has the potential to be very effective. Second, verbal RJPs are virtually cost-free. Although on-site visits and orientation sessions certainly have costs associated with them, the cost of answering a question honestly or offering a bit of realistic information verbally is negligible when compared to printing a pamphlet or producing a video.

Nevertheless, verbal RJPs have disadvantages as well. First, it is difficult to control the content of impromptu verbal RJPs. When an applicant asks a question of a line worker during an on-site visit, the organization has little control over what that person will say. The honesty expressed during that interchange can be very helpful to the applicant, but the organization has no way of tracking the information. Second, given the first disadvantage, it is very difficult to ensure consistency among verbal RJPs. When an applicant speaks with several different people during a typical application process, she will most likely be given different information about the same topic. The applicant is then left to judge the information based on the perceived credibility of the source.

The organization must decide who will meet the potential newcomer, because each of these people will be a potential contributor of verbal RJPs. Coworkers, employment interviewers, human resources managers, supervisors, and other organizational insiders are all viable candidates for offering verbal RJPs.

Two very important considerations for the organization when considering verbal RJPs, then, are source credibility and consistency of messages.

Verbal RJPs have been shown to be associated with the greatest reduction in both voluntary and involuntary turnover (as compared with written and video RJPs). Verbal RJPs are also the only kind with a positive relationship to job satisfaction. Research has shown that of all three media, spoken words are the most successful in reducing turnover and are the only medium whose use seems to increase the job satisfaction of the applicant.

Time of Administration of the RJP

In addition to deciding the optimal form of an RJP, an organization must determine the best time to administer it. An RJP can be administered during any of the following points in the hiring process:

- When the applicant first makes contact about the job opening
- After the job offer has been made but before the job is accepted
- After the newcomer starts the job

The research related to time of administration is complicated, but several issues are relevant. First, some researchers argue that RJPs administered after the newcomer starts the job are not RJPs at all. Because RJPs given after hiring do not allow for the opportunity to self-select out of the process, they should be considered efforts at "realistic socialization" rather than realistic job previews (Phillips, 1998). We agree. Although realistic information is useful at any point in the process, by definition, information given after the newcomer starts the job is not an RJP.

Second, Phillips' (1998) research has shown that RJPs presented before the job offer is accepted have stronger relationships with important outcome variables, such as job performance. Therefore, it would seem most appropriate for the organization to invest time and resources into producing and administering RJPs early in the recruitment process, before the job offer is accepted (Griffeth & Hom, 2001). Although many organizations do not wish to expend time or money on applicants who will not become members, the research and arguments presented here indicate that the cost of turnover could be greater down the line if RJPs are not given at this stage.

Realistic Recruitment and the Communicative Organization

The practice of realistic recruitment is well suited to the communicative organization. As we have shown throughout this chapter, traditional recruitment practices can contribute to unmet expectations, dissatisfaction, and turnover. Realistic recruitment is an attempt to treat recruits in a more ethical manner, with the hope that expectations will come close to matching reality, and as a result satisfaction, performance, and job retention will be increased. In other words, realistic recruitment is an attempt to anticipate and address misunderstandings before they occur.

Perhaps the most important characteristic of the communicative organization is that misunderstandings are a central feature of organizational life and can occur for a variety of reasons, including conflict in values and lack of information. These two causes of misunderstandings are especially relevant to the recruitment process in that potential employees need realistic information about the job and the organization, including its values, if they are to make an informed decision about their "fit." Throughout this chapter, we have included many examples of situations where a lack of information or misleading information led to misunderstandings for both the applicant and the organization.

Just as important as anticipating misunderstandings is strategic communication planning, which provides a variety of strategies to handle misunderstandings when they do occur. The *construct strategy* is perhaps most relevant to the move from traditional recruitment to realistic recruitment. If an organization followed the precepts of the communicative organization, it would recognize that misunderstandings were occurring as a result of their traditional recruiting practices. Implementing the construct strategy would provide an opportunity for the organization to learn from the misunderstandings of the past, discover where and how misleading information was being communicated, and engage in more realistic recruitment. The construct strategy encourages the move from problem to solution and is particularly useful during the recruiting process.

Realistic recruitment is not a simple process; it requires dedication to changing entrenched practices and an attention to communication skills. It brings into play several of the characteristics of social interaction advocated in the CO model, particularly exchange assessment and psychological immediacy. Whenever RJPs are used, the principle of exchange assessment needs to be incorporated. Exchange assessment encourages the communicator to consider the most appropriate medium—written, video, or verbal—for the message, as well as the best time to communicate it.

As discussed earlier, verbal RJPs presented by a credible source have the strongest relationship to relevant outcomes. To have a positive impact, however, it must be delivered in a competent manner. As communication students understand, communication does not happen effortlessly; it is a skill that needs to be developed. Psychological immediacy is a necessary skill in the implementation of verbal RJPs.

Summary

Recruitment is a vital component of organizational behavior. The information exchanged (or not exchanged) during this process can affect important factors such as applicant satisfaction, job performance, and turnover. Although historically both the applicant and the organization have tended to misrepresent themselves during this process, it seems more beneficial to both in the long run to engage in realistic, honest communication. The potential benefits of realistic recruitment (by both parties) include met expectations, increased job satisfaction, increased performance, and reduced turnover.

Realistic recruitment, although not the cure-all for dissatisfaction, poor performance, and turnover, is important in the communicative organization. With the fluctuations in the job market and economy that are commonplace in the United States, both applicants and organizations will feel pressure to misrepresent themselves. In a slow economy, applicants may think they have to make themselves appear more qualified than they really are if they are to secure a place in a tight job market. During times of economic boom, when organizations are vying for qualified workers, managers may try to lure applicants in with overly positive portrayals of the organization and position. We hope that both applicants and organizations remember that in the long run exaggerating important information will potentially lead to negative consequences for everyone involved. The communicative organization urges thoughtful and ethical behavior, and realistic recruitment practices meet these criteria.

CHAPTER
8

Socialization of New Members

In the previous chapter, we explored the recruitment of new employees and ways to make that process more honest and realistic. Once a new employee enters the organization, she tries hard to become established as a helpful, cooperative employee. Therefore, she takes for granted that initial information received is accurate and correctly indicates how time should be divided among various job tasks. In an interview with one manager, we learned about Sharon Stiles, an employee who made this assumption and ended up doing other people's work for them. She accepted requests from individuals because the previous individual in her position "used to do this for us." John Lewis is 59 years old and an executive director of an association that deals with food and drugs. He told us the story of Sharon's first days on the job:

> Sharon was experiencing a lot of stress. She had replaced a previous employee, Linda, who had left for another job. Linda, who had many years of experience in this job, had done a lot of extra work for people in other divisions because she was so accommodating and so capable, but it was not required in her job. Linda was not willing to say no, so she did a lot of extra work for people. When these same people came to Sharon with their usual requests, Sharon became overwhelmed with all the extra work. People were coming up to her and saying, "Linda used to do this for me."

As a newcomer to this organization, Sharon did not have the experience to distinguish between those tasks that were truly important and those that she could legitimately refuse to do. She felt nervous approaching John and admitting there was too much work, because she did not want to appear incompetent or uncooperative. This failure to admit a problem led to a misunderstanding on Sharon's part. According to our definition, which we introduced in Chapter 1 and again in Chapter 6, *misunderstandings* involve more than ineffective communication between members of an organization. It is an umbrella term used to connote the problematic nature of interaction in organizational settings. We identified three possibilities for creating misunderstandings: conflict in values, lack of information, and strategic misinterpretations. In this case, the cause of the misunderstanding was a lack of information.

Sharon's predicament is not atypical for organizational newcomers. New-comers regularly are confronted with situations characterized by uncertainty and ambiguity in many areas, including formal job duties, formal and informal role requirements, status differences, and myriad cultural constructs. Given this situation, the organization and the individual expend energy to address these issues. The organization attempts to *socialize* the individual into the culture of the organization and to the requirements of her position and role. At the same time, the newcomer attempts to influence the organizational situation by bringing to bear her own personal characteristics, values, beliefs, skills, and attitudes as she conducts her daily activities.

In this chapter, we focus mainly on the efforts of the organization to socialize the newcomer, relegating discussions of how the newcomer attempts to influence the organization to future chapters. Also, although socialization attempts are relevant throughout a member's time with an organization (especially at boundary passages, such as promotion and transfer), we devote the majority of this chapter to the socialization of newcomers. We begin with an overview of a newcomer's information needs. Next, we situate organizational socialization within a broader context—organizational assimilation. We then move to a discussion of two factors that affect socialization and then move to an overview of socialization processes. We conclude the chapter with a discussion of the relationship between socialization and emotion in organizations.

The Need for Information

A new employee generally receives more information about initial job tasks than about the organization's culture. Information that comes from the top of the organization down to the lowest-level employee contains directions about how to accomplish a job or task, as well as a sense of the values and culture of the organization (see Hafen, 2004, for the role gossip plays in this process). Information about tasks is usually specific and narrowly defined. Cultural information is vague or sometimes implied; yet it is cultural information that affects the way people are able to integrate and use the information about tasks. In other words, the values or principles of the organization and the kind of supportive or non-supportive environment in which people exist will have a direct bearing on an individual's ability to understand the task and its importance. For example, in some organizations collaborative work is valued and rewarded, whereas in other organizations only individual effort is recognized. Sharon needed that information before agreeing to take on additional assignments from other units. She also needed to know the difference between the formal requirements of her role and the way her predecessor defined them.

Unfortunately, organizations spend less time communicating their cultures, mission, and values than they do explaining the details of the task. Time pressure is often the reason cited for this. Meiners (2004) concluded that if a newcomer needs to be integrated into the flow of work quickly and the supervisor has limited time due to other obligations, this may limit their interactions to "critical" matters, which tend to involve task information. This imbalance leads to the kind of trap in which Sharon found herself. No one had explained the way Linda had personalized the formal role requirements or the culture of the organization so that Sharon could make good decisions about how much work she should do for other units in that organization. And she did not ask.

It is easy to say, "Why didn't Sharon just ask what she should do?" Remember, she was a new employee trying hard to make a good impression. Often, new employees are reticent about speaking up; they do not want to appear to be complaining from the very beginning. What did Sharon do to handle this problem? Let's return to John's story.

Sharon attempted to do it all by staying extra hours and giving up her lunch hour. However, the strain of all this began to cause her health problems. I, as her supervisor, had no idea what was going on, because Sharon never came to talk to me. One of Sharon's friends came to me and told me confidentially that Sharon was experiencing a lot of stress. I have an open-door policy in the office, so that people are always free to come and speak to me confidentially, without fear of reprisal. However, Sharon was not aware of my open-door policy or she was afraid to use it, so she kept her feelings bottled in. Meantime, she was getting more stressed out. I don't want my employees to be treated unfairly or not come to work. The problem was that Sharon would not communicate with me.

Most managers will tell you they have an open-door policy, and yet it is not surprising that, as a new employee, Sharon felt uncomfortable taking advantage of it. If she was unaware of the policy, then that was a serious problem as well. Information comes to new employees in many forms, from the supervisor, from peers, from subordinates, and even from outside the organization. This information varies in terms of accuracy and completeness. We know that as information is passed from one individual to another several adjustments are made to the content. First, if the information is not complete, the recipients tend to fill in with their own interpretations of what was meant or they add details where none were provided. In Sharon's case, lacking information about how much units worked together, she filled in the rest of the information on her own and concluded that helping out was what she was supposed to do.

Second, information is distorted. If you have ever played the child's game of "telephone," where a message starts at one end of a group and people whisper the message from one person to the next, you know that if there are more than three people, the message can become garbled by the time it reaches the end of the line. Of course, the same thing happens in organizations. People leave out details that do not sound important, and they pay attention to what seems salient to them.

Third, people substitute information. Perhaps they have forgotten one detail but draw from memory something that is similar to the piece of information they received.

Consequently, a new employee attempts to fill in the gaps in her knowledge base. She is called upon to perform tasks immediately that require a great deal more information, and yet it is impossible to give a new person all the information needed from the beginning. We cannot remember everything someone might need to know to perform the job well. So, the new employee makes assumptions, as Sharon did. She assumed that, because people told her the previous employee did this extra work for them, she was expected to do the same. The fear of sounding like someone who complains was stronger than the stress she was feeling, even to the point of affecting her health.

One of the major functions of communication is the reduction of uncertainty. Communication researchers have known for a long time that the most difficult situation to respond to is an uncertain one. If a person always ignores you, you develop coping strategies to handle the feelings of rejection. What really throws you off balance is when that same person all of a sudden starts talking to you in a kind way. You do not have a set of strategies with which to respond. Therefore, the more information newcomers can collect about individuals and the organization and its mission, the more uncertainty is reduced.

Karl Weick, in his classic text *The Social Psychology of Organizing* (1979), asserted that the more equivocal (uncertain) the message, the more the recipient needs help from others to understand it: "Organizations have developed as social systems for resolving equivocality and increasing the certainty of life. Organizations are established to undertake many of the more difficult tasks human beings face" (p. 111). Communication strategies help increase certainty. When the situation presented has little equivocality, organizational members can depend on rules to guide their behavior. As equivocality increases, they will need more communication to respond to it. If these rules have been written from a majority view of the world, then minority employees will have a difficult time understanding and following them.

Being "different" from the dominant group in the workplace creates additional barriers to being successful. Those differences may be the result of race, gender, age, religion, ethnicity, disability, sexual orientation, or language. During the assimilation process, new employees may begin to feel they must "sell out" their own culture in order to adopt the culture of the organization. Two authors, Renee Blank and Sandra Slipp (2000), have identified three guidelines for consideration in "buying in" instead of "selling out" (p. 105). They suggest there are ways to become assimilated into the organizational culture without giving up your own identity. These guidelines will help you determine which you are attempting to do:

- Your fundamental value system, that which you hold close to your heart, is the final arbiter of "right." If your values—which you learned as a child, tested as an adolescent, and solidified as an adult—are in direct violation of or contradiction with the organization's values, and you discard your values, you could be in danger of "selling out."

- If you know yourself—that is, have validated your talents, skills, and abilities—and perform a function or accept a position well beneath your talents, you could be in danger of "selling out."
- If you accept, without question, the culture of an organization that flaunts its discrimination against or disrespect for your culture, you could be in danger of "selling out."

This issue is a very personal matter. The organization is trying to help new employees assimilate into the organization, and you must decide if that assimilation is asking you to give up too much of your culture. Several options are available. First, you may decide that you will not be accepted no matter what you do and therefore you seek employment elsewhere. Another is to remain in the organization but dramatically change your style. A third is to adopt the organization's values and politics. Finally, you can adapt to the organization's culture while maintaining your own sense of identity. You go as far as you can to fit in without giving up your core values and political views. This last choice implies mutual accommodation between yourself and the organization. The type and structure of the organization you find yourself in and the structure of that organization will determine how much flexibility you have to make these changes.

According to Chapters 2 and 3, "traditional" organizations spend a great deal of time figuring out how to be precise in their actions—thus the reason for time-and-motion studies and bureaucratic rules. They tend to rely heavily on policies and procedure manuals, thinking that if it is all written down, certainly a new employee need only turn to the appropriate page in the manual to find the answer to any question. The quantity of information shared, however, does not necessarily indicate its quality. Employees, no matter how much information might be shared, can still be disappointed with their knowledge about the company. It is the kind of information that is shared, and the context in which it is shared, that make it meaningful. Often employees feel there is no legitimate way for them to provide feedback about working conditions or concerns about tasks they are being asked to perform.

Members of a "humanistic" organization might spend a lot of time socializing with new employees, believing that the best way for them to learn about the organization is through informal conversation. They are likely to be much more concerned with the newcomer's level of comfort, personal needs, and goals than are other types of organizations.

The communicative organization, by contrast, focuses on communication practices during the socialization stage and encourages specific communication behaviors to improve work relationships. Misunderstandings are expected, and strategies are developed to address them. Communication becomes the central feature of organized activity. Employees in this organization will be encouraged to pay attention to relationship development in such a way that there is less confusion about the status of organizational relationships. For example, we suggested in Chapter 6 that psychological immediacy would be encouraged. In this case, one person is involved psychologically with another person's message to the point that he is intently aware of the issues the other person is discussing and indicates that he has heard what she has said. The listener indicates that he appreciates the extent to which this topic or issue is important to the speaker.

The situation John and Sharon faced would be dramatically influenced by the type of organization in which they work. How did they resolve their dilemma? John continues his story:

> I talked to Sharon's direct supervisor about it. I'm one step up from her direct supervisor. I never told him, though, how I became aware of the problem. We agreed that Sharon should develop a list of all jobs she was being asked to do. Then we would all sit down and discuss it. We would divide the list into jobs she should not do and jobs she should do. Then we would decide if someone else in the office needed to help with the extra work. The meeting with Sharon was the first time I had discussed the situation with her. I thought it might be more appropriate for her direct supervisor to talk to her about the problem and tell her to write the list, since he had more contact with her and it seemed Sharon was frightened to talk to me. We made the list, worked it out, and Sharon and I finally talked. I informed her that she could always come and talk to me, a policy she said she knew I had. She said, however, that she did not want to disturb me, so she did not come to talk to me. I explained to Sharon that problems are solved better when everyone involved can work on them, and in the future, she should come talk to me. She seemed relieved and the talk cleared the air.

Another portion of the discussion of the communicative organization in Chapter 6 included the strategies available to organizational members for addressing misunderstandings (i.e., contain, cope, and construct). The conclusion of Sharon's story is a perfect example of the construct strategy. In this situation, communicative action promoted learning, the result of which was new understandings and new procedures for both parties involved.

This one talk, of course, did not solve all of Sharon's problems or answer all the questions she might have had, but it was a beginning. Sharon will only believe John's open-door policy if he comes through the door to reach out to others instead of always waiting for others to come to him. As Sharon moves through the process of becoming a full-fledged member, a variety of factors will influence her success and ultimately contribute to how long she stays in this organization.

Organizational Assimilation

A useful context for a discussion of organizational socialization is provided by the concept of *organizational assimilation*, put forward by Jablin (2001). Jablin defined *assimilation* as "the process by which an individual becomes integrated into the culture of an organization" (2001, p. 755); in other words, how well the new member adapts to norms of behavior and adopts new attitudes valued by the organization.

Assimilation generally consists of

> two dynamic interrelated processes: (1) planned as well as unintentional efforts by the organization to "socialize" employees, and (2) the attempts of organizational members to "individualize" or change their roles and work environments to better satisfy their values, attitudes, and needs. (Jablin, 2001, p. 755)

For example, the organization may plan an orientation session for new employees in which rules and regulations are discussed; however, the employee may learn a great deal about what is expected of her from informal conversations she has over coffee with her colleagues.

Bullis and Stout (2000) posited three assumptions upon which the concept of assimilation is based. First, as evident in the description by Jablin, "individuals as well as organizations are active agents" (p. 51). Assimilation is a dual process in which organizations and individuals influence one another. Often, *assimilation* is used as a synonym for *socialization*, but this is an incorrect use of the term. Socialization is but one-half of the assimilation process; individualization efforts by the newcomer must also be considered when discussing assimilation. Second, "organizations are bounded entities" (p. 49). Bullis and Stout argued that as we adopt language of "outsiders" and "insiders," we "assume that organizations have boundaries through which individuals cross" (p. 49). Research, then, which likens the organization to a machine, organism, or culture, has been concerned with articulating the processes that lead to a "successful" boundary crossing. The third assumption regarding assimilation is that it occurs in phases: "a relationship develops over time, in stages, between the organization and individual" (p. 49). The stages typically consist of anticipatory socialization, encounter, and metamorphosis (Jablin, 2001).

Anticipatory Socialization

Anticipatory socialization is the first phase of assimilation. During this phase, newcomers form expectations regarding particular occupations and what it would be like to be a member of a particular organization. Anticipatory socialization typically takes two forms: (1) vocational anticipatory socialization and (2) organizational anticipatory socialization. Vocational anticipatory socialization includes the information gathered during childhood and adolescence from a variety of sources, including family, peers and friends, educational institutions, media, and part-time employment (Jablin, 1987, 2001; Vangelisti, 1988). Such information may affect both occupational choice and expectations for organizational behavior, including communication. This is the information that enables a person to form impressions of what it would be like to be a teacher, a lawyer, or an artist. It is all the general impressions that have been formed over the years through exposure to mass media as well as attitudes expressed by those in a person's immediate environment.

Organizational anticipatory socialization includes the information intentionally and unintentionally gathered as the job seeker interacts with potential employing organizations. This information serves to socialize job seekers even before they become members of a particular organization. Information can come from a variety of sources, including organizational literature (e.g., formal job postings, annual reports, company brochures, etc.) and interpersonal interactions, such as job interviews, company visits, and interactions with incumbents (see Jablin, 2001, for an extensive review of the research on anticipatory socialization). A good example of this comes from Gibson and Papa (2000); they investigated communication during assimilation among blue-collar workers at an organization they labeled "Industry International." Workers in this organization had strong productivity, low turnover, and often worked 50- to 55-hour work weeks with no personal days, no sick days, and few vacations. The interviews that the researchers conducted with workers revealed that more than two-thirds of them had family, friends, and community members who also worked there. These influences led to the workers' assimilation and served to mold their perceptions of the company as well as their commitment to it.

Anyone interviewing for a position is advised to do careful research on the organization in an attempt to answer the following kinds of questions: What would it be like to work in this organization? Does it operate on a worldwide basis? What is exciting about being in this organization? Could I become enthusiastic about this organization's product or service? What could I bring to the organization that it would value? Our discussion of realistic recruitment and realistic job previews in Chapter 7 is illustrative of the activities relevant to organizational anticipatory socialization.

Organizational Encounter

The *encounter* phase, also known as the *entry phase*, of the assimilation process occurs when "the newcomer confronts the reality of his or her organizational role" (Jablin, 1987, p. 694). Although the individual is a formal member of the organization at this point, she has yet to gain the status of "insider," because she has not been socialized by the organization nor has she been given the opportunity to individualize role requirements. This was the situation with Carol, a 49-year-old payroll and accounts payable manager, whose difficulty with the entry phase took several years to resolve:

> The first problem I encountered was really one that took four years to get over. This issue was because of my length of service. Our facility is one in which the average years of service is 15 years. When I first arrived, employees felt that I could not be trusted and that I could not possibly know what I was doing. After all, I was brand new. My predecessor had retired from the position after 20 years, and I had her blessing as the new replacement. Still, I was viewed as an interloper and an incompetent by most of the employees, including some management personnel. There was a huge misunderstanding

there. What they did not know was that I had been doing this work for 19 years before ever coming here. The problem resolved itself after about four years, but it was very troubling at the start.

Although the length of time it took to resolve this situation was a bit extreme, the point of Carol's story is a good one: Trust is not easily earned in many institutions for newcomers.

Jablin (2001), in reviewing the research on communication processes during this phase, indicated that information is shared between the individual and the organization in a variety of ways: formal orientation programs, socialization strategies (discussed in the next section of this chapter), training programs, formal mentoring, informal mentoring, and so on. Waldeck, Seibold, and Flanagin (2004) commented on this list of traditional information channels and argued that new members will most likely also learn from more advanced media sources such as e-mail, web pages, voicemail, instant messages, videoconferencing, and cell phones. They called these sources *advanced communication and information technologies* (or ACITs).

Regardless of the channel used, organizational encounter is characterized by information giving to the newcomer as well as information seeking by the newcomer. Information giving and information seeking are particularly interesting behaviors because they involve active attempts by the newcomer to affect her organizational situation. Vernon Miller and Fred Jablin (1991) identified seven general information-seeking tactics used by newcomers during the encounter phase of assimilation:

- *Overt questioning* is asking for information in a direct manner.
- *Indirect questioning* is getting another person to respond to hints and noninterrogative questions.
- *Third-party questioning* is asking someone other than the primary information source.
- *Testing* is breaking a rule and then monitoring the target person's response for information.
- *Disguising conversations* use jokes and self-disclosure to ease information from a source without being obvious.
- *Observation* is watching another's action in order to model that behavior.
- *Surveillance* is reflecting retrospectively on conversations and activities to determine the information needed.

Miller (1996) later determined that the use of any of these tactics depended on the level of uncertainty experienced by the newcomer and the social costs incurred from seeking the information. For example, a person asking questions might be seen as bothersome or lacking in the necessary job knowledge. Testing might be dangerous because breaking a rule to seek information could easily be seen as being insubordinate. The tactics used also varied according to the source of the information (coworker vs. boss), as well as the type of information requested (job instructions, job performance, and how others feel about the newcomer). Miller's research indicated that the seven information-seeking tactics could be reduced to five. Because they are so closely associated, disguising conversation and indirect questions were reduced to one category, "indirect." For the same reason, observation and surveillance were combined into the category termed "observed." In general, Miller found that newcomers use overt questions and observation tactics most often, third-party and indirect tactics a bit less, and testing tactics infrequently. These are the tactics that are available in the information-seeking process. Knowledge about such tactics makes people more flexible, which is one of the goals of the communicative organization.

Metamorphosis

The final stage, *metamorphosis*, is when the new employee actually begins to change some of his behaviors and expectations in order to meet the standards of the new environment and begins to alter the requirements of his role to match his needs, desires, and skills. It is at this point that the newcomer makes the transition to an organizational insider. Perhaps this new organization expects people to come to work early and stay late. Without saying anything, the new employee quickly learns that he is the only one going home at five. It is also during this stage that the new employee may attempt to put his stamp on the organization, create an individual identity within the organization, stake out his territory, or obligate the organization to adapt to the new member's values in some other way. For example, college graduates are eager to put what they have learned to work and to help their new organization benefit from what they have learned in school. Older employees may resent this "newcomer" trying to show them how to do something they have been doing for years. Working out this tension is part of the metamorphosis process.

Vanessa, a college senior, helps us see the progression from organizational encounter to metamorphosis, and the changes that occur in feelings, commitments, and relationships:

This past summer I started a new job at a locally owned gift shop in my town. Growing up I always wanted to work at the gift shop, I just thought it was the cutest little shop and have always thought highly of the man who owns it. I assumed that to work there it would not take much skill and it would not feel like a real job; it would be more like hanging out and talking to all the people who came in throughout the day. When the owner approached me about possibly working there for him this summer, he had me come into the shop one day and just talk to a few of the other employees, he showed me around and went over a little of what I would be doing.

When I actually started working there, it was a difficult adjustment. Work was not easy. We had shipments coming everyday with new items that had to be priced, put away, or displayed, (and order items) for customers. I had to take down and either move or rearrange displays. Then, there was the café that I had to worry about on top of the gift shop side. Also, when it came to my coworkers there was a little tension at first. One woman resented me and was never helpful when I had questions or needed help. Another woman tended to push all of her work on me, saying that there were other jobs she had to do while I was doing hers.

Over the next few weeks I had gotten to work with everyone several times and had become comfortable with them. They were letting me in on the conversations and inside gossip, they were quicker to jump to my aid if they saw that I needed something, and even started asking for my input on displays. Also, I began thinking about and promoting the shop much the way the others who had been working there did. It sort of became my second family for the summer because of the way everyone worked together and socialized with one another. I became a part of the shop and was known for my individual personality. I found myself to be more conscious of the attitudes I presented when I was working at the shop. Also, I started mirroring the behaviors of my coworkers in handling certain customers.

The values of the shop also became my values, or I came to appreciate them more than what I had inside and outside of the shop: small-town pride, reputation, and customer satisfaction (leading to town satisfaction). All of this could be seen in how we were expected to interact with the customers, partner with other businesses or schools to promote town events, and make sure we did what we could to make sure the customer left happy. Long-time customers eventually started calling me by my first name instead of "the new girl for the summer." That is an important issue as well—". . . for the summer." I was hired with the fact in mind it was only until I moved back to college. Even though I was a temporary employee, all the other employees and the boss let me in as if I had been there and was going to continue to be there. In fact, since I was only temporary, I worked harder to "leave my mark" so that in the future there could be the possibility of returning during breaks. Also to be an example for others—to have the coworkers say "Well, Vanessa, who worked here over the summer, did it this way . . . " or "When Vanessa was here she was . . . " I had become such a part of it that the coworkers and customers who know me from there will now refer to my personality and ways of doing different projects.

Vanessa describes the transition from encounter to metamorphosis wonderfully. It is a time of growth, acceptance, increased role responsibility, and becoming a true insider.

This is also a time of ethical dilemmas for a new employee. Although ethical decisions are a personal and confidential matter between individuals and their consciences these judgments are influenced by the organizational environment. White and Lam (2000) suggested that individuals are more likely to face ethical dilemmas if "(1) organizations do not provide the means to prevent unethical behavior, (2) individuals have personal 'motivation' to be benefited from behaving unethically, and (3) job positions provide the 'opportunity' to engage in unethical practices" (p. 38). During assimilation the new employee will be assessing these factors and making ethical choices about how to behave in the organization.

Criticisms of the Assimilation Approach

Organizational assimilation has been a very useful way of conceptualizing individual experience in organizational life. Recently, however, research and assumptions in this area have come under scrutiny. For example, Bullis (1999) and Turner (1999) have suggested that the term *assimilation* is an improper label for the process that it denotes. Turner argued that the term *assimilation* is often considered in everyday usage to "denote absorption into the whole" (1999, p. 384) and does not indicate the dual agency notion that Jablin proposed. Bullis (1999) agreed and argued that, despite Jablin's lucid definition, the term *assimilation* has negative connotations (i.e., absorption of a minority group by a culturally dominant group). To remedy this language problem, Bullis suggested reversing the terms *assimilation* and *socialization*, with socialization representing the broader concept and assimilation representing the organization's efforts to transform the newcomer into a fully functioning organizational member. Kramer and Miller (1999) answered this criticism by suggesting that the terms remain the same but that we do a better job in the discipline of promoting the idea that assimilation "involves the *interaction* of socialization and individualization" (p. 360).

Other criticisms have been levied against assimilation research (e.g., Kroman, Myers, & Oetzel, 2003). Most notably, Bullis and Stout (2000) claimed that although Jablin contended that the stage model characterizes a "common" experience in U.S. society, it does not represent everyone's experience; those who do not fit into this pattern are "irrelevant" (p. 63). Those deemed "irrelevant" often are members of subordinated groups, be they part-time or temporary workers or workers in nontraditional organizations (e.g., nonprofit or volunteer organizations). Jablin (2001) addressed this criticism by indicating his intentions: "This focus is not intended to diminish the importance and legitimacy of nonpaid work in the family [or] assimilation into jobs in volunteer and nonprofit organizations" (p. 733).

We now turn our attention to the next step in the process of integrating new employees into the organization—*organizational socialization*. These are the processes in which organizations engage to assist newcomers in assuming their new roles. This is also the stage where the organizational culture is explained.

Organizational Socialization

Organizational socialization represents the efforts of the organization in the assimilation process. John Van Maanen and Edgar Schein (1979) defined *organizational socialization* as "the process by which an individual acquires the social knowledge and skills necessary to assume an organizational role" (p. 211). Bullis (1993) extended this notion and suggested that socialization is a "process through which newcomers become organizational members" (p. 10). Socialization processes are considered important to other relevant issues such as "newcomer acculturation, employee attitudes and behaviors, and the shaping of newcomers' identities" (p. 10). Organizational socialization, then, is the organization's attempts to transform an organizational newcomer into a full-fledged member by instilling into the person the organization's norms, values, and beliefs as well as the formal and informal role requirements associated with the person's position.

Factors Affecting Socialization: Loyalty and Congruency

Yoash Wiener (1988) identified two factors that affect socialization of employees and that could determine the success of socialization efforts—loyalty and congruency. Several other factors are also associated with socialization, such as self-efficacy, motivational orientation, previous work experience, and demographic variables (see Saks & Ashforth, 1997, for a review).

The first factor is the individual's belief that he has a moral obligation to engage in a mode of conduct reflecting loyalty and duty in all social situations in which he has a significant personal involvement (Wiener, 1988). Someone who is high in loyalty is likely to believe you should stick by your friends no matter what, and that you owe the organization your loyalty because you have been supported by that organization. These individuals are more likely to adapt to the prevailing organizational culture.

The second factor is the degree of congruency between core values held by the organization and by the individual. When the degree of congruency is high, members are more likely to adopt the organizational value system. We have developed a grid that represents how these two factors might contribute to very different types of employees with different levels of commitment (see Figure 8.1).

	High Loyalty	**Low Loyalty**
High Congruence	*Motivator* ──────── Socialization process: maintenance	*Activist* ──────── Socialization process: utilitarian
Low Congruence	*Loyalist* ──────── Socialization process: guilt-ridden	*Loner* ──────── Socialization process: protracted

FIGURE 8.1   Loyalty–Congruency Socialization Process Grid

We identify the possible combinations of these two factors and indicate the potential effect on the socialization process. This grid is intended to be descriptive, not a guide for future behavior.

In Quadrant I, the new employee has a high sense of loyalty and duty, and therefore will feel some sense of obligation to adapt to the organization. At the same time, this individual's values are highly congruent with the organization's values. If the organization wants a new employee to adopt the current culture, this individual, identified as a *motivator*, is the easiest to socialize. The socialization process is a matter of "maintenance" of the individual's loyalty and the congruency between individual and organizational goals. For example, Marta, who is passionate about the environment, believes in being loyal to those who support her and joins Greenpeace. She will integrate into that organization very quickly. The socialization process will only require "triggers" to remind her of the organization's goal and how important it is to support it.

In Quadrant II, the newcomer ranks low in loyalty but believes in the organization's mission. This person is more loyal to a cause in which he believes than to any organization and is driven by that cause, thus meriting the title *activist*. The most effective socialization process to use with this individual is "utilitarian," in that socialization efforts focus on what is of most use to the employee. As long as the organization's goal remains similar to the employee's personal values, the employee will adapt to the organization. If the organizational goal changes, he is less likely to remain with the organization. For example, Karl joined an organization that was on the cutting edge of technology, working with the latest advancements. Because he was innovative and interested in the newest technologies, this organization suited his needs. However, when the organization decided to stop developing new technology, Karl lost interest and eventually left. The mission of the organization no longer matched Karl's personal values, and because he had a low level of general loyalty to a group, there was little to hold him to the organization.

In Quadrant III, the new employee has high loyalty to the organization but discovers that her personal goals and the goals of the organization are not compatible. The employee is a *loyalist* as far as the organization and its people are concerned, but she has difficulty accepting the specific mission. This employee faces a moral dilemma. On the one hand, she wants to remain loyal to the organization, but on the other hand she finds that she cannot tolerate the clash of values. Consider the case of John. John has just started working for a large public relations firm. He feels a great sense of loyalty to the firm and to its founder, who hired him. Then he is asked to develop a PR campaign for a major tobacco company. John does not smoke and believes the tobacco industry is selling a product that kills people. John's tenure with this organization will depend on which is stronger: his loyalty to the organization or his commitment to his personal values. It will also depend on how well the organization socializes John in its belief that it should not judge its clients as long as the clients' service or product is legal. The organization keeps John on board by using "guilt" to increase his sense of loyalty to the organization in the hopes that loyalty will overcome the lack of congruence between his values and the organization's goals.

In Quadrant IV is an individual who has a low level of loyalty and no congruency between personal goals and the organization's goals. This person is likely to have a short stay in the organization and has been identified as the *loner*. The assimilation process for such employees is protracted; it is continuous and usually fails to keep the individual embedded in the work of the organization. Consider Anita. She took a job selling cosmetics in a store while she was waiting for a job to open up in a cosmetics house. She has little or no commitment to this store because, after all, she expects to be there a very short period of time.

The socialization process applies primarily to new members because their needs for cultural adaptation are most salient, but it also serves as a means of support and renewal for an existing value system and longer-term employees. In fact, this process occurs at every level of the organization and at each change the employee makes throughout her career. As the organization changes, the socialization process continues for all its members.

Van Maanen and Schein (1979) suggested that the socialization process is critical to the survival of the organization:

> The more experienced (organizational) members must find ways to insure that the newcomer does not disrupt the ongoing activity on the scene, embarrass or cast a disparaging light on others, or question too many of the established cultural solutions worked out previously. Put bluntly, new members must be taught to see the organizational world as do their more experienced colleagues if the traditions of the organization are to survive. (p. 211)

As new members are "tested" in this setting for their skills and degree of commitment to the organization and the work, they can receive a number of benefits. Van Maanen and Schein pointed out these benefits. Once having passed these tests, these new members are granted inclusionary rights, which then permit them

> (1) to share organizational secrets, (2) to separate the *presentational* rhetoric used on outsiders to speak of what goes on in the setting from the *operational* rhetoric used by insiders to communicate with one another as to the matters-at-hand, and/or (3) to understand the unofficial yet recognized norms associated with the actual work going on and the moral conduct expected of people in the particular organizational segment. (p. 222)

In short, the socialization process allows new members more and more access to the internal workings of the organization.

Socialization Processes

As indicated in Chapter 7, organizations expend significant resources on recruiting, hiring, and training new employees. Consequently, they have a considerable interest in ensuring that newcomers perform their roles in the intended manner and understand and adapt to the organization's culture. A sizable amount of research has been conducted investigating socialization processes and their effects on relevant outcomes such as uncertainty reduction, role ambiguity, and turnover (see Saks & Ashforth, 1997; Jablin, 2001; Bullis & Stout, 2000, for reviews of this research).

Much of the research on socialization processes has stemmed from work conducted by Van Maanen and Schein, who argued that an organization has a variety of processes available for socializing newcomers and that these processes have different potential effects. The authors were particularly concerned with the effect socialization may have on newcomers' response to their roles, which they defined as having three components: (1) a "content or knowledge base," which involves the range of possible solutions to problems that are encountered on a daily basis in the role; (2) a "strategic base," "which suggests the ground rules for the choosing of particular solutions" (p. 227); and (3) an "explicit and implicit mission, purpose, or mandate," which involves the relationship of the particular role to the overall mission of the organization. Also important is the notion of a *role boundary*, which "refers to whatever delineates the perimeter—and thereby the scope—of a role" (Ashforth, Kreiner, & Fugate, 2000, p. 474).

Van Maanen and Schein contended that how an organization socializes its newcomers will affect the manner in which the newcomer approaches her role. The authors refer to this connection as the newcomer's "response to socialization." A newcomer could accept the role as it is presented, without questioning the status quo, which is considered a "custodial response." Another response possibility is an "innovative response," in which the newcomer makes substantive changes to the knowledge base or strategy associated with the role, or redefines the purpose of role functions (i.e., the mission). In either case, the socialization tactics that the organization employs should affect the response, either custodial or innovative. If the employee assumes the custodial response to socialization, on the one hand the organization will lose those skills and special abilities that the new employee may have brought to the position and the organization. On the other hand, the newcomer should not ignore the role that the organization expects to be filled.

To complete their argument, Van Maanen and Schein (1979) offered six pairs of socialization tactics that organizations could employ. They are presented as oppositional pairs. The list of tactics is not considered by the researchers to be exhaustive or mutually exclusive. The following sections discuss the tactics, integrating the concepts of loyalty and congruency offered earlier in this chapter.

Collective versus Individual Socialization Processes. *Collective socialization* involves putting a group of recruits through a common set of experiences together. Peer pressure serves to "promote and intensify the demands of the socializing agents" (p. 233). Military boot camps are an excellent example of this type of socialization. In the corporate world, many large organizations conduct group training where new recruits are put together at an off-site location to learn the task and the organization's cultural requirements. This tactic is often used when the organization wants to build a collective sense of reality. Obviously, any type of organization that has large numbers of new members entering the organization at the same time could employ this socialization tactic. Kristie, a college senior, described how her professional business campus fraternity used collective socialization.

> Once the active members have defined a pledge class, the pledges are given a list of tasks that they must complete within their pledge period of five to six weeks. As a group, the pledges must hold a fundraiser, perform a philanthropy event, and obtain a speaker to speak to the entire chapter. Each of these assignments is designed to test the abilities of each pledge and the pledges as a group and to introduce them to the values and mission of our fraternity.
>
> In completing the pledge process, the pledges learn a great deal about the fraternity and also begin to feel as though they are part of the group without being thrown into an organization with which they are unfamiliar. In organizing each of the events, cohesion is built, which contributes to their sense of loyalty to their pledge class and ultimately the whole fraternity. After members have completed the pledge process and are active members, cohesion remains because each member has gone through the same process and completed the same tasks to get where they are. All members hold similar goals and experiences within the area of business and this aids in developing and maintaining a working, healthy environment for our business fraternity to thrive in.

As evidenced by Kristie's story, the power of collective peer pressure would make this an appropriate socialization process for those individuals who have high congruency with the organization's mission but who do not yet have any sense of loyalty to the organization (those identified in Figure 8-1 as "activists").

Individual socialization occurs when recruits are brought into the organization in relative isolation from one another and put through a unique set of experiences. Examples would be apprenticeship programs, trainee assignments, and on-the-job training. The views of those socialized individually are likely to be far less homogeneous than the views of those socialized collectively.

Formal versus Informal Socialization Processes. *Formal socialization* occurs when newcomers are segregated, in one form or another, from regular organizational members. This tactic is used "in organizations where specific preparation for new status is involved and where it is deemed important that a newcomer learn the 'correct' attitudes, values, and protocol associated with the new role" (p. 237). Segregation can involve actual physical separation from normal daily procedures, or it could involve designating the individual as a "newcomer" in some way, such as with special uniforms or badges. Police departments, for example, often segregate newcomers from incumbents by having the recruit wear a different uniform from that of a full-fledged officer. This tactic may be most appropriate for the individual we have identified as having low congruency with the organizational mission but high loyalty to the organization itself—the loyalist.

Informal socialization processes do not segregate the newcomer in any special way or distinguish the newcomer's role specifically, but instead use informal, laissez-faire socialization for recruits. It is important to realize that because the newcomer is not distinguished from other organizational members, the mistakes that person makes are "real" mistakes. When a recruit is segregated from other organizational members and thereby designated a "newcomer," mistakes are expected and more easily excused.

Sequential versus Random Socialization Processes.   *Sequential socialization* is the degree to which the organization specifies a certain set of steps to be completed in order to advance to the target role. Professional training programs such as medical school require a series of steps that the aspiring doctor must complete before being allowed to practice. Loners would benefit from a set of specific steps in the hope that they would follow them initially. However, as we predicted earlier in the chapter, loners would probably not stay long with the organization. Motivators, with high levels of congruency and loyalty, may be willing to adhere to strict steps set forth by the organization in an attempt to groom them for a long career.

Random socialization "occurs when the sequence of steps leading to the target role is unknown, ambiguous, or continually changing" (p. 241). In this situation, the newcomer must provide her own sense of logic to the information provided about reaching the target role. In some extreme circumstances, the newcomer is personally responsible for creating the steps. A potential consequence of random socialization is that the newcomer is exposed to a variety of viewpoints within the organization as she attempts to negotiate her way through the process of establishing and clarifying the necessary steps.

Fixed versus Variable Socialization Processes.   When an organization uses *fixed socialization*, it provides the newcomer with a precise timetable for when to expect progression to the target role. For example, many organizations tell newcomers that they should expect a probationary period (e.g., six months or a year) when they begin employment, after which they can expect an increase in pay, benefits, and job duties.

Variable socialization processes provide no real cues to the newcomer as to when to expect movement to the target role. Van Maanen and Schein contend that most modern organizations operate more on a variable basis than a fixed basis because of the constantly changing environment and internal structures. Additionally, they argue that different people may progress at different rates, making it very difficult to predict when a particular boundary passage may occur.

Serial versus Disjunctive Socialization Processes.   If an organization uses *serial socialization*, it uses an experienced organizational member, who occupies a similar role to the one the newcomer will occupy, to help "groom" the newcomer (p. 247). An experienced member serves as a role model or perhaps a mentor for the newcomer. In some educational institutions, for example, new faculty members are paired with a senior faculty member who helps them negotiate their way through the first few years on the job, "showing them the ropes" with regard to the different demands of the position. This system would work especially well with motivators, who already have a high degree of motivation toward the organization and its mission. Motivators may not need the reinforcement of some of the other recruits and can be initiated into those specialized positions sooner.

However, when an organization uses *disjunctive socialization* processes, no role models are available or provided for the newcomer. In this situation, the newcomer is left alone to discover the ins and outs of the position. Disjunctive socialization may occur, for example, when the organization has undergone a major restructuring. Often, restructuring is accompanied by a "house cleaning" of sorts, and new personnel are brought in to occupy open positions.

Investiture versus Divestiture Socialization Processes. The *investiture socialization* tactic affirms the personal characteristics and identity that the newcomer brings to the organization. In essence, the organization is saying, "We like you the way you are." Investiture socialization attempts to make the transition to the new organization as comfortable as possible for the new employee. By welcoming the individual and everything she has to offer, the stress accompanying the transition should be reduced. An organization may apply this process to the loyalist, because she already comes with a high level of commitment to the organization and its mission.

Divestiture socialization, however, seeks to deny and strip away certain personal characteristics of a newcomer: "Many occupational and organizational communities almost require a recruit to sever old friendships, undergo extensive harassment from experienced members, and engage in long periods of time in doing the 'dirty work' of the trade" (p. 250). Boot camp is the prototypical example of divestiture socialization. In the military, the organization is attempting to increase predictability and standardization; one way to do that is to strip away individuality and rebuild the members in a particular way.

Van Maanen and Schein's argument is that the type of socialization processes employed will affect the response of newcomers to their roles (i.e., custodial or innovative). Reviews of the extant research conducted on this topic (see Saks & Ashforth, 1997; Jablin, 2001) indicate the following connections:

- Collective, formal, sequential, fixed, and serial tactics tend to be correlated with custodial responses.
- Individual, informal, random, variable, and disjunctive tactics tend to be related to innovative responses.

Jablin (2001) maintained that research has not been consistent in correlating the investiture–divestiture pair with a particular response.

It is important to recognize two main points in the previous discussion of socialization tactics and responses. First, this view of socialization represents a *one-way* view that minimizes the interactive nature of the communication aspects of these tactics and processes. Second, the relationships between the tactics and responses presented should in no way be construed as *causal*. In other words, use of certain socialization tactics will not guarantee a certain type of response. Given the ability of human beings to exercise choice and the fact that each person is unique, there will never be a direct causal relationship that applies to every case.

The view of the socialization process we have presented incorporates attitudes on the part of the newcomer toward both the organization and its mission and offers a variety of socialization processes that might be applied depending on the employee's attitude. Obviously, what works best is for new organizational members to join organizations in whose mission they believe and to which they can remain loyal. Frequently, however, the organization must work with uncommitted members. At the very least, the organization needs to focus on the kind of information being shared with employees that ensures adequate understanding.

Assimilation and socialization depend on adequate information being shared. When employees are given conflicting messages about the organization's culture and/or their role requirements, it is difficult for them to determine how they should behave. In writing, superiors may say one thing but mean something entirely different. For example, a manager may say, as did John in our earlier story, "I want employees to come to me with any problem," but not really expect them to need constant reassurance on a daily basis. Or employees may be overburdened with information that they cannot process or absorb. Because new employees (and longer-term employees, for that matter) may not want to take the risk of sending negative feedback to a supervisor, managers often are not aware that information is not getting through or that it is being sent in such a way that the employee cannot make sense of it. Assumptions are made and decisions carried out that are based on erroneous perceptions.

New members, as well as managers, must monitor carefully what happens during the encounter stage of socialization when the new member enters the organization for the first time. The degree of loyalty, as well as how similar the newcomer's views are to the values of the organization, will determine the kind of socialization process he is likely to experience. Organizations want to hold on to productive employees; therefore, assimilation is important to maintaining new employees' loyalty and contentment. Both newcomers and managers need to take the following measures:

- New employees should collect as much information about the organization as possible, both formally and informally, by talking with current employees about what it is like to work for the organization.
- Managers need to take special note of the progress new employees are making in the first few days and weeks toward adopting the values of the organization as their own.
- New employees must assess how much of their own culture they are being asked to set aside in order to adopt the culture of the organization. Ultimately, each new employee must decide if the request is acceptable or too great.

■ Managers need to consider each new employee and determine what approach will work best, remembering that the organization must make some adaptations to its new members as well as expecting adjustments from them.

Ultimately, it is the individual who decides the degree of loyalty to give to a particular organization or a particular field. People with a good sense of their core values, those things they believe in that cut across time and situation, will be able to make good decisions about the type of organization for which they want to work. At the same time, the organization needs to identify clearly its mission and goals so employees can make wise choices about where they will spend their career.

As discussed earlier in the chapter, loyalty, commitment, and other issues, such as identification, performance, and satisfaction, are important aspects of the new organizational member's experience. There are myriad ways in which these issues are affected for each person, but two that are of particular importance in the assimilation process are *emotions* and *work-family balance*. New organizational members must learn what role emotions play in a particular culture and what the emotional demands are for a particular job. They must also learn how the organization responds to the attempts of the worker to manage the demands of work and family. We now turn our attention to these two important parts of organizational life.

Emotions in Organizational Settings

When considering all of the different things that one must learn in order to be successful at a new job, one of the last things people consider is what is expected emotionally. According to Rafaeli and Sutton (1989), it is important to know the rules for emotional management in order to understand organizational culture. Appropriate emotional management will help an individual develop relationships, and it can increase an individual's chances of achieving career success (Staw, Sutton, & Pelled, 1984; Waldron 2000).

Socialization research on a variety of service industries (e.g., flight attendants in Hochschild, 1983; cruise ship staff in Tracy, 2000; and bill collectors in Sutton, 1991) suggests that organizations choose employees who seem able to conform to certain emotional display rules. Once hired, these employees are formally taught (socialized) emotional display rules (Kramer & Hess, 2002). Managing one's emotions relies in part on *emotion regulation*, which is the efforts to increase, maintain, or decrease one or more components of an emotion (Gross, 1999). Two forms of emotion regulation exist: deep acting and surface acting.

Deep acting is an emotional display that stems from more of a conditioned internal state. In deep acting, the "display is a natural result of working on feeling; the actor does not try to seem happy or sad but rather expresses spontaneously a real feeling that has been self-induced" (Hochschild, 1983, p. 35). In other words, in deep acting employees draw upon emotional memories to produce the desired emotion or emotional display. Emotional memories alone, however, are not enough to produce these emotional displays; individuals must make themselves believe they are reliving that particular experience. The emotion is genuine, but its origin is somewhere other than the employee's immediate context.

Surface acting deals more with the external state of emotion; it is the public display of emotions. The expression of surface acting according to Hochschild (1983) "is in the body language" (p. 35). The appropriate emotions are displayed for others to see, but they are not actually felt by the individual. The employee's display is a mask deemed appropriate by the employee's organization, but it has no reflection on the employee's current emotional state. For example, an angry employee can reduce her appearance of anger while leaving her internal state of anger in tact. She appears calm and in control of the situation, but internally she is still angry.

In addition to these internal and external states, emotion regulation also involves the amplification and suppression of emotion. According to Cote (2005), *amplification* involves initiating or enhancing public displays of emotion, whereas *suppression* consists of reducing or eliminating public displays of emotion. For example, a sales clerk may need to intensify his support of a product and a life insurance agent may need to reduce her excitement on a given day. Regulation does not involve the complete suppression or intensification of a particular emotion, just an enhancement so that the emotion matches organizational expectations.

The organizational expectation usually involves a degree of emotional professionalism. Interestingly, Cote's (2005) research found that most individuals relied on the terms *professional* or *unprofessional* "to define appropriate and inappropriate control of emotions without providing specific explanation" (p. 75). This is a great example of practical consciousness from Gidden's *Theory of Structuration* discussed in Chapter 6 (i.e., activities or emotions that employees are able to engage in but not necessarily explain). Many aspects of the socialization process involve learning what is appropriate or inappropriate by observing others and experiencing positive or negative consequences resulting from particular behaviors. In other words, employees learn what is considered professional but may not necessarily be able to explain what or why emotional professionalism is beyond the display of appropriate emotions.

The learning of emotional professionalism or regulation is an important aspect of organizational socialization. Research has indicated that organizational emotional display expectations have implications for employee selection, socialization processes, employee rewards and punishments, and organizational culture (Kramer & Hess, 2002). Emotional regulation, though, can have adverse affects on the employee. According to research by Ashforth and Humphrey (1993), Grandey and Brauburger (2002), and Pugh (2002), emotion regulation is an important predicator of strain. Strain represents a variety of emotional, physical, and behavioral states, including anxiety, low commitment, elevated heart rate, and absenteeism (Cote, 2005). One source of strain stems from emotional dissonance.

Emotional dissonance is when conflict exists between the emotions an individual genuinely feels and those required to be displayed within the organization. Strain increases when the job's display rules or emotional regulation expectations significantly differ from the employee's felt feelings. For example, a hospice worker may experience emotional dissonance when she is trying to display emotional neutrality when one of her favorite patients is dying. Another example of emotional dissonance would be an incredibly outgoing and enthusiastic individual who must continually suppress those emotions in favor of being somber and serious while attempting to collect overdue bills for a collection action. The greater the amount of dissonance felt, as well as the more time spent displaying the inconsistent feelings, the greater the overall strain felt by the employee will be.

Emotional dissonance is generally only felt by employees engaged in surface acting. In deep acting, the feeling displayed is consistent with the feeling felt, although the emotion is being drawn for another experience or context. In surface acting, however, the emotional display is potentially inconsistent with the employee's internal state. Brotheridge and Grandey (2002) found that the more an employee must engage in surface acting, the higher the possibility of work-related strain. Self-reports of emotional dissonance are related to burnout, anxiety, depression, and job dissatisfaction (Cote, 2005).

Emotional Labor

The U.S. economy is becoming increasingly service based; most U.S. employees work to provide services rather than products or goods (Meyer & DeTore, 1999). Increased interaction with clients and the public results in an increased need for organizations to prescribe appropriate emotional responses in employee–client interactions. The process of managing one's emotions in the organizational setting is known as *emotional labor*. Unlike emotion regulation, emotional labor deals with the emotional management of the client's emotions, not the employee's, although the employee's emotions are used to elicit the desired client response.

At its core, emotional labor is the management of one's emotions in order to induce a desired reaction in another individual. Hochschild (1983) developed this concept after investigating the ways in which flight attendants and bill collectors managed their own emotions in order to manage the emotions of their particular public associates. Flight attendants were expected by the airlines to create a warm and inviting environment for their customers, while bill collectors attempted to be assertive and create fear in the individuals with whom they were dealing. Emotional labor, then, involves managing not only one's own feelings, but the emotions of others to create an organizationally deemed appropriate response from both the employee and the client. This activity becomes known as emotional labor when it is done for a wage in the public sphere and is reactive to the interactional environment.

Scott and Myers (2005) conducted research on emotion management and emotional labor at a fire station. This research indicated a strong link between the emergency response worker's emotional displays and the emotions displayed by the clients. The very nature of emergency-response work dictates that employees will be dealing with clients experiencing distress, tragedy, and incredibly high levels of stress: "Firefighters are keenly aware that their customers could judge the gravity of a situation based on emergency workers' emotion displays" (p. 76).

As demonstrated in Scott and Myers' (2005) research, emotional labor can be an intense process. Hochschild (1983) identified three positions that employees can take toward their work and the potential consequences of each: overidentification, separation with guilt, and estrangement. The first stance that an employee can have toward work involving emotional labor is that she may *overidentify* with the work that she is doing. This type of worker does not see her work as acting, and she has little sense of "false-self" (Hochschild, 1983, p. 187). Without this distinction, the worker is unable to distinguish between personalized interactions and everyday routine work encounters. Overidentification can lead to high levels of stress and increased risk of burnout.

Some workers will try to compensate for overidentification by separating themselves from the work that they are doing. Although these workers may be less likely to burn out, they often feel guilty over the gap between their ideal feelings and their displayed feelings. Many report "feeling phony because at a given moment they feel that they should not be acting at all or that they are not acting well enough" (Hochschild, 1983, p. 188). The separation of self from an occupational role may reduce burnout likelihood, but the guilt associated with this type of separation often leads to increased stress levels.

Finally, workers can compensate for the costs of emotional labor by *estranging* themselves from all levels of acting. Burnout and job-related stress are minimized, but the employee does risk losing a job, because the job itself calls for some form of acting. If overidentification means that the employees are too much a part of the job, these workers are too little a part of the job. Therefore, the goal for employees cannot be to totally mask feelings, but to find a balance that meets their own needs as well as organizational needs. This is particularly true in the previously described research on emergency response workers.

By this point, you may be overwhelmed by the prospect of burnout, job stress, and the other negative factors associated with emotional labor given the prevalence of service-oriented jobs in the United States. Morris and Feldman (1996) conceptualized emotional labor in terms beyond emotional management. These dimensions include frequency of appropriate emotional display, attentiveness to required display rules, variety of emotions required to be displayed, and emotional dissonance. The first dimension, *frequency of appropriate emotional display*, simply refers to the number of interactions and emotional displays between service providers and their clients. The second dimension, *attentiveness to required display rules*, refers to the intensity or attention that the display rules require of the employee. For example, brief emotional interactions are more likely to be scripted (e.g., please, thank you, a smile) and require less emotional intensity than more extended interactions (e.g., helping a client make burial arrangements).

The third dimension of emotional labor is the *variety of emotion required to be expressed*. Morris and Feldman (1996) argue that the greater the variety of emotions to be displayed, the more emotional labor that is involved for the employee. For example, some jobs require that the employee constantly switch between "positive emotions to build enthusiasm, negative emotions to support discipline, and neutrality of emotions to demonstrate fairness and professionalism" (p. 991). A job requiring such emotional variety requires more planning, skill, and, at times, more intensity.

The final dimension, *emotional dissonance*, has already been discussed. The more conflict an employee feels between her felt and displayed feelings, the more intense the emotional labor process is going to be for her. These dimensions demonstrate that not all service-intensive jobs are going to be emotionally problematic for their employees; instead, a number of factors must be considered when determining the effects of emotional labor on an employee.

Research has indicated that emotional labor can be harmful for employees. Hochschild (1983) argued that emotional labor can lead to *emotional alienation* or an "estrangement between what a person senses as her true self and her inner and outer acting" (p. 136). Van Maanen and Kunda (1989) also argued that emotional labor increases physical illness, burnout, and emotional numbness. Noe's (1995) research on emergency medical technicians expanded this argument by concluding that emotional labor can also cause problems in an employee's personal relationships outside of work. Other negative consequences that have been associated with emotional labor include burnout (Wharton, 1999) and depression, cynicism, and role alienation (Ashforth & Humphrey, 1993; Fineman, 1993).

Although many examples exist that demonstrate the negative effects of emotional labor, several researchers have argued that emotional labor can actually enhance the work experience. Conrad and Witte (1994) argued that there are possible health benefits to displaying positive emotions at work, even when those emotions are not genuine. Others have argued that the emotional labor has a performative nature and can be enjoyable, as can be the experience of positively influencing a client's emotional state during the interaction. Shuler and Sypher (2000) conducted research on 9-1-1 operators and found that although emotional labor is trying, employees often find ways to positively manage the emotional labor, such as through humor or storytelling. In fact, some individuals may even be drawn to jobs that require emotional challenges because they enjoy the thrill of the challenge.

Finally, it is important to realize that the socialization process plays an important role in the ways that employees perceive and respond to emotional labor demands. The selection process has been identified in research as the "primary mechanism [for] ensuring that members would be able [to] adequately enact preferred emotion management strategies" (Scott & Myers, 2005, p. 77). Job candidates are often subjected to personality and psychological tests in addition to formal and informal job interviews. Scenarios are often presented during job interviews to gauge how the employee might respond to a given situation. The socialization process continues after an employee is hired through both formal and informal interactions. Employees will often be subjected to repeated exposure to emotionally intense stimuli (i.e., bank tellers may watch films re-creating robberies and then be expected to respond to them; flight attendants will practice emergency evacuation procedures) to condition them to the organizationally deemed appropriate response. Numerous organizations will use simulations and role-playing activities to socialize employees on the appropriate emotional displays to a variety of employee–client interactions.

One major contributor to an organizational member's emotional state at any given moment is the extent to which there is a conflict or balance between the demands of the workplace and the demands of home. In the final section of this chapter, we discuss the interconnections between work and family.

The Challenges of Work and Family

Thus far, you have learned that the socialization process begins prior to the employment interview and continues throughout an employee's career. It includes learning everything about the organization—from its culture to the appropriate emotional displays expected in a given occupation. The last area of this process that we ask you to consider is work-family balance. Workforce participation by women, including mothers, has continued to grow over the last several decades. According to the U.S. Department of Labor, the 2005 employment rate of mothers with children under one year of age is 53.8 percent. "Dual-career families" and "dual-career couples" are hot topics in academic journals, popular press newspapers, and HR offices around the United States. This prevalence, though, does not mean that the phenomenon of balancing work and family is without conflict.

In her 1989 book *The Second Shift*, Arlie Hochschild offered the term *second shift* to describe the experiences of many working women. Hochschild described a condition in which women work full time outside of the home and then return home to start their second shift, which includes the responsibilities for their home and families. This focus on the often inequitable division of domestic labor between spouses led to research on the *glass ceiling* and the *mommy track*. Both terms describe the difficulties that women have had in climbing the corporate ladder because they either need to take time off to take care of their children or because they are viewed as less serious workers who will at some time need to take time away from work to have and care for children.

According to the Bureau of Health Professions (2004), women enter careers such as nursing at a higher rate than men. Although nursing is viewed as a family-friendly occupation for women, studies have indicated that nurses who are mothers advance through the ranks much more slowly than women who do not have children (Davies & Rossner, 1986; Lane, 2000). Career advancement is often based upon the ability to work long hours and hold an uninterrupted work history. Not being able to take late shifts or work overtime because of family obligations negatively impacts an individual's career advancement.

Additionally, the second shift may take more of a toll on individuals in particular occupations. Occupations that require caregiving, such as daycare, nursing, social work, and elementary education, demand that individuals provide an intense form of caregiving that often mimics the type of care that they also must provide to their spouses and children (Bullock & Morales Waugh, 2004). Stress may come from the need to provide highly intensive care at both work and home.

In interviews with in-home daycare providers conducted by one of the authors, providers often referenced the stress associated with meeting their own family's needs after an 8- to 10-hour day of caring for others' children. One provider commented that she simply could not handle having additional people in the home when she was not working, the implication being that she did not permit her children to have friends over to play. Another daycare provider felt that she was unable to really enjoy the time she had with her spouse and children in the evening because she was emotionally drained and often felt unable to provide the emotional and physical care that her husband and children needed. She stated that while she always served home-cooked meals to her daycare children, her family often ate frozen or fast food. This fact bothered her and was indicative of her struggle to balance work and family needs.

More recent organizational communication research has focused on workplace accommodations for working parents. These accommodations include on-site dependant care, alternative workplaces, and flexible scheduling. These policies, though, have not eliminated the struggle that working parents feel when attempting to balance work and family. Sandberg (1999) found that gender still plays a significant role in determining who will utilize family leave policies, with women more likely than men to take family leave (Kim, 1998). Because men are often viewed more negatively than women for taking advantage of alternative work arrangements and family leave (Allen & Russell, 1999), these accommodations are underutilized by men, single workers, and career-oriented mothers (Baily, Fletcher, & Kolb, 1997). Consequently, although the policies do exist in many organizations, working parents are still conflicted as to how to balance their work and family lives in such a way that meets the needs of both their employees and their own families (Kirby, Golden, Medved, Jorgenson, & Buzzanell, 2003).

As with other socialization processes, much learning comes from watching coworkers and how they respond to a variety of situations. As Kirby and Krone (2000) found, coworkers exert a great deal of influence over whether an individual chooses to utilize a particular family policy. Individuals will often choose to ignore an existing policy because they fear how their coworkers or supervisors will perceive them if they utilize it. Consequently, the existence of such policies may do little to alleviate the work-family balance for a significant number of individuals.

However, not all research focuses on the negative or conflictual nature of work-family balance. In 2006, Greenhaus and Powell argued that this balance can positively impact individuals in a number of ways. First, the balance of roles may be beneficial for an individual's mental and physical health. Research has indicated that participating in a variety of roles can contribute to a person's happiness, satisfaction, and perceived quality of life (e.g., Rice, Frone, & McFarlin, 1992). Rather than becoming consumed by work or family issues, an individual participating in multiple roles has the opportunity to switch between roles that contribute to their sense of well-being in different ways. Second, individuals who participate in both work and family roles are buffered from distress in one particular role. For example, an individual without a family to focus on who has had a particularly negative day at work might go home and continue to focus on that negative experience, whereas an individual with a family at home is able to go home and be distracted by positive interactions with a spouse and/or children. The reverse may be true as well. Work can afford spouses or parents with an opportunity to solve problems and interact on a professional level in ways that they are unable to with their family members.

Finally, "experiences in one role can produce positive experiences and out-comes in the other role" (Greenhaus & Powell, 2005, p. 73). Participation in one role can help an individual become more successful in another role. An employee may learn interactional skills at work that improve family interactions as well, or vice versa. A parent may learn patience that can, in turn, translate into patience with coworkers or employees. An employee may learn organizational skills that may contribute to her becoming a more organized, less stressed parent of teenagers with hectic social calendars.

Summary

The socialization process in organizations is critical to maintaining a dedicated and loyal workforce. How seriously the organization takes its obligation to socialize new members may determine the degree of turnover, and ultimately, productivity. The individual member must decide how important the organizational mission is to his contentment and enthusiasm for working in that environment.

The assimilation process combines the interrelated concerns of the socializa-tion goals of the organization and the individualization goals of the worker. Throughout this process, which begins before the worker joins the organization and continues to the end of employment, the organization adapts to the new worker and the new worker adapts to the job and cultural demands of the new organization.

As the worker confronts the reality of his new organization, he will learn the expectations of the organization regarding a whole host of things, including how he should, or should not, express emotion. He will also find that his work life will be influenced by his family or home life, and vice versa. All of these realities pose challenges that may motivate some employees, but paralyze others. Organiza-tions and individuals need to work together to balance the needs of the individ-ual and the needs of the organization in a way that is productive and healthy for both parties. The success of this enterprise is closely tied to the energy and effec-tiveness of the assimilation process.

CHAPTER

9 Conflict in the Organization

Organizational conflict can take the form of mild tensions between coworkers or involve persistent warlike behavior, as exhibited in the following two stories.

> The New Jersey governor and general assembly had one task before them: balancing a $31 billion state budget. Without a budget, no state monies could be spent, and Governor Jon Corzine threatened to shut down the state government. Such threats had been made in the past, but on July 1, 2006, the threat became a reality. The shutdown closed state-operated beaches, parks, and casinos. In addition, road crews were idle, and state offices and all state court proceedings, with the exception of emergencies, were closed. According to the *New York Times* (July 8, 2006), 100,000 workers, including 45,000 state employees, were out of work without pay. The New Jersey State Casino Industry lost approximately $16 to $20 million dollars a day in revenues, causing the state to lose $1.2 million dollars a day from lack of casino tax revenues. Additionally, according to the *New York Daily News* (July 9, 2006) the state lost around $2 million dollars each day from missed lottery revenues. Although the governor and general assembly eventually reached a mutually acceptable state budget, millions of dollars had already been lost, and hundreds of workers were financially hurt by lost income that they could not make recoup.

This example represents the extreme; however, consider the following story provided by Trischa, a research scientist in the pathology and laboratory medicine division of a major medical clinic, who describes a conflict typical of everyday life in organizations:

> I have a coworker who, I'm guessing, but I think her level of training is probably a level or two below mine. But the biggest issue is that she is Chinese, ethnic, and she was in her position maybe a half a year or so before I was. So, I was the newcomer, per se, and in her eyes she saw that as a hierarchical thing. She thought she could run the show even through her level of training and knowledge was a couple of steps below what I have.

> Early on I didn't feel that we were utilizing the small space that we had very well, and I suggested some changes that she was not open to at all. So from those minor little things it continued to escalate. We'd be given projects. We collaborate with an outside company. The outside company sends us materials that we need to do testing on, and rather than taking a team approach to it she wants to segregate; she wanted to have her own projects that only she worked on. She kind of adhered to this individual approach to everything from the very start.
>
> I have had it. In encounters with her where I try to address an issue or a problem or just have an open dialogue she would really just fly off the handle. She would get really outraged, talking in an elevated tone of voice and just keep circling around saying two or three sentences over and over again. I sat one day for 45 minutes and listened to the same thing over and over just to see how long it would take before she would stop. I've gone from really liking what I do to, "okay, I can get by." It's knocked down a notch.

These examples illustrate how conflict can erupt and disrupt the work environment. The conflict between the governor and the general assembly that led to the New Jersey government shutdown had catastrophic effects on the state's economy and workforce. Trischa described a situation that is more like those that most of us will face in our everyday work lives. In this case, differences between coworkers led to diminished satisfaction levels and performance for both. Although this particular conflict did not affect thousands of lives and millions of dollars, the participants involved certainly had their lives affected.

Just as in our personal relationships, workplace conflict can make employees miserable and less productive or it can be the impetus for creative change. When one is enmeshed in a conflict, the possibility of creative change may seem far-fetched, and, indeed, it sometimes can be impossible. However, with energy, anticipation, and communication, new ways of thinking, acting, believing, or feeling can emerge. Knowing which conflicts have this potential is an important part of organizational life.

Conflict can permeate our lives; our understanding of it is critical to our success as communicators and organizational members. Our communication skills will make the difference between success and failure at work relationships and personal relationships. According to Putnam and Poole (1987):

> Communication constitutes the essence of conflict in that it undergirds the formation of opposing issues, frames perceptions of the felt conflict, translates emotions and perceptions into conflict behaviors, and sets the stage for future conflicts. (p. 552)

In this chapter, we offer a brief overview of the literature relating to conflict and organizational life. We begin by offering several definitions of conflict and describe how conflict can start and then we discuss the negative and positive consequences associated with it. Next we outline several models of conflict styles. We conclude the chapter by reviewing the organizational responses to conflict and the individual skills and organizational strategies associated with conflict processes. The research and theory on conflict is vast and broad; our intention here is to provide a useful introduction to the topic.

Defining Conflict

Conflict is the "competition between interdependent parties who perceive that they have incompatible needs, goals, desires, or ideas" (Van Slyke, 1999, p. 5). "Interdependent parties" are two people who have some connection to each other and depend on each other in some way to accomplish tasks. If the parties were completely independent, with no connection to each other, there would be no impetus for conflict to develop. When two people work together, one might have a stronger need to finish a task on time than the other or one person's goal might be to use the task to establish ties to another project, whereas the other person only wants to complete the immediate task. These different goals can eventually pit the two people against each other. Putnam and Poole (1987) have defined conflict as "the interaction of interdependent people who perceive opposition of goals, aims, and values, and who see the other party as potentially interfering with the realization of these goals" (p. 552).

Interaction is central to these definitions. Social interaction is the way conflict is identified and framed. Until individuals discuss the issues in the conflict, it remains a conflict only in a person's mind. In conflict, individuals know that they oppose each other and have different goals. This situation is different from misunderstandings, which of course can lead to conflict. Misunderstandings occur when there are differences or uncertainty or ambiguity about values, goals, or courses of action. Instances in which people who are communicating do not share meaning would be misunderstandings. Conflict is when they are in direct opposition to each other.

Conflict, similar to an interaction, can be viewed as an emergent process (Felstiner, Abel, & Sarat, 1980–1981). Conflict, in this emergent view, is *subjective* because it is interpreted and evaluated by individuals who may not show their feelings about the conflict in their behaviors. It is *unstable* because continued interactions will influence and change an individual's reaction to the perceived conflict. It is *reactive* because individuals will continue to respond to these new interactional developments. Finally, given the unstable and reactive nature of conflict, parties may and will avoid closure because new claims continue to surface (Kusztal, 2002).

Conflict may be either substantive or affective. *Substantive conflict* occurs when organizational members disagree on a task or content issues. *Affective conflict* deals with inconsistencies within interpersonal relationships. This form of conflict occurs when organizational members realize that their feelings and emotions regarding one or more issues are incompatible (Rahim, 2001). For example, if Joe and Bobby are working on a project together, substantive conflict occurs if they cannot agree on the order in which they should complete tasks. Affective conflict occurs if they have differing ethical standards upon which each wants to proceed to complete the task.

Within an organization, three types of conflict can occur: interpersonal, intragroup, and intergroup (Rahim, 2001). *Interpersonal conflict* refers to conflict that occurs between two or more people that may or may not have to do with organizational tasks or task-related feelings. Interpersonal conflict is similar to conflict that would occur in relationships outside of the organization. *Intragroup conflict*, sometimes referred to as *intradepartmental conflict*, occurs among members of a group, often between subgroups that have interdependence in terms of goals, tasks, and procedures. This type of conflict can occur when individuals within a group disagree on how best to solve a problem or approach a task and the group divides into sides because of this disagreement. *Intergroup conflict*, or *interdepartmental conflict*, occurs when two or more units or groups within an organization disagree over a specific task, behavior, or procedure. A well-known example of intergroup conflict is conflict that occurs between labor and management.

Just as we expect misunderstandings to occur, we should also expect conflict to be a part of our work and private lives. The communicative organization (CO) model presented in Chapter 6 starts with the premise that we should anticipate misunderstandings and expect that they will occur. Similarly, we should expect that conflict will occur and anticipate it.

How Does Conflict Start?

Certain behaviors or events can initiate a conflict, and there are environmental conditions or contexts in which conflict can occur. We shall identify those events and contexts so we can anticipate when conflict will likely erupt.

Peterson (1983) has delineated four events that are thought to precipitate interpersonal conflict: rebuffs, illegitimate demands, criticisms, and cumulative annoyances. A *rebuff* occurs when one person appeals to the other for a desired reaction and the other fails to respond as expected. An *illegitimate demand* is a request made by one person that is perceived by the other as being unjust or outside the normal range of requests. *Criticisms* are verbal or nonverbal acts performed by one person that are perceived by the other as unfavorable or demeaning. *Cumulative annoyances* occur when sheer repetition of instances of some activity performed by one person crosses a threshold of tolerance and becomes unacceptable to the other person. These initial behaviors may lead to conflict.

Jim Williams, a member of the human resources department of a large manufacturing company, provided us with an excellent example of what Peterson referred to as "criticism."

> I had a message on my voice mail from an employee at one of our facilities. This facility is well known to me, since I have done at least nine harassment or discrimination investigations over the past several years there. The employee didn't leave any substantive reason for his call, so I asked the operations manager for input.

> The operations manager explained the following: The employee was reprimanded for causing a slip zone on the shop floor. The employee was warned that causing safety hazards would result in discipline in the future. The unsafe condition was brought to management's attention by another employee (who happened to be feuding with the employee that called me). The feud with this other employee was worsening, and the supervisor was having difficulty managing that coworker relationship.
>
> When I finally talked to the employee, I was expecting a very lengthy call. Employees come to HR when they have a lot to unload. The employee, however, said four words that seemed to address his main issue: "He yelled at me." The employee was talking about our operations manager (who later confessed that he did yell at the employee). The employee also mentioned that the operations manager didn't listen and didn't respect the workers. However, the overriding theme was, "He yelled at me."
>
> I asked the employee what resolution he thought was appropriate. Instead of saying, "I want to file a complaint" (words I'm all too familiar with from that plant), instead of threatening to file an unfair-labor-practice charge, instead of asking me to visit and resolve, instead of pointing the finger at his coworker, he said: "Just talk to the operations manager and tell him I don't like to be yelled at."

This is a perfect example of how a verbal act accompanied by a demeaning non-verbal tone can escalate a conflict. The conclusion of the story also shows how communication can help alleviate conflict. However, as will be described later, more talk does not always decrease conflict.

Several factors contribute to the likelihood that conflict will occur (Rahim, 2001). First, the likelihood of conflict increases when individuals are required to engage in a behavior that is inconsistent with their needs or interests. Conflicts regarding overtime or not being granted leave for family events are examples of this factor. Second, the likelihood of conflict increases when individuals are forced to compete for scarce resources that they either desire personally or need in order to successfully do their job. One example of this would be a preferred customer list in a telemarketing firm; conflict could occur when one individual or group of individuals has access to such a list while another individual or group of individuals is forced to rely on randomly generated lists of potential customers. Third, organizational conflict is more likely when an individual possesses attitudes, values, skills, or goals that are exclusive of another party's. One example might be a manager who holds racially or sexually discriminatory attitudes toward other organizational members. Finally, the likelihood of organizational conflict is increased when parties who are interdependent have at least partially exclusive behavioral preferences regarding joint activities. If one sales agent likes to conduct business over dinner and drinks in the evening whereas another sales agent likes to maintain traditional working hours and does not believe in the use of alcohol, the potential for conflict based on behavioral preferences greatly increases, particularly if the two agents are teamed together.

We can also examine the different relational contexts from which conflict is likely to occur. Whitteman (1992) identified five contexts that favor the development of conflict. First is *frequency of occurrence*, which is the degree to which a person experiencing a conflict perceives it to be repetitive. Some conflicts never seem to be resolved and are always present in a relationship. Second, *goal mutuality* is the degree to which one person perceives that the other person wants, or is willing to let, the first person achieve her goals, which can be in sharp contrast to those of the second person. Third, *goal-path uncertainty* is realizing the level of doubt or uncertainty regarding how to resolve the problem. Uncertainty is often the most difficult context with which to cope. The fourth context is *attribution of cause*, which is the degree to which one perceives the other person as the source of a conflict. The final context is *negative feelings* that one person has about the other. Any one of these contexts can lead to negative consequences.

One last context that favors conflict development is an organizational structure in which ambiguity is high. For example, Warters (2000) researched conflict that occurred in university settings. The researcher found that conflict was high "although universities often carry an overarching mission . . . each unit may have its own definition of these missions and sense of priority these missions should receive" (p. 162). These differing definitions of missions and priorities create ambiguity for organizational members. Ambiguity, when used appropriately, can lead to creativity; alternatively, it can cause stress and conflict. Another context in which ambiguity may be high is organizational merger or acquisition. Ambiguity and the resultant conflict revolve around financial matters, organizational resources, changing power and authority, cultural changes, and emotional reactions to the merger or acquisition (Cohen, Virkin, Cohen, Garfield, & Webb, 2006).

As you anticipate future interactions with coworkers and friends or family members, think about the events and conditions that are likely to create conflict. Are you likely to be rebuffing someone, making an illegitimate demand, or providing criticisms? Is this interaction likely to be repetitive of previous interactions where conflict occurred? Do you and the other individuals have mutually exclusive goals? Are you uncertain about the path you will take to your goal? Will the other person attribute the cause of the conflict to you? As you examine an upcoming interaction, try to anticipate conflict and take steps to diminish its negative impact.

Consequences of Conflict

Conflict, as noted, can have either negative or positive consequences for the individual and the organization.

Negative Consequences of Conflict

Much research has been done on the negative consequences of conflict. When group members have interpersonal problems and are angry with one another, they work less effectively, produce suboptimal products, and cognitive functioning is inhibited (Jehn, 1995). Resolving interpersonal conflict takes time and psychological energy. Much of the group's efforts are focused on resolving the conflict, thereby limiting productivity. Think about the last time you were in conflict with someone. You probably worried about how to resolve it. Your concentration on anything else was diminished. In a work team, the tension between two or more members spreads to the entire group.

Even when a group thinks it has reached agreement on resolving conflicts, it can be betrayed. One group with which the authors worked was directed by an administrator and two assistants who wanted to rebuild trust among the group members. Over the years, the finances of the group had come into question, and the administrators wanted to disclose fully the budget decision-making process and invite members' input. After a lengthy meeting in which the entire budget was explained and comments were invited, the group agreed on some guidelines that would not only balance the budget, but also allow for an enrichment program for new projects. Three days after this discussion, the three administrators announced budget cuts that did not follow the guidelines to which they had agreed. This decision was never a part of the budget discussion; consequently, mistrust and anger on the part of the members quickly replaced a sense of accomplishment that the previous budget discussion had established.

The results of these actions may have a long-term effect on the group. Members will refer to this event in future years as an example of how particular individuals cannot be trusted. Trust can be lost quickly, and it can take years to gain it back: "In some organizations, disputes may have a long history, decisions and actions in the present being shaped by conflicts, grudges, or differences that others believe are long forgotten or settled" (Morgan, 1997, p. 170).

Recall that we previously stated that organizational conflict can be either substantive (task) or affective (relational). Affective conflict has the greater potential for causing negative consequences. Because this conflict is based in relational matters, it has the potential to leave organizational members with negative feelings, leaving them irritable, suspicious, or resentful (Jehn, 1997). Group members are less likely to compromise on affective matters, thus hindering group performance and limiting the information-processing abilities and the cognitive functioning of the group (Amason, 1996; Baron, 1997; Jehn, 1995; Wall & Nolan, 1986). Affective conflict can also negatively influence group loyalty and job satisfaction while increasing individual and organizational stress and anxiety.

When you enter a new organization, typically you have no knowledge of the history of prior disputes, and therefore you should be careful not to fall into a dispute by accident. You do not want to step unknowingly on a land mine. Therefore, as a newcomer, you should avoid taking a position until you know more of the facts and information. Becoming involved in a conflict early in your career can affect other people's perceptions of you for your entire time in that organization. As much as individuals dislike conflict, there are some surprising positive consequences of conflict. If you find yourself enmeshed in a conflict, the best alternative is to attempt to turn it into a positive outcome.

Positive Consequences of Conflict

Despite the obvious negative consequences of conflict, there are many positive outcomes as well. Whereas affective conflict often results in negative consequences, substantive conflict can yield positive outcomes. Groups, as well as individuals, who experience conflict are able to make better decisions (Amason, 1996; Fiol, 1994; Putnam, 1994; Schweiger, Sandberg, & Ragan, 1986). Conflict over tasks can help people identify and better understand the issues involved (Putnam, 1992). Opposing points of view, when expressed, can actually clarify issues and uncover problems that have been less obvious or unknown. Critiquing solutions helps a group avoid groupthink. *Groupthink* occurs when a group does not allow opposing viewpoints to be expressed and believes that its decisions are invincible or not subject to criticism. Open discussions of opposing views about the task can be associated with completing tasks and using resources more effectively (Tjosvold, Darr, & Wong, 1992). One group in conflict over a work schedule discovered additional criteria to be used in developing the schedule only after making the conflicting issues more obvious. Discussions aroused by conflict can lead to creative solutions.

Conflict can improve decision making by encouraging individuals to use creative problem solving. Conflict, and the resulting creative process, can help keep the work environment lively and interesting. Constructive conflict can stimulate thinking about otherwise mundane tasks or behaviors. At the same time, conflict can cause marginal employees who are not willing to be team oriented or use creative problem solving and task resolution to decide to leave the organization, thus increasing the group's cohesiveness and effectiveness (Shell, 2003). This can also promote healthy change for individuals as well as organizational growth (Darling & Brownlee, 1984). Part of this change and growth may come from management taking a critical look at the organization and its members and making strategic changes (Shell, 2003). All of this combined can serve as a motivational force for all levels of organizational members.

In Chapter 6, we developed the communicative organization model where an organization expects and anticipates misunderstandings and conflict in order to use those problems to the advantage, rather than the detriment, of the organization and the individuals involved. In this model, the advantage of conflict and its ability to move a group forward is fully explored. To be better prepared to move conflict to a positive discussion, it is necessary to understand the different conflict styles that organizational members may enact.

Individual Conflict Styles

No one conflict style fits every situation in the organization. Individuals involved in conflicts need to be flexible in their approach to resolution. If you, as a student, were to resolve your conflict with a professor the same way you would with a roommate, it is possible your success ratio would be quite different given the power differences involved. According to Putnam and Poole (1987), the effectiveness of a particular strategy

> hinges on the disputants' abilities to adapt to the situation, their fairness and objectivity in approaching the conflict, and the way in which they communicate the strategy. Successful use of a particular strategy also hinges on mutual awareness of the conflict, open-minded attitudes, willingness to ignore power issues, and existence of problem-solving procedures. (p. 561)

Blake and Mouton (1978) developed a managerial grid (see Chapter 3) that has influenced the way researchers have characterized conflict styles of superiors and subordinates. The five basic conflict styles generated by this grid are (1) *withdrawing* (also called *avoiding*); (2) *smoothing* (also called *accommodating*); (3) *forcing* (also called *dominating and competing*); (4) *confronting* (also called *collaborating, problem solving, and integrating*); and (5) *compromising*.

In early literature, the focus was on how managers should use these styles to generate various outcomes. Depending on the ethical climate of the organization, some of these conflict styles may be more or less acceptable; that is, they would meet organizational expectations of proper conduct. For example, one researcher (Vardi, 2001) identified an ethical climate of rules and regulations. Such a climate "reflects the importance of following rules and procedure, the strict obedience to rules, and the suggestion that successful people go by the book" (p. 334). If there is a formal procedure for resolving complaints or disputes, many of the interpersonal approaches to conflict may be seen as inappropriate in an organization that goes strictly by the rules.

Some individuals withdraw from or avoid conflict at all costs. They dislike arguments and would tend to ignore conflict for as long as possible. Someone with a *smoothing* or *accommodating* style will usually give in to another's demands, because he does not want to hurt anyone's feelings. That person may resent the outcome personally but superficially appear to be going along with the other's demands. A *forcing* style is often characteristic of a bully, or a person who wants to get his way no matter what happens to others. Most people have worked with someone like this; the bully fails to see that meeting others' needs can actually help him accomplish his own objectives faster and more effectively. *Compromising and confronting* are styles that lead to problem solving. Although both attempt to recognize the needs of both sides in the conflict, the difference resides in where each style begins the discussion. With compromise, the starting point is with the question, "What do you want to do about this problem?" With confrontation, the initial question is, "What is the problem we need to address?" This question is followed by, "What are the criteria that we should use in judging proposed solutions?" Only after addressing those questions do you turn to "What would you like to see accomplished?"

Another conflict style classification system was advanced by Ann Nicotera (1994); she used people's detailed descriptions of how they handle conflict as the basis for her model. The model (an adaptation of one developed by Ross &

DeWine, 1988) includes the following styles: *evasive* (avoiding the conflict and not disrupting the relationship), *estranged* (also avoids the conflict but manages to disrupt the relationship), *accommodating* (considers other's view over one's own view but without resentment), *patronizing* (considers other's view over own view but maintains a grudge for giving up own view), *assertive* (focuses on own view over the other's view but without anger), *aggressive* (focuses on own view in a hostile or threatening manner), *consolidating* (gives equal consideration to both views in a nondisruptive way), and *begrudging* (considers both views but in a disruptive manner). One might use a variety of these styles, depending on conditions of the conflict. For example, avoiding a conflict might be best when emotions are high and individuals need time to cool off. Or there might be occasions when one starts out the conflict in an assertive mode, but when no response comes from the other party, quickly moves to an aggressive style.

Another way of thinking about the conflict management styles is through the use of distributive and integrative dimensions:

> Distributive conflict resolution promotes winning through the use of negative behaviors and disagreement to prevent others from reaching their goals. Integrative behaviors foster cooperation and shared solutions, such as modifying ideas and bargaining for an acceptable compromise. (Franz & Jin, 1995, p. 111).

The distributive dimension includes the conflict management styles of confronting and withdrawing; the integrative dimension includes forcing and smoothing (Walton & McKersie, 1965). These dimensions indicate the communicator's concern for satisfaction of outcome for one's self and for others on a continuum of low to high. In the distributive dimension, forcing represents a high concern for self-satisfaction; smoothing represents a high concern for others. In the integrative dimension, confronting attempts to satisfy both the self and the other by finding creative solutions to the problem presented; withdrawal yields lower satisfaction for both the self and the other by avoiding the problem all together. In other words, the distributive dimension includes those conflict management styles that are concerned with either the self or the other, whereas the integrative dimension includes conflict management styles that attempt to satisfy the concerns of both parties (Rahim, 2001). Compromise is the middle ground between these two dimensions and represents partial satisfaction by both parties of the conflict outcome.

Observations of group interactions have revealed that individuals progress through a period of distributive conflict followed by subsequent integrative activities. Initially, organizational members engage in distributive conflict because that serves their personal needs and goals at the expense of others. In this setting, conflict is defined from a win-lose perspective. In other words, each person wants to win at the expense of others, who must lose. Group members engage in extended debates and persuasive appeals to promote their position.

When group members use integrative behaviors, they reduce their efforts to persuade others to change their ideas. Instead, they search for solutions to problems and provide support for others: "Integrative strategies thus are cooperative and not mutually exclusive . . . the objective is to share values, highlight common objectives, and help achieve consensus" (p. 111).

The transition from distributive to integrative conflict resolution occurs when the need to accomplish a common goal is recognized. Once individuals realize that it will be impossible to achieve the desired goal without resources and abilities beyond their own, the transition can begin to take place. A sense of urgency to get on with the task and complete it triggers the move toward integrative conflict resolution.

Diversity and Gender as Related to Conflict Styles

Diversity in the workplace has had a great impact on the way in which conflict is resolved and handled. Given the rapidly changing demographics of the U.S. workforce and the expanding globalization of U.S. businesses, "this issue is, in fact, a phenomenon of great strategic and operational consequence for both public and private organizations" (Witherspoon & Wohlert, 1996, p. 375).

Diversity in the workplace and different orientations toward conflict can heighten the frequency and intensity of conflict situations. Background and training can have a large impact on people's attitudes toward conflict. Shuter and Turner (1997) found that European American women were less likely to become directly involved in conflict than African American women were. In addition, African American women believed in using direct communication to mitigate conflict, whereas European American women advocated the use of less direct conflict reduction strategies. This general finding no doubt changes based on the other person in the dispute and one's relationship to that person.

An example of how a lack of understanding of cultural differences can result in conflict is the joint venture research team established by IBM in collaboration with companies from Japan and Germany. Problems among the more than 100 scientists from the three countries began early in the project. They were housed in a research facility in Long Island. Individuals wanted to associate only with team members from their own country, thus jeopardizing the project's success. In addition, other conflicts emerged:

> An observer noted that the Japanese disliked the office setup, which consisted of many small offices and few open spaces, and they had difficulty conversing in English. The Germans covered the glass walls of their offices to maintain privacy, thus offending both the Japanese and Americans. The Japanese liked to go out drinking after work, during which time they tended to develop strong group norms. The Americans, however, preferred to go home to their families. Furthermore, the Americans complained that the Germans planned too much and that the Japanese would not make decisions. (Gannon, 2001, p. 108)

It might also be expected that men and women would respond to conflict differently. The Myers-Briggs instrument was used to assess personality types as compared to conflict types. Male respondents were found to be predominantly "thinkers," and female respondents were predominantly "feelers." Psychological type influenced conflict management for only one of the five conflict style preferences. "Feelers" were more likely to choose an obliging style than were "thinkers." Similarly, gender influenced conflict style preferences for only one of five conflict-management choices. Male respondents had a higher "obliging" score than did female respondents (Sorenson, Hawkins, & Sorenson, 1995). This finding suggests that personality has a greater impact on conflict-resolution style than biological sex.

Some researchers have found that in the workplace women must often adopt competing styles of conflict resolution in order to survive, particularly in male-dominated organizations (Burrell, Buzzanell, & McMillan, 1992). Even though they prefer not to use a competing style, women employees tend to perceive conflict situations as "going to war" with others. In such a situation, negotiation skills might be more valuable to an individual who finds herself at a disadvantage by taking the conflict more personally than others.

Next we turn our attention away from conflict styles to the different ways that organizations can respond to conflict.

Organizational Responses to Conflict

As should be obvious by now, conflict in organizational settings is messy. Individual relationships and organizational constraints all come together in the context of a workplace, thus it is inevitable that conflict will occur. This should not be a surprise to those in power positions in organizations, who should be ready with a variety of responses once conflict emerges.

Resolution or Management

The organizational response to conflict is to either resolve or manage it. The difference between the two is not merely word choice (Rahim, 2001). *Conflict resolution* involves reduction, elimination, or termination of conflict. Alternative dispute resolution is usually aimed at conflict resolution. It may include negotiation, bargaining, mediation, or arbitration. If the situation is deemed detrimental or serious enough, resolution may be necessary for both individuals and the organization. Examples of such situations would be *ad hominem* attacks (attacking the person instead of the idea), threatening comments, or discriminatory remarks. Reduction strategies include changing the context of the conflict, altering the issues in the dispute, or removing or relocating one of the individuals involved in the conflict (Shell, 2003).

Sometimes though, as previously discussed, conflict can generate positive outcomes for both individuals and organizations. In such situations, conflict management may be the desirable course of action. *Conflict management* involves implementing strategies to decrease the negative effects of conflict and creating an environment in which conflict can enhance the learning and effectiveness of individuals and the organization (Rahim, 2001). The organizational socialization process may include teaching new members how to deal with conflict constructively and presenting conflict management styles that work best in a variety of situations. For conflict management strategies to be successful, they should satisfy the following three criteria: (1) contribute to organizational learning and long-term effectiveness, (2) satisfy social needs, and (3) fulfill moral and ethical needs of members (Rahim, Garrett, & Buntzman, 1992).

A number of factors influence the outcome of a situation involving conflict as well as the organization's decision to either resolve or manage it. One factor is whether a conflict is substantive or affective (Rahim, 2001). Affective conflict can become intense more quickly, because individuals may feel that they are under attack. For example, a personal attack may occur when two coworkers are both up for promotion. Each believes the other to be less worthy and a source of competition.

A second factor is the size of the conflict. Conflict size can be measured by incompatibility, annoyance, disputes, or disagreements (Rahim, 2001). The extent of the infiltration of a conflict into a person's life will determine how that person responds. For example, if a person has a one-time conflict with a salesperson, the size of the conflict is relatively small. However, a conflict with a team member with whom the person must interact on a daily basis could have long-term effects, and therefore is more important to resolve.

A third factor that influences the outcome of a conflict is the rigidity of the issue. If it is an old conflict that has been debated many times over a long period, the positions each party takes can be quite rigid. To the extent that each party is somewhat flexible, there will be a better chance of resolution. The longer the conflict goes on without resolution, the more rigid it becomes. Therefore, it is usually better to confront a conflict in its early stages rather than hoping it will go away; it usually does not.

The power differences present in the relationship and the history of the relationship itself are other factors that will influence individuals' ability to resolve a conflict. Obviously, a conflict between a boss and a subordinate will be more difficult for the subordinate to negotiate than for the boss. If the history of the relationship has been calm, with infrequent conflict, then the two sides are less likely to move to a conflict stage. However, if the relationship is fragile, with many past conflicts, then the parties will move to conflict much more quickly. The same issue, brought up in the context of different relationships, will have dramatically different outcomes.

Finally, individual personalities, traits, and dispositions influence the outcome of conflict. When many individuals are involved in a conflict, it is difficult to resolve, because each person will come to the conflict with unique personalities and ways of coping with dissent. When the group suggests it is in internal conflict, one that should not go "public," it will depend on the individual members of the group to keep it private. For example, a sorority had an all-day retreat to resolve internal decision-making problems. Internal conflicts were making the members less productive as a group. After eight hours of intense discussion, with the help of a facilitator, everyone present expressed satisfaction with the results. Two days later, a front-page article in the student newspaper detailed the internal struggles the group was having. The writer listed an "unnamed group member" as the source of the information. Although only one member broke the trust of the group by going to the newspaper, accusations were soon being hurled at many of the members of the group. This conflict was influenced by the nature of this group's relationships. The group had established a pattern of behavior, and each person had her own particular style of dealing with conflict. Understanding conflict style will help people adapt to the particular characteristics of a conflict situation.

Alternative Forms of Dispute Resolution

Alternatives are available to the basic forms of conflict management and resolution mentioned previously. Here we turn our attention to specific forms of resolution—bargaining and negotiation—as well as forms that require a third party—mediation and arbitration.

Bargaining and Negotiation. In one sense, bargaining is an example of the compromise style of conflict management. Putnam and Poole (1987) define *bargaining* as "a unique form of conflict management in that participants negotiate mutually shared rules and then cooperate within these rules to gain a competitive advantage over their opponent" (p. 563). This is different from other conflict-management approaches in that there is an exchange of proposals in an attempt to reach a joint settlement. Bargaining and negotiation, from this perspective, are interchangeable and are both aimed at settling disputes over the distribution of scarce resources, contractual relationships, and policy.

Bargaining may take one of two forms: distributive or integrative. In *distributive bargaining*, the goal is to maximize individual gains and minimize losses. Distributive negotiations tend to deal with fixed-sum issues "characterized by mutually exclusive positions and by an inherent conflict of interest between two sides" (Putnam & Poole, 1987, p. 566). Examples of distributive negotiations include those dealing with issues such as wages, work hours, and the distribution of scarce organizational resources. Additional distributive bargaining topics include compromises, trade-offs, and win-lose results. Distributive negotiation and bargaining are characterized by closed communication. Closed communication strategies are less direct than open ones. For example, an individual involved in distributive bargaining is less likely to put all the options on the table immediately that she is willing to accept and is more likely to use obscure responses and guarded nonverbal signals that disguise the range of acceptable solutions.

Integrative negotiating involves maximizing joint gains and is more appropriate for conflicts dealing with variable-sum issues. Examples of *variable-sum issues* include dealing with rights, obligations, overlapping interests, and flexible initial interests (Putnam & Poole, 1987). Integrative bargaining topics would entail those conflicts in which creative solutions could be utilized and would be acceptable to both parties. Integrative bargaining involves using open and direct communication that encourages dialogue and continued problem solving. Parties generally approach the negotiating table with their defenses lowered and a willingness to listen to the other side's proposal.

Examining conflict from a broader organizational view, Calvin Morrill and Cheryl Thomas (1992) identified the dispute process in an organization. Their typologies result in the following organization-wide responses:

- *Aggressiveness* is the degree to which an aggrieved party attempts to achieve a desired outcome at the expense of an opposing party at any stage in a dispute process.
- *Authoritativeness* is the extent to which an aggrieved party attempts to improve an outcome at any stage in a dispute process using the resources his social position affords.
- *Observability* is the likelihood that the stages of a dispute process will be visible to any social audience.

Dennis Mumby and Cynthia Stohl (1996a) described the negotiation process in organizations as a deliberative process in which the participants create knowledge about their situation. They view the goal of negotiation as

> no longer exclusively getting an effective settlement, but also as the redefinition of the problem, a perceptual change in the elements of the problem, and a new appreciation of the socio/historical context of the dispute. From the perspective of organizational communication, communication-as-negotiation has a transformative power that transcends notions of technical and instrumental rationality. (p. 62)

This perspective on negotiation in the organization views the participants as engaged in the process of themselves defining the conflict and its environment. The two themes of rationality and effectiveness help define many aspects of organizational life.

Involving a Third Party: Mediation and Arbitration.   Mediation and arbitration are forms of alternative dispute resolution that involve third parties. Research has indicated that successful managers spend more time mediating conflict than unsuccessful managers (Luthans, Rosenkrantz, & Hennessey, 1985). Mediation involves balancing power between disputing individuals, full participation of the individuals involved in the conflict, flattened lines of communication that allow all voices to be heard, and a democratic decision-making process (Wiseman & Poitras, 2002). The mediator has no decision-making authority but guides the disputing parties through a process of reaching an acceptable outcome for both. Although the mediation process is designed to have a neutral third party, this poses an inherent dilemma for managers. Recognizing the struggle to navigate between hierarchal power distribution and the power balance needed for successful conflict mediation, many organizations are offering or requiring managers to attend mediation workshops and training sessions.

It is important to note that although much research has focused on managerial mediation, mediators can be outside parties to the conflict. In third-party mediation, the mediator seeks to assist the disputants in resolving their conflict but has no decision-making power. Arbitrators, however, often have legal authority to make decisions for conflicting parties when a decision cannot be reached in other ways. Arbitrators make formal binding decisions based on evidence collected during initial negotiating processes (Putnam & Poole, 1987).

We conclude this chapter with a discussion of individual skills and organizational strategies for approaching organizational conflict.

Individual and Organizational Conflict Management and Resolution Strategies

As conflicts emerge, actions and behaviors must be engaged in at both the individual and organizational level. In this section of the chapter, we discuss individual skills that are useful during conflict episodes, as well as organizational strategies for addressing conflict.

Individual-Level Strategies

Van Slyke (1999) identified specific skills that will help an individual resolve organizational conflict. First, the individual must have the ability to establish effective working relationships. At the base of conflict resolution is the ability to build trust and respect. If individuals can manage to separate the issues from the people involved, then they can disagree without attacking each other. The ability to build those kinds of relationships is critical to success.

Next, participants must have cooperative and problem-solution attitudes. They must want to solve the problem. Of course, sometimes a party does not intend to solve a problem by meeting the other side's demands. For example, in a courtroom, an individual's goals usually do not include compromise and solving the other person's problem.

The individual must also be able to manage the group process and group decision making and be knowledgeable about the issues (Van Slyke, 1999). Understanding the communication process that takes place between individuals in dyads or in groups is a critical skill. Knowledge relevant to the issues under discussion is a prerequisite to managing the discussion.

Interpersonal relationships are at the core of our ability to resolve conflict. Morrill and Thomas (1992) discovered the importance of interpersonal relationships when they found that conflicts between employees who were "weakly tied" (meaning they had casual or nonexistent interpersonal relationships and did not care much about each other) were more likely to be sustained at the grievance level or elevated to third-party intervention than conflicts between employees with stronger interpersonal ties. Thus, effective development of interpersonal relationships among coworkers can potentially decrease the severity of grievances filed.

An interesting approach was taken by Patrice Buzzanell and Nancy Burrell (1997), who used metaphors to describe individuals' attitudes toward conflict. They analyzed the use of three metaphors: conflict as war, conflict as impotence, and conflict as a rational process. The *conflict-as-war* metaphor depicted conflict as a battle proceeding at great personal cost. Individuals described themselves and others as adversaries actively engaged in struggles and battles. The focus was on winning the battle. Some of the phrases used by their subjects included the following: "guerrilla warfare," "the One Hundred Years War," "the clash of the Titans," and "fighting cats and dogs."

The *conflict-as-impotence* metaphor was described as a victimizing process in which participants are powerless to alter events. Participants view themselves as lacking control in their interactions with others. Some phrases used by individuals to describe this approach to conflict were "a bear preying on a defenseless infant," "having a tooth pulled," and "running up a steep hill with lead weights in my pockets."

Finally, the *conflict-as-a-rational-process* metaphor presented conflict as a collaborative experience with potentially positive outcomes for all participants. Participants resolve conflict through debate, negotiation, talking, and exploring issues. Phrases used by participants to describe this approach were "an opportunity to deal with issues," "pleasantly negotiating an important business deal," and "the comedy cabaret, we end up laughing most of the time."

Interestingly, Buzzanell and Burrell's participants reported that they used conflict-as-impotence most frequently. Therefore, having skills and knowledge of different approaches to conflict may help one overcome a sense of helplessness in conflict settings.

Organizational-Level Strategies

Organizations can employ several strategies to reduce destructive or negative forms of conflict. Bryne (1993) suggests that organizations organize around process instead of task so that employees know to work through problems and challenges when they encounter them as they accomplish their organizational tasks. Organizations should employ teams whenever possible to avoid groupthink and to utilize maximum group decision-making ability. Consequently, teams should be rewarded for creatively and effectively solving problems and overcoming challenges. All employees, regardless of their place in the hierarchy, should be trained and socialized in constructive conflict processes and be made aware of conflict management styles and their potential uses and misuses.

As discussed elsewhere in the text, conflict levels tend to rise in times of merger and acquisition. To minimize the negative consequences of such activities, Cohen et al. (2006) found that the tone in which the initial merger/acquisition message was made set the stage for future conflict implications. If the process was handled well and information was announced by the organization rather than leaked through informal networks and gossip, affective conflict was reduced. Open and continual communication from the top down appeared to offset much organizational tension and reduce the likelihood for negative conflict. Although this research focused on mergers and acquisitions, common sense dictates that the same would be true for any organizational environment. In addition to open lines of communication, a clear line of authority and responsibility also decreases affective conflict (Shell, 2003).

Summary

In previous chapters, we have discussed talk as structure. Recall that in structuration theory, organizational structure is (re)produced through interactions as agents draw upon rules and resources and make communicative choices. One's attitude toward conflict and how it should be resolved or managed will influence an individual's reaction and behavior in interactions, which will, in turn, influence future interactions. Given the individual's role in creating structure and the unintended consequences that are a part of any interaction, we must anticipate conflict and treat it as a part of our daily personal and organizational lives.

Organizational conflict can be one of the most frustrating and difficult aspects of working in an organization. It is particularly frustrating when the people involved feel they have little or no control over the outcome. It helps to be sensitive to one's own style of interacting and managing conflict situations and pay attention to the style of others. In the communicative organization, conflict is expected and anticipated. It will occur. The only unknown is how the parties will respond to it.

What steps might be taken so that organizational conflict does not make a group dysfunctional? Suggestions for dealing with organizational conflict include the following and are an extension of the communicative organization (CO). First, attempt to step back from the conflict and analyze what part is the content of the conflict and what is based on personal issues. Personal issues need to be set aside while the content is addressed first. This is a part of the planning stage for strategic communication in the CO model. Second, be aware of your own preferred style of conflict resolution. If you tend to avoid conflict, be sensitive to signs that avoidance has allowed the conflict to become more intense. The sooner parties address the conflict, the less likely it will escalate. In the CO model, we suggested that individuals plan, recognize, contain, cope, and construct new approaches to misunderstandings; the same should be done with conflict.

Third, distinguish symptoms from causes. We often waste time trying to resolve symptoms instead of the real underlying cause of the conflict. Symptoms let you know that a conflict is present; causes of conflict are issues underlying the symptoms. Fourth, identify the methods used thus far. We must be aware of our basic coping techniques for handling conflict. What have we already tried to do to resolve the conflict (e.g., ignore the problem and hope it will go away; try to win the argument through persuasion or compromise; give in and let the other person win)? Identify the methods used and the success of each technique. Finally, be sensitive to different approaches and views of conflict based on gender and cultural diversity. People's backgrounds and particular situations may structure their view of the conflict. Everyone will not view the conflict, or its intensity, to the same degree.

In this chapter, you have learned the basic definitions of organizational conflict and how conflict can start. Additionally, you have seen the consequences, both positive and negative, of conflict, and how different individuals have different styles for approaching conflict. As conflict emerges, organizations must respond in a measured and appropriate fashion (bargaining, negotiation, mediation, or arbitration). Importantly, conflict involves individual skills and organizational strategies if the outcomes are to be acceptable and productive for all parties.

CHAPTER
10 Superior–Subordinate Communication

Perhaps no relationship in the workplace is as important as the one between a superior and a subordinate, the supervisor and the worker. The success of both parties, as well as the success of the organization, is dependent upon an effective and efficient relationship between these two people. As important as this relationship is, it is often fraught with problems, particularly misunderstandings.

Differences are inherent in the superior–subordinate relationship; differences based on status, hierarchical level, power, access to resources, age, sex, gender, experience, technical expertise, ethnicity, commitment to the organization, ethical perspectives, and values, and so on. Whatever the basis, supervisors and subordinates readily express a feeling of separation caused by these differences. Studs Terkel, a famous radio personality and author based in Chicago, wrote an insightful book called *Working* (1972). In it, he presented people's thoughts and feelings regarding work life in a variety of professions. One of the themes throughout the book is the relationship between the boss and the worker. Consider the following excerpts:

> Nancy, a bank teller, speaks her mind: My supervisor yells at me. He's about 50, in a position that he doesn't really enjoy. He's been there for a long time and hasn't really advanced that much. He's supposed to have authority over a lot of things but he hasn't really kept informed of changes. . . . You can ask him a question without getting "I'm too busy." Yet you ask a question a lot of times and you don't get the answer you need. Like he doesn't listen. (p. 257)

According to Wheeler, a general foreman:

> There's a few [workers] on the line you can associate with. I haven't as yet. When you get familiarity it causes—the more you get to know somebody, it's hard to distinguish between boss and friend. This isn't good for my profession. But I don't think we ever change much. Like I like to say, "We put our pants on the same way." We work together. But they always gotta realize you're the boss. (p. 183)

Dave, a factory owner, gives his view:

A man comes in and I'm working like a worker, he tells me everything. He talks from the bottom of his heart. You can break bread with him, you can swear. Anything that comes out of your heart. The minute he finds out you're in charge, he looks up to you. Actually he hates you. (p. 397)

As is obvious from these stories, relations between superiors and subordinates often are fragile; both parties must exert energy (particularly communicative energy) to construct and maintain a productive (if not minimally adequate) relationship.

In this chapter, we discuss various aspects of the superior–subordinate relationship. We begin with a general overview of the relationship, and then move to a discussion of misunderstandings in this context. Following that, we discuss a prevalent theory regarding the relationship, Leader–Member Exchange Theory. Next, we explore communication from superiors to subordinates and from subordinates to superiors. We conclude the chapter with a discussion of biological sex as it relates to the relationship between the two parties.

As you read this chapter and learn about superior–subordinate communication, please keep the following story from one of our interviews in mind. The interviewee, Glen Phillips, was a 50-year-old engineer at the time this incident took place:

I was working on detailed engineering specs for a client. I had already done two other specs for this client, and the client had told me they were the best looking, detailed specs he had ever seen. So I was doing something right. I move on to the third set of specs. I take them into the boss to review. He tells me that I need to change the format. I told him that the way we had done it before was better for the client. I explained that the client loved the previous specs so we should not change our format. I asked why they were a problem. He told me that the specs had to be changed. He wouldn't tell me why, just that they had to be changed. Then he told me to leave the office and change them.

If I wanted to keep my job, I had to change them. So I did, but I was very confused and angry. I think that boss was power hungry. He refused to communicate with me and explain why they needed to be changed. And he wouldn't listen to me when I tried to reason with him and explain why they shouldn't be changed. He absolutely would not listen to me. He had his mind made up and didn't want to hear me at all. He blocked me out and made me leave. He would hear nothing of it. After that, we did the specs the new way, although no one knew why and he wouldn't tell us.

The client thought that the specs were no longer the best he'd ever seen. He asked why they were redone, and I told the client that my supervisor told me to do it that way. It was a hard decision, but I was representing my boss. And if he told me to do the specs a certain way, I had to do them that way. The client was disappointed, though, because he had two previous sets of specs that he loved and the third set was a disappointment. And I couldn't even tell why they had to be different since my boss wouldn't tell me.

As you can tell from this story, the superior–subordinate relationship is a complicated one. For reasons that will become clearer as the chapter unfolds, Glen found it difficult to state his opinion strongly to his boss, a situation that eventually served to harm relations with a client. As you read, apply the concepts already covered to help shed light on what occurred. At the end of the chapter, we offer several questions for you to consider about Glen's situation in light of the material covered.

Nature and Importance of the Superior–Subordinate Relationship

Fred Jablin (1979) defined superior–subordinate communication as "those exchanges of information and influence between organizational members at least one of whom has formal (as defined by official organizational sources) authority to direct and evaluate the activities of other organizational members" (p. 1,202). As we discuss superior–subordinate communication throughout this chapter and the remainder of the text, keep in mind that it is not necessarily limited to relationships that are distinguished by only one level in the hierarchy. Superior–subordinate relationships exist, as defined by Jablin, whenever one person has formal authority to regulate the behavior of another.

Exchanges of information and influence between superiors and subordinates can take many forms (see Table 10.1). Katz and Kahn (1978) offered a variety of topics about which superiors might communicate to subordinates and vice versa.

These lists provide valuable insight into the nature of communication between superiors and subordinates. Two points, however, should be noted. First, the lists might be interpreted as saying that the superior tends to communicate only task-related information to the subordinate, whereas the subordinate communicates both task-related and personal information to the superior. As we will show in this chapter, both parties can share both kinds of information during their communication but the extent to which they do so depends on the type of rela-

TABLE 10.1   Forms of Communication between Superiors and Subordinates

Communication from Superior to Subordinate	Communication from Subordinate to Superior
Job instructions	Information about the subordinate
Job rationale	Information about the coworkers
Organizational procedures and practices	Information about organizational policies
Feedback about subordinate performance	Information on what needs to be done and how it can be done
Indoctrination of goals	

tionship they have established. Second, the communications are framed as information-sharing, to the exclusion of information-seeking or collaboration. Again, we will demonstrate in this chapter that, depending on the relationship type, superiors and subordinates often engage in communicative behavior other than information-sharing. Whatever form it might take, Jablin estimated, based on prior research, that "supervisors spend one-third to two-thirds of their time communicating with subordinates" (1990, p. 177).

A critical role of communication is the maintenance of an acceptable relationship between the subordinate and the supervisor (Waldron, 1991). For an organizational newcomer, this relationship is particularly crucial for four reasons (Jablin, 1982):

1. The supervisor may serve as a role model for the subordinate.
2. The supervisor has formal power to reward and punish the subordinate.
3. The supervisor mediates the formal downward communication flow to the subordinate.
4. The supervisor may develop a personal relationship with the subordinate.

From our perspective, maintaining an acceptable relationship with a subordinate is crucial for the supervisor, for the following additional reasons:

1. The subordinate serves as an important channel of informal communication to the supervisor from other subordinates regarding both task-related and personal issues.
2. The subordinate's satisfaction with the relationship may have a direct impact on the supervisor's satisfaction with the relationship as well as on the subordinate's overall job satisfaction.
3. The supervisor's performance is eventually dependent on the performance of the subordinate, which may be directly or indirectly tied to the quality of the superior-subordinate relationship.

As you can see, this critical relationship becomes complicated quite easily. In the next section, we discuss the idea that the relationship is often mired in misunderstandings.

The Prevalance of Misunderstandings in the Superior–Subordinate Relationship

Research regarding the superior–subordinate relationship has demonstrated that superiors and subordinates often have vastly different perceptions of and meanings for important behavioral and organizational activities. In 1962, Phillip Tompkins coined the term *semantic-information distance* to represent this idea (Jablin, 1990). Semantic-information distance is the "gap in information and understanding that exists between superior and subordinate on specified issues" (Dansereau

& Markham, 1987. Semantic-information distance is also known as *perceptual incongruence*. However termed, this phenomenon has the ability to stunt the growth of the superior–subordinate relationship and seriously hinder organizational effectiveness (Jablin, 1979; 1984).

Perceptual incongruence can occur in a variety of issues relevant to the superior–subordinate relationship. Jablin (1984) reported that superiors have an inaccurate view of their subordinates' satisfaction with their jobs and the organization, with supervisors reporting that their subordinates are less satisfied than they actually are. Schnake, Dumler, Cochran, and Barnett (1990) found that there was perceptual incongruence regarding subordinate participation, communication openness, and feedback to subordinates regarding performance; supervisors viewed these subjects more positively than their subordinates.

Perceptual incongruence can have negative individual, relational, and organizational effects. It may be related to such issues as relationship development between the superior and a subordinate (Jablin, 1984), lower intrinsic job satisfaction for the subordinates, a higher level of perceived conflict, and negative perceptions of the organizational climate (Schnake et al., 1990). By contrast, perceptual *congruence* has been shown to have a positive impact on subordinate job satisfaction and subordinate satisfaction with the communication relationship with the supervisor.

Semantic-information distance, or perceptual incongruence, is often considered a natural byproduct of the superior–subordinate relationship. Because superiors and subordinates differ with regard to so many variables and do not always communicate effectively, gaps in understanding and perception tend to occur. Dawson Hendricks, a 53-year-old supervisor of a chain of grocery stores, illustrates this point:

> Some of these workers just treat the job as a 9 to 5 job that pays their bills. A lot of employees at the store are young kids, and I'm not saying that they aren't good workers, but at the retail level sales don't affect them. They are going to get paid no matter what, but on my end of the industry, on the wholesale part, I have to worry about sales revenue and keeping the customers as satisfied as possible. Some employees don't understand that if they dissatisfy a customer that could stem into more than one customer and really hurt the store. There is a reason why we (as the supervisors and managers) stress customer service and overall efficiency of the store, and that is to keep the store running successfully. Sales may not affect a minimum-wage employee, but it definitely affects us on the higher end of the business.

Although communication difficulties may arise between superiors and subordinates because of differences between them, in some situations either party may deliberately communicate in a manner that distorts information or is strategically ambiguous.

No one likes to be the bearer of bad news. This precept is particularly true for the subordinate. *Upward distortion* is a term used to describe the hesitancy of subordinates to communicate negative news up the chain of command and their tendency to distort such news to place it in a more positive light (Dansereau & Markham, 1987).

A number of explanations explain the occurrence of upward distortion. First, subordinates may think that if they communicate negative news to the supervisor, they will be held personally responsible for it. Whether they are the cause of the negative news or not, they may think that the boss will blame them. As a result, they are likely to distort the information. Second, if the negative news is related to the superior's performance in some way it might be interpreted as criticism of the superior. Subordinates might present negative information in a positive manner because they are unwilling to criticize their supervisors openly. Finally, Jablin (1990) noted that several variables may moderate the occurrence of upward distortion, including the subordinate's desire for promotion, need for security, level of trust in the supervisor, and level of motivation.

Whereas subordinates might use upward distortion with their superiors to manage either perceptions or their relationship, in some situations supervisors may consciously use ambiguity in communicating with a subordinate, not to mislead, but to promote positive outcomes. Eric Eisenberg (1984) forwarded the concept of *strategic ambiguity* as a potentially productive communicative tool in organizations. Strategic ambiguity is a situation in which contextual cues are purposefully omitted from communication to "allow for multiple interpretations on the part of the receiver" (p. 230). For Eisenberg, clarity in communication is not always necessary for effectiveness. In fact, on some occasions purposeful ambiguity will benefit the situation, leading to improved relationships and creative problem solving.

Consider the following e-mail sent from Marcus, a manager of human resources, to the CEO of his company. Upon learning of the concept of strategic ambiguity, Marcus began thinking about the company's vision statement and how it could be improved with this concept in mind. The vision statement at the time was "20/0/100," standing for 20-percent growth, zero errors, and 100-percent, on-time delivery. Marcus shared his e-mail to the CEO with the authors:

> I would like to present my desire for a more unifying vision statement. I know in the recent past 20/0/100 has been a vision that has been shared. However, as an employee, I haven't been able to become "passionate" about this goal. There are several reasons: in some respects it is unattainable—a finish line not to be crossed. It is a vision that is not personal to me, and the sum of the masses (from feedback I have received) has not bought into the concept.
>
> I think one of the reasons this concept has not been successful for me (while I'm sure it has provided some value to the company) is that it does not contain a key ingredient—strategic ambiguity, a vision that, in its ambiguity, can be redefined and made personal to each employee. Prior to 20/0/100, I recall seeing other vision statements that included the concept of "continuous improvement." This statement, perhaps, had a bit more strategic ambiguity in it.
>
> I would like to share a vision that my own department has come up with. It is the vision of development—"develop paper, develop process, and

develop people." These general terms of development can be defined and understood by each person in his or her own personal way. The actions that become attached to these general terms become the employee's own. And the result? Maybe 20/0/100, maybe something else! The concept of development can be applied everywhere: develop relationships, develop customers, etc.

On a creative level, picture the photographer in his lab developing film: the incredible process of developing a negative and making a picture out of it with color and faces and memories. *Development* becomes an action word. It becomes something exciting. I think that if our charge was to develop ourselves, our customers, our company, we could have a single team thinking about a single word. This could lead to rewards that are not dictated by a preset goal, but by the worth, value, and ideas of the employees.

Marcus seemed to understand the possible benefits of strategically ambiguous communication. In his case, the "clarity" of the existing vision statement left him out of the picture; it did not mean anything to him. Strategic ambiguity, then, although potentially a contributor to misunderstandings in organizations, can be used to promote identification and the sense of a shared vision.

Although Eisenberg does not limit the use of strategic ambiguity in organizations, we think that it is particularly useful in connection with the relationship between superior and subordinate. In particular, given the power differential, it would seem that the supervisor would have more freedom to be strategically ambiguous than would a subordinate. At the same time, if the superior and the subordinate have a particularly close relationship, it is more than likely that strategic ambiguity could be employed by the subordinate and tolerated by the supervisor.

Eisenberg identified several outcomes associated with the use of strategic ambiguity in organizations, but the following are perhaps most relevant to the superior–subordinate relationship:

- **Strategic ambiguity allows for meaning projection.** When a supervisor is ambiguous about the interpretation of an event, value, or behavior, subordinates must fill in the blanks, so to speak. As they do so, they may project a meaning that is consistent with their own beliefs, which would lead to a perception of similarity with the supervisor. A worker's level of perceived similarity with the supervisor is considered to be a contributor to the worker's satisfaction with the relationship with the supervisor.
- **Strategic ambiguity leads to a restricted code.** As relationships grow deeper between individuals, the need to be clear and direct often diminishes. What emerges is often a conversational shorthand that makes little sense to an outsider. Strategic ambiguity, when successfully employed, may serve to strengthen the relationship between the superior and the subordinate, while simultaneously limiting access to the relationship by outsiders.
- **Strategic ambiguity allows people to regulate what and how much they want to share.** For a variety of reasons, superiors and subordinates may want to limit the amount and type of information they share with each

other. Strategic ambiguity allows for communication on a particular topic, while at the same time limiting each party's disclosure of personal, or even confidential, information.

Upward distortion and strategic ambiguity are two very different communication tactics used for very different reasons. Both could contribute to the gap in understanding between superior and subordinate. As such, the ethics involved should be examined. Upward distortion is certainly the more ethically suspect of the two, because it is a conscious effort to mislead another through misrepresentation of reality. Strategic ambiguity, if used appropriately, should be considered an ethical tactic because it seeks neither to mislead nor to cause damage to the recipient. If, however, it is used with the intention of harming the recipient or if it causes the recipient undue stress, then it should be considered unethical.

A Dyadic View of the Superior–Subordinate Relationship

Perhaps the most popular theory of the past quarter century regarding superior–subordinate relationships is the Leader–Member Exchange Theory. Originally called the Vertical Dyadic Linkage Theory (VDL) and proposed by Graen and his colleagues (e.g., Dansereau, Graen, & Haga, 1975), this theory posited that leadership consists of a dyadic relationship and that "work roles are developed and negotiated over time through a series of exchanges, or 'interacts,' between leader and member" (Bauer & Green, 1996). Vertical Dyadic Linkage Theory is now known as the *Leader–Member Exchange (LMX) Theory,* a label that connotes the bidirectional nature of the superior–subordinate relationship. With its focus on individual relationships, LMX Theory considers the supervisor to have many individual relationships with a heterogeneous group of subordinates.

LMX Theory begins with the assumption that supervisors have a limited amount of time and resources. As a result, the supervisor cannot expend the same amount of energy on every subordinate. Therefore, distinct relationships will form with individual subordinates (Bauer & Green, 1996). The relationships can be placed on a continuum, ranging from *leader–member exchange* (LMX), or *in-group,* relationships, to *supervisory exchange* (SX), or *out-group,* relationships. In between the two types is a third type—*middle-group* relationships. The terms *in-group* and *out-group* were most prevalent during the early years of this strain of research, when the theory was referred to as Vertical Dyadic Linkage Theory. As the label Leader–Member Exchange Theory emerged, the terms LMX and SX replaced the terms *in-group* and *out-group* (see Fairhurst, 2001, for an extended discussion of the stages of this strain of research).

LMX (in-group) relationships are characterized by mutual trust, reciprocal support, liking, and greater interaction. Conversely, SX (out-group) relationships are primarily role defined and contractually based (Bauer & Green, 1996). Middle-group relationships vary in their levels of the above characteristics.

As described by Bauer and Green (1996), LMX relationships are related to several important outcomes:

- Subordinate turnover
- Subordinate satisfaction and promotions
- Ratings of subordinate performance
- Subordinate extra-role performance

In other words, subordinates in LMX relationships with their supervisors tend to stay in the organization longer, are more satisfied, and receive higher performance ratings than subordinates in either middle-group or out-group relationships.

What determines which type of relationship a subordinate will be in with a supervisor? Although it is difficult to determine, one study has examined the role of the initial interaction in the formation of LMX relationships. Dockery and Steiner (1990) found that two factors affected the development of LMX relationships during the first time the pair interacted in their official positions: *liking* by the leader and *perceived ability* of the subordinate by the leader. Liking was defined by Dockery and Steiner as "mutual affection the leader and member have for each other based primarily on interpersonal attraction" (p. 397), which includes demographic similarity and similarity in values. "Perceived ability" involves the extent to which the supervisor believes that the subordinate will be able to perform the assigned tasks with little or no difficulty. Other factors, such as trust, perceived similarity, and the level of centralized decision making are linked to the formation of the various member exchange relationships (Bauer and Green, 1996; Krone, 1994). It does not appear, based on at least one research study (Lamude et al., 2004), that demographic characteristics such as subordinate job classification and biological sex are related to becoming involved in an LMX relationship.

Once a relationship has been established, energy must be exerted to *maintain* that relationship, particularly on the part of the subordinate (Lee & Jablin, 1995; Waldron, 1991). *Maintenance communication* is the term Waldron (1991) applied to the "messages and behaviors used to preserve an acceptable and lasting relational state" (p. 289). Waldron noted four tactics associated with maintenance communication. They could vary depending on the type of relationships being maintained. Subordinates have the following tactics available (pp. 296–298):

- **Personal.** Informal interaction used to build and maintain a friendship
- **Contractual.** Conformity to formal role requirements, expectations held by the supervisor, and general communication conventions
- **Regulative.** Strategic regulation—of messages, impressions, emotions, and contacts with the supervisor
- **Direct.** Direct negotiation of the terms of the relationship and explicit discussion of perceived relational injustices

Waldron found that in-group subordinates tended to use more personal, contractual, and directness-maintenance communication tactics, whereas out-group members used more regulative tactics. Following the same line of research, Lee and Jablin (1995) found that despite having a large repertoire of maintenance tactics available, supervisors did not vary their tactics based on relational type. Consistent with Waldron's findings, however, subordinates did vary their maintenance communication tactics based on the type of exchange relationship in which they were involved. Using a different theoretical base (i.e., influence techniques), Lamude et al. (2004) found that supervisors did vary techniques between the two groups. Their research indicated that supervisors tended to use more *prosocial techniques* (e.g., immediate reward, self-esteem, responsibility to others, supervisor modeling, and supervisor feedback) with those in LMX relationships, and *autosocial techniques* (e.g., punishment, guilt, legitimate supervisor authority) were less likely to be used with this group.

As can be seen from our discussion of relational maintenance, communication plays an integral role in the superior–subordinate relationship. Communication not only affects the relationship (as evidenced by maintenance communication), but is also affected by the relationship. In other words, how superiors and subordinates communicate with others is based on the type of relationship they have (i.e., in-, out-, or middle-group).

Fairhurst and Chandler (1989) found that the superiors and subordinates in in-group relationships tended to influence each other through mutual persuasion. Subordinates felt comfortable challenging the authority of the supervisor. In middle-group relationships, supervisors invoked their authority more often than with the in-group as a means of resolving challenges. Finally, as would be expected with the out-group, supervisor communication was characterized by more directives and the invoking of authority than with the other two groups.

Gail Fairhurst (1993) continued this line of research by examining the communication of women leaders and how it changed based on the type of membership exchange. She found that supervisors in high to medium LMX relationships sought to minimize power differences through the following communication patterns:

- **Value congruence.** Interaction that demonstrates similarity in values
- **Nonroutine problem solving.** Creatively approaching problems
- **Insider markers.** Indicators of group membership, such as inside jokes
- **Support.** Explicit and implicit markers of social and professional support
- **Coaching.** Aiding the subordinate in mastering a particular skill or concept

Fairhurst also identified four communication patterns that supervisors used to maximize power differences in out-group relationships:

- **Performance monitoring.** Consistent checking of work and progress
- **Face-threatening acts.** Communication characterized by criticism and rebuke
- **Competitive conflict.** Use of interruptions and nonsupportive statements
- **Power games.** Arguing for the sake of arguing

Interestingly, several of the behaviors used to minimize power differences in LMX relational types are supported by the CO model (particularly support and coaching), whereas those used to maximize power differences in SX relationships seem to violate the demands of the CO model. The CO model encourages the use of the behaviors on the former list in *all* organizational relationships, however, not just those marked as LMX. It would seem that engaging in behaviors found in the latter list would only serve to reduce employee satisfaction and performance, an effect that would benefit personal or organizational ends.

Leader–Member Exchange Theory offers valuable insight into the dyadic nature of the superior–subordinate relationship. Research in this area has moved past the one-to-many theory of leadership posited by both trait and behavior research. The LMX Theory demonstrates that each relationship is unique, that the relationship type affects important outcomes, and that communication plays a central role in the formation and maintenance of the relationship. In the next section of this chapter, we discuss issues relevant to communication from the supervisor to the subordinate.

Communication Activities: Superior to Subordinate

As stated earlier in the chapter, supervisors spend one-third to two-thirds of their time communicating with their subordinates. General topics of communication have already been discussed, but other activities are going on concurrently. For instance, while a supervisor might be communicating with a subordinate about the job rationale or organizational values, the supervisor might at the same time be establishing trust, conveying immediacy (i.e., care), giving feedback, or seeking feedback regarding her own performance. Supervisors must also determine how to communicate each message, and one aspect they must consider is their use of humor. We now turn to a discussion of each of these issues.

Trust

Trust is an important ingredient in the superior–subordinate relationship. Both parties are vulnerable; trust helps to alleviate some of the vulnerability and provide for a mutually beneficial situation. According to Whitener, Brodt, Korsgaard, and Werner (1998), managers can have a significant impact on building trust through "managerial trustworthy behavior" (p. 513). According to these researchers, trust has three facets (p. 513):

1. Expectation that the other will act benevolently.
2. A willingness to be vulnerable and risk that the other will not act accordingly (i.e., will not take advantage of that vulnerability).
3. Some level of dependence on the other.

Whitener et al. (1998) suggested five categories of managerial behavior that influence the subordinate's perception of a supervisor's trustworthiness:

1. *Behavioral consistency* enables the subordinate to predict future behavior.
2. *Behavioral integrity* involves telling the truth and keeping promises.
3. *Sharing and delegating of control* satisfies subordinates with their level of participation in decision making.
4. *Communication* conveys accurate information, explains decisions, and demonstrates openness.
5. *Demonstration of concern* makes evident benevolence toward others.

Glen's story at the beginning of the chapter should come to mind at this point. Glen's supervisor did not seem to incorporate any of the listed behaviors. Particularly absent were behavioral consistency, sharing and delegating of control, and communication. As a result, Glen will have trouble trusting his supervisor in the future.

It is important to remember that trust is a relational construction; both parties must contribute to the development, maintenance, and growth of trust. Lara, a 54-year-old dental assistant, shows us this point:

> I have worked with Dr. Stedler for 34 years. He has total respect for my judgment. And I pretty much can use my own thought. I make a lot of decisions without even consulting him about it, but he trusts my decisions and judgments, and he has given me those rights. However, I definitely know my limits with that. It's going to be difficult not having that respect when the new doctor joins us. We have worked together for 34 years, and we know how to work with each other and what to expect from each other. It is so easy for us because I don't have to run back and ask him about every decision, and it helps him because I don't have to expose him to other problems and decision making, which causes less stress for him.

Lara's story points out that trust (and respect) are created through time as the relationship grows. Thirty-four years of working together and learning each others' styles, ethics, and values has led to mutual trust. With a new doctor coming in, trust will need to be built; it will not be immediately present, because there is no relational history.

As changes in the workplace continue, trust will become that much more important. With allegiance to workers eroding and workers changing jobs more often than ever before, trust will become harder to establish. Trust is also difficult to establish when supervisors attempt to appear concerned and caring, but in reality are willing to do whatever they can to achieve a goal [a concept known as *Machiavellianism* (Teven et al., 2006)]. As we adjust to the norms of the twenty-first-century workplace, we must try harder to trust those around us. Communication is the central feature in this challenge.

Immediacy

Let's begin this section with a quick story from Bojinka:

> I have noticed, as a manager, the different levels of communication in the office. It's interesting because I work with all women, and I don't know what it is, but I try not to come off as an intimidating boss. We are all friends, but the communication is lacking I think. I have tried a lot more to talk with the women, maybe when we are on a coffee break or something. Making the setting more informal and less pressured I feel really allows the communication to flow better and I learn so much more and gain so much more feedback. The women are a lot more comfortable talking to me in that setting.

What Bojinka noticed is that relationships and deep communication are not established automatically just because you work with someone. As indicated in the previous section, one way to build trust with a subordinate is to demonstrate concern. A particular element of communication that is closely associated with the demonstration of concern—*immediacy*—has been studied in the context of the superior–subordinate relationship. *Immediacy* is "any communication that indicates interpersonal warmth and closeness" (Koermer, Goldstein, & Fortson, 1993, p. 269), either conscious or not (Richmond & McCroskey, 2000). Immediacy can be expressed both verbally and nonverbally and in both cases may affect a subordinate's perception of his supervisor, and hence, his level of trust in that person. Supervisors' use of nonverbal immediacy, for example, can enhance perceptions of the supervisor by the subordinate (i.e., their credibility and interpersonal attractiveness), the subordinate's satisfaction with the supervisor, and communication with the supervisor.

How, then, is immediacy conveyed in this relationship? Koermer, Goldstein, and Fortson (1993) conducted an exploratory qualitative research study that unveiled six ways in which a supervisor conveys immediacy to a subordinate:

1. Values subordinate input on job and in personal matters.
2. Attentive to subordinate both verbally and nonverbally.
3. Expresses confidence in the subordinate's ability.
4. Shows a personal interest in the subordinate.
5. Expresses verbal appreciation for commendable work.
6. Demonstrates a willingness to assist the subordinate.

Again, Glen's story should come to mind. Glen's supervisor failed to convey immediacy through his communication. He did not show Glen that he valued Glen's input, that he was attentive, or that he had confidence in Glen's ability. As a result, Glen's performance and satisfaction suffered, as well as his relationship with his supervisor. If supervisors can communicate immediacy and help to establish trust, the expected outcome is an effective relationship, one in which both superior and subordinate parties are able to function at their highest levels and contribute to each other's success.

Feedback

One behavior that is vital to the relationship is the giving of feedback from the supervisor to the subordinate. Wiener (1954) introduced the general concept of feedback to the communication discipline in 1948 and later defined it as "a method of controlling a system" (p. 61). Since that time, the concept has been applied to the general communication model, the public-speaking context, interpersonal relationships, systems approaches, and the organizational context, particularly as it is relevant to superior–subordinate communication. In this context, *feedback* is any communication between organizational members that implicitly or explicitly provides task guidance, personal evaluation, or other guidance. Important to this definition is the notion that feedback can involve both task elements (what needs to be done and how) and personal elements (social and psychological development), what Kim and Miller (1990) refer to as "work-oriented" and "altruism-oriented" elements, respectively. Often, feedback is conceived of just in terms of tasks, but given the new climate of "coaching" in the workplace, personal feedback is becoming more expected. Feedback is especially relevant to the communicative organization, because it is a prime mechanism for addressing misunderstandings. Also, as will be noted in the following sections, it can create them as well.

Providing Feedback.   Feedback from a supervisor to a subordinate has been shown to have a positive impact on motivation, satisfaction, commitment, and performance (Geddes, 1993). These outcomes will be affected positively, however, only if the feedback is provided in a manner that is considered acceptable by the subordinate. If not, the outcomes could be negatively affected. Consider the following two stories from Latasha, a sales representative. Latasha described two instances of performance feedback that had very different results:

> We were at a sales meeting and it was right after the new management had bought us. My supervisor was always a person who was very into presentation and appearances and so forth, and she wasn't pleased with me and another salesperson on two issues. Basically, what she did was put us into a room and proceed to sit down and talk about all the things we were doing wrong. Instead of saying, "You guys are doing a good job," it was total criticism. Then we had to go into a meeting directly after that, which was very hard, because when you feel totally criticized and you are around other people and have to put on a face, it can be a very difficult thing to do.

In this instance, the feedback that Latasha received from her supervisor was communicated in such a threatening manner that Latasha was negatively affected. Contrast this with another feedback situation she described:

> My company has been coming in with a lot of orders from South America and China. It is kind of exciting getting into markets where we haven't been

before. So I told my supervisor about that, and he said, "That's great!" He told me later that he had talked to the sector president and told him that I was doing a great job with the company and gave me credit for that, whereas my old boss would never have given me that credit or any sort of encouragement. It is not that I think people need a pat on the back all the time, but when I heard that he gave me credit, that just made me feel good. It made me want to do an even better job.

In comparing the two stories, you should notice several points. First, feedback can have different consequences depending on how it is phrased and how it is communicated. In the first instance, Latasha was demoralized because she was criticized so harshly. In the second instance, the feedback she received was provided in such a manner that it made her feel proud and want to perform at an even higher level. Second, feedback can be either negative or positive. In the first instance, the feedback was quite negative: the supervisor told Latasha that her performance was not up to par. In the second case, the feedback was much more positive: the supervisor praised her efforts and gave her credit to upper-level management.

The equation for the relationship between type of criticism and its effect on relevant outcomes is not as simple as these examples portray, however. Certainly, negative feedback can be communicated in a way that allows for improved performance and motivation, whereas positive feedback can sometimes contribute to negative outcomes, especially if it is unwarranted or from a noncredible source. Nevertheless, how the feedback (of either type) is communicated is of particular importance.

Geddes and Linnehan (1996) conducted research that showed that positive feedback is less communicatively complex (i.e., simpler for the receiver to process) than negative feedback, which often involves balancing information on task, role, and ego. As a result, they suggested adding complexity to the positive feedback, because "it is likely recipients will engage in more controlled processing of *guidance* rather than *praise*" (p. 339). In other words, for positive feedback to have longer-lasting effects than momentary good feelings, it should be cast in a way that engages the subordinate in thoughts about how to improve performance (or attitude) even further.

Delivering negative feedback is difficult. Supervisors regularly avoid communicating negative feedback or bad news in order to "manage employee emotions, minimize negativity, and preserve relationships" (Wagoner & Waldron, 1999, p. 193). In other words, just as subordinates may engage in upward distortion to reduce the likelihood of being blamed for bad news, supervisors may engage in downward distortion to protect themselves, their subordinates, and their relationships.

Negative feedback can be about many things, but it typically involves such matters as poor performance, denied requests, and broken rules. As managers communicate negative feedback to subordinates, they have many possible ways to approach the conversation. For example, Wagoner and Waldron (1999) in a study at UPS found that when managers had to convey negative feedback about broken rules to their subordinates, they did so by stressing the need to conform to group standards. In this way, the feedback was designed to evoke commitment to coworkers and the organization rather than the supervisor. This approach allowed the supervisor to act more as a channel of news than as a critic, thereby reducing the possibility that the subordinate would have negative feelings in return toward her.

Providing feedback to a subordinate is a complicated matter that involves much more than we have room to discuss here [see Fairhurst (2001) for a useful review]. As feedback is given, the supervisor must balance the type of feedback with timing, appropriate phrasing, goals, needs of the subordinate, and a whole host of other concerns.

Seeking Feedback. Although providing feedback is an essential part of the superior–subordinate relationship, seeking feedback is just as important. In order to determine if she is performing well, a superior needs to receive feedback from subordinates. Feedback is important for managerial effectiveness. Although formal mechanisms of performance appraisal are in place in most organizations that allow subordinates and supervisors to evaluate a manager [see Walker & Smither (1999) for an interesting article on this topic], candid and time-specific informal feedback also is necessary. However, seeking informal feedback from subordinates has risks. First, subordinates are often hesitant to provide negative information to their supervisors (recall the discussion of upward distortion) for fear of repercussions. As a result, they tend to provide positive feedback more frequently (Baron, 1996) or to couch negative feedback in overly positive terms to avoid the possibility of retribution. Second, if supervisors seek positive feedback, they may run the risk of seeming needy and high maintenance.

There are obvious benefits to seeking negative feedback. For instance, if a supervisor seeks constructive criticism regarding his communication behavior during meetings, the chances of getting accurate information may increase. That, of course, may be true only if the subordinate trusts that the supervisor will not retaliate in some manner and is genuinely concerned with improving performance.

Ashford and Tsui (1991) investigated feedback-seeking behavior by managers as a way of improving managerial effectiveness. They found that although managers sought both negative and positive feedback from their own supervisors, they tended to seek positive feedback from their peers and negative feedback from their subordinates. Results also indicated that seeking negative feedback was associated with more accurate knowledge. In addition, it resulted in a perception of effectiveness, whereas seeking positive feedback decreased this perception. Finally, managers were more likely to seek feedback from their own supervisor than from either their peers or their subordinates.

Given its potential benefits, it would seem that seeking feedback from subordinates, particularly negative feedback, should be done more often. A July 18, 2005, edition of *Investor's Business Daily* said, for example, that successful mid-level managers seek feedback—they ask open-ended questions and welcome critique. Subordinates seem to be a relatively untapped wealth of informal information regarding managerial performance. Seeking negative feedback, however, should occur only within the confines of a trusting relationship; otherwise the supervisor runs the risk of getting positively couched information and the subordinate may experience undue stress.

Compliance-Gaining

Another prototypical behavior of a supervisor is getting the subordinate to perform as a fully functioning organizational member, complying with organizational directives, policies, and procedures. As supervisors attempt to influence their subordinates, they may use a variety of tactics broadly referred to as *compliance-gaining techniques*. The use of particular tactics is associated with many factors, such as the subordinate's communication style. It is also related to various outcomes, including perception of the supervisor's communication competence.

A supervisor's choice of a particular compliance-gaining tactic is related to the subordinate's communication style. Garko (1992) conducted a study that showed a relationship between the supervisor's compliance-gaining tactics and the subordinate's communication style, particularly the use of an attractive or unattractive style. An *attractive style* is considered to be attentive, friendly, and relaxed; an *unattractive style* is inattentive, unfriendly, and unrelaxed. Garko's results indicated that supervisors were more likely to use the compliance-gaining tactics of assertiveness, coalition, and higher authority with subordinates who communicated in an unattractive style. When subordinates communicated using an attractive style, supervisors were more likely to use the compliance-gaining tactic of friendliness. Supervisors were likely to rely on reason and bargaining for either attractive or unattractive styles.

A supervisor's use of particular compliance-gaining tactics can also affect her subordinate's perceptions of her communication competence. For example, Johnson (1992) found that when supervisors employed "prosocial" tactics, their subordinates' perceptions of their communication competence increased. Prosocial tactics are those that "attempt to gain relational rewards by explaining or justifying the actor's position and attitude" (p. 56). Just as with the delivery of feedback, how supervisors attempt to gain compliance has effects more far-reaching than the particular situation.

The literature on compliance-gaining is too large to cover adequately in this section, but our brief discussion of it suggests its complexity and importance. Research indicates that issuing direct orders is not always an adequate or effective means of gaining employee compliance. Supervisors must take into account both the attributes of the individual subordinate and the relevant outcomes before choosing an appropriate tactic. It should also be evident that the effective implementation of compliance-gaining techniques is not a given; it involves a set of skills that need to be learned and practiced.

An interesting way to think of the communication from supervisor to subordinate was forwarded by Kelly Crawford, who told her story earlier in this chapter: "A supervisor is in a teaching position. There needs to be somebody to say, 'Okay, this was a mistake,' not necessarily 'This was a mistake, correct it or I'm going to fire you' but 'this was a mistake, learn from it.' "

Humor

Researchers have gained interest in the use of humor in the superior–subordinate relationship over the past two decades. The use of humor in any relationship is a complex enterprise. Using humor requires an understanding of the nature of the relationship, the boundaries of the relationship, the values and sense of humor of the other person, and knowledge of their general humor-orientation. Humor appears to have several uses in the organizational context (Martin, Rich, & Gayle, 2004, p. 25):

- **Relieves stress.** Effective and context-relevant uses of humor can create relational cohesion (stronger relationships), which can help reduce tension.
- **Communicate difficult information.** Self-detrimental or face-threatening information can be communicated through humor in a way that reduces the negative impact of the message by surprising the other person or communicating the message in an unexpected or incongruous way.
- **Make one feel superior.** Making the other person the source of the humor or butt of the joke can reduce their relational power.

In addition, humor in organizational contexts also promotes creativity, encourages group cohesion, and is related to effective leadership styles; those who use humor at work have reduced turnover and higher job involvement and job satisfaction (Rizzo, Wanzer, & Booth-Butterfield, 1999).

As you can imagine, the context of the superior–subordinate relationship makes the use of humor a bit trickier. Supervisors must be aware of how their use of humor can easily be translated into negative circumstances for subordinates if it crosses the line of good taste or the boundaries of the relationship; such humor could be interpreted as harassment (Duncan, Smeltzer, & Leap, 1990). Humor can, however, have positive effects when used by the supervisor. Research has shown that employees reported liking managers whom they perceived as being humorous. In addition, those managers who are perceived as being more humor oriented are also perceived as being more effective. Finally, employees' job satisfaction is higher if they perceive their manager to have a humor orientation (Rizzo et al., 1999).

Some supervisors consciously employ humor as part of their style of leadership. Different types of humor can be used, and use of these types is connected to organizational power as well as the sex of the interactants. *Positive* humor involves playfulness or friendship. *Expressive* humor involves self-disclosure that is done in a self-ridiculing way, whereas *negative* humor is that which belittles others or is otherwise hurtful. Martin et al. (2004) found in their research that those with formal organizational power (supervisors) and males use all forms of humor, whereas their female counterparts are limited to a narrower range of humor usage.

We now turn our attention to communication activities of the subordinate to the supervisor.

Communication Activities: Subordinate to Superior

As indicated by the Leader–Member Exchange Theory, the frequency, type, and personal nature of communication from a subordinate to a superior will depend on the type of relationship in which they are involved. In an LMX relationship, a subordinate will feel comfortable communicating frequently with the supervisor, about topics both personal and professional, in a manner that is not always deferential, but perhaps challenging. In an SX relationship, a subordinate will probably communicate less frequently, mainly about task-oriented topics, and will offer relatively few challenges to the supervisor's authority.

With the emergence of the participative workplace, the opportunities for subordinates to communicate up the hierarchy have increased. As traditional managerial practices wane, including one-way downward influence, subordinates have had to learn to employ upward-influence tactics.

Upward Influence

Attempts at upward influence by subordinates is an issue that is confounded by a variety of variables other than the relationship itself, such as the sex of the participants, organizational hierarchy, and the capacity of the supervisor to exert influence upward (Dansereau & Markham, 1987). This last variable is referred to as the *Pelz effect* (Pelz, 1952) and indicates that "subordinates would initiate more upward messages if they believed their superiors had upward influence" (Putnam & Cheney, 1992, p. 74). In the following discussion of research on *upward influence*, keep in mind that its use is more than a matter of an individual subordinate's comfort and skill level.

Krone (1991) adopted a model of political behavior in organizations to help explain upward influence by subordinates. She argued that subordinates would differ in their upward-influence tactics based on whether they were in an LMX or an SX relationship. She posited three potential strategies:

■ **Open persuasion.** An overt form of influence where the desired outcomes are fully disclosed. It is characterized by empathic listening, open argument for a proposed course of action, and logical reasoning.

- **Strategic persuasion.** An influence technique that uses either open influence or clearly stated outcomes. There is only partial openness in revealing the ends that are sought.
- **Manipulation.** A disguised attempt at upward influence.

The results indicated that people in LMX relationships tended to use more open and strategic persuasion than did those in SX relationships.

Infante and Gorden (1987; 1991) have forwarded a line of research that has investigated the role of argumentativeness as well as a cluster of other traits in upward influence and employee voice. They define *voice* as "effort to correct unacceptable situations; . . . value of freedom to communicate supportively and critically" (1991, p. 294). The results of their study indicate that employee voice will be responded to if subordinates display argumentativeness, but also are affirming.

In a related study, Infante and Gorden (1987) argued that organizations will become stronger if they foster independent-mindedness in their employees. Independent-mindedness is associated with the tendency to exert upward influence. The results of this study demonstrated that a supervisor's upward effectiveness was predicted by his or her argumentative and relaxed style.

Upward influence, sometimes associated with the concept of voice, is a complicated subject. Even though traditional hierarchical structures are slowly being replaced by more decentralized, participative environments, subordinates still find it difficult to express their opinions to their superiors.

In the final section, we cover the issue of women and the impact of biological sex on the elements discussed in this chapter.

Women and the Superior–Subordinate Relationship

Much has been written about the plight of women in the organization. It is certainly no surprise that women's ways of communicating, thinking, and acting are often not valued in the workplace and that women are severely underrepresented in managerial positions throughout the world. For example, in May 2006, only eight women were CEOs in *Fortune* 500 companies. Additionally, according to a February 18, 2005, article in *The Boston Globe*, women are in charge of only 14 of the nation's 1,000 largest publicly traded companies. When they do break the glass ceiling, it tends to be slippery; the average tenure for a male CEO is 8.2 years, whereas a female CEO lasts only 4.8 years. Myerson and Fletcher (2000) proposed the idea that "gender inequity is rooted in our culture patterns and therefore in our organizational systems" (p. 131). With roots so deep, it is obvious why such vast differences still exist, despite the increasing numbers of women in the workforce.

What is a bit surprising, though, is that with regard to some of the critical issues we have discussed in this chapter, traditional research has shown that the sex of the participants in the superior–subordinate relationship, with a few exceptions, does not appear to be relevant to the outcomes. In a study designed to determine if sex differences exist in supervisors' evaluations of their subordinates' (who are also managers) leadership skills, Knott and Natalle (1997) found that men and women managers were rated essentially the same in all leadership skills but one. The only skill on which women managers were rated higher was "putting people at ease." Interestingly, hierarchical position did affect the evaluations; upper-level managers were rated higher than lower-level managers. From this study, it appears that one's position in the hierarchy is more predictive of differences in evaluation of leadership skills than one's sex.

Lamude, Daniels, and Graham (1988) investigated the role of sex on perceptual incongruence between superior and subordinate. Prior to the study, they proposed the notion that the sex of the parties of the dyad may be one of the most influential factors affecting perceptual incongruence. They were particularly interested in determining if perceptual incongruence was higher for mixed-sex superior–subordinate relationships than for same-sex ones. The results of their study provided no evidence for greater perceptual incongruence on the basis of sex composition.

Compliance-gaining is another area investigated with regard to sex differences among supervisors. According to a study by Hirokawa, Kodama, and Harper (1990), when controlling for the relative amount of power possessed by men and women supervisors, men and women do not differ significantly in the types of persuasive strategies they would use with subordinates to gain compliance. Level of power seemed to be the relevant variable; high-power supervisors used more punishment-based strategies, such as warnings, threats, and ultimatums, whereas low-power supervisors used more altruistic or rational tactics such as counseling or explanation. In other words, level of power, not sex, was a better predictor of the type of compliance-gaining tactic used by supervisors.

Other studies present similar results regarding the lack of impact of biological sex on various issues. Bauer and Green's (1996) research on the development of leader–member exchange relationships showed that sex did not play a role in relevant outcomes. Johnson's (1994) study showed that legitimate authority was a better predictor of communication differences in the workplace than sex.

One interesting exception to these findings regarding sex differences in the superior–subordinate relationship is the study by Lamude and Daniels (1990). They examined evaluations of communication competence in superior–subordinate relationships to determine if there is a pro-male bias. They found that women supervisors were rated lower in communication competence than men supervisors were by their subordinates. Ironically, women subordinates rated women supervisors less favorably than they rated men supervisors. In addition, supervisors rated women subordinates lower in communication competence than they rated men.

This brief discussion was not intended to minimize the oppressive circumstances that many women face in today's workforce, but to show the role that sex plays in many of the issues covered in this chapter.

Summary

In this chapter, we examined many aspects of communication and the superior–subordinate relationship. The relationship between a superior and a subordinate is crucial to the success of both parties, particularly the organizational newcomer. Despite its importance, the relationship is still characterized by a gap in understanding between the parties regarding important organizational activities and outcomes. The relationship is a relational construction best thought of as a dyad that can be characterized by varying levels of trust, support, and frequency of interaction.

Now that you have negotiated your way through the different aspects of the superior–subordinate relationship presented in this chapter, reflect on the story recounted by our interviewee Glen at the beginning of this chapter in light of the following discussion questions:

1. Describe this situation in terms of perceptual incongruence (semantic-information distance). Could it have been an instance of the use of strategic ambiguity? Why or why not?
2. On the basis of this story, would you say that this is an LMX, an SX, or a middle-group relationship? Explain your reasoning. If it is an LMX relationship, would this event hurt or help the maintenance of that relationship? What if it is an SX relationship?
3. If you were Glen, what would you do next? How would you approach your boss from this point forward? Would you attempt any upward influence? If yes, how would you do it?

The superior–subordinate relationship is undergoing significant changes in the modern workplace. Organizations that have adopted decentralized structures, participative decision making, and project teams have experienced a shift from traditional hierarchical relationships between supervisor and subordinate to relationships characterized by blurred lines of authority, increased communication, and a more equal distribution of power. These changes demand new skills. Whereas authority and control were the tools of traditional supervisors, managers in this new atmosphere must be accomplished communicators, able to develop interpersonal relationships with each worker. Despite endeavors in this direction, however, misunderstandings will undoubtedly occur. Therefore, we recommend that organizations turn to the CO model. Recognizing that there is an inherent gap in understanding between supervisor and subordinate should sensitize both parties to seize opportunities to construct learning and could enhance the possibility of success in the future.

11 Peer and Coworker Communication

Communication with coworkers can create one of the strongest connections between you and your job and between you and the organization. As people feel more connected to one another, morale and organizational commitment significantly increase. Peer relationships can provide a source of intrinsic reward for the employee, buffer job-related stress, and reduce job dissatisfaction and turnover (Kram & Isabella, 1985). These personal relationships are also connected to innovation in the organization. Albrecht and Hall (1991) discovered that coworker relationships characterized by trust, credibility, influence, and relationship importance were directly related to supportiveness of one's new ideas for the organization. Thus, it is in the organization's best interest to foster coworker relationships.

Rosabeth Moss Kanter, a well-known management consultant and writer, suggests the importance of interpersonal relationships at work: "Intercompany relationships are a key business asset and knowing how to nurture them is an essential management skill" (1997, p. 245). Much of her research suggests strategies for managers to nurture such relationships, leading to increased organizational effectiveness.

We begin this chapter by examining the nature of relationships in organizations. Next, we offer an overview of factors influencing the development of relationships in the workplace and the positive and negative consequences of work relationships. Then we examine workplace romance, an organizational perspective on office romance, and potential reasons for deterioration of workplace relationships. The chapter concludes with strategies you can use to manage your own workplace relationships.

Nature of Relationships in Organizations

We begin our discussion of coworker relationships by identifying their parameters. *Interpersonal relationships* in the organization may be defined as follows:

> two people who interact face-to-face for any length of time who assume the roles of sender and receiver of messages simultaneously. Compared to a small group the

dyadic nature of interpersonal relationships provides each participant with more involvement, more satisfaction, and more participation. (Tortoriello, Blatt, and DeWine, 1978, p. 90)

Interpersonal relationships in the organization may take two forms: organizational or personal. An *organizational interpersonal relationship* is based on the organizational structure. For example, two women are assigned to work on a particular project. Because the organizational structure has forced them to spend time together on a mutual task, they are participating in a dyadic relationship. This relationship may remain mostly task oriented or it may move outside the immediate task concern and become a personal relationship. A *personal relationship*, or friendship, develops because two people choose to spend time with each other owing to mutual emotional needs. One main difference between these two types of organizational relationships is the voluntary or involuntary nature of each: "Friendship cannot be imposed on people; it is an ongoing human association voluntarily developed and privately negotiated" (Rawlins, 1992, p. 9). Friendships develop by choice, not by required association. They may, however, begin as a required association and develop into something more complex and interrelated to others in the organization. An example of how complicated it can be to manage coworker relationships is found in a story told by Carrie Miller, a 35-year-old office administrator:

> Sallie, who is an office administrator like me, and I were sent an e-mail from Denise, our supervisor, asking us to go to lunch. Sallie and I never want to make waves, we always just try to go with the flow. So we said yes and accepted the invitation for lunch at a new Mexican restaurant. We returned and I walked to the office of a coworker, Lisa, to remove some things I had left in her office refrigerator.
>
> Lisa asked me where I had been and I told her that I had had lunch with Denise. Lisa started ranting and raving about Denise. I went back to my office, and Denise appeared and asked where I had just been. I told her I had gotten something from Lisa's refrigerator. She asked if Lisa had asked me about the lunch. I said yes. This put Denise over the edge and she began going on about how she was sick of everyone in the office having to know her business. Denise said that she was going to put a stop to this and walked away. She then sent an e-mail to Lisa and to Joan, another secretary who she thought had been gossiping about her. The e-mail said that if anyone had any problems with the lunch, they should have come to her [Denise]. She also said she thought that it was nobody's business with whom she had lunch. I went to Sallie, and Sallie reassured me that we had done nothing wrong.
>
> I called Lisa and Joan and told them about the e-mail sent to Sallie and me. Denise then called me into her office and asked me what Lisa and I talked about exactly. I told her that I just said to her, "We [Sallie, Denise, and Carrie] went to lunch." Then Lisa came to me and asked me what I had just told Denise about her. I told Lisa that I told Denise that we discussed lunch and I

did not tell Denise that Lisa was ranting and raving about her. Lisa and Joan went into Denise's office to find out about the problem. Denise began interrogating Lisa about her conversation, trying to get Lisa caught in a lie. Lisa and Joan were both furious and left Denise's office. From that point on, for four days, none of us communicated but there was pressure brewing.

A simple lunch turned into a major battle. The situation becomes more complex when all the relationships involved are added together: the supervisor (Denise) has independent relationships with Carrie, Sallie, Lisa, and Joan. Each of them has relationships with one another and in various combinations with Denise. Ten possible dyadic relationships are possible among these four people. Add to that the possible number of triads (30) and possible four-person combinations (80), and a total of 120 different combinations among these five people are possible. As shown in Carrie's story, many of these relationships were involved in this conflict.

A look at some basic principles of developing interpersonal relationships at work may help us understand the complex situation that Carrie described.

Proxemics

Often interpersonal relationships form because a person simply has more opportunities to interact with some people than with others within the organizational setting. The research on *proxemics* (the distance between people) provides a strong indication that people develop friendships based on which individuals happen to share the same space. In an organization, individuals are more likely to develop relationships with those with who they are in constant contact rather than with those they seldom see or hear.

Researchers have discovered that proximity is a major factor not only in forming the relationship, but in increasing the closeness of the two partners as well (Sias & Cahill, 1998). Therefore, simply placing individuals within the same physical space will increase the likelihood that they will develop a personal relationship. Part of what made Carrie's situation more intense was that Sallie, Lisa, Joan, and Carrie all shared the same office area and were therefore more aware of planned activities that occurred outside the office. Knowing how physical space positively and negatively affects office relationships will help managers figure out ways to improve relationships by changing that space. We need to pay attention to how the physical space negatively and positively influences our communication. Criteria in addition to proxemics contribute to the endurance of an interpersonal relationship at work. In this next section, we will discuss how we convey information about the nature of the relationship through our messages.

Relational Communication

Four decades ago, researchers identified two levels of messages being communicated in a relationship. Watzlawick, Beavin, and Jackson (1967) concluded that the *content* of a message conveys information. It may be about anything that is capable of being communicated (e.g., job instructions, task information, or personal information). The second level of communication is sometimes referred to as the *command* aspect, or the relationship level of communication, meaning what sort of a message it is. This second level ultimately defines the relationship between the two individuals. Here a person is saying, "This is how I see myself" or "This is how I see you in our relationship."

For example, in one company where two individuals were working together on a joint project, Jim made it clear he saw their coworker relationship as unequal. He told Bob that they needed to finish the project by the end of the week. The content of this message seemed simple enough; however, its timing and presentation also made a clear statement about their relationship. Jim's stern tone of voice, frowning expression, and the fact that *he* had chosen the date for completion made it clear that, as far as he was concerned, he was the dominant person in this relationship and would make most decisions by himself. He was communicating on two levels: one dealt with the subject matter and the other established some rules for the relationship. Returning to the opening story, Denise's e-mail to Joan and Lisa clearly contained information about her relationship with them. The structure of the language said, "I'm in charge. Don't question what I do." Most messages say as much about the relationships as they do the actual content.

Relational Balance

The third principle has to do with the balance of the relationship. Interpersonal relationships are identified as *symmetrical* when the two partners are equal in the relationship. In such a relationship, they participate equally in decision making and share control over what they do together. Other relationships are *complementary*, meaning that one person's behavior complements the other person's behavior. For example, one may be dominant, whereas the other is submissive. Thus, this second type of relationship is based on a maximization of differences between two people: one plays the "one-up position" and the other plays the "one-down position." Superior–subordinate relationships appear complementary, whereas coworker relationships appear symmetrical. In most relationships, however, the individuals shift in and out of these roles at various times.

In Carrie's story, Denise appeared to have a symmetrical relationship with each of the others until she invited Carrie and Sallie to lunch. Joan and Lisa then perceived her relationship with Carrie and Sallie as more equal than their relationship with her, feeling that Carrie and Sallie had been given special access to Denise. This change in relationships caused the friction and became an important issue to resolve.

Interpersonal Needs

The fourth principle concerns need. In any interpersonal relationship, both partners come to the relationship with the same psychological needs but at different levels of strength. Each partner is expressing three kinds of needs to some degree:

the need for affection, the need for inclusion, and the need to control others (Schutz, 1966). First, everyone needs to feel included by others, to feel like a full partner in a relationship. This is an expression of the human desire to be a member of some relationship or group. Second, everyone has a need to give and receive affection from others, even in a work environment. Affection can range from feeling liked by others to more intimate feelings. Finally, people want to feel that they have the power to affect outcomes in relationships. Everyone needs to control others. Each individual feels these needs to a different degree.

For example, at work some people have a strong need to control others; other people want specific job instructions and feel little need to be "in charge." Some people want to take the lead, and others are happy to follow. Schutz's hypothesis is that the better the fit between individuals and their respective needs, the more productive the relationship will be. If a person has a high need for inclusion, her most satisfying relationship will be with someone who has a high need to include others. Part of what caused the frustration among the office workers in Carrie's story was Joan and Lisa's need to be included, Denise's need to control, and Carrie and Sallie's need for affection.

Relational Control

The fifth principle deals with control. Research on power in the workplace suggests that coworker relationships can serve as a powerful control over an employee's behavior. Melissa Gibson (1998) discovered this fact in an extensive study of blue-collar workers. At Industry International, an incentive plan that included every organizational worker provided the backbone of the company's success. The company maintained high profitability and superior work levels for almost a century because of the incentive program, which was designed to make workers feel like independent entrepreneurs. In this situation, the workers controlled one another's behaviors because the income of all was dependent on the work of all. The disadvantage was that "industry workers labor through long work weeks, dangerous job tasks, and adverse working conditions" (p. 14). The workers have received from 55 percent to 107 percent of their base salary as additional income at the annual "bonus day."

However, there was a cost to the workers to produce such high earnings for the company. These workers never took sick leave; they came to work sick. They did not take vacation days, and they worked an average of 60 to 70 hours per week without overtime pay. What Gibson discovered was that this incentive plan had become a major way that coworkers controlled one another's behavior, and it had become quite constraining. As Cheney (1995) pointed out, "There really is no empowerment in the increased responsibility for employees with 1½ or 2 jobs to do" (p. 168). This is an excellent example of concertive control, which was discussed in Chapter 5.

Being sensitive to these principles will make you better able to manage your work relationships successfully. Knowing that proxemics can encourage the development of a relationship may make us more sensitive to the design of offices. Knowing that the way in which you convey information may actually contribute to controlling someone's behavior will make you more aware of how you are communicating that information. Knowing that the other person in the relationship may have a higher need to control, be included, or be liked may make us more tolerant of the differences between us.

Using this information to manipulate others for your own gain or to damage others would be unethical behavior. Consider Kreps' ethical principles discussed in Chapter 1. Control used in this way would certainly violate the principle of not inflicting harm on another, and would thereby be considered unethical behavior. One role of all organizational members, but particularly management, is to be aware of the possibility of such behavior and to foster an atmosphere where it is not tolerated: "Managers who fail to provide proper leadership and to institute systems that facilitate ethical conduct share responsibility with those who conceive, execute and knowingly benefit from corporate misdeeds" (White & Lam, 2000).

These five principles of coworker relationships can help us to understand how these relationships function; however, it is also important to know how they develop. The communication process changes as the relationship develops over several stages.

Relationship Development in the Workplace

Coworker relationships can take one of three primary forms: information peer, collegial peer, and special peer (Kram & Isabella, 1985). An *information-peer relationship* is characterized by low levels of self-disclosure and trust. Individuals in such a relationship tend to focus on work-related issues and share little intimacy beyond polite conversation. *Collegial peers* share moderate levels of trust, self-disclosure, emotional support, and friendship. These friends share information beyond that of an acquaintance, but not as much information as a close friend. Conversation could range from work-related issues and difficulties to information about one's personal life. The third form, *special peer*, is a relationship that is characterized by high levels of emotional support, trust, self-disclosure, and intimacy. These individuals are able to share feedback about work as well as personal issues and the content and depth of discussions is almost limitless (Sias, 2005).

Patricia Sias and Daniel Cahill (1998) have traced the development of coworker relationships and corresponding changes in communication patterns. They have identified three transitions in coworker relationships: *transition 1—* acquaintance to friend; *transition 2*—friend to close friend; and *transition 3*—close friend to almost best friend. Organizational relationships will vary across these transitions. Some work relationships will remain at the acquaintance stage despite the fact that the individuals may have worked together for some time. They simply lacked sufficient mutual attraction or shared life events to move the relationship to the next stage. Some will move to the friendship stage, whereas others will become close friends. In other words, not all relationships move through all three stages. During each of these transitions, some patterns of communication are more obvious than others.

The first transition, from acquaintance to friend, is primarily caused by contextual (environmental) factors such as being in the same physical space, sharing tasks, and socializing outside of work. For many, this transition is caused simply by working with the other person for extended periods of time in close proximity. An increase in perceived similarity is an important reason as well. The communication between the partners focuses more on nonwork and personal topics and is less and less cautious.

The second transition, from friend to close friend, is driven primarily by problems or events in both personal life and work life. Socializing becomes more intimate in that coworkers spend more time together outside of work and with each other's families. Communication becomes more intimate and more open. People discuss more work-related problems than they did prior to becoming close friends.

The third transition, moving from close friend to almost best friend, is associated primarily with socializing outside work and shared life events and work-related problems. Trust increases and coworkers feel freer to share opinions and feelings, especially about work frustrations. Discussions about work and personal life become much more detailed.

> In sum, coworker friendships tended to develop early due to the coworkers simply being around one another, working together on shared projects and tasks, and perceiving common ground. At this point, the variety of communication topics discussed increased; however, the coworkers were somewhat cautious about sharing information and opinions with one another. Relationships developed into close friendships, usually because of important personal or work-related problems . . . until the coworker became a trusted source of support with communication becoming increasingly more intimate and less cautious. (Sias & Cahill, 1998, p. 289)

Given the benefits of coworker relationships mentioned earlier, coupled with the information from this study that proximity plays a large role in the development of such relationships, organizations may need to take another look at the use of telecommuting and "virtual offices." Many companies today, in order to decrease costs, hire new employees to work out of their cars or their homes, that is, to have "movable" offices. Movable offices are accomplished by having fewer offices overall and making no permanent office assignments. Thus, when an employee needs to spend a day at the office and is not traveling, she "signs out" the office space needed for that day and files are delivered to that location for that time. These trends may incur significant costs in terms of human relationships. Stohl (1995) concluded that "when workers are no longer simultaneously at the work site, there is less overlap and interaction among specializations, people are less identified with the organization, and coworkers are not available for task and social support" (p. 9). We discuss the impact of technology and telework on relationships and other organizational issues in Chapter 14.

Think back to the information presented on assimilation in the organization. For a new employee who is trying to begin the process of identification with the organization, movable offices could be a serious drawback. Those first weeks are an important time for the organization to begin the process of socializing the new member into its culture. With diverse populations in the workforce, this process will become even more important. If employees are isolated from the organizational environment, it is likely that organizational commitment and loyalty will decrease significantly.

A second critical factor in the development of coworker relationships is how superiors treat coworkers. Patricia Sias and Fred Jablin (1995) have studied how superior–subordinate relationships influence the communication characteristics of coworker relationships; specifically, how perceived differential superior–subordinate treatment affects coworker relationships. They found, through extensive interviews and analysis of incidents reported by participants, that when a subordinate received treatment perceived as undeserved, *favorable*, and differential (i.e., others perceived this person as a "brownnoser"), then group members developed distrust and dislike of that subordinate. They communicated with that person less often and became more cautious about what topics they would discuss with him or her: "In sum, the target became isolated from the rest of the group communication network" (p. 23). Sasha Holmgren, a 46-year-old financial consultant, tells us the following story that demonstrates Sias and Jablin's findings:

> There was a time when it was my son's senior year soccer season. I had privately asked my boss that, for the next month, could I get out of work at most an hour early on days when the soccer games were away. We worked out this agreement, and I had to pick up a few extra responsibilities, but it was no big deal, and I was very appreciative of it. But, there was this one woman that I worked with that saw me leaving at certain times during the week and really got mad about it. First of all, it was none of her business, and second, she had no idea what kind of agreement I had with our boss.
>
> She became very hostile towards me and made the working environment very uncomfortable. There was so much tension between us, yet, she never confronted me about it; she just gave me attitude. So one day I confronted her. I told her exactly what I was feeling and that it was none of her business what I had worked out with our boss. She had never taken into consideration the times when she asked our boss for some kind of special treatment. Eventually, the tension decreased, but it was so hostile because of the lack of communication between us.

Sasha's situation is a clear example of how the perception of favorable or differential treatment by supervisors can cause major relational and organizational concerns. The hostile environment that was created due to this situation certainly had to affect both the productivity of these employees and their levels of satisfaction and commitment.

When the target was perceived to be receiving undeserved, *negative*, and differential treatment, the effect was to increase group cohesiveness and the frequency of communication among coworkers. The intensity of their relationships increased, and they felt free to discuss a wider variety of topics: "There was an increase in communication frequency and intensity, along with a decrease in editing of communication with the target" (p. 24).

Often, unfavorable differential treatment of a subordinate was perceived by coworkers to be fair because the person was a poor performer. In this situation, communication significantly decreased as coworkers attempted to distance themselves from the "problem" employee. In the opposite situation, where a coworker was perceived to deserve favorable treatment because he "earned" it, others tended to respect that person and regard him with approval. The person actually became a conduit between other coworkers and the supervisor.

Sias and Jablin's study shows that the different ways in which the supervisor treats employees have serious consequences for coworker relationships. Some of these consequences can have a negative effect on the productivity of the entire work group, whereas others serve to isolate an individual from the rest of the group. Personal relationships of all forms in organizations are complicated enterprises; both positive and negative consequences can emerge from these situations.

Positive Consequences of Workplace Relationships

Workplace friendships can provide a number of benefits to both of the individuals involved in them as well as to the organization. Friendships are a unique workplace relationship in that they are formed voluntarily; that is, friendship is a relationship that individuals choose to involve themselves in beyond the expected and anticipated work relationships. Friendships also are unique because they afford individuals an opportunity to know one another outside of the organizationally prescribed role and status (Sias & Cahill, 1998). This unique feature actually provides one of the benefits of the relationship: individuals are able to share workplace experiences and help one another make sense of them. Individuals can talk to their coworkers about organizational phenomena that friends outside of the organization might not understand or be able to relate to. These shared experiences can provide valuable emotional, social, and task support to individuals and, in turn, benefit the organization by potentially reducing employee burnout and turnover.

Friendships at work can also provide a support system that supplies information and feedback people might not otherwise receive. Peers, particularly those with higher levels of trust and intimacy, can be valuable sources of important organizational information as well as gossip (Rawlins, 1994). The more connected someone is to other individuals in the organization, the greater that person's loyalty is to the organization. This combination of organizational information and loyalty can lead to further career development, which can benefit not only the worker but also the organization.

Coworkers can also exert a great deal of influence over how their peers view organizational attitudes, behaviors, and policies (Kirby & Krone, 2002). This influence can determine whether an individual chooses to utilize family medical leave, paternity leave, or flex time. An individual is less likely to use a benefit that is available to him if he feels that his coworkers will think less of him for doing so.

Sometimes having someone befriend another employee is just what that employee needs to be successful. Consider the following example where one comment made a difference (Blank & Slipp, 2000):

Albert, a Polish immigrant, has been for 10 years a department manager in a nursing home and rehabilitation center that is part of a national chain. In this time he has seen several directors come and go but has never felt equal to the director. Also he has noticed that his peers—other department heads—do not consider him a professional. They are responsible for nursing, finance, food, and administration. He is head of maintenance, including housekeeping and laundry. At several staff meetings he was not only ignored but told that his department was "full of uneducated ghetto hoods or illegal aliens."

Albert tells his story:

> I know my people aren't as educated as many of the other staff and that some of them are immigrants—all legal—but they work hard and take pride in their jobs. And frankly, they usually show more respect and care for the residents than do the so-called professionals whose job it is to take care of them. I felt continually isolated by the other department heads, but I wanted to break the ice. I noticed that during some of the staff meetings two of the people did not take part in the "trashing" of my department. Outside the meetings, I began to reach out to these potential allies by chatting with them when I saw them in the halls. Finally, I confided in Pat, who seemed the friendliest, and told her how I felt in the meetings. Pat reminded me that I could "catch more flies with honey than vinegar." I was familiar with the expression but didn't quite see how I could apply it. Every day for a week Pat would ask me, "Use any honey yet, Al?" I would just smile and say, "I don't know what kind to buy." One day, just before a staff meeting I put together several bunches of fresh-cut flowers from my garden and gave them to the other department heads with a note. The note said, "Thank you for all your support and professionalism. It makes me strive even harder to exceed our goals for the residents." Well, the "honey" worked! Everyone immediately started asking me questions about the flowers and gardening. People were surprised and impressed about how much I knew about plants. Within a few weeks, I was greeted in a warm and friendly way whenever the other department heads saw me, and the negative comments about my staff stopped. (pp. 37–38)

The relationships Albert was building not only affected him in a positive way, but his entire staff began to benefit from the respect he was gaining. Relationship-building is especially important for minority members of an organization. They may already feel alienated, so building links to others in the organization is critical. Such links will help them feel that they belong and that the organization has accepted them. Without those personal connections, they could feel cut off. Work relationships can also have negative consequences; thus, it is important to emphasize the positive attributes and develop ways to mediate or resolve the negative consequences.

Negative Consequences of Workplace Relationships

Coworker relationships are not without negative consequences. Eileen Berlin-Ray (1993) has articulated some of the potential negative results of support in coworker relationships. She contends that such support can be misused in four ways: as a commodity, for information retrieval, as a cause of codependency, and against one's own interest.

First, support can be used as a *commodity*—given by one person in order to be "owed" support at some future time. Such support may act as political currency, allowing the provider to dictate to recipients when the provider is ready to "cash in his chips." This exchange is often referred to as "social costs," or the cost of a relationship in terms of time and energy.

Second, support can be used as *information retrieval* provided in order to make the other person feel she should give the supporter some information not ordinarily available to the supporter. For example, Paula invites Sarah for coffee and appears to be supportive while Sarah shares a work problem. Only later does Sarah realize that Paula has shared nothing about herself. In this instance, Paula obtained information she wanted, and Sarah may end up feeling used, which will damage the relationship. Rules about confidentiality in the workplace may negatively affect friendships because they place individuals who are used to disclosure between friends in awkward positions. Consequently, managing organizational information becomes more difficult.

Third, support can lead to *codependency*, a situation in which a coworker becomes dependent on the relationship to the extent that he is no longer able to act independently. For example, Latha and Anne have a close friendship at work. They can depend on each other to share gossip and accompany each other to any office function. When Latha is approached about a special assignment, she turns down this opportunity because it would involve moving to another unit in the organization and separate her from her friend, whom she has come to depend on to such an extent that she is unsure if she could handle this new assignment on her own. Besides, it's comfortable to continue doing what she and Anne have always done. Thus, Latha has missed an opportunity because she and Anne have become too dependent on each other. Some individuals report that their performance at work suffers because of friendships, either because more socializing occurs or because they can get by doing less work due to assistance from friends.

Finally, giving support *may work against the person* providing it. For example, Paula tells Sarah about an opportunity Paula was hoping to get herself. Because she feels obligated to Sarah, she tells her about it too, even though she knows it will not be in her own best interest.

Romantic Relationships in the Workplace

Clearly, developing friendships at work can be beneficial, as well as detrimental, to both the individuals and the organization. When these friendships turn into romantic relationships, both these consequences are heightened and additional complications can develop. A relationship that begins as a romantic one has the potential to turn into sexual harassment. For example, if Minoko decides the romantic relationship should end, and Gary still feels there is a chance to develop it, Minoko could perceive Gary's continued attention as unwanted and contributing to creating a hostile work environment. The fear of repercussions from sexual harassment charges puts a strain on all workplace relationships. When coworkers believe a colleague has harassed someone, or do not believe the person claiming harassment, tension in the workplace becomes the predominant emotion.

However, these potential pitfalls are not a deterrent to workplace romances. One study conducted by the Bureau of National Affairs suggested that approximately one-third of all romantic relationships begin in the workplace (Karl & Sutton, 2000). *The Wall Street Journal's* online career website (2006) states that 40 percent of all employees report being involved in a workplace romance at some point in their career. An article in the April 2006 edition of *USA Today Magazine* reported estimates as high as 20,000,000 workplace romances currently taking place in the United States. According to Fisher (1994), the workplace is an ideal environment for romances to begin because coworkers tend to have similar educational backgrounds, interests, and abilities. Additionally, the workplace provides opportunities for frequent interaction and close contact. Small group and interpersonal communication research has suggested that working closely with another individual that you perceive to be capable and talented increases affinity. Add in similar interests and daily experiences, and you have the perfect recipe for romance.

Like friendships, these relationships have the potential to either benefit or harm the individuals involved. Romantic relationships can increase teamwork, communication flow, and job satisfaction. However, they can also distract the couple from organizational responsibilities as well as other organizational relationships (Hovick, Meyers, & Timmerman, 2003). For example, as Tracy and Logan's romantic relationship develops, they may exclude other team member's ideas or ignore aspects of their jobs that would require them spending time apart. Furthermore, if the organization prohibits coworker romances, then Tracy and Logan may further distance themselves in an attempt to hide their relationship. In the absence of such a policy, the relationship will still be subject to the scrutiny and attention of coworkers and superiors. This attention may be uncomfortable for both the couple and the individuals around them.

As previously mentioned, deterioration of the romance can greatly strain the work environment. Although several newspaper polls have indicated that fewer individuals fear punishment for becoming involved in a romantic relationship in the workplace, the fear of reprisal after a break-up has greatly increased. According to a February 9, 2006, article in *USA Today*, although concern "about sexual harassment related to office romance fell from 95 percent of those polled in 2001 to 77 percent four years later, fear of reprisal after a romance ends grew from 12 percent in 2001 to 67 percent in 2005." In daily life, we know that individuals often seek revenge after a break-up. Revenge in the workplace can involve charges of sexual harassment, negative performance reviews, or the creation of a hostile work environment. Whereas the relationship had the potential to increase job satisfaction and comfort, failed workplace romances can cause the individuals involved to feel insecure, unmotivated, unproductive, nervous, angry, or intimidated (Soloman & Williams, 1997). Additionally coworkers may feel caught in the middle of the break-up, resulting in the deterioration of additional relationships.

The break-up of relationships that are not mutually romantic can have the same consequences as when romantic partners in the workplace break up. In some situations, intimate feelings are not reciprocated and perceptions of the nature of the relationship may differ for the parties involved. This can be especially difficult when there is a supervisory relationship between the two. Take for example the situation described by Amelia, a 21-year-old intern at a radio station. She had worked at the radio station for two years on and off, but one summer she interned with the sales department, and that is the setting for this story:

> When I asked to do sales at the station instead of promotions, my advisors agreed and paired me up with one of the top sales executives. He was 38 and very successful and a fun person to be around. I had known him since I started at the station two years earlier, but didn't know him on a personal basis. Things started out fine. He interviewed me, and I got the internship, then he had me watch a series of videos for a few weeks. After that, I began to go with him on sales calls and began working on my own projects.
>
> During the sales call it was just the two of us in his car driving from place to place. We would have lunch together while he explained the business to me and talked about his clients. But he would also talk to me about myself and school and just life in general. We would talk about our social lives, like dating and partying. I never thought much of it. He mentioned that we should hang out sometime at the bars downtown, and I thought that was normal because I had hung out with so many people from the office before at concerts or promotions we had at the bars.
>
> After I went back to school, he would call me sometimes or I would call him to discuss how things were going at the station and how his clients were. Then I'd talk about my classes that term. He knew that I went home every weekend to work, so he mentioned us finally hanging out sometime. Then he called me one day saying he had tickets to a concert and his friend was going and so were some people from the station. So I went, but we were mostly with his friend and his girlfriend the whole time, so it felt kind of weird, but not too weird, because his friend was closer to my age.
>
> When I was at work one Saturday, my Mom left me a message that I had just received flowers for Sweetest Day. So I rushed home after work to see who they were from, and they were from him. I began crying because he was my mentor and I knew that I didn't have feelings towards him in that way. I thought he was fun and a friend, but apparently he thought more. It made me very uncomfortable. Especially since he was supposed to be like my boss and he was almost twice my age.

> It just scared me and frustrated me because I knew that I wanted to work for this organization one day, but I felt that my chances were being taken away once I let him know that I was not interested and didn't mean to send the wrong intentions to him. He hasn't really spoken to me since, and now I just feel like I've lost a tie with the sales division of the organization.

Amelia now finds herself in a very difficult situation. On one hand, she has lost someone she thought was a good friend and mentor to her who could help her succeed at the radio station in the future. On the other hand, though she did not characterize it as such, she was perhaps a victim of sexual harassment, depending on how it is defined in the company's policies and procedures. The sales executive also found himself in a very difficult situation, though he clearly overstepped the boundaries of acceptable behavior. He had been developing what he thought was an intimate relationship with this person, whom he thought by her calling him and going out on a "date" was reciprocating. This misunderstanding led to extremely negative personal and professional consequences for both parties. Amelia has lost a mentor, an important connection in the sales department, and her confidence was been shaken. The sales executive lost a solid worker and a chance to mentor a younger worker; he could have gained a sexual harassment charge. The organization now must suffer the consequences of lost productivity, strained relationships, and inevitable gossip. Romantic relationships in the workplace are indeed complicated.

The Organizational Perspective on Workplace Romance

As with friendships, workplace romances have the potential to either benefit or harm the organization. These relationships are different though in that the potential for harm greatly increases if the relationship results in a break-up. In our daily lives, we are much more tolerant of ex-friends than we are of ex-lovers. Given the potential for disaster, you would expect organizations to have firm and clear policies on dealing with workplace romance. Over the years, organizational management styles have seemed to progress from a strict no-fraternization policy to a "don't ask, don't tell" policy to a surprising mixture of unclear and unresolved policies. An article on February 9, 2006, in *USA Today* reported that 72 percent of companies polled did not have policies in place on office romances. An article in the April 2006 edition of *USA Today Magazine* quoted the American Management Association as stating that only 12 percent of companies maintain a written policy on employee dating. Among those having policies, 92 percent prohibited employees from dating a subordinate, 69 percent disallowed dating a supervisor, and 11 percent banned all workplace romances.

It is surprising that more organizations do not have office romance policies in place given the personnel, as well as legal, problems such relationships can cause for the organization. In addition to the morale problems previously discussed, Hovick, Meyers, and Timmerman (2003) found that workplace couples tend to exchange a great deal of personal information while on the company clock. Their study indicated that the average couple spoke face-to-face approximately five times, exchanged a little over four emails, and spoke on the phone several times in the course of an average work day. Practically speaking, this means that during an eight-hour work day, couples are e-mailing one another at least once every two hours. Obviously, time spent on personal issues is time not spent on organizational issues. As we know from our daily lives, sending the e-mail is the least time-consuming part of the process; we must also think about and compose the e-mail in addition to reading and digesting the e-mail that we receive. Therefore, the total time away from work-related duties is much greater than just the time involved in hitting the send button.

Organizations that allow office romances to occur may face legal consequences. As previously discussed, sexual harassment charges are one possible legal consequence. Another possibility though is the potential for lawsuits based on preferential treatment. *The New York Times* reported on July 24, 2005, that the California Supreme Court ruled that "workers can sue when a colleague who is sleeping with the boss is shown repeated preferential treatment." Workers often are concerned that romantic relationships between superiors and subordinates may result in unfair raises, unjust promotions, better assignments, and breaches in confidentiality. Coworkers are afraid that information they share with the colleague or boss may automatically be shared with the intimate partner.

To reduce the potential of these lawsuits, while also recognizing that the potential for office romance is high, some companies have become creative in their efforts to minimize potential problems. One such solution is to require a relationship contract. These contracts can include a statement that both parties are willingly and voluntarily involved in the relationship and an agreement to comply with all organizational sexual harassment policies. These contracts can also require that the individuals participate in mediation to resolve any complaints that come out of the relationship either during the course of the relationship or at its dissolution.

Companies that do not want to prohibit office romances can also establish clear guidelines for pursing such relationships. According to John Challenger, CEO of a global outplacement firm, these guidelines should include the following:

1. *Clear definitions of what types of relationships are allowed.* In other words, are relationships permitted between superiors and subordinates as well as coworkers? Are only individuals in different units permitted to date?
2. *Definitions of what behaviors are considered appropriate in the work environment.* Will couples be allowed to hold hands or share e-mails and telephone calls during work hours and on company property?
3. *Have in place alternative assessment opportunities if the couple involves a superior.* To eliminate the perception of unfairness, it is best if a couple involved in a romantic relationship do not evaluate one another or decide salary raises or promotions.

4. *Managers should meet with romantically involved couples to be assured that the relationship is indeed consensual and not violating any organizational sexual harassment policies.* Managers should also monitor post–break-up couples to ensure that no company policies dealing with sexual harassment or violence are being violated.

Relationship Deterioration

Given the importance of workplace relationships to both individuals and the organization, it makes sense that the loss or deterioration of such relationships would have the potential to impede workplace processes. In extreme scenarios, the work process could halt if individuals feel the need to seek other employment because they no longer feel comfortable or able to work with their former friend. In daily life, everyone has had an experience where a friendship can no longer be maintained and the ex-friend is avoided at any and every cost. Now imagine if that ex-friend is a coworker, superior, or subordinate, and you can see how such a situation could strain work processes, if not entirely halt them. Sias, Heath, Perry, Silva, and Fix (2004) identified five primary reasons that friendships deteriorate in the workplace. These reasons include personality issues, life events, conflicting expectations, promotions, and betrayal.

As with nonworkplace friendships, personality issues can cause friendships to deteriorate. Traits that were once endearing may become annoying or more extreme than one individual wants to manage. For example, an individual may be drawn to another person because of her ability to speak her mind, but over time that individual may become more outspoken than the other can handle. Individuals, as in daily life, may start to see more differences than similarities and no longer have a basis on which to maintain or continue the friendship. Additionally, being together at work challenges friends' needs for some autonomy and distance from each other. It is possible that friends can share too much time together and strain the need for independence in the relationship.

Loss of similarities may also occur because of changing life events. Kirby and Krone's (2002) research found that coworkers often cluster into subgroups based on family status (i.e., married/unmarried, children/childless). As an individual's family status changes, he may no longer find social support from his former friends, but instead seek friendships from new subgroups. Family status changes could include the birth or death of a child, marriage or divorce, or the challenge of caring for an elderly or ill parent. These life changes can be one source of conflicting expectations.

As individuals' life events change, so may their attitudes towards flex-time, family medical leave, maternity/paternity leave, and so on. Whereas they and their friends once agreed that flex-time was unfair and only rewarded individuals with children, the addition of a child to the family may change their perception of such a benefit. This expectation of what is fair and unfair may cause conflict with a former friend.

Another source of conflicting expectations can come when individuals change work responsibilities or status. Friendships can deteriorate over unexpected evaluations, reprimands, or differing opinions. In most friendships, people seek to find acceptance. If one member of the relationship has to provide negative feedback to the other at work, this can certainly result in a strain on acceptance. The demands of the job, such as an annual review, can cause conflicting expectations as individuals attempt to negotiate their expectations of their friend as well as coworker or superior. If individuals are unable to negotiate these conflicting roles and expectations, the friendship is likely to deteriorate.

If one friend advances through the organizational ranks faster than another friend the friendship can suffer. Sias et al. (2004) found that individuals often have difficulty negotiating changes in status when one individual receives a promotion that places them in a position of authority or greater rank than the other. We generally expect that our friends are our equals and that we share the same difficulties and challenges. However, this same study found that individuals who lose a friendship because of promotion experience less anger and frustration than those who lose friendships for other reasons. Individuals tend to perceive promotion as a natural evolutionary work process, and although they may mourn the loss of the friendship, promotions and the changes that they bring with them are considered to be part of a natural progression.

Given the importance of trust in any friendship, it seems logical that a betrayal of trust would be the last reason for the loss of friendship. Betrayal can come in many forms, including those already discussed. For example, an individual could be perceived as stealing a client, inappropriately disclosing personal information, not supporting a friend's suggestion or idea, or a multitude of other behaviors that can lead to one person feeling betrayed by the other. Once betrayed, most individuals find it difficult, if not impossible, to trust the other again, leading to the demise of the friendship.

Strengthening Workplace Relationships

The following discussion describes approaches to increasing satisfaction at work. Because strong, positive coworker relationships have many benefits for individuals, as well as the organization as a whole, the authors recommend reinforcing the following behaviors of both managers and employees. One can provide positive feedback; work to mediate conflict, discuss communication (or metacommunication); help employees manage peer, friend, and romantic relationships; and finally, incorporate coworker relationships in total quality programs.

Provide Positive Feedback

Positive feedback not only raises morale among your peers, it also helps to ensure the type of support you would like to receive in return. Everyone needs encouragement to keep going and to keep improving. Technology such as e-mail makes providing feedback quick and easy to do. One corporate leader we talked with described it this way: "I always say 'thank you' or 'congratulations' to peers, as well as superiors. This is not only the kind thing to do but also the smart thing to do. I will remember when they notice my achievements, and when they need my help I will be much more likely to want to respond."

Mediate Conflict

Earlier in this book, we discussed conflict and how to cope with, resolve, and mediate it. Here we identify mediating conflict as an especially useful skill in the communicative organization. A person who is able to mediate conflict between peers will often be chosen as the leader of a group. No one wants to be miserable at work, and anyone who can intervene to stop the "pain" of a conflict is often identified as the leader.

Diversity at work may require additional skills at developing coworker relationships: "If managed well, a diverse work force can boost productivity and creativity, increase market share and make your organization more responsive to diverse markets" (Kunigis, 1997, p. 12). As an organizational member, you should be concerned about your organization's level of awareness and support of a diverse workforce. Such awareness will add to the vitality of a communicative organization and ultimately result in making it more successful and a richer place to work. You will need to be sensitive to different cultures and ways of resolving conflict so that diversity remains a positive attribute of the organization.

Discuss Communication

Metacommunication is talking about how you talk to each other; it is about the communication process itself. Thus "meta" communication is one step removed from the actual communication event: communicating about communication. If you are able to talk to peers about the way in which you are communicating with one another, you may find other people have the same perceptions about situations. Usually this discovery serves to identify potential conflicts before they must be mediated. For example, you might say to a coworker, "I was thinking about our staff meeting this morning and I'm wondering if I was clear about cost-containment. Did that make sense to you? I saw you frowning and I wondered if I wasn't being clear or if you disagreed with the point. I'd really like your opinion."

Help Manage Relationships

Managing all the possible work relationships is difficult. Sometimes only a fine line separates professional relationships, platonic friendships, and romance. No matter how fair one person may attempt to be, others' perceptions of that fairness will always be tarnished by their observation of those close, personal conversations that are likely to occur in informal surroundings. It is difficult to draw that line, especially because we are spending so much time at work that it naturally becomes the place where friendships are formed. For some people in the organization, interpersonal relationships are of prime importance, whereas to others, work always comes first. Neither approach is right or wrong, simply different. In a previous publication, one of the authors suggested the following guidelines for developing friendships at work (DeWine, 1994, pp. 340–341).

- Develop your closest friendships outside of work. Everyone needs someone in whom to confide. Those confidences must not affect the work relationships that already exist. Consequently, they should be shared with individuals not in the immediate work environment. Of course, you must restrain yourself from betraying the confidentiality entrusted to you by peers. Information shared with friends at work should be more general, and specific individuals should not be named.
- Don't start an intimate relationship at work unless you are prepared to cope with the consequences. Those consequences may include one of the partners leaving the company if the relationship interferes with people's ability to work together. Other consequences, such as a lack of trust by coworkers, perceived favoritism leading to resentment, and breakdown in relationships among coworkers, may not be so obvious.
- Recognize that males and females will cope with friendships at work differently. This difference may not have as much to do with biological sex as with psychological sex. One individual will approach the office secretary with friendly overtures, maintaining the relationship first and asking for help second. Others will think first of the work to be done, and only when it is completed will they turn to maintaining the relationship with "small talk." Understanding this difference allows us to be more tolerant of these differences rather than rejecting one approach or the other.

Some organizational incentives, such as total quality management (TQM), work to improve coworker relationships. TQM places people on teams where they must work closely together on organizational issues. Two researchers (Allen & Brady, 1997) discovered that organizations with TQM experienced more positive coworker relationships than those without TQM. An organization-wide initiative such as TQM may enhance personal relationships.

The best organizational relationships, like the best marriages, are true partnerships that tend to meet certain criteria. Kanter (1997, p. 246) has identified a series of these criteria for healthy work relationships:

1. *Individual excellence.* Both partners are strong and have something of value to contribute to the relationship. Their motives for entering into the relationship are positive (to pursue future opportunities), not negative (to mask weaknesses or escape a difficult situation).
2. *Importance.* The relationship fits major strategic objectives of the partners, so they want to make it work. Partners have long-term goals in which the relationship plays a key role.
3. *Interdependence.* The partners need each other. They have complementary assets and skills. Neither can accomplish alone what both can together.

4. *Investment.* The partners invest in each other (e.g., through equity swaps, cross-ownership, or mutual board service) to demonstrate their respective stakes in the relationship and each other. They show tangible signs of long-term commitment by devoting financial and other resources to the relationship.

5. *Information.* Communication is reasonably open. Partners share information required to make the relationship work, including their objectives and goals, technical data, and knowledge of conflicts, trouble spots, or changing situations.

6. *Integration.* The partners develop linkages and shared ways of operating so they can work together smoothly. They build broad connections between many people at many organizational levels. Partners become both teachers and learners.

7. *Institutionalization.* The relationship is given a formal status, with clear responsibilities and decision processes. It extends beyond the particular people who formed it, and it cannot be broken on a whim.

8. *Integrity.* The partners behave toward each other in honorable ways that justify and enhance mutual trust. They do not abuse the information they gain, nor do they undermine each other.

Summary

Communication with peers at work creates a strong bond between the employee and the organization. When people feel more connected to each other, morale and organizational commitment increase significantly.

In this chapter, we discussed how organizational and personal relationships at work differ. We explored the principles behind developing work relationships, including proxemics, symmetrical and complementary relationships, interpersonal needs, and power. We examined relationship development, the positive and negative consequences of peer relationships, and strategies for strengthening relationships. We also looked at romantic relationships as well as the reasons that workplace relationships tend to deteriorate, which include personality issues, changing life events, conflicting expectations, promotion, and betrayal.

Keep in mind the powerful impact of personal relationships on your own job performance as well as the success of the entire organization. Providing positive feedback to peers, mediating conflict, talking about the relationship and communication in the relationship, and developing approaches to managing the various types of relationships at work will be important skills for you to acquire.

The success with which you manage your interpersonal relationships at work can make the difference between looking forward to going to work each day or dreading the next negative interaction you may have with colleagues. We hope the information in this chapter will help you create an enjoyable working environment.

CHAPTER 12

Organizational Teams

Teams are permanent fixtures in organizational life. Much of the work done in organizations is done by teams, committees, or some other sort of small group: "The proliferation of groups as units of organizational activity extends beyond decision making into such arenas as planning, policy implementation, innovation, and conflict management" (Putnam, 1992). Organizations attempt to develop small groups into organizational teams with a sharper focus to accomplish organizational projects. Why do organizations put so much energy into developing teams? The synergy and nonsummativity that comes with an effective team enables the organization to respond to a dynamic business environment that demands constant innovation and change balanced with stability (McKinney Jr., Barker, Davis, & Smith, 2005). Specifically, research has shown that teams have many benefits, including increased productivity and employee empowerment (Shonk, 1992).

It is quite likely that you, as a newcomer to an organization, will be placed on more than one team at a time. One team might be allocated the task of developing a marketing plan to launch a new product or service and may be disbanded once the product is on the market. Another team might be a more permanent work team in a regional office. The result could be that you report to two different people at once.

Teams serve to link employees to the organization and can increase their loyalty. In fact, in one study researchers found that employees identified more with their teams than with the larger organization (Barker & Tompkins, 1994). The implications for the organization are clear: Productive teams are critical not only to the success of the organization but to the satisfaction of individuals as well.

As you can imagine, definitions of what constitutes a team abound. We offer the following definition of a *team*, which is a mild adaptation of one forwarded by Katzenbach and Smith (1993): *A team is a small group (three to nine) of interdependent people with complementary skills who are committed to a common purpose, performance goals, and approach for which they hold themselves mutually accountable.* Several important aspects of this definition make this a definition of not just any team, but an *effective* one. First, a team must be larger than a dyad (otherwise it is simply an interpersonal relationship), but not too large so that direct communication among all members becomes impossible. Research seems to indicate that the breaking point for team effectiveness is 10 members. Second, the members of the team are interdependent, which means that the success or failure of one member is dependent on the success or failure of the others. If the members of a team are not interdependent, then the time and energy it takes to form and maintain the team is not necessary; work could instead be done independently. Third, members must be committed to each other and to the goals, objectives, and processes of the team. Without this commitment, the team will be burdened by either unproductive or insubordinate members or conflict that does not allow the members to move forward in their tasks. This is not to imply, however, that conflict should be or will be avoided in a healthy team. As we discovered in the previous chapter and will discuss further here, conflict on the appropriate levels and handled positively can be very constructive. Finally, the real strength of a team comes from the mutual accountability of the team members as they hold each other responsible to meeting and exceeding expectations. These expectations involve process concerns (e.g., communication, meeting deadlines, attending meetings, etc.) and outcomes (e.g., quality of work, satisfaction, etc.).

We begin this chapter by outlining the characteristics of teams. Next, we discuss teams in the workplace, followed by descriptions of two types of workplace teams—self-managed work teams and virtual teams. We conclude by discussing effective teams and showing how misunderstandings are a part of team life.

Characteristics of Teams

Certain factors are inherent in any team. The way in which the team manages these characteristics is critical to its success. Relational communication, decision making, norms, cohesiveness, diversity, satisfaction, and stuckness are all characteristics explored in the following sections.

Relational Communication

In addition to completing tasks, teams also serve social, or relationship, goals. First, relationships are formed that help employees feel more connected to the team. These personal relationships make the link between the employee and the organization stronger. Many people talk about the organization as a collection of individuals that work with one another. It is those personal relationships that keep them connected to the organization and give the organization a personality. Second, individuals receive support from others to face difficult challenges. This supportive climate can help members solve personal as well as work-related problems. Colleagues are a good source of comfort when facing a difficult decision, an unusual task, or some new problem.

Third, the team provides opportunities for members to demonstrate leadership abilities. Working with a team gives individuals a chance to step forward and organize tasks as well as provide vision for the future. Leadership demonstrated in a team can be repeated as the employee's level of responsibility shifts to include a larger portion of the organization.

Finally, teams provide a setting in which new ideas can be tested before going "public." Trying out ideas in a team can give an indication of how those ideas might be received by a larger audience. People seem to be more accepting of failed ideas in this smaller setting than when an idea is launched "publicly."

We need interpersonal relationships in order to feel engaged, to test our ideas and abilities, and for moral support. Without team interaction we are isolated, cut off from the advantages of teamwork. We need the support of others to face life's challenges, both at work and in our personal lives.

At the same time, poor relationships can lead to dysfunctional teams. Sometimes the dysfunction is caused by one individual whose behavior is inconsistent. Stohl and Schell (1991) called this person the "farrago":

> We choose to call our focal actor a farrago because (a) interactions with this type of problematic person often result in confusion as to responsibilities, group tasks, decision-making procedures, and so on, and (b) these interactions cause the group itself to become such a confused mixture. . . . [I]nteractions with this type of person often result in confusion as to responsibilities, group tasks, and decision making. (p. 95)

Inconsistent behavior is the most difficult form with which to cope. When a relationship with someone goes from negative to positive to negative again, it is more difficult to respond than if the relationship is always negative. At least if the person's behavior is predictable, even if it is always negative, we can establish ways of limiting the impact of that behavior. It is when the behavior changes dramatically and for no apparent reason that we are caught off guard.

Keyton (1999) has used the term *primary provoker* to identify the initial dysfunctional member and *secondary provoker* for the team members who actively support that person's dysfunctional behavior. When the team members give that support, it compromises the decision-making process. Members must either *avoid* or *accommodate* the focal person. Either reaction takes a great deal of energy, which is diverted from the team's task. Clearly the team accomplishes less. Often the team becomes consumed with the underlying relationships rather than the task:

> Because the primary provoker must have others on which to dispel his or her negativity and others for which to perform, other group members earn the secondary provoker distinction by creating and maintaining (even ineffective) relationships with the primary provoker. (Keyton, 1999, p. 368)

The primary provoker can play the role of scapegoat for the team. Placing blame on one member allows the rest of the team members to ignore their own behavior, which supports the dysfunctional actions. When team members do not "own" their contribution to the failure of the team, they avoid being labeled themselves.

The result of such dysfunctional relationships in the team can include the following: (1) decision-making procedures are compromised to avoid conflict; (2)

issues are defined according to the poor relationship or the weak member; (3) a great deal of energy is consumed trying to resolve issues relative to the primary provoker; (4) confusing behaviors are exhibited in response to this conflict; (5) time and energy is consumed in mending the relationships; and finally, (6) negative emotions are displayed toward the team as a whole (Keyton, 1999, p. 370). Teams trying to solve relationship issues can spend a majority of their time and energy trying to resolve those issues and far less time and energy accomplishing the task.

Decision Making

The process the team goes through to make decisions is critical to its success. If the process is flawed, the decision is weak. For example, if the process allows for one talkative member to dominate all discussions, it is possible the team never hears an opposing viewpoint that could lead to a better decision. Thus, the actual level of team productivity is a product of its potential for success minus the losses due to a flawed process. Steiner (1972, p. 9) offers an equation that illustrates this principle:

Actual productivity = Potential productivity − Losses due to faulty processes

Two well-known authors in group dynamics, Randy Gouran and Dennis Hirokawa (1983), have tried to explain this phenomenon through the development of their *vigilant interaction theory*, which has applications in the work team context. The theory suggests that team interaction affects decision-making performance by directly shaping the quality of vigilance (or critical thinking) that leads to a final team choice. The way in which team members talk about issues affects the way they think about these issues, which, in turn, determines the quality of the choices they make as a team. Gouran and Hirokawa suggest that the final decision is based on four previous subdecisions: (1) Is there something about the status quo that requires improvement or change? (2) What do we want to achieve or accomplish? (3) What are the choices available to us? (4) What are the positive and negative aspects of those choices?

One finding of their research is that the quality of team decisions is less dependent on the team's efforts to develop criteria than it is on the absence of efforts to hinder or retard criteria development. In other words, negative actions have a greater ability to disrupt the team's performance than do positive actions to make the team successful. Another way to state this premise is that continuing to emphasize positive actions, without eliminating negative ones, will not work as well as simply eliminating negative ones.

Norms

Norms are the informal rules that teams establish to govern their activities and behaviors. Teams need to agree on how they will operate. Will they meet weekly?

Will they send written comments to one another or rely on oral discussion exclusively? Will what they say in meetings be confidential? Must they reach consensus or simply take a majority vote? In short, how will they function?

Decisions on such questions are the norms that become a part of the team's culture made up of shared values, beliefs, rituals, and stories about the team. Sometimes these norms emerge gradually and naturally, and other times the team directly discusses early in its history what norms or rules it wants to establish. Either way, norms contribute to the establishment of a pattern of interaction that helps or hinders the work of the team. For example, if the team establishes the norm that the meeting does not begin until 10 or 15 minutes after the hour set for the meeting and that the first 10 to 15 minutes are usually for social conversation, this decision can become a huge barrier to productivity. If, on the one hand, the team establishes taking a vote on controversial issues, this procedure could inhibit the potential for reaching consensus. If, on the other hand, it agrees that every decision and discussion must reach consensus, then the amount of time necessary to complete tasks may be greatly extended. It is important that a team determine the norms that will govern its behavior.

In one of the interviews for this book, a college student, Frank, talked about what happens when team norms are broken. His fraternity had one person assigned to plan social events. The norm was that new recruits were responsible for informing the rest of the chapter about these events. According to Frank:

> We had a social planned with a sorority uptown. It was a failure from the beginning. Our social chair picked one location, then changed it. The person in charge told the recruits and left town that weekend, assuming the recruits would inform the rest of the fraternity of the change, as had been the custom. They did and we showed up, but the sorority did not. No one told them of the change. They went to the first place we had picked. The bar owner was disappointed because he was losing money since half the people didn't show up. The fraternity members were frustrated, as were the sorority members. Normally the socials are supposed to be planned in advance. Everyone is supposed to be at our chapter meetings and we announce the social calendar for the week at the meeting on Sunday. When we changed the way we normally do things it was sure to fail.

Norms should be discussed, and the team needs to be aware of how its norms are contributing to its overall success. In this story, norms were broken, and misinformation resulted. People should learn the particular norms of the team they join and be cautious about breaking them, because there may be negative consequences.

Cohesiveness

Cohesiveness is the degree to which members feel connected to the team. The members' identification with the team and its goals is accomplished through "forging, maintenance, and alteration of linkages between persons and groups" (Scott, Corman, & Cheney, 1998, p. 304). The more these linkages are identified and reinforced, the greater team cohesiveness. For example, an individual might feel a link to a team because he believes in the task on which the team is working. That task could further the organizational goal or advance the success of the team itself. Another individual might feel connected to the team because of relationships formed there. If people are attracted to other team members as friends and colleagues, they will want to work for the team's success.

Fred Jablin's work on organizational assimilation is consistent with team cohesiveness as well. He suggested that the "newcomer attempts to become an accepted, participating member of the organization by learning new attitudes and behaviors or modifying existing ones to be consistent with the organization's expectations" (1984, p. 596). This happens on a smaller scale in organizational teams. Team members adapt to the norms of the team, learn new attitudes and behaviors, and increase team cohesiveness. When members are not able to forge these linkages with the team, then cohesiveness is affected. Can a team function that is not cohesive? In some cases, yes, but it is much more difficult for team members to focus on the team goal. Cohesiveness in teams has been linked to many different positive outcomes, such as increased cooperation and decreased absenteeism (Sanders & Nauta, 2004).

Diversity

The diversity of a team will directly affect cohesiveness. *Diversity* is "not a passing fad. It is, rather, a current trend and a future reality that may determine, in part, the performance, productivity, and success of today's and tomorrow's organizations" (Witherspoon & Wohlert, 1996, p. 376). To the extent that team members can embrace multiculturalism, which involves "increasing the consciousness and appreciation of differences associated with the heritage, characteristics, and values of many different groups, as well as respecting the uniqueness of each individual" (p. 377), those teams will have a greater chance of working collaboratively successfully. When team members feel that their personal or cultural values are dissimilar to the teams' values, there tends to be increased task and relationship conflict and decreased team involvement (Hobman, Bordia, & Gallois, 2003).

Cross-cultural teams have the potential to be the most successful, given the diversity of ideas and contributions they can generate. Solutions are likely to be more inclusive of all possible outcomes. One author examined 800 teams of four to six members and discovered a wide disparity in the effectiveness of multicultural teams (Gannon, 2001). It is critical to examine conflicting values and attitudes directly and openly in the team, or the advantage of having a variety of points of view will be diminished by the conflict they cause. For example, in some cultures, individuals are comfortable working without specific knowledge about tasks, whereas in other cultures they would be very uncomfortable. According to one study, Japan ranks first among 53 national cultures on avoidance of uncertainty, or the need for precision and complete information about how to do tasks.

In response to the question, "Who agrees that managers should have precise answers to questions of subordinates?" different nationalities agreed to the following degree (see Figure 12.1).

Clearly, if there were team members from Japan, Sweden, and the United States on the same team, they would have to resolve the need for clarity and answers to all questions. There would certainly be different tolerance levels for the way in which individuals respond to ambiguity.

Satisfaction

Satisfaction means the team feels it has accomplished its task and members have been recognized individually for their contributions. Satisfaction and rewards are uniquely tied to each other. A team feels satisfied with its work to the degree that the work has been accepted and recognized. The rewards can be external or internal. External rewards can be recognition by a boss, resulting in an increase in salary or promotion. Internal rewards can include meeting individual goals and expectations. In addition to task accomplishment, team members also

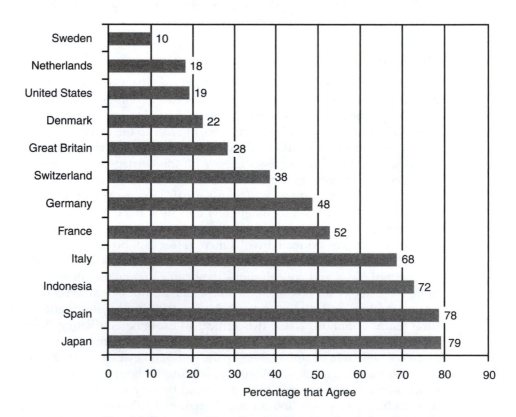

FIGURE 12.1   **Should Managers Have Precise Answers for Subordinates?**

increase satisfaction based on their own social needs. To the extent that one's needs to interact with others, be accepted by others, and be appreciated by others are met by being a member of a team, then satisfaction with the team will increase.

Barker and Tompkins (1994) report an interesting example of how team members begin to identify with and feel satisfied about their team's work. When asked what is different about working in a team environment, one subject in their study reported the following: "You look at your work more as a personal thing than as a company thing" (p. 234). Another example of this linkage to the team was revealed in the following situation:

> One day on the shop floor, Barker met Tim, a new temporary worker. Barker noticed that Tim had his clip-on ID tag turned backwards, hiding the photo. Barker asked him why he wore it this way, to which Tim replied, "That's the way I always wear it." Then he turned the tag around to reveal a capital "T" where the photo should be, which indicated that he was one of many temporary employees and not yet a full-fledged team member. "When you're a temp you don't have a picture on your ID card. You just have a big T there. Your last name is 0123. I'm going to wear it this way until I get full-time status." Tim's desire to identify with the team was so strong that he felt compelled to hide the stigma of not yet being a complete team member. (Barker and Tompkins, 1994, p. 234)

Clearly, team membership in organizations can have compelling effects on our behaviors and attitudes. Membership can lead to higher productivity and loyalty to the company. At the same time, some team characteristics can work against the success of the team, and consequently against the organization.

Stress

Working with others requires coordination and compromise. Conflict is a natural outcome. We experience *stress* because of our own desire to perform and the strain of negotiating with others. Negotiating conflict is psychologically exhausting. It takes a great deal of energy and attention, which creates stress. Because you assume the other party is angry or will be angry, you place yourself in a stressful situation. In self-managed teams (discussed later in this chapter), members tend to put that kind of stress on one another. Self-managed teams are more susceptible to team peer pressure, because instead of one supervisor the team member now has six or eight managers: "Team members expect each other to identify with the team and to behave according to the team's norms and rules. By violating team norms or exhibiting elements of dis-identification a team member risks punishment by the team" (Barker & Tompkins, 1994, p. 226). The resulting stress for the individual team member can be quite high.

Teams, as a collective, are also subjected to many stressors. Morgan Jr. and Bowers (1995) identified several types of team stressors and their potential effects (p. 270):

- *Team training load* (i.e., replacing trained members with untrained members) can reduce decision-making effectiveness.

- *Team workload* can complicate communication patterns, leading to decreased performance.
- *Team size* can lead to decreased information sharing needed to make decisions as size increases.
- *Team cohesion*, when low, can lead to decreased decision-making ability.
- *Goal structure*, when focused on the individual rather than the team, can lead to decreased performance.

Clearly, individual- and team-level stress can affect performance when stress exceeds optimal levels.

Stuckness

Joann Keyton has described another characteristic of teams that can have a negative impact on the team's success—*stuckness*. According to Keyton (2000), "Stuckness refers to the repetitive, often unconscious tensions that prevent a group from even doing the work of problem solving on scarce resources or compromising about conflicting needs" (p. 202). When the team is unable to break a pattern of behavior that keeps it from moving forward, it continues to make the same mistakes. Sometimes the team tends to repeat old patterns of interaction and behavior instead of confronting the opposing forces or beliefs within the team and finding connections between them. This is a situation where changing old norms might be helpful rather than harmful. If those norms are allowing the team to remain "stuck," then trying a new process, changing the environment or climate, or shifting the resources may be the solution. A team may be very willing but unable to perform a task, or it may be quite able but unwilling to do so. Either way, the team is stuck in one position, unable to move forward. It is the challenge of the leader to determine what kind of leadership style would best motivate the team and move it in the right direction.

Therefore, teams can be characterized by relational communication, the decision-making process, the norms they follow, the cohesiveness of the team, the degree to which members are satisfied with the actions of the team, how open the team is to outside opinions and information, how the team handles stress, and the team's degree of "stuckness." All of these traits make each team unique, with its own history and behavior patterns. Examine the teams to which you belong and try to describe the characteristics that define them.

With that general description of the characteristics of teams, we now turn our attention to a more specific discussion of teams in the workplace.

Teams at Work

Although it is difficult to determine exactly what percentage of organizations are using teams today, researchers and practitioners alike agree that a vast number of organizations use them and that their use will only continue to grow. One study published in 1999 (Devine, et al.) claimed that of all U.S. organizations, 48 percent used one or more teams. Another study based on a 1993 survey of *Fortune* 1000 companies (Lawler, Mohrman, & Ledford, 1995) demonstrated that 68 percent use self-managed teams and 91 percent use some form of employee participation group.

Because of the growing demands for flexibility and adaptability to rapidly changing environments, the prevalence of teams in organizations will only continue to grow. For more than 50 years, some organizational theorists have been arguing for making teams the basic work unit. This has been traced by one researcher back to the work of Eric Trist and his coal mine experiments in 1951 (Shonk, 1992). The call for such an organizational structure is still being heeded and repeated with even more strength by current writers, such as Katzenbach and Smith (1993), who said: "we believe that teams—real teams, not just groups that management calls 'teams'—should be the basic unit of performance for most organizations regardless of size" (p. 15).

So what would a team-based organization look like? Team-based organizations can take on several appearances and follow a variety of processes, but they must make cultural shifts in order to support teams. Sherriton and Stern (1997) said that the following cultural shifts must occur:

- **From hierarchical to flat.** Organizations must decentralize their decision-making and power structures; in other words, power and authority must be disturbed throughout the organization.
- **From fragmentation to cohesion.** Cultures that had previously segmented different factions of the organization from one another (e.g., management and workers; accounting and distribution), must now become comfortable with these groups being thrown together.
- **From independence to interdependence.** Individual organizational members will no longer work on projects in singular, isolated ways; their processes and products will be interlinked with other organizational and extra-organizational members.
- **From competition to cooperation.** Many organizations tend to breed competition among coworkers as a means of motivating them to work harder; however, a team-based culture must replace the ethic of competition with one of cooperation, as team members will need to rely on one another, build trust, and increase cohesiveness to have an effective and satisfied team.
- **From tried-and-true to risk-taking.** When individuals work in relative isolation from one another they tend to go with what they know works best and works best for them; however, moving into the realm of teams means that diversity of thought, process, and execution increases, and therefore so does the need to break out of old habits and take risks on new ideas, processes, and products.

Although this cultural shift will take time and will necessarily cause misunderstandings, the move to teams as basic work units should increase performance. Teams tend to perform well for several reasons. First, they bring more skills and experiences to bear on the situation than a single individual. Second, because of the diversity of skills and experiences, teams are more flexible and responsive to change than individuals tend to be. Third, teams afford the members opportunities for close, interpersonal relationships, which, as we described earlier, can significantly affect their quality of work and personal lives. Finally, teams offer the possibility of fun as interpersonal relationships are developed and hardships and successes bring social rewards (Katzenbach & Smith, 1993).

Types of Organizational Teams

Organizational teams can be of a variety of types, and those types can take different forms. There are four major types of organizational teams (Cohen & Bailey, 1997): work teams, parallel teams, project teams, and management teams. These types can take different forms (e.g., supervised, self-directed, virtual). Let's first turn to the four major types of organizational teams.

Although organizational teams can be classified in a number of different ways, researchers Cohen and Bailey (1997) provide a useful and manageable typology. *Work teams* are "continuing work units responsible for producing goods or providing services" (p. 242). Membership in these teams is relatively stable and is full time. These teams have traditionally been directed by supervisors, but currently there is a movement toward self-management. Examples of this type of team are mining crews or apparel manufacturing teams.

Parallel teams "pull together people from different work units or jobs to perform functions that the regular organization is not equipped to perform well" (p. 242). Membership in these teams is a bit more flexible and short-lived than membership in work teams. These teams have limited authority and tend to make recommendations rather than final decisions. Parallel teams tend to be used for problem-solving and improvement activities. Typical examples of parallel teams include quality circles and task forces.

The third type of team described by Cohen and Bailey is a project team. *Project teams* produce one-time outputs and are time limited. Members tend to have specialized expertise, and each member of the team is recruited (and should be valued) for that expertise. A typical example of a project team is a new-product development team that brings together experts from a variety of areas to combine their efforts in the development of a new product.

Finally, *management teams* "coordinate and provide direction to subunits under their jurisdiction, laterally integrating interdependent subunits across key business processes" (p. 243). Often, as other types of teams are assembled that require different specialties or functional differentiation, it is helpful to have teams of managers who have the ability to understand and direct their activities. Management teams are designed to do just that.

Connecting Teams with the Environment

Regardless of the type of team being discussed, one important element of their survival and effectiveness is their connection with the relevant environment. Too often teams are treated as closed systems, more concerned with internal functioning than understanding their connections to external demands. As we discuss in the chapter on systems theory, a system (in this case a team) must be considered in relationship to its relevant environment, otherwise the complexities of the team and its survival are minimized.

Leaders of teams have several options for interacting with the environment. Acona Gladstein (1990) set forth three basic leadership strategies for connecting the team to the larger environment. The *informing* strategy involves concentration on internal team process until the team was ready to inform outsiders of its intentions" (p. 344). With this strategy, the leader decides that maintenance of the team is the most important goal, and that no input is necessary from the environment until the team has completed its decision-making process. Sports teams that shut the doors to the media during difficult times or during times of internal turbulence (e.g., coach being fired, brawl, losing record) could be considered to be using the informing strategy. When the doors are opened to the locker room, the leader generally informs the public as to the future direction of the team, and leaves the team-process issues behind closed doors.

The *parading* strategy places "simultaneous emphasis on internal team building and achieving visibility that would allow outsiders to see that members know and cared about them" (p. 344). This strategy attempts to balance the internal needs of the team with the external needs of the environment. As you can imagine, this can be a taxing effort as the leader attempts to regulate communication and information flow within the team and between the team and the environment.

The last leader strategy for connecting the team with the environment is *probing*. In this strategy, the leader "stressed external processes, requiring team members to have a lot of interaction with outsiders to diagnose their needs and experiment with solutions" (p. 344). This type of strategy can be employed for several purposes. The probing strategy can be useful in that it virtually ensures that the outcome of the team's process will attend to the demands and needs of the environment. Second, constant attention to the various constituencies in the environment can be a valuable public relations tool that shows that they are truly "cared" for. However, giving full attention to the environment while not attending to internal processes can degrade the quality of team performance and satisfaction.

The balance between internal and external foci depends, in part, on the demands of the environment. The real lesson to be learned from these strategies is that the traditional way of thinking about teams (focusing on internal processes) may not lead to the best performance. Team leaders need to understand the demands of the environment and the status of internal processes and then determine the most effective strategy. It is possible (and likely) that the strategy adopted could change as internal and external needs change.

Now that we have discussed the basic nature of organizational teams, we turn our attention to two of the most popular forms that teams are taking in today's organizational environment—self-managed work teams and virtual teams.

Self-Managed Work Teams

Self-managed work teams, also known as *self-directed work teams*, are gaining popularity in organizations of all forms. *Self-managed work teams* (SMWTs) have responsibility for their own work. They set out tasks for themselves and monitor their own performance instead of a supervisor doing these things (Thomas, Pinto, Parente, & Druskat, 2002). Examples of SMWTs include: quality circles, new venture teams, communication teams, task forces, and so on (Barry, 1995). Members of SMWTs should "take responsibility for their work, monitor their own performance, and alter their performance strategies as needed to solve problems and adapt to changing conditions" (Wageman, 1997, p. 49). As workers become involved in SMWTs, they tend to lose their individual-task orientation and define their work roles in regard to how they can personally contribute to the mission and goals of the team (Manz & Sims Jr., 1987).

SMWTs differ from traditional, supervised teams in a variety of ways, but three are of most importance: job categories, authority, and the reward system. First, SMWTs differ from traditional teams in the way that *job categories* are enacted. In traditional teams, employees are detached from the final product due to many narrow job categories (i.e., here's what you do, and here's what I do), but with SMWTs there are a few broad categories with cross-trained members. Second, *authority* is different between the two types of teams. In traditional teams, authority lies with the supervisor, but in SMWTs authority comes from team control (see discussion of concertive control in Chapter 5). Finally, the *reward system* for traditional teams is based on individual performance and seniority, whereas rewards for SMWTs are based on team performance (Barry, 1995).

Why would organizations use SMWTs instead of traditional teams? SMWTs are thought to increase employees' commitment to the organization because participation in decision-making should increase support for those decisions. A self-managed team has special characteristics:

> These groups make all the decisions, do all the coordination, and perform all the work required to complete an end product. Self-managing teams (theoretically) have no first-line supervisors; the team does its own supervising of self and other, thus multiplying the number of potential supervisors. The team hires and disciplines its own members, coordinates directly with other departments for supplies and information, and negotiates with other teams to solve production problems and overcome obstacles. (Barker & Tompkins, 1994, p. 225)

In addition to increasing employee commitment, the use of SMWTs is related to the following important outcomes: competence, productivity, innovative problem solving, increased job satisfaction, increased quality of workers' lives, increased flexibility, and increased customer satisfaction (Chansler, Swammidass, & Cammann, 2003; Kauffeld, 2006; Thomas et al., 2002).

Clearly, SMWTs offer many benefits; however, they are not to be used in every situation. Orsburn and Moran (2000) argued that SMWTs are inappropriate in two situations. First, SMWTs should not be used when interdependence is not required for the outcome. This is useful advice for organizations considering the development of any type of team, but particularly SMWTs. Second, they should not be used in situations where challenging deeply held organizational assumptions would be detrimental. SMWTs are prime organizational contexts for double-loop (generative) learning (discussed in Chapter 6), which involves questioning the way things have been done and the assumptions upon which they are based. Sometimes organizations are not prepared for such challenges, and at other times they are not stable enough to survive them. In these cases, SMWTs, which tend to challenge basic assumptions, should not be used.

By now you might be wondering: If SMWTs do not have a supervisor, what role does leadership play? Barry (1995) tells us that although a SMWT is a "boss-less team," it still requires leadership. This leadership is needed in the areas of task-based processes, as well as in group development. A number of broad types of leadership roles and behaviors are needed in SMWTs (Barry, 1995, pp. 58–59):

- **Envisioning**—creation of new and compelling visions, which involves generating ideas and defining goals.
- **Organizing**—coordination of the many elements that are connected to the team's tasks, which involves attention to deadlines, efficiency, and structure.
- **Spanning**—connection of the team's activities with the important constituents in the relevant environment, which includes networking, securing resources, and being politically aware.
- **Social**—concern for the social and psychological needs of the team members, which includes interpreting and paraphrasing, using humor, and mediating conflicts.

These leadership roles and behaviors, which are enacted by various members within the SMWT, vary in importance depending on the type of project. For example, when working on a problem-solving project such as how to decrease harmful emissions from a manufacturing plant, the behaviors of organizing and spanning may be most relevant as the SMWT begins work. However, with a project-based SMWT, goals will need to be set at the outset, which requires envisioning.

The ultimate success of SMWTs, as with all teams, depends on myriad factors and conditions. Research has pointed to several of these issues, which we will cover as a way of concluding our discussion of SMWTs. Successful SMWTs must have control of the resources they need, such as money, human resources, office supplies, communication equipment, travel, and so on. Without the ability to control these resources, the SMWT has no fuel, and therefore no chance to succeed. A successful SMWT must also have team members who have the necessary cross-functional skills to accomplish the task. All the resources in the world will not help a team that does not have the skills demanded by the situation. The SMWT must also have the support of the organization as well as all of the information necessary to accomplish its goal. Although information tends to be a guarded resource in some organizations, withholding it from a SMWT dooms it to failure. Finally, SMWTs must be cohesive. Cohesiveness in SMWTs has been shown to be related to two primary factors: (1) having control or influence over staffing and training of new team members and (2) the perception of fair treatment by the leadership of the organization. Although there are many other contributors to the success of SMWTs, the following have been identified as the most critical (Chansler et al., 2003, pp. 101–102):

Virtual Teams

As globalization, geographically disparate workforces, and the need to balance work-family lives have all begun to define modern organizational life, organizations have relied on new communication technologies to facilitate teamwork:

> Distance-spanning communication tools open up vast new fertile territory for "working together apart." For the first time since nomads moved into towns, work is diffusing rather than concentrating as we move from predominantly industrial to information products and services. (Lipnack & Stamps, 1997, p. 2)

What Lipnack and Stamps are referring to is the creation of virtual teams. A *virtual team* "works across space, time, and organizational boundaries with links strengthened by webs of communication technologies" (Lipnack & Stamps, 1997, p. 7). The members of virtual teams may have never met face-to-face, or they may have offices in the same building. Membership in virtual teams is limited only by communication technology and a common language.

The tremendous strides made in communication and information technologies have spurred the use of virtual teams to new heights. Obviously, the lack of such technologies would seriously restrict the extent to which virtual teams could function or exist. Technologies such as wide area networks, voice-over internet protocol, virtual private networks, the Internet, and computer-mediated communication software serve as the platform upon which virtual teams are built (Beranek & Martz, 2005). The different needs of virtual teams are met with different technology. For example, according to Chinowsky and Rojas (2003) the need to *communicate or interact* with virtual team members can be accomplished using the telephone, cellular phone, teleconference, fax, e-mail, and instant messaging. If team members need to engage in *cooperation*, they can use project websites, discussion boards, or work sharing. Finally, if they need to *collaborate* they can use videoconferencing with data sharing and virtual teaming.

The use of such technology does of course bring with it concerns. First is the need to ensure that all members are trained and comfortable with using the full range of technology that might be necessary for the team to function effectively and efficiently. Second, security is a major concern for virtual teams. As hackers, viruses, and data theft proliferate, virtual team processes, data, communication, and outcomes are all at risk. Finally, technology can just simply break or malfunction, and when teamwork is all done virtually this can be detrimental to the team.

In addition, the use of virtual teams can be financially costly. Leonard et al. (1998) point out the potential costs of the use of virtual teams:

> There are some extra costs to operating . . . virtual teams, however. While business is being transacted across ever-expanding distances, much of it still requires the high degree of interaction traditionally offered by face-to-face transactions. Distance and time zone differences between team members exacerbate the challenges of development, rendering difficult the coordination of even simple tasks. Complex problem solving or brainstorming seems nearly impossible at a long distance. (p. 286)

Of course, the challenges of any team many only become bigger when the team is a virtual one. A June 1, 2005, online article in *Training Magazine* discussed the difficulties that individual team members can face in the virtual team environment:

> "Oh, yeah, virtual teams—whoop-de-do," groans a mid-level manager for an insurance company, who prefers to remain nameless. She currently works on two permanent teams and two project teams, all with members scattered in up to seven different states. "If you're lucky," she says, "you get the e-mail with the agenda for a team meeting a few hours ahead of the [regularly scheduled] conference call." If she isn't lucky, she sees the agenda for the first time when the call begins. "So then it's, 'OK, let me read this stuff and also try to discuss it intelligently while I do.' And everybody is so busy that you know they're all multitasking during the call," she adds. "When I'm the one leading a meeting, I'm pretty sure half of them are checking their e-mail. Nobody pays much attention."

As with any team, the challenges of the virtual team can be met with certain values and practices that will help promote effectiveness and efficiency in the hopes that the mid-level manager's experience just presented is not the norm in virtual teams. Duarte and Snyder (2006, pp. 10–23) offered eight critical success factors for virtual teams:

1. **Human resources policies.** Policies that support career development, support cross-boundary work, and provide technical support for virtual team members must be established.
2. **Training and on-the-job education and development.** Virtual team members must be trained on the relevant technology, how to facilitate meetings in a virtual environment, and how to share knowledge via technology.
3. **Standard organizational and team processes.** Virtual teams must attend to creating team charters, goals, and objectives; project planning; developing cost estimates; and defining job and role requirements.
4. **Electronic collaboration and communication technology.** Appropriate technology for the virtual team environment requires significant commitments of money, information technology staff, and solid modeling behaviors by organizational leaders.

5. **Organizational culture.** Norms of collaboration, respect, and information-seeking must be fostered within the virtual team culture and between the virtual team and the organization.
6. **Leadership.** The organization's leadership must value teamwork, learning, communication, diversity, and outcome-based performance.
7. **Team leader competencies.** Leadership in virtual teams requires coaching, cross-cultural abilities, building and maintaining trust (see Aubert & Kelsey, 2003), media selection, and networking.
8. **Team member competencies.** Team members must be competent in networking, technology skills, time and career management, cross-cultural skills, interpersonal awareness, and project management.

Effective Teams

Organizations use teams because they believe they will produce high-quality work. However, some teams fail, whereas others succeed. In a major study, Wageman (1997) identified characteristics that separated "superb" teams from "ineffective" teams. *Superb teams* consistently met the needs of their customers, appeared to be operating with increasing effectiveness over time, and were made up of members who were engaged in and satisfied with their work. *Ineffective teams* frequently failed to meet customer needs, appeared to be operating increasingly poorly over time, and were made up of members who were alienated from or dissatisfied with their work (Wageman, 1997, p. 52). When team members feel alienated from their work, it is impossible for them to engage customers and convince them that the organization will be responsive to their needs. Soon the team is not even listening to customers, because the team does not believe in the organization themselves.

Wageman identified seven features of superb teams (1997, p. 53):

1. **They have a clear and engaging direction.** They have a sense of why the team exists, and they understand their goal and know what direction to take. They have a strong determination to accomplish the task.
2. **The basic work is designed to be done by a team.** Members work together to complete significant tasks. The team recognizes, however, that some tasks are better done by an individual. For example, a routine project in which it is important that details be completed in exactly the same way each time is often best done by an individual. It is only frustrating to try to make a team perform as if it were one person.
3. **Team rewards are strongly associated with team effort.** A national car dealership wanted salespeople to work in teams to provide better coverage for their customers, but it continued to reward the individual salesperson for the number of cars sold. The reward system was in direct competition with the organizational goal. If a team is to work well together, there must be rewards for team efforts.

4. **Physical resources are readily available.** Tools, appropriate meeting space, access to computing services, and other resources must be present if the team is to work in a timely, proactive, and effective fashion.
5. **The team, not the leader, has the authority to make decisions over basic work strategies.** If the team is to perform at a high level, it must feel it has the power to make decisions about how its work is done.
6. **The team can articulate clear goals that fit the organization's goals and can be measured within a specific time period.** It is the leader's task to ensure that fit. The team must set realistic goals that are measurable so that it knows when it has accomplished the task. For example, if a team's goal is to improve the working climate of the organization, it must establish criteria for how it will know when that aim has been accomplished. Otherwise, its efforts will simply lead to frustration.
7. **The team establishes norms that promote strategic thinking.** To be innovative, the team must set norms that allow it to think ahead and define future actions instead of reacting to current conditions.

Clearly, successful teams recognize the team goal and feel their members' individual fates are linked directly with the success of the team. This is a difficult concept to instill in the United States, where individualism is a strong value. The organization must create rewards based on the success of the team as a whole to establish successful teams.

In addition, team members have certain characteristics that can lead to the success of the team as a whole. Sometimes members put forth great effort with little success because they lack the necessary skills. Other members are skilled and knowledgeable but lack the desire to put forth great effort. Finally, some members have the skills, put forth the effort, but have not been trained in the use of certain performance strategies that could be used to solve the problem (Hackman, 1990). All three—effort, skills, and strategies—are necessary for success. These are the characteristics to which leaders must pay attention. Failure to attend to these issues can lead to problems, or as we have termed them, misunderstandings.

Misunderstandings and Organizational Teams

Recall the definition of a team that we presented at the beginning of this chapter: *A team is a small group (three to nine) of interdependent people with complementary skills who are committed to a common purpose, performance goals, and approach for which they hold themselves mutually accountable.* This definition points to several ways in which misunderstandings could arise (though the possibilities are indeed endless). We conclude this chapter with a discussion of misunderstandings in the team environment, which include misunderstandings that arise from team size, interdependence, and the acceptance of common goals.

The first area of misunderstandings in the team environment we will examine comes from the concept of team size. As the size of the team increases, so does the potential diversity of thought, values, background, personality, and so on, which can be productive, but also a source of misunderstandings. As team members interact, they may find themselves in situations where the person next to them (or on their video screen in the case of virtual teams) has divergent and perhaps seemingly irreconcilable differences regarding communication or task process. These differences, if not attended to in a constructive manner, can be harmful to the team as team members attempt to complete their tasks. Another potential misunderstanding that can arise from team size is that as team size increases, so, too, does the likelihood that cliques might form. The formation of cliques in work teams is potentially damaging to team cohesion, and subsequently to satisfaction and performance.

The second area of misunderstandings stems from the concept of interdependence. A lack of understanding, appreciation, or commitment to the notion of interdependence leads to the team not taking advantage of the synergy and non-summativity that are the prime benefits of teamwork. For example, consider this story from Noreen, a 26-year-old systems engineer:

> My team gets a job from one of our customers. Management divides up the overall project into three parts with one project manager, but three different groups working on each part. The team has a deadline for which all sections are to be compiled together, tested, and sent to the customer. Each group works on their own section and no major issues are found. The time comes for all groups to combine their work and send it off. All of a sudden there are problems combining everything into one complete working project. Individually, everything is fine, but together it does not work. The deadline is approaching and everyone spends a lot of time redesigning parts and reworking parts so they can be combined together.

This team did not understand or appreciate the concept of interdependence. The effects were many: project quality suffered, the organization lost time and resources because of the extra energy these team members had to expend to re-do their work, and the individuals certainly suffered as they dealt with the stress and extended hours needed to meet the deadline.

The final area of misunderstandings that we will examine involves the acceptance of common goals. Perhaps the biggest complaint we hear from team members around the country is that they cannot handle that their team members are more interested in looking out for themselves than they are for accomplishing the goals of the team. What we are really talking about here are the power plays that individual members bring into the team environment. Oftentimes, members are more interested in pursuing their individual goals as a means of acquiring or wielding power than they are in subduing their personal goals to the goals of the collective. This inevitably leads to conflicts among team members and the complication of team decision-making processes and resource allocation.

Misunderstandings also come about when team members accept what they *perceive* to be common goals and processes in an effort to avoid conflict. This form of misunderstanding is known as groupthink. The concept of *groupthink* was first developed by Irving Janis in 1972 to describe what happens when a group tries to maintain cohesiveness and avoid conflict in the extreme. This type of thinking overlooks contradictory opinions. One characteristic of groupthink is the belief that the group is invulnerable. Invulnerability means thinking one cannot be wrong, that one's ideas are right despite information that is contradictory. When the group begins to believe it is so knowledgeable, and so "right" in its decisions, it concludes that the group cannot be open to criticism or change. Additionally, groupthink leads to believing unanimity, or agreement, exists when it doesn't. "So we're all agreed?" might be asked, and when no response is made everyone leaves the meeting thinking they are all in agreement. Sometimes we ask questions not really expecting to receive an answer.

Summary

Organizational work teams will continue to be a part of organizational life. As a future employee your challenge is to understand how you can make a significant contribution to team activities and help the organization provide systems that will enhance the likelihood that the teams you serve on will be successful. This chapter presented the characteristics of organizational teams, how teams have emerged in the modern workplace, two forms of teams (self-directed work teams and virtual teams), and the misunderstandings that can arise in the team environment.

In summary, we would suggest that you remember the following:

- Learn the norms unique to each team before causing unintentional disruption.
- Help the team avoid groupthink by pointing out information it may be ignoring.
- Work to encourage cultural diversity in the team and be sensitive to the potential misunderstandings that can be caused by cultural differences. Work to resolve those differences.
- Help teams avoid "stuckness" by changing the environment or by changing the pattern of behaviors of other team members.
- Encourage a collaborative climate to help generate a unified commitment of team members.

Understanding the general characteristics of teams, what makes them successful, and how a member can contribute to that success will improve members' ability to function in the team-based workplace of the twenty-first century.

CHAPTER
13 Leaders and Leadership

This chapter is not just about the "official" leaders in the organization, such as the boss, the supervisor, and the CEO. It is about the characteristics, behaviors, attitudes, and values of leadership that can be exhibited by any organizational member depending on the situation. Given the right set of circumstances, any organizational member can contribute to the success of the group by providing leadership when needed. As expressed by Raelin (2003):

> In the twenty-first-century organization we need to establish the experience of serving as a leader, not sequentially, but concurrently and collectively. In other words, leaders coexist at the same time and all together. In addition, we expect each member of a community to make a unique contribution to the growth of that community, both independently and interdependently with others. (p. XI)

Consider the following two stories that exhibit extraordinary as well as everyday instances of leadership. The first comes from a news article written by Bird for the *University of Texas McCombs School of Business Magazine* (2003) regarding Herb Kelleher, cofounder and former CEO of Southwest Airlines.

> After successfully battling prostate cancer and seeing his company through its 28th consecutive year of profitability (a feat completely unprecedented in the airline industry), Kelleher planned to "throttle down" on Oct 1, 2001.
>
> As he tells it, October 1 and reducing his hours never came. "After September 11th it was an emergency situation where everybody was supposed to pitch in," said Kelleher. "It was an unprecedented crisis in the airline industry, and survival literally was at stake."
>
> Southwest not only survived, it thrived. At the request of new CEO Jim Parker and COO Colleen Barrett, Kelleher retained several key areas of responsibility while remaining active as chairman. Under their joint stewardship, Southwest audaciously pursued a growth strategy even as other carriers scaled back.
>
> While the big three—American, United, and Delta—laid off nearly 50,000 employees in 2001, Southwest, the fourth largest U.S. carrier, maintained a no-layoffs policy. This February [2003] the airline that started as a business plan on a cocktail napkin announced its 30th consecutive year of profitability.

Kelleher's approach to management offers a series of paradoxes. Consider, for example, his philosophy on shareholders. In 2002, Morningstar Inc. recognized Kelleher and Parker as co-CEOs of the Year for their record of maximizing shareholder value. And yet, as Kelleher explains, he has always placed the needs of shareholders last, after employees and customers.

The second story was told to us by a 20-year-old college student regarding his experience as the leader of a campus-based honors fraternity.

> I think delegation skills are the most important thing a leader can have. I think one person can't do everything; everyone knows that. I think delegation skills are so much more important especially when you're dealing with a group as big as this fraternity. For example, we have a person in the group that sends out e-mails. I compose the e-mails, but she sends them out—that's her job. That's not a waste of my time, but that's time that I can spend doing other things with the group rather than typing every e-mail and sending it out. I know I hear stories about last year's president where she did everything. I don't think that's a good leader; that's being way too dependent on yourself, and not trusting of others. These fraternity members are smart, and they are people that I can trust. I know they'll do a good job.

Although these stories represent two very different organizational situations and scopes of leadership, we put them side-by-side to demonstrate two things. First, leadership happens wherever and whenever it is needed, whether in major public companies or small, local organizations. Second, leadership is about understanding and addressing the needs of organizational members and helping them move forward in meeting their personal and professional goals.

This chapter presents major issues related to organizational leadership and communication as they have developed over the years. We begin with a general overview of the nature of leadership and then move to a brief summary of how leadership theories have emerged and developed over the past century. Next, we discuss the responsibilities of leadership, and then how power and ethics are related to the context. We conclude this chapter with a brief discussion of passion as related to leadership.

Overview of Leadership

Leadership is a complex subject; in this section, we point to a few basic aspects that highlight its communicative and interactive aspects. The following is an important concept central to the notion of this way of viewing leadership: *Leadership is not a particular trait some people have and others do not. It is a process that takes place in every human interaction.* Kouzes & Posner (2001) extended this point as they argued:

Myth associates leadership with superior position. It assumes that leadership starts with a capital 'L' and that when you're on top you're automatically a leader. But leadership isn't a place, it's a process—and this becomes all the more important to appreciate going forward in time. Leadership involves skills and abilities that are useful whether one is in the executive suite or in the front line, on Wall Street or Main Street, on college campuses, community centers, or corporations. (p. 82)

Leadership, therefore, is interactional (it takes place through communication), contextual (different people contribute leadership in different circumstances), and it is a process (changing as the needs of the people and situation change).

Leadership can happen in any setting with any combination of individuals. There is no age limit or required background. Leaders can emerge at any time and be anyone. For example, a young girl, Melissa Poe of St. Henry's School in Nashville, Tennessee, wrote a letter to the President of the United States asking his assistance with her campaign to save the environment. This fourth-grade student got the president's attention by getting her letter posted on a billboard:

Through sheer diligence and hard work this nine-year-old got her letter placed on a billboard free of charge and founded Kids for a Clean Environment (Kids FACE). When she eventually got the disappointing form letter from the President, she had 250 billboards across the country and over 200,000 members and 2,000 chapters. In her own school she had developed a manual on recycling. She is proof that you don't have to wait for someone else to lead. (Kouzes & Posner, 2001, p. 83)

Rather than certain required traits for leaders there are some essential elements that are often present for leadership to emerge. Melissa Poe demonstrated those elements, as will be discussed in the remainder of this chapter.

How do we know a leader when we see one? One definition is the following: *A leader is a person who takes charge of the situation and influences the attitudes and actions of others*. Watching young children arguing over who will be the leader of a game or activity can be instructive. Often, one of them will finally say, "OK. You (pointing to one youngster) be a leader, and you (pointing to the other youngster) be a leader, too. Now follow me." The person who acts to move the group forward, with or without the title of leader, will be the true leader in this setting. The person who sees a need or has a possible answer and is not afraid to give voice to her ideas will emerge as a leader. However, if the goal is only to get others to do what one wants, it may be a case of propaganda or persuasion, not leadership.

Based on research and as observed through practical experience, we can say that leadership demonstrates another element: *The leader influences the behavior of others to reach a common goal that benefits the group, not just an individual*. Warren Bennis, a well-known author on management, defined the difference between *leadership* and *management* by saying that the manager does things right, whereas the leader does the right thing (Bennis & Nanus, 1985). In other words, the manager may know all the policies and procedures to follow and perform them correctly, but the leader will know how to do the right thing even if it is not spelled out in the policy manual. In their survey of 90 successful corporate and public leaders, Bennis and Nanus found that managers are problem solvers who are efficient, whereas leaders are effective problem identifiers who focus on all available resources to move a group forward.

For example, a director in a company had an employee with an extended illness who ran out of sick days. Her colleagues in the office volunteered to give their sick days to her so she could recover fully before coming back to work. The employee manual did not have a provision on this, but it was the right thing to do. The director allowed the employee's colleagues to help her through this difficult time and cover her sick time by giving away their own. Later, it turned into a policy that this company adopted so others in crisis situations could benefit from the generosity of their colleagues. This leader demonstrated the elements of leadership described above and also exemplifies what we will call *leadership as serving*. The leader removed bureaucratic barriers in an attempt to ensure a successful and humane outcome for her employees—the essence of leadership as serving.

Development of Leadership Theories

Authors have developed theories of leadership to expand on the basic elements discussed above and to capture the complexities of the concept. First explored in the early twentieth century, leadership theory has seen many changes over the last 100 years. Literally thousands of studies have been conducted and pages have been written about leadership in an attempt to help us understand how leadership emerges and what makes it effective. In this section of the chapter, we provide a brief outline of some of the major developments in theories of leadership.

Trait Approach to Leadership

Early research on leadership was primarily concerned with identifying traits that differentiated effective from ineffective leaders. *Traits* are characteristics, either psychological or physical, that affect behavior (House & Baetz, 1979). From this perspective, "leaders are born rather than made" (Bryman, 1996, p. 277). Trait research began around 1904 and continued for approximately 50 years (Owens, 1992). By mid-century, researchers realized that identifying a definitive set of traits as markers of effective leadership in all situations was probably impossible.

Although no definitive traits of leaders were identified that could be carried across all leadership situations, several traits were found with relative consistency across studies (House & Baetz, 1979, p. 348):

- Intelligence
- Dominance
- Self-confidence
- Energy, activity
- Task-related knowledge

Trait research continued through the mid-1900s when researchers began to identify other factors in addition to individual personality traits that contribute to effective leadership. Ralph Stogdill (1974) reviewed over 3,000 books and articles that had been written in the 1940s, 1950s, and 1960s. One of his conclusions was, "Theorists no longer explain leadership solely in terms of the individual or the group. Rather it is believed that characteristics of the individual and demands of the situation interact in such a manner as to permit one, or perhaps a few, persons to rise to leadership status" (p. 23). Instead of focusing on traits of a leader, researchers began to identify leader behaviors and the impact on group outcomes.

Situational Approach to Leadership

As trait research started to taper off in the mid-1900s, researchers began examining *behaviors* as markers of effective leadership. This work was pioneered by the Ohio State Leadership Studies, beginning in 1954 (Owens, 1992). The results of these studies led to the notion of the "average leadership style"; that is, leaders were assumed to have a "typical" style that was used with all subordinates (Dockery & Steiner, 1990; Fairhurst & Chandler, 1989).

From these beginnings, a theory of leadership emerged that suggested shifts in leadership behavior depending on variables in the group setting. This approach was referred to as *situational leadership*. It assumes that the leader's behavior depends on a variety of circumstances in the specific situation. A number of early writers identified possible situational variables, including how followers interact, the relationship of the leader to the followers, the motivations of both, and the task itself (e.g., see the discussion of Blake and Mouton's Managerial Grid in Chapter 3).

One situational variable was identified by researchers as two distinct needs of a group: getting the *task* completed and developing strong *relationships* in the group. For example, some projects require a great deal of attention to accomplishing the task, whereas others need strong relationships among the team members. If the leader spends all his time getting the task done without any attention to relationships, then the team members may not work well together for the next task, even if this task was accomplished. However, if the leader only focuses on relationships everyone may feel good about the experience, but not get the job done. A leader who does not focus on either and basically leaves the group to their own devices is called a *laissez-faire leader*. Alternatively, the leader may try to control all aspects of the group, as the following interview demonstrates. This interview was with a 25-year-old female who works in development at a nonprofit organization.

> I do think the term "micro-manager" gets thrown around a lot, but in my case I do think it applies. My boss is a good boss in that she gets things done, but she does not foster a very independent work environment. When I am given a task to fulfill, at times she will outline exactly what I should say, as if I had no idea how to achieve the desired outcome. If I write an annual campaign letter or grant proposal, she rewrites half of it in her own words.

When a leader is so directive, as in the example above, the individual work-ing with her is not allowed to learn and grow on her own. The employee will not be prepared to take steps to ensure success with the projects she is working on. This young woman went on to point out how this style of leadership had an impact on her behavior.

> The result is a lack of confidence on my part to make decisions without consulting her first . . . She currently has complete control of the development department. I think she is hesitant to relinquish any of that control. This may be ideal for her, but as a developing professional it does not serve me very well. I have had to realize this on my own, and now have to very consciously decide what decisions I can make on my own and which I should consult her about. If I had not realized this, I would have gone on to another position and had a boss who thought I was incapable of doing things independently. I am a very capable and independent person, and I think to myself, "If I am not the right person to do this job effectively, then why do I get great reviews and the highest percentage merit raise possible?"

Clearly, micromanagement has not allowed this individual to learn and grow in her job. She will not perform as well as she could because she has been supervised so closely. Her leader/manager did not demonstrate trust in her ability or in her willingness to do the job. It is clear that the ability of the follower to carry out the task can determine the style of leadership that is effective.

Paul Hersey, Kenneth Blanchard, and Dewey Johnson (2001) extended the situational approach to leadership and coupled the task and relationship behav-iors of leaders with what they termed the "readiness level" of the followers. They posited that leadership style should depend on the "extent to which a follower demonstrates the ability and willingness to accomplish a specific task" (p. 175). A follower's readiness level should not be considered a personal trait or character-istic, but something that varies by task. Since readiness level varies based on the situation, so too should the extent to which the leader exhibits task and/or rela-tionship behaviors. Figure 13.1 shows the interrelationships between leader behaviors and follower readiness.

As you can see from the model, there are four basic follower readiness lev-els (R1, R2, R3, and R4) that determine which leadership style (S1, S2, S3, S4) is most appropriate. The four leadership styles can be characterized by the extent to which they include task and relationship behaviors (p. 174):

- **Style 1 (S1):** above average amounts of task behavior and below average amounts of relationship behavior
- **Style 2 (S2):** above average amounts of both task and relationship behaviors
- **Style 3 (S3):** above average amounts of relationship behavior and below average amounts of task behavior
- **Style 4 (S4):** below average amounts of both relationship and task behaviors

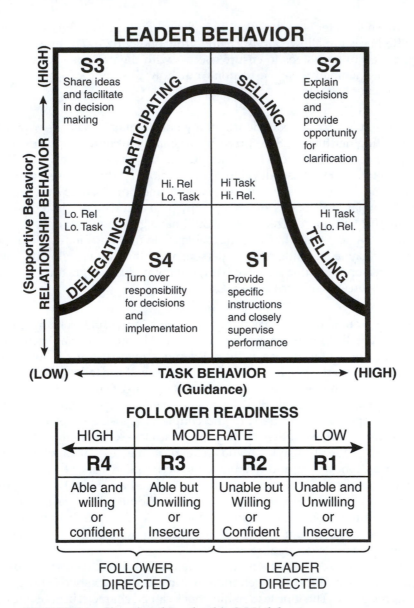

FIGURE 13.1   Situational Leadership® Model

Source: From Hersey, P., Blanchard, K., & Johnson, D. (2001). *Management of organizational behavior* (8th ed.), p. 178. Englewood Cliffs, NJ: Prentice Hall. Reprinted with permission.

With these behaviors available, the leader must determine the extent of follower readiness for the particular situation at hand. There are four basic readiness levels (pp. 177–178):

■ **Readiness Level 1 (R1):** the follower is unable and unwilling to complete the task, or is unable and insecure regarding the situation

- **Readiness Level 2 (R2):** the follower is unable but willing to complete the task, or is unable but confident that she can complete it
- **Readiness Level 3 (R3):** the follower is able but unwilling or able but insecure about completing the task
- **Readiness Level 4 (R4):** the follower is both able and confident about completing the task

With the readiness level of the follower determined, the leader must select the leadership style that best matches the particular readiness level. In a situation where the follower is unable and unwilling (or insecure) regarding the task (R1), the leader should employ the *telling* style (S1). When using the telling style the leader issues task guidance and direction by focusing on facts and consequences. This would be most effective since the follower will have no self-motivation or previous positive experience with completing this type of task. The *selling* style (S2) will be an appropriate style when the follower feels he can complete the task but is actually unable to do (R2). This style of leadership will have the leader providing guidance but also emotional support by opening up dialogue to help bring the follower along and to allow for questions. The addition of emotional support will afford the extra motivation to keep the follower going when his abilities may cause frustration.

The *participating* style (S3), which involves encouragement and open communication, is useful in situations where the follower is able but unwilling or insecure regarding the task (R3). In this situation, the follower may have the necessary skills to complete the task, but they are usually newly developed and therefore confidence levels are not sufficiently high. With appropriate emotional support from the leader and opportunities for asking questions and seeking feedback, the follower will become more confident and able to complete the task. Finally, in situations where the follower is both able and confident with regard to the task (R4), the leader should choose the *delegating* style (S4). The follower knows how and wants to the task so the leader should let her do it. The follower's activities should still be monitored, but the leader should not micro-manage the situation.

The most important contribution made by Hersey and Blanchard was the notion that leaders can change their style of interacting with followers depending on the followers' ability and involvement in the task. We find this to be extremely beneficial to anyone who wants to emerge as a leader or be a successful leader. The leader should not treat all individuals as if they are driven by the same motivation or have the same level of skill or interest. The best leaders adapt to the traits of the group members and the particular situation [see Jacobson (1981) for a useful instrument to measure one's ability to select the best leadership style given the needs of followers].

Charismatic Leadership

Since the early 1980s, the number of "new" leadership theories has exploded. The root of the contemporary theories that we will discuss next, such as transformational leadership, can be found in House's (1977) charismatic leadership theory. Further developing Weber's (1947) work on charismatic authority, House defined *charisma* as the effect a leader has on his or her followers. Charisma, from this view, entails followers' identification with the leader as well as the leader's ability to communicate emotional involvement with the organization's mission. The personal characteristics of a charismatic leader include having a strong presence, a desire to influence others, demonstrating self-confidence, and displaying a strong sense of one's own moral values (Northouse, 2001).

Charismatic leadership, though, is not only about personality traits, but also specific behaviors (Northouse, 2001). Charismatic leaders must be strong role models for their followers, and their actions and behaviors must match at all times. Second, charismatic leaders must appear competent and able to handle any situation in front of their followers. These leaders must be able to communicate rhetorical visions and ideological goals with a strong moral overtone to their followers in a clear, concise, and passionate manner. They must be able to convey to their followers that they have high moral and performance standards for them. Finally, they must be able to provoke task-relevant motives, such as affiliation, power, or esteem in their followers.

Transactional and Transformational Leadership

In the mid-1980s, Bass (1985) expanded the notion of charismatic leadership into what is now known as *transformational leadership*. This leadership approach focused not only on what characteristics a leader needed to possess, but also the attributes the followers needed from a leader. Much attention is paid by this theory to the role that follower perceptions of the leader play in the leadership process. Additionally, communication and communication practices are foregrounded in the transformational leadership approach.

Bass (1985) began by arguing that there are two types of leaders: transactional leaders and transformational leaders. *Transactional leaders* utilize three leadership factors. First, they are focused on *contingent rewards*. Followers have specific performance goals to meet and are either rewarded or punished based on their ability to either meet or not meet these goals. Leaders employ either management by exception-active or management by exception-passive to instill and maintain contingent rewards. Management by exception in its *active* form requires the leader to actively monitor the follower's progress and take corrective action as soon as necessary. The corrective process is designed to bring the follower back on track. The *passive* form of management by exception also involves corrective action, but the leader waits until deviances or problems occur before taking any action. Little monitoring occurs in the passive form, because the leader is waiting for problems to occur. The essence of transactional leadership is the motivation of followers through a system of rewards and punishments based on performance that may be more or less monitored (Gardner & Cleavenger, 1998).

Transformational leadership, as previously mentioned, is an expanded version of charismatic leadership. Unlike transactional leadership, which is grounded in the more mundane exchanges that occur between leaders and followers, *transformational leaders* appeal to the higher-order needs of their followers (Reardon & Reardon, 1999). Transformational leadership involves several factors (Bass & Avolio, 1994). First, the leader must have *attributed charisma*, or the ability to gain trust, respect, and confidence from his or her followers. Second, this leader must be able to demonstrate *idealized influence*, or the perception of being a role model to the followers. If successful at demonstrating idealized influence, followers will often look up to or want to emulate the leader. The transformational leader must be able to instill *inspirational motivation*, which is the ability to encourage followers to pursue a goal and persevere through times of change or difficulty. This aspect of the leadership model demands that leaders be able to draw upon a wide emotional range to convey inspiration, commitment, or dedication to the organization's mission and the end result. *Intellectual stimulation* is also necessary and requires a leader who is able to think creatively and envision a variety of solutions. Intellectual stimulation also demands a leader who is willing and able to consider every solution that is brought forward by followers and to fully explore their usefulness. Finally, the transformational leader must be able to communicate *individualized consideration*, or concern for each of his or her followers.

Raelin (2003) wrote of the *leaderful organization*, which is an extension and modification of the transformational leader:

> Leaderful practice is unique compared to empowerment models . . . in that it does not merely present a consultative model wherein leaders in authority allow "followers" to participate in their leadership. Nor does it equate to stewardship approaches that see the leader step aside and allow others to take over when necessary. Instead, it offers a true mutual model that transforms leadership from an individual property into a new paradigm that redefines leadership as a collective practice. (p. 5)

Raelin (2003) provides the following example of this model of leadership: A vice president of a small company on the West coast planned to resign because his family was planning a move to a city some 500 miles away. The president of the company scheduled a meeting of top management to talk about how to replace him. Prior to the meeting, a member of the leadership team started a campaign to keep "James," the vice president, because of the difficulty of replacing him and because he added a great deal to the success of the organization. She wanted others to think about alternatives to see if they could reach a consensus on what might keep James a part of the company. Some people came up with ways for his work to be done by audio and video technology. James also indicated that he would be willing to travel back to the company's location for critical meetings. By the time the meeting occurred to discuss how to replace James, everyone, including the president, believed that the topic of the meeting had shifted to how to work with James from a remote location. In this case, the president was not the only organizational leader. In fact, the management team member who worked for this solution contributed strong leadership to the group (p. 189). This solution demonstrates collective and collaborative action that results in a compassionate response to a problem. It goes beyond consulting with others and creates an environment in which employees feel empowered to take the lead in critical decision-making processes.

Feminist Perspectives on Leadership

With the leaderful organization viewpoint on leadership, we begin to see a perspective on the topic that encourages leaders to empower followers to make decisions and act independently. Organizational members are encouraged to work for collective goals rather than focusing only on personal ones (Bass, Avolio, & Atwater, 1996). Empowering the followers reinforces current thinking about the need for organizations to have a less hierarchical structure and be more flexible and team oriented. Some authors believe that this style of leadership is tied to the increase of female leaders in organizations:

> This concept of leadership can be readily associated, at least partially, with stereotypes of women and how they would be expected to behave as leaders . . . and may have triggered the growing interest in the study of the intersection of transformational leadership and gender. Furthermore, the massive entry of women into the workforce in the last half-century, followed by their movement to management roles, might have contributed to changes in the conceptualization of leadership, towards transformational leadership theory and empowerment of followers. (Kark & Gan, 2004, p. 161)

One leadership theory, executive leadership development, serves as a theoretical transition point that begins the turn toward feminist perspectives on leadership. Executive leadership development entails ongoing socialization processes that begin in childhood and continue throughout the organizational socialization and assimilation process (Avolio & Gibbons, 1998). Researchers who study executive leadership development (e.g., Bass, 1990; Burns, 1978; Gibbons, 1986; Kotter, 1982) argue that factors such as family, culture, and social factors influence the development of leadership capacity. Early family experiences, school, part-time jobs, religious involvement, and community activities influence leadership development (Parker, 2003). Tannen (1990) argued that women and men are socialized from early childhood to engage in distinctively different communication styles with different purposes, rules, and understandings of how to interpret interactions. These differences may lead to two different leadership models: one based on masculine instrumentality and the other on feminine collaboration. Whereas this can be useful to an organization, many feminist scholars argue that the feminine model has historically been rejected by male-dominated organizational structuring processes (i.e., Grossman & Chester, 1990; Helgesen, 1990). With the influx of women into positions of higher authority and leadership in organizations, it is possible that the feminine model is beginning to obtain credibility in leadership circles.

Several forms of feminism, including radical feminism, focus on the positive value of those qualities normally associated with female leaders: sensitivity, nurturing, and expressing emotions. They would argue that these characteristics and voices should not be marginalized in the organization, but rather should be highlighted, welcomed, and, in some cases, used as a replacement for the traditional male perspective. We would like to conclude this section by highlighting one feminist perspective on leadership—leadership as serving.

Leadership as serving (Fine & Buzzanell, 2000) means "doing things for others that enable them to do their jobs; serving means taking obstacles out of employees' way rather than putting them up" (Fine & Buzzanell, 2000, p. 131). According to Fine & Buzzanell, some suggest that this "softer" view of leadership actually can be more productive. Rather than have the leader be the person who solves problems, the leader becomes the person who facilitates others' ability to solve their own problems.

In describing leadership as serving, Fine and Buzzanell (2000) argued that this perspective on leadership revises the concept of serving by removing the domination intonations present in the term *servant*:

> In a different constellation of meanings, service is an honorable term that suggests providing gifts from the self and giving of oneself for the good of others in the *service* of some greater good. Using the Greek root word for service, *diakoneo*, which includes the office of helper *and* helped as agent, we invest serving or service with the accoutrements of both agent and agency to displace the harmful feminine characteristics. Those who serve are no longer servants or slaves bereft of the freedom to choose what they do. (p. 152)

According to Fine and Buzzanell (2000, p. 157), leaders who serve exhibit:

- *Hopefulness* for fundamental change
- *Strength* in the feminist vision
- *Watchfulness* lest service become servitude
- *Humbleness* in knowledge that the server is an instrument of change
- *Wonderment* at the passages of self, other, community, and principal growth

Leadership as serving involves a personally and professionally involved approach. A leader must be willing to think of other organizational members first and to remove bureaucratic barriers that stand in the way of their success. The serving approach can be quite trying and tiring for some who attempt it, but it offers the opportunity to inject the feminist ethic into a traditionally male-defined skill set.

Rather than argue that one model is more effective than another, we suggest that a leadership model that embraces a wide range of possible leadership behaviors should be accessible to any individual engaged in leadership practice. The designated leader should use many perspectives and approaches and surround herself with those who operate differently from her. To the greatest extent possible, she should adapt her leadership approach to the needs of the team members and the situation.

It is important to challenge our concepts of how leaders behave. As stated earlier in the chapter, leadership comes in all sizes, shapes, colors, and forms. You cannot afford to ignore contributions to the success of the group or organization because the contribution is coming from an unexpected source.

Communication Concepts and Effective Leadership

Although leadership can come from all types of individuals, some basic underlying concepts cut across all models of leadership; here we will focus on those most related to *communication*. Research on leadership from a communication perspective includes attention to traditional interpersonal communication concepts, such as message content and delivery, impression management, communicator style, and trust. These concepts could be applied in any of the models of leadership we have discussed. We believe they form the foundation for creating vision for others.

Message Delivery: Impression Management and Communicator Style

Leadership theories, particularly charismatic and transformational theories, rely heavily not only on personality, but also on the leaders' communication behaviors. Leader effectiveness and follower satisfaction also rely upon the follower's perception of the leader and how well the leader can communicatively manage this perception. The leader must also possess a degree of self-awareness. Sosik and Jung (2003) define *self-awareness* as self-directed attention. This attention to one's self enables the leader to adopt the appropriate impression management strategies and communication styles necessary to manage followers' perceptions.

Successful leaders must pay careful attention to both the content of the message they send and the manner in which it is delivered. Content is important because it provides the followers with a sense of either the leader's or the organization's vision. The content of the message should inspire followers to strive to achieve more and work harder than they would have on their own or if they were acting in their own self-interest. Essentially, content becomes the leader and followers' focal point.

Crafting a message (i.e., content) is only half the process. The leader must be able to deliver that message to the followers. The body of research in this area ties message delivery to many important outcomes; for example, Gardner (2003) has demonstrated a positive correlation between strong delivery and perceived charisma. In the next section, we will discuss delivery in terms of impression management and communication style.

Impression Management

In any situation, particularly as a leader, we want to present ourselves in the best possible light, and we often employ impression-management strategies to help facilitate this process. *Impression management* entails those strategies that people engage in to manage the perceptions of others. Jones and Pittman (1982) identified five impression-management strategies that have since been integrated into the study of leadership: ingratiation, self-promotion, intimidation, exemplification, and supplication. *Ingratiation* is the individual's attempt to present himself as more attractive and likeable to others. When successfully conveyed, ingratiation makes the leader appear warm and charming and highly charismatic. Research has indicated that if an ingratiator's efforts are perceived as genuine, leader effectiveness and follower satisfaction rates are high (Gardner & Cleavenger, 1998). The ingratiator appears to like everyone and wants everyone to like him in return. If misused, an "ingratiator's dilemma" occurs, and the individual can appear manipulative and fake.

Self-promotion is when an individual attempts to present himself as being a highly competent leader or individual. In other words, no matter what the situation, he is able to communicatively and behaviorally handle it. Like the ingratiator style though, this technique can yield either highly positive or highly negative results. If the leader's credibility is even slightly damaged, a "self-promoter's paradox" can occur, which often results in perceptions of leader ineffectiveness and follower dissatisfaction (Gardner & Cleavenger, 1998).

Exemplification is an impression management strategy that relies on the individual's ability to present herself as a person of high moral worth. The leader attempts to convey her morality in terms that encourage followers to pursue like-minded endeavors. Exemplification, with its basis in morality and ethics, has been highly associated with perceived leader effectiveness and follower satisfaction. However, notable scandals, such as those involving Enron and the Catholic Church, demonstrate that exemplification, like other strategies, can have a serious impact on the leader if it is misused.

Intimidation and supplication are very different impression management strategies from the three previously discussed. *Intimidation* relies on the creation of a dangerous individual who is not to be crossed. In a leadership role, intimidation could be based on a variety of threats ranging from termination, being cast out from the organization, physical or mental harm, or some other form of punishment. Numerous bodies of research have demonstrated that intimidation is an ineffective leadership style, because it is associated with lower perceptions of leader effectiveness and follower satisfaction. *Supplication* involves an individual presenting himself as being helpless so that others will rescue him. Followers rarely find much confidence or leadership ability in an individual displaying such a trait.

In summary, studies conducted by Sosik and Jung (2003) found that the impression management style used most commonly by leaders is exemplification followed by ingratiation, intimidation, self-promotion, and, finally, supplication.

Communicator Style

Impression-management strategies attempt to manage follower's perceptions. The second part of perception management involves the leader's communicator style. Research suggests that differences in delivery lead to different perceptions about a leader. Robert Norton (1983) identified nine different communicator styles. According to Norton, an individual is not limited to only one communicator style; a successful communicator can draw upon a variety of communicator styles depending on the interactional context. The communicator styles, as identified by Norton, are animated, attentive, contentious, dominant, dramatic, friendly, open, relaxed, and impression leaving.

An *animated* communicator relies on nonverbal communication, including gesturing, eye contact, and facial expressions. An animated style may help a leader convey the inspirational motivation necessary to persevere in times of change or difficulty or to rally the troops whenever necessary. An *attentive* communicator demonstrates good listening skills and can demonstrate empathy through both nonverbal and verbal cues. A transformational leader might use attentive communication to demonstrate the individualized consideration that followers want and need to stay focused on the organizational vision and mission.

A *contentious* communicator likes to argue and often challenges others to demonstrate proof. Although this communicator style can cause heated arguments if taken too far, the transformational leader could use contention in moderation to intellectually stimulate the followers to think outside of the box. The *dominant* communicator tends to take charge of interactions and speaks frequently in a strong manner. Although appropriate in certain circumstances for a transformational leader, this style is most aptly suited for the transactional leader who needs to establish a system of rewards and punishment and administer corrective actions as necessary.

The *dramatic* leader likes to make her point both verbally and nonverbally in an exaggerated or picturesque tone. This communicator will rely upon expressive language and storytelling to convey the point. Like the animated communicator, a leader could use this style to rhetorically create the vision and message necessary to inspire followers as well as attain attributed charisma. Charisma and individualized consideration can also be attained through the use of the friendly communicator style. The *friendly* communicator is one who frequently gives positive feedback and recognition to others. Along the same lines, the *open* communicator openly expresses emotion and personal information. This style could help a leader foster idealized influence and attributed charisma by using his own life as an example and demonstrating his own commitment to the vision and mission of the organization.

The *relaxed* communicator generally comes across as calm during interactions. This communicator rarely displays nervousness or tension, and this style is ideal for demonstrating charisma and idealized influence in times of organizational flux or uncertainty. The final communicator style—*impression leaving*—refers to the leader's ability to say things in a memorable way and to leave others thinking about the interaction after he has gone. This style fits perfectly with the notion of charisma and attempts to instill respect, trust, and confidence in followers.

As stated previously, there is not a one size fits all communicator style, nor is there only one perfect communicator style for a leader. An adept leader, through self-awareness, must ascertain her follower's perceptions and adapt the message and delivery to fit the followers and circumstances.

Building Trust

The most important foundation for good leadership practice is building trust. If individuals believe others are acting in good faith and on their behalf, they will respond to requests. If mistrust exists, individuals will always look for a hidden agenda and try to protect themselves against possible retribution. It is critical that you learn how to build trust with your colleagues so that you can make leadership contributions. In fact, organizational policies and rules are created to safeguard employees against untrustworthy behavior. The topic of trust was presented briefly in Chapter 10 in our discussion of superior–subordinate relationships. Trust is so critical to leadership that we want to revisit it in this context as well.

According to Stewart (2001), "Real trust is hard even between people who have chosen to be together and have years to work on it, like spouses. It's harder still where they have little or no say in selecting their colleagues and where time is short. Impossible where an organization is large" (p. 67).

Because trust is so difficult to develop and maintain in an organizational setting, the organization must put trust-strengthening mechanisms in place. Training workshops for employees that focus on trust issues can help. But what can you personally do to enhance others' trust in you as a leader? Keep the following five strategies in mind when you are trying to build trust among those with whom you work.

First, *maintain confidences*. The quickest way for someone to lose all trust in you is to hear something told to you in private come back to them through several other sources. Why would that person ever share something with you again? Despite how seductive it might be to share a bit of gossip, what you stand to lose is far greater than what you would gain in short-term notoriety. Sometimes individuals will test their trust in you as a leader by telling you a small piece of confidential information to see if you share it with anyone else. How you treat that small amount of information will determine if the person trusts you enough to tell you more.

Second, *always follow through*. This doesn't mean that when someone asks you to do something you always do it for them. However, it does mean that you always respond in some way to a request. If you are unable to comply with the request, don't ignore it, hoping it will go away. Respond and let the person know why you can't meet the request. People dislike ambiguity more than they do negative feedback. Remaining silent usually will not make the issue go away. It only serves to frustrate those who are waiting for an answer. Think back to the CO model; what we are describing here is related to the notion of timely feedback that is a part of that model.

Third, *be honest*. Nothing is worse than trying to cover up bad news by lying. You are better off just saying you can't talk about a certain topic than to lie about it. Once you lie, it is unlikely that others will believe you in the future. It is better to disagree than to remain silent and with your silence imply consent. Of the great corporate scandals of the twenty-first century, the cover-up operations in many cases were worse than the original act. Leaders who use the impression management style of exemplification may suffer from this very problem. Being honest also means possessing a certain amount of self-knowledge and knowing your strengths and weaknesses. Being honest with others about those things you cannot do will be as welcome as demonstrating those things that you can do. Effective leaders surround themselves with people who have the strengths they do not.

Fourth, *listen with respect*. This does not necessarily mean that you agree with a person. It does mean you respect that person's right to explain his position and his thinking. Give the speaker the courtesy you would expect by listening intently to his position. People are usually much more willing to hear your arguments once they have had a chance to explain their own position, but they have to feel that they have been given a full and respectful hearing. This means not interrupting people before they are finished, no matter how tempting that is. It means repeating back to them what you think you heard to be sure you understand their position. It means respecting their right to a different opinion.

Finally, *what you say and what you do must be consistent*. It's not fair to say you support someone's position and then act as if you do not. If you say you support an idea in private, then you should support it publicly. No one wants to march into battle with troops behind them, only to turn around and find that everyone has left the field! Trust is easily dissolved when this behavior is not practiced.

If followed, these five behaviors will be extremely useful to you as you participate in leadership opportunities. Maintaining others' confidences, following through, being honest, listening, and being consistent will help others build trust in you. Once you have others' trust, you must guard against losing it. Trust is very difficult to develop, and extremely easy to lose. It can take months or years to carefully build trust among colleagues, and it can be destroyed in just a few moments when a confidence is shared or someone lies. Once lost, trust is difficult, if not impossible, to regain.

Responsibilities of Leadership

Some areas of responsibility for leaders are easily identified and provide a framework for a variety of theoretical approaches to leadership. The first responsibility of the leader is *to act*. One of the least effective reactions to a problem is to take no action at all. Leadership is represented by the person who is present in the moment and takes action. Kouzes and Posner (2001) provide an excellent example of such a situation. Charlie Mae Knight was the new superintendent of a school district in California where 50 percent of the schools were closed and 98 percent of the children were performing in the lowest percentile for academic achievement in the state. The facilities were in terrible shape, and there was a 10-year-old lawsuit threatening to dissolve the district and force the children to transfer to schools outside the community.

One has to wonder why anyone would accept a position in an organization with such critical problems, but Knight was not discouraged. She managed to get local companies and community foundations to provide needed resources and asked parents to volunteer time to help improve the schools. Within two years of her arrival, the district's students performed in the 51st percentile on achievement tests; today student performance has climbed to the 70th percentile. The lawsuit to dissolve the district was dropped, and for the first time the district received the state's Distinguished School Award.

Knight was a leader who was clearly present and took action. For too many years the district had suffered under leadership that was inactive and viewed problems as insurmountable barriers. Knight saw them as challenges and opportunities:

> Leadership is less and less a state of being and more and more a process of doing a set of actions. Tomorrow's leaders will have less time for planning and forecasting. They will need to build the bridge as they walk on it . . . Leaders don't make excuses for inaction. They are first movers and early adopters. They make things happen. (Spreitzer & Cummings, 2001, p. 246)

Leaders get others to act and challenge their thinking. They cannot act alone, and they must create the environment for action. In June 1967 Robert Kennedy said, "Few will have the greatness to bend history itself. But each of us can work to change a small portion of events. And in the total of all those acts, will be written the history of this generation" (p. 237). Knight is only one small example of a person working to change a small part of history by acting with conviction.

A second critical leadership responsibility is *building a team* from among the members of the group. John Wooden, former head basketball coach for UCLA who had one of the most winning records over a period of close to 30 years, used sports to identify key characteristics of leaders in his book (2005):

> I wanted a powerful and efficient machine but one that also had heart and soul. The words I chose to describe the presence of this powerful block are "Team Spirit." Initially, I defined "Team Spirit" as a willingness to sacrifice personal interests or glory for the welfare of all, but there was something in the definition that bothered me, something not quite right . . . When it came to team spirit willingness was not enough; eagerness was the exact description of what I sought in my self and in those I coached. A willingness to be selfless suggests a begrudging aspect of doing what is required for the team. I wanted each player to be eager to sacrifice personal interest for the good of the group. To me, there is all the difference in the world between willingness and eagerness. Thus, I changed that single word in the definition. Team spirit—an eagerness to sacrifice personal interests or glory for the welfare of all—is a tangible driving force that transforms individuals who are "doing their jobs correctly" into an organization whose members are totally

committed to working at their highest levels for the good of the group. Members of such an organization are unselfish, considerate, and put the goals of the organization above their own, even at the expense of their own personal desires. When this happens—and the leader is the one who makes it happen—the result is almost magical. (p. 47)

In sports, the notion of sacrifice of personal goals for the larger goal of the group is often played out on the field or the court. Those players who do not support the goal of the team over their own personal achievements may soon be sitting on the sidelines. This key component—developing a team—is a central responsibility of a leader.

A third responsibility of leadership is *asking the right questions* and continuing to search for responses instead of responding with an answer immediately. Karl Weick is a well-known author on organizational development and interpersonal interactions in the organization. He has also been good at asking the right questions of researchers. According to Weick (2001):

The effective leader is someone who searches for the better questions, accepts inexperience, stays in motion, channels decisions to those with the best knowledge of the matter at hand, crafts good stories, is obsessed with updating, encourages improvisation, and is deeply aware of personal ignorance. (p. 94)

Because organizational uncertainty will become more dominant in the years to come, leaders need to be able to adapt to conditions and constantly seek new answers. Weick predicts that there will be more unpredictability as we move further into the twenty-first century, the result being fewer experts and more novices, the migration of decision-making duties to those with the expertise, more improvisation and fewer routine tasks, and more plausibility and less accuracy.

A fourth responsibility for leaders is *effective decision making*. How leaders go about the process of making decisions is as important as the decision itself. An organization's decision-making process, as directed by the leader, can have a huge impact on the organization. For example, Steven Sample, the 10th president of the University of Southern California, wrote a widely popular book on leadership entitled *The Contrarian's Guide to Leadership* (2005). He advises that a leader "needs to be able to see the shades of gray inherent in a situation in order to make wise decisions as to how to proceed" (p. 7). He encourages leaders to examine all arguments without forming an opinion, using an F. Scott Fitzgerald quote for support: "The test of a first-rate mind is the ability to hold two opposing thoughts at the same time while still retaining the ability to function" (p. 8). Sample goes on to suggest that leaders who delegate almost all decisions to lieutenants have an opportunity to build a much stronger and coherent organization. The leader, however, must be careful not to delegate the most critical decisions.

Finally, the leader must practice *constant and continuous communication*. Often, those individuals who have the information others need emerge as leaders. In general, people do not like ambiguity. If a leader does not provide the information people seek, then they will fill in the missing information with rumors and supposition. This is an unhealthy situation. Individuals who forget that they must constantly keep others informed about their actions, decisions, and key events might find themselves in the role of the band director marching down the street only to turn around and find that the band turned left at the last intersection.

Power and Ethics in Leadership

Individuals who assume leadership roles often acquire power as a function of the role; how they handle that power can determine their successes and failures. James Michener (1978), in his book *Chesapeake*, describes the leaders of the Eastern shore at Patamoke and Choptank. From 1583 to 1978, he chronicles their successes and failures. It is his last chapter that seems to address most directly the issue of moral leadership. Pursy Paxmore and Owen Steed were two characters caught up in the White House scandals of President Richard Nixon. President Nixon was the only U.S. president to resign office because of scandals in his administration. The famous Watergate break-in was complicated when the president's office attempted to cover it up. At the end of the book, Steed and Paxmore discuss what goes wrong when people in positions of power are corrupt:

> PAXMORE: "A group of California adventurers without political apprentice-ship saw a chance to bend things their way when they saw how easy it was to manipulate the system."
>
> STEED: "How do you explain the corruptions, the near-treason?"
>
> PAXMORE: "Men without character slip from one position to the next and never comprehend the awful downward course they're on."
>
> STEED: "Couldn't Nixon have stopped it?"
>
> PAXMORE: "Woodrow Wilson could have. Or Teddy Roosevelt. And does thee know why? Because they had accumulated through years of appren-ticeship a theory of government. A theory of democracy, if thee will. And they would have detected the rot the minute it started."
>
> STEED: "Why didn't the Californians?"
>
> PAXMORE: "For a simple reason. They were deficient in education. They'd gone to those chrome-and-mirrors schools where procedures are taught, not principles. I doubt if any one of them had ever contemplated a real moral problem, in the abstract where character is formed." (p. 837)

After serving a prison term for laundering illegal funds and participating in other illegal political activities related to the Nixon administration's scandals, Pax-more reflected on his inability to resist being caught up in the corruption, ". . . because I stood so close to power, to the greatest power in the world, the pres-idency. It obliterated judgments. I knew, but I was powerless to react because I was poisoned by power" (p. 837). In the end, he could not live with his own behavior and took his own life.

Unfortunately, some leaders use their power to instill fear in employees. One of our interviewees revealed this type of leadership and the impact it has on the organizational member. This interview was with a production assistant to a major national TV talk show host.

> The work environment at (the show) was run by a manager who basically ran his employees with fear. Not rewards or encouragement, fear. They also made us compete with each other, for promotions, and for more hours and a fear of losing our jobs. We were never awarded, no "Oh that was a great show." He only talked to us when the show went bad. They even would call us in the office and verbally abuse us. They would say stuff like, you're lucky you even have a job here, or, you are never going to get promoted. There was one time when the boss asked me to do something that I wasn't comfortable with. Sometimes when a guest can't get to the show, they send people to get them. My boss wanted me to go to a very bad part of (town) by myself to pick up a guest. As a very young woman, I wasn't comfortable with that. But I went, and it was very scary for me. When I came back, I was like, listen, don't ever ask me to do that again. You sent a young girl into the middle of the ghetto! I said. He almost fired me because I protested to do it, but because other people had brought up that issue, eventually, because I spoke up, they would not allow women to go by themselves anymore. I mean there was no motivation in the company with the way he ran it. They just wanted total control over every-thing.
>
> There weren't a lot of jobs in that city for me. I needed something to pay the bills, and I did feel that I was lucky to be working on a nationally televised program. They would also bring up the possibility of promotion to keep you hanging. They also used things like Christmas as a big motivator. Each year you got a big bonus and $500 worth of gift certificates. Plus, we got the summer off. So whenever I felt like quitting, I told myself, oh, Christmas is almost here, I'll wait till then, or summer's coming, I can tough it out.

Why do people tolerate bad leaders? Jean Lipman-Bluman (2001) suggests it is because of people's insecurities: "To acknowledge their ineptitude, even their malevolence, will only stir up our dreaded insecurities" (p. 129). In fact, she con-cludes that bad leaders are at least predictable. They can be counted on to behave poorly, and this does provide some security. However, the price paid is quite high in terms of lack of freedom and submission to the leader's dictates:

> So, in our eagerness to quell our anxiety, we are often less willing to surrender our-selves to good leaders, who "tell it to us straight," than to put up with dishonest, incompetent, perchance evil leaders. For what does the good leader do but dispel our illusions, or at least make us aware of them, thereby opening our eyes and heightening our tension? (Lipman-Bluman, 2001, p. 129)

Lipman-Bluman's advice is to confront our anxieties so that we may discover the leader within ourselves. When many organizational members do this, the organization as a whole becomes much stronger.

In our experience as employees, leaders, and consultants, issues of power and control—more than any other emotions—create the greatest conflicts and most unpleasant work environments. Unfortunately, some individuals are motivated by power alone to seek positions of leadership. There may be situations in your career that you cannot control. If your superior (and everyone has a boss—even the CEO must report to a board of directors) falls into the category we have been discussing, you must seriously consider how much you can tolerate. As we mentioned earlier, today's workers must be prepared for a number of job changes over their careers. You should constantly be preparing yourself to adapt to new environments and new job requirements. One author provides insight into becoming what he calls a "courageous follower" (Chaleff, 2003, p. 4). He suggests that the sooner we become comfortable with the "idea of powerful followers supporting powerful leaders, the sooner we can fully develop and test models for dynamic, self-responsible, synergistic relationships in our organizations" (p. 3). We suspect that his suggestions to assume responsibility, to challenge, to participate in transformation, take moral action and to listen, is what we have been talking about under the general notion of leadership.

Passion

One critical aspect of outstanding leadership that we have not yet mentioned is passion—passion for a job, for an organization, and for the people in the organization. A leader has to love what she is doing. Warren Bennis (2001) writes about a point in his career when he had an epiphany about being the president of the University of Cincinnati. He was asked in an open session by a colleague, "Warren, do you love being president of the University of Cincinnati?" Warren paused for what seemed like many minutes and finally answered, "I don't know." Later he wrote that he realized that he no longer had the passion for the job and resigned. He concluded, ". . . if there is one single thing I have found out about leaders is that, by and large, if not every day, they seem to love what they're doing." (p. 275). He went back to doing what he loved: teaching and writing. All outstanding leaders find their calling and their voice and identify how they can have an impact on the world. If they don't love what they are doing, then they probably are doing the wrong thing.

Charles Handy (2001) wrote about the world of "fleas and elephants," or large and small organizations. He believes that we must look to the fleas for imaginative new ideas because the elephants must work toward efficiency. He believes that at the heart of every flea organization is a creative individual. In a study of such individuals, he discovered that the one defining and common characteristic of all the leaders he studied was passion:

These individuals were passionate about what they were doing, whether they were building new airlines, new eateries in New York and London, new theatre companies or health centers, this passion for what they did enabled them to endure anything—the long hours necessitated by starting a venture, the failures and mistakes that inevitably occur, and that they speak of as lessons learned rather than failures . . . passion, not reason, provided the driving force. (pp. 31–32)

Leaders who don't love what they are doing often fail, cause others to be miserable, and are constantly looking for something that is missing. Be sure you choose to do something with your life and your career that you love doing. You want to wake up every morning eager to start a new day doing the things you love.

Summary

The way we ended this chapter is perhaps how we should have begun. Start with something you love. Ground yourself in a theoretical foundation that makes the most sense to you and the needs of your followers. Pay attention to the needs of team members and adapt your message delivery accordingly. Build trust among your colleagues, be present, and take action. Communicate and ask the right questions, and remember that a leader has power over others only to the extent that he is given that power by those who are supervised. In fact, giving power to others increases the willingness of the followers to embrace the leader's goals and ideas. It is the authors' hope that by implementing some of the suggestions and approaches to leadership in this chapter, there will be fewer individuals leading with fear and intimidation in our work world.

Lao Tzu, the author of *Tao Te Ching*, sums up our final thought on leadership: Some leaders accomplish a great deal and are loved and praised by followers:

Lesser leaders use threat and fear to get results. The worst leaders use force and lie; they are despised. But the best leaders, when work is done and the good attained, the people say "We did it ourselves!" (quoted in Sashkin & Sashkin, 2003, p. 7)

14 Communication Technology in the Organization

Without a doubt, the single greatest change in organizations in the past few decades has been the increasing pervasiveness of technology. Word processing, e-mail, the Internet, voice mail, discussion boards, chat rooms, instant messaging, online training, videoconferencing, and virtual reality have changed the very nature of work. Fifteen years ago, when predictions were made that the twenty-first century would be the information age, we had no idea how much information would someday be available to organizations and individuals. When they said the United States would move into a global society, they could not have anticipated how technology would heighten the need for every industry to become responsive to the global marketplace.

In short, communication technology now pervades all aspects of organizational life, bringing both benefits and challenges. Consider the following story from Teresa, a 29-year-old human resources generalist:

> One of the major communication obstacles that we face everyday is the variety of communication delivery systems and the comfort levels of those using the systems. For example, some managers prefer direct conversation and won't even leave a message if a "live" person doesn't answer the phone, some communicate via voice mail only, and others do all of their communication via e-mail. Because important information is communicated from the corporate office via e-mail as well as voice mail, managers must be proficient in both delivery systems. Issues do arise when you have individuals who are not comfortable because they may not check their e-mail as often as they should. Likewise, a person who prefers e-mail may not place a priority on checking voice mail. Our company's managers are expected to maintain at least two voice mailboxes, a cell phone and/or pager, as well as e-mail. Sometimes I think we just give them information overload and things get missed.

Teresa's story demonstrates the complex nature of communication technology in organizations. This example points to some of the primary areas of interest when it comes to communication technology in organizations: employees' skill and comfort level with technology; information (over)load; media choice; the infiltration of communication into private lives; and the effects of technology on communication, and vice-versa.

In this chapter, we provide an overview of communication technology in organizations, including a discussion of the basic forms of this technology and how organizational members make choices regarding their use. Next, we discuss the concept of virtual work and issues related to it, such as telework, telecommuting, work-family balance, and monitoring of employee use of communication technology. We conclude the chapter by revisiting two theories covered earlier in this text, showing how they have been used to help understand the relationship between organizations and communication technology.

Overview of Communication Technology

The integration of communication technology into organizations over the past few decades has indeed been staggering, and it is quite easy to become paralyzed by the language that has accompanied this revolution. A few key definitions, points, and trends may help orient you to the communication technology landscape. Perhaps one of the most relevant acronyms to our discussion here is ICT, which stands for *information and communication technology*. Two elements are subsumed under this term. First, *telecommunication* includes "technologies that are used to establish communication over a distance" (Bouwman, van den Hooff, van de Wijngaert, & van Dijk, 2005, p. 22). Second, *information technology* refers to "technologies that are used to store, process and provide data" (Bouwman et al., 2005, p. 22). *ICT*, then, is concerned with moving data (whether video, audio, numbers, words, databases, graphics, etc.) across space and time so that it can be received, edited, processed, or stored.

The study of ICT can be approached in a number of ways, but here we are most concerned with the relationship between technology and communication in the organization. Although communication and technology mutually affect one another, it is safe to say that the ways in which technology has affected organizational communication are the most visible:

> In the early days of computers, visionaries foresaw offices and factories humming with self-propelled robots. Today, a more likely vision has the firm humming with communicating employees. Many large organizations have installed a complex network of computer-based telephone, facsimile, printing, voice mail, email, and even videoconferencing technologies. The technologies increase the potential for communication in the organization. (Hinds & Kiesler, 1995, p. 373)

ICT affects where and when work can be done, how work is done, how employees interact with each other and with the relevant environment (e.g., customers, suppliers, the media, competition, etc.), and how the messages themselves are constructed. With regard to the latter, Rice and Gattiker (2001) argued that communication technology transforms messages in three ways. First, the *nature of messages* is affected; messages may be more task-related, focus on content rather than the identity of the sender, and attend less to closing signatures (e-mail) than messages written in more traditional forms. Second, the *form of content* has changed with technology; multiple threads in discussion boards lead to a loss of coherence, but they also demonstrate visually how ideas are fleshed out. In addition, hyperlinks interrupt (both positively and negatively) traditional notions of text structure. Finally, *temporal aspects of content* have changed. Certain media, such as cell phones and videoconferencing, enable synchronous (sender and receiver communicating at the same time) communication, whereas other media, such as fax and e-mail, are asynchronous (sender and receiver are communicating with a delay). What is driving the ever-increasing use of ICT in organizations? Fulk and DeSanctis (1995) offered five features of new communication technologies that have enabled organizations to integrate ICT more easily:

1. Increases in the speed of communication
2. Dramatic reductions in the costs of communication
3. Increases in communication bandwidth (i.e., the amount of information that can be pumped through a communication line)
4. Vastly expanded connectivity, which is the extent to which people and computers are linked
5. Integration of communication computing technologies, which enables groups of people to share information and develop community

These features have spurred numerous trends, including the digitization of print-based content, such as books, newspapers, archival materials, speeches, etc.; the increased presence of mobile communication equipment, such as personal data assistants (PDAs) and multifunction cellular phones; and the increased use of location technology, such as GPS (global positioning systems), to monitor employee work processes and output (Bleecker, 1998).

As the proliferation and use of communication technologies continues to advance in modern organizations, scholars and practitioners alike are concerned with their unintended consequences. The following are just a few areas that are being investigated by communication scholars regarding communication technology in the workplace (also see Flanagin & Waldeck, 2004; O'Kane, Hargie, & Tourish, 2004; Wiesenfeld, Raghuram, & Garud, 1999):

- How do communication technologies affect employee stress, productivity, satisfaction, and identification?
- How may communication technologies assist, and perhaps modify, traditional approaches to the socialization process?
- How do communication technologies help and hinder employees as they attempt to balance their work and family lives?
- To what extent is the monitoring of employee use of communication technologies ethical?
- How do organizational members decide which communication medium to use to communicate a particular message?

- How do communication technologies both liberate and constrain organizational members?

Basic Forms of Communication Technology

An array of technological tools are available to organizations. The types of technologies available will only continue to increase. What is available today could not have been imagined 10, or even 5, years ago. Advances in technology occur on a daily basis; this chapter could be updated weekly. Rather than trying to predict what new technologies might be available to organizations in the immediate future, we will review some dominant considerations that permeate the choice of any technology, using current technologies as examples.

Although this portion of the chapter covers certain forms of communication technology that are related to message delivery and reception, we would be remiss if we did not provide an overview of a few typical devices and technological advances that have made those forms much more feasible (Table 14-1). Cellular phone technology, for example, has progressed to the point where basic cell phone users can send and receive voice, video, and data messages. Recent advances in this area have bundled web, voice, data, and e-mail together in one mobile unit that can be linked to a personal computer through a simple connection (i.e., Blackberry). This mobile technology has made it possible for organizational members to be virtually anywhere in the world and yet still be connected to their work. In addition, laptop computers have become much more powerful, smaller, and lightweight, and can now be connected to the Internet through wireless capabilities. Wireless technology has helped fuel the communication and information explosion in organizations.

Voice Mail.   *Voice mail* is a convenient form of communication when one person hopes to have an interactive conversation and finds that the other person is unavailable. More and more corporations have turned to voice mail to cut costs. Although this measure may have reduced expenses, it has also "cost" many organizations in terms of public relations. The following excerpt from a December 10, 1999, *Athens* (Ohio) *Messenger* news story describes the anger experienced by many customers attempting to reach a human being by phone:

> We're sorry, but all the lines are busy. Please hold for the next available operator. Thank you for your patience. Remember, your call is very important to us.
>   Seriously.
>   If you'd like to listen to a continuous loop of music by the Bee Gees, push 1 now. If you'd like to leave a message that will undoubtedly be ignored, push 2 now. If you are ready to implode in frustrated anger, push 3 now.
>   Like its cousin, road rage, phone rage raises blood pressure and causes outbursts. And as companies increasingly rely on voice-mail systems to handle customer service, more and more people are seething in silence, or slamming down the phone.

Although leaving voice messages makes the work of connecting with others easier, it is not a substitute for an interactive conversation in which people share

TABLE 14.1   Communication Media Technology

Media Type	Description	Participants	Advantages	Challenges
Voice mail	Spoken messages for retrieval	One-to-one; one-to-many	Efficient message transmission	Noninteractive
Internet, intranet, and extranet	Text, video, images, audio, interactivity, and data sharing	Local and global	Global access with ability to restrict access	Resource allocation to maintain and develop
E-mail	Written messages with file attachment	One-to-one; one-to-many	Ease of use	Can be too quick to allow forethought
Instant messaging	Written messages with minimal delay	One-to-one	Ease of use; more immediate than e-mail	Can be too quick to allow forethought
Videoconference and videostream	Video and audio interaction	One-to-one; group	Allows for multiple communication cues	Arranging connections; professional production
Virtual reality	Video, audio, and simulation	Individual or group	Hands-on learning	Expensive setup and maintenance

information and meaning. For example, earlier in the text we talked about the synergy present in team decision making. One person's idea may cause another to be more innovative than she would have been alone. A person's facial expressions and tone of voice, as well as the environment, can impact the communication process. Mediated communication limits these more subtle forms of communicating.

The Internet, Intranets, and Extranets.   The *Internet*, which is the worldwide system of linked computers, was developed in conjunction with the U.S. Department of Defense in the 1960s (O'Kane et al., 2004). The Internet has changed the nature of organizational life; a company's reach can now quite literally be global. Company websites can be used for myriad purposes, including product sales and services, recruitment, public relations, entertainment, and internal communication through secured sites. Regardless of a website's purpose, O'Kane et al. (2004) suggest that web developers keep three things in mind as they develop sites:

1. **audience**—What do different demographic groups need/want/expect from the site?
2. **resources**—Are adequate resources in place for site maintenance, staff training, and organizational support for sales in a global market?

3. **product**—Are product quality and availability in place to meet the demands of the global marketplace?

Organizations also have the possibility of adopting intranet and extranet technologies. An *intranet* "facilitates increased collaboration among employees, as it flattens the organization structure and introduces 'any-to-any' connectivity within the company" (O'Kane et al., 2004, p. 82). Resources and applications on an organization's intranet are protected from external users and are exclusive to organization members. In contrast, an *extranet* "extends this [an intranet's capabilities] to encompass external stakeholders such as specific customers or shareholders" (O'Kane et al., 2004, p. 82). Internet, intranet, and extranet technologies all allow for dynamic communication and facilitate connections among employees and between the organization and the relevant environment.

E-mail.   *E-mail* has become the preferred way to send written messages. It is estimated that as of 1996, 80 percent of all U.S. corporations were using e-mail (Greengrad, 1996). That number can only have increased over the past several years; we estimate that today it is probably more than 90 percent. E-mail messages are immediately available to the recipients, and it avoids instances of "phone tag." In fact, e-mail is so convenient that sometimes people send messages that might not have been generated in the absence of e-mail or that would have been written but not sent. Consider the employee who thought he was sending a personal message to a colleague, wishing him success in fighting a battle against "that SOB controller," but accidentally used the wrong distribution list. This private message was sent to the entire organizational distribution list, including the "SOB controller" and the president. In that sense, e-mail is almost too easy. People send messages without carefully thinking through the contents, just to get the message off their desk and onto someone else's computer screen. E-mail messages are also more informal than would be acceptable in a written memo. Therefore, when a message should sound more formal or more definite, a written memo placed in mailboxes may convey that subtle message in a way that an e-mail message cannot.

Sometimes the use of e-mail is perceived negatively because it is an unsuitable medium for a particular message. One example occurred late in 1999 with the replacement of the CEO of a major corporation. Employees received the following e-mail:

> To: All _____ Personnel
> Subject: Moving Forward
>   This past Sunday evening, _____ (CEO of the company) informed members of the senior management that he had decided to retire, effective immediately. He will be joining a company that will be identified in a coordinated press release later today. Attached at the bottom of this note is a copy of the news release we are sending to the news media globally.
>   In the last two weeks, _____ was presented with what he believes to be an extraordinary opportunity to lead a new business venture into the e-Commerce world. He believes that our established, dominant place in the market coupled

with the very favorable position in the arbitration make this the right time and the right choice for him to retire.

Today, we began the transition to new leadership at _____. The _____ Committee of the Board has asked me to be the interim Managing Partner and CEO. I am honored to be asked and pleased to serve.

We are grateful for _____'s 11 years at the helm of our fine organization and we recognize that a transition of leadership was inevitable. As you know, we are experiencing the most successful year in our history, with revenues expected to exceed nine billion. That success is directly a result of the hard work of each and every one of you.

Personnel in this *Fortune* 500 company were surprised to receive this news via e-mail. They expected that vice presidents and partners would tell managers, who would then communicate this information to staff in a more personal way. Later, managers did make phone calls to try to provide more information about expected changes in the company. In a large corporation, however, sometimes a message needs to be delivered before employees read about it in the newspaper. It is difficult to decide which method is the most effective and efficient for the delivery of important information throughout a large organization.

Instant Messaging.   Another communication technology that is being adopted by organizations is instant messaging, which has been adopted by more than half the U.S. workforce (Holtz, 2006). *Instant messaging* enables users who are online simultaneously to send messages back and forth through a messaging window with little to no delay. Although some companies have adopted instant messaging as a way to enhance communication among employees, some workers have opted to use this technology to work around company restrictions on e-mail use (e.g., no personal e-mail at work). Instant messaging is primarily a text-based system, but some service providers feature video and audio capabilities. A number of instant messaging systems also allow for collaborative work on documents, which increases its utility in organizations.

Videoconferencing and Videostreaming.   *Videoconferencing,* which involves voice and video transmissions involving several people, has been marketed as a cost-saving technique over face-to-face meetings (e.g., due to expenses related to travel and lost time). Videoconferencing capabilities are now widely available thanks to high-speed Internet connections, inexpensive web cameras, and increased bandwidth.

The precursor to the videoconference, the teleconference (voice over a telephone line), was first introduced by AT&T at the New York World's Fair in 1964. In 1981, the same company introduced the picturephone, which allowed groups to go to a teleconference room that was rented out at $2,300 per hour (Bulkeley, 1992). Its use ended that same year as corporations developed their own on-site capabilities. Since the mid-1980s, the cost of videoconferencing equipment has been decreasing. That fact, coupled with increased travel costs, has stimulated a good deal of videoconference activity among corporations.

But are videoconferences effective? In a recent study, videoconferencing meetings were perceived as more structured and more task-focused than face-to-face meetings. Videoconferences required participants to know the agenda before-hand and to have completed tasks ahead of time. However, the videoconferences did not appear to have a strong impact on productivity or consensus (Hart, Sven-ning, & Ruchinskas, 1995). Thus, although the use of technology may force people to be more organized and structured, it does not necessarily improve their ability to perform.

Another form of voice and video transmission that occurs over the Internet or intranet is videostreaming. *Videostreaming* is a one-way transmission (as opposed to the two-way transmission in videoconferencing) of voice and video that can be viewed by multiple viewers simultaneously. Organizations are now using videostreaming to communicate messages to internal and external constituents. Videostreams can be highly produced or occur in real-time, but both allow for widespread and repeated distribution of important information, such as a CEO discussing a new product initiative or her intentions to take the company public. A survey on company communication conducted by Vanson Bourne in a July 22, 2004, issue of *New Media Age* stated that only 1 in 10 CEOs had tried videostream-ing technology, but 64 percent thought it could be a useful business tool.

Virtual Reality.   *Virtual reality* will become an increasingly important technol-ogy for organizations. It already has had a huge impact on the training profession, because it preserves the visual-spatial characteristics of simulated work (Regian, Shebilske, & Monk, 1992). Virtual technology enables collaboration among geo-graphically dispersed organizational members. They can organize their work, col-laborate on tasks, simulate an organizational environment, and share information, all online. The 2000 American Society for Training and Development's State of the Industry Report indicates that from 1997 to 1998 there was a 50 percent increase in the amount of training delivered by technology rather than in the classroom. From 1998 to the present, however, the use of virtual reality technology for train-ing has leveled off:

> This leveling off in the growth of learning technologies suggests that perhaps organ-izations are finding technology-based training difficult to do well. Challenges that companies may be facing include technological barriers, cultural resistance to a new way of learning, and the challenge of ensuring that technology-based training is cost-effective and produces results that truly enhance individual and firm perform-ance. (McMurrer, Van Buren, & Woodwell, 2000, p. 15)

Nevertheless, there is no doubt that organizations are making huge investments in learning technologies. It is interesting to note that the highest use of learning technologies to deliver training occurred in manufacturing (13 percent of training time), trade (12.5 percent), and technology (11 percent). According to the report, the two industries predicting the largest increases in the use of learning technolo-gies were health care and the government.

For the final part of this introductory section, we now turn our attention to summarizing a few of the major theories related to how individuals make choices regarding which communication technology to employ. While we do not cover the breadth of theory related to this topic, you will gain an understanding of the basic issues related to media selection.

Criteria for Selection of Mediated Communication

Two characteristics most likely determine when and how a particular technology is used: social presence and media richness. *Social presence* refers to the degree of sociability present in the use of the media. Characteristics such as warmth, personalness, and sensitivity (Rice, Chang, & Torobin, 1992) are aspects of the social presence of a medium. For example, face-to-face conversation supports the use of facial expressions, touch, posture, and numerous nonverbal cues to communicate a message. The people participating in the conversation feel that both parties are involved and present in the dialogue. With e-mail, despite the fact that users can use "nonverbal" signals such as the smiling face (☺), it is much harder for a recipient to interpret a message. Consequently, the recipient may feel that a dialogue is not occurring, just one-way communication answered by another one-way message. Face-to-face communication has a high degree of social presence; written messages have a low amount. What types of messages require a high degree of social presence? Certainly, conflicts should be dealt with face-to-face, and bad news might be made worse if delivered in a medium with low social presence.

Commercial Financial Services Incorporated sent an e-mail to 1,450 people in June 1999 to let them know they had been fired, shortly before the Oklahoma company declared bankruptcy. When asked about the rationale for using e-mail for the mass firing, one top-level executive explained, "Companies today have people all over the globe. When something catastrophic happens, they want everyone to hear it at the same time, if possible" (Seminerio, 1999). Of course, many employees thought, "The whole thing is classless. It lacks sensitivity." In a medium with low social presence, it is easy for people to construe things differently from what the sender of the message intended. This difference can create workplace tensions. In the Commercial Financial Services example, the way the fired employees were treated had a profound impact on the performance of those who were not fired.

At the same time, we also have learned that sometimes giving bad news is easier when the sender does not have to be present when the other person receives it. Researchers at Case Western Reserve University concluded in a study that people are more comfortable using e-mail to communicate bad news than doing so in person or on the telephone. "People are usually more honest and distort the bad news less" in e-mail messages than in spoken communication. "With e-mail becoming, in many offices, the primary vehicle for communication between workers and employers, the workplace dynamic has changed for good. What this means for employees' relationships with their employers is unclear" (Seminerio, 1999).

The second important characteristic that determines which form of technology one is likely to use is *media richness*. Media vary in terms of the speed of feedback (how quickly you can reasonably expect a reply from the person receiving your message), the degree of formality and structure in the language, the variety of language used, and the tone of voice and facial expressions (Daft & Lengel, 1986; Donabedian, McKinnon, & Burns, 1998). For example, a response to a written memo may take a couple of days, by the time it is delivered and handled, whereas a response to an e-mail message may take just a few minutes. The language in a written memo is often more formal and more structured than the language in a quick e-mail message.

When communicating ambiguous information, which might be subject to many interpretations, a rich media is necessary. Face-to-face communication has the highest level of media richness; it provides immediate feedback and personal interaction and uses natural language high in variety (Lengel & Daft, 1988). For example, when the boss says, "This report needs your attention" and her voice is high pitched, her eye contact intense, and she is leaning toward you, there is more information to process than just the message itself. In addition, when you look back at her with your raised eyebrows and a questioning look on your face she responds with, "That means today if possible." Her face-to-face message is much richer in information than a memo delivered to your mailbox. Face-to-face communication enables immediate feedback and personal interaction, which helps to define the message. If a message can be misunderstood, it is more likely to be misunderstood in the absence of face-to-face contact.

Another factor influencing the choice of communication media is *accessibility*. The speed and ease with which one can send messages to multiple audiences has seduced many people who thought they would never use e-mail. People send messages via e-mail that they would never take the time to write out in a formal memo. Tom, a unit manager, tells a story of one such occasion:

> Saul Lawrence was angry with June, a colleague. At a meeting she had publicly criticized a project he had been working on for some time without, he thought, justification. He had not had a chance to defend himself and thought it was important for others to hear his side of the situation. It was very easy to create a distribution list of everyone who had been at the meeting, and because he assumed others had probably heard about the criticism he included six other individuals who were in some way involved in the project. His e-mail memo read, "Contrary to what you may have heard, Project X is on time and will be brought in under budget. It would be much better if people got their facts straight before criticizing the work of others."
>
> Susan, who read the memo but had not been at the meeting, thought he was referring to a comment she had made in a report delivered to top management the day before about projects in general often being underestimated in terms of time to completion. She answered Saul's e-mail, and of course sent it to the same distribution list: "If we are going to take any comment about outcome measures so personally, then we will never be able

> to excel at what we do." Thus started a barrage of e-mail messages, none of which addressed the original issue. The two people involved in the original conflict (Saul and June) never did discuss their differences with each other.
>
> The messages got so out of control that finally the unit manager had to issue an e-mail message that read: "This public forum will not be used to air personal attacks."

It is hard to believe that professionals can get so personal and negative, yet it happens often. As communication consultants, the authors are frequently asked to help solve exactly these types of conflicts. Communication technologies such as e-mail have made it easier to escalate conflicts in a very short period of time. If Saul's only option had been to call each person on the phone, or even type out a formal memo and distribute it to everyone's mailbox, it is unlikely he would have done so. But because technology has made the distribution of messages so easy and quick, sometimes messages are sent that would be best left unsent.

Charles Steinfield (1992) is a communication researcher who has completed extensive research on human and technology communication. He has concluded: "Problems will occur when media that are low in social presence are used for communication tasks requiring significant interpersonal involvement, such as negotiations or conflict resolution" (p. 351). That is exactly what happened to Saul in our example. To negotiate a conflict with a colleague takes a high degree of involvement and social presence. Using inflammatory language without the opportunity to interact and defend oneself only leads to more misunderstandings. The accessibility of e-mail is just too tempting. People sometimes use it without thinking through the consequences of the message. Writing a memo, copying it, and distributing it is a more deliberative process, causing the sender to think more carefully about the words and how they will be interpreted.

Another factor in technology usage is *position in the hierarchy*. As Rice, Chang, and Torobin (1992) have pointed out:

> In general the higher one's level in the organization, the greater percentage time [is] spent interacting with other people, the more that communication is oral (especially face-to-face) and the more the task demands involve equivocal and rapid-feedback communication. (p. 6)

The president of a major university and the CEO of a *Fortune* 500 company with whom we have worked do not follow this pattern, however. One answers hundreds of individual e-mail messages a day, and the other frequently sends out e-mail messages to thousands of employees each week. Many leaders are allowing e-mail to substitute for face-to-face encounters.

In one large organization, however, e-mail has actually increased personal contact. Richard Brown, former CEO of Electronic Data Systems (EDS), recently described a situation in which he needed to reach all employees of EDS quickly about a matter of great importance to the company. His e-mail began, "It is 3 A.M. in the morning and I have just landed in Pango, Pango, and since I can't sleep I had some thoughts I wanted to share with you" (Brown, personal communication, April 15, 2000). He proceeded to let all 140,000 employees of EDS know about a recent breach in confidentiality to which everyone needed to be sensitive. Had he waited until he returned to corporate headquarters in Texas, called a meeting of top-level managers, and asked them to get the word out, it would have been at least two weeks, and he would have had no guarantee that the message would be communicated exactly as he wanted. By e-mail, in seconds, every EDS employee around the world read the same message from the CEO.

Researchers have discovered no clear patterns among various communication styles and the use of communication technology. Individuals with high-energy styles, who are rather dramatic and animated, as well as those with a more relaxed style of interacting use different technologies equally: "Communicator style plays quite a small role in explaining adoption, usage, and evaluation of computer mediated communication" (Rice et al., 1992, p. 22).

Some researchers believe that contingency theory addresses the most appropriate medium for use in a given situation. The degree of equivocality, or uncertainty, in a situation; the need for quick feedback; and the personalness of the source may be better predictors of the type of mediated communication used: "At some point there will be enough users so that the perceived benefits of using the system exceed the costs. This in turn results in a rapid growth in the number of users until usage becomes universal within the community" (Steinfield, 1992, p. 354). Steinfield refers to this situation as the critical-mass theory.

Communication Technology and Virtual Ways of Working

With communication technology now being so affordable, reliable, and accessible, many organizations have started to question the basic assumption that workers must be in the same physical location to do their work. Workers can now work together while being separated by space and time:

> Spurred by advances in information technologies, many organizations have begun experimenting with virtual ways of working. Included in these ways of working are modes such as telecommuting, working from satellite centers, mobile work, and the like. Indeed, in some organizations, it is no longer important when you work and where you work, as long as the work gets done. (Wiesenfeld et al., 1999, p. 7)

Virtual work, as we will call it here, can certainly benefit the organization and the individual. In their review of literature on the topic, Bailey & Kurland (2002) demonstrate that there are at least four macro-level benefits to this type of virtual work. First, virtual work can significantly reduce real estate costs for organizations, because they no longer have to house each and every employee physically. Second, employees can use virtual work as a way of attempting to balance the demands of work and family. This is a widely researched area of virtual work, which we will return to later in the chapter. Third, virtual work helps organizations comply with the 1990 Americans with Disabilities Act. Organizations can now more easily hire individuals with disabilities who may not be able to perform a job in a traditional manner, but can work effectively and efficiently with the assistance of communication technology and a familiar environment. Finally, with the reduction in travel for employees (car, plane, bus, train, etc.), both traffic and air pollution can be positively affected.

The idea of working away from a central location is not new in and of itself, though its popularity has certainly increased dramatically in recent years. One of the first organizations to experiment with virtual work was IBM in 1989. IBM developed an approach called "hoteling" that was designed to reduce the amount of time salespeople spent traveling to meet with customers and to reduce real estate costs (Neuhauser, Bender, & Stromberg, 2000):

> The sales representatives or systems engineers gave up their desks and vehicles and moved to alternate workplaces, usually in their homes. If the employee needed to do work at a desk or in a meeting room, they would call to make a reservation, just as if it were a hotel. (p. 58)

Since IBM's initial experiment with virtual work two decades ago, other organizations have adopted the practice and modernized it, leading to a new breed of worker: "The new, ultra-mobile workforce, nicknamed 'road warriors,' are message-intensive. They talk on the go and go where the action is" (Bleecker, 1998, p. 47).

Telework and Telecommuting

Perhaps the most popular descriptors associated with virtual work are telework and telecommuting. Though associated, these two terms represent different phenomena. Jack Nilles is credited with first introducing these terms, defining them as follows: *Telework* is "*any* form of substitution of information technologies (such as telecommunications and computers) for work-related travel" (1998, p. 1). He considered telework to be moving the work to the workers, instead of the workers to the work. He defines *telecommuting* as "Periodic work out of the principal office, one or more days per week either at home, a client's site, or in a telework center" (p. 1). A May 5, 2006, article in the *Los Angeles Times* reported that, according to the U.S. Chamber of Commerce, 20 million people in the U.S. telecommute and that one in six U.S. employees works from home at least once per week.

Not all employees who can telecommute do, however. A July 12, 2006, article in *PC Magazine* reported that 25 percent of the U.S. workforce could work from home, but doesn't. Why might an employee not work from home given the flexibility, time and cost savings, and potential for increased productivity and satisfaction? A number of reasons have been cited, but three deserve our special attention. First, despite having telecommuting as an option, individual managers may be biased against telecommuting, thereby making the employee reticent to use it. For example, Gross (2006) described how certain managers in the U.S. government question telecommuting because they do not know that employees will be more productive and they do not know how to supervise off-site workers. This pessimism by managers may lead to pressure on the workforce not to take the option of telecommuting. Second, some telecommuters can become isolated professionally, and this can limit the extent to which they use the telecommuting option (Cooper & Kurland, 2002; Ford & Kondrasuk, 2002). Finally, telecommuting can lead to fragmentation of core organizational values, causing those who do not telecommute to look down on those who do. This can lead to personal and professional isolation, but also to the work of those who telecommute being considered less legitimate than that produced by on-site employees (Hylmo, 2006). As a result of these pressures, a worker may decide not to telecommute. While there are certainly many more reasons why employees may not take the option to telecommute, these three are most prevalent in the communication research at the current time.

Telecommuting and Work-Family Balance. Telework and telecommuting have opened up possibilities for how employees balance the needs and demands of work and family. However, workers who have taken the option to work from home have found that drawbacks may accompany the benefits:

> We have entered a new era of workplace connectivity through the advent of portable wireless technologies. These tools will provide needed flexibility to juggle work and family aspects of our self-identities and provide the needed control to preserve this sense of self. However, in this fast-forward age, they may also blur traditional boundaries to such a degree that the lines delineating our sense of self will become shadowy and inconsequential. (Schlosser, 2002, p. 401)

Let's consider the positive and negative implications of telework in relationship to work-family balance.

Duxbury, Higgins, and Neufeld (1998) have researched a variety of ways that telework can help employees manage work-family balance as well as increase work-family conflict. The positive and negative aspects of telework with regards to work-family balance are summarized in Table 14-2.

Telework can aid the work-family balance in four ways. First, it can provide *flexibility* with regard to when and where work will be completed, making it possible for the employee to attend to family needs during the typical work day if necessary. Second, telework affords *control* over family and work schedules and responsibilities such that the employee does not have to feel overly constrained by a traditional work schedule/location. Third, *dependent care*, whether for children, a spouse, significant other, or other family member, can be more easily maintained, because the employee can work from home or while traveling. Finally,

TABLE 14.2   Positive and Negative Aspects of Telework with Regard to Work-Family Balance

Positive Aspects	Negative Aspects
Flexibility	Role overload
Control	Workaholism
Dependent care	Blurring of boundaries between work-family
Relationships at home	Negative impact on relationships at home
	Child care

relationships at home can be attended to throughout the day, leading to increased interaction with family members.

Telework can also increase work-family conflict. Duxbury et al. (1998) describes five ways that this can happen. First, the person doing the telework can experience *role overload* by having too much to do on a daily basis. Not only does the employee need to attend to the demands of work, but she simultaneously needs to attend to the demands of the home. Second, engaging in telework has been associated with *workaholism* as work takes over family time and family needs. Some who telework at home find themselves unable to stop working in an effort to prove to themselves and their employers that the alternative work arrangement in no way hinders their performance. Third, telework can *blur boundaries between work and family*, such that the demands of both are compromised. No longer can work be left at the office and family left at the front door—they now coexist in the same location, and that blurring of boundaries can be paralyzing to some workers. Fourth, employees working from home may find that family-time actually decreases, leading to a *negative impact on relationships at home*. Finally, *childcare* is of concern as employees find that telework is not a substitute for caring for the needs of one's children. Hill, Ferris, and Martinson (2003) spoke of this issue when they noted that telework "is associated with lower work/life balance and less success in personal/family life [which] is cause for personal and family concern" (p. 236).

Is there anything that can be done to help a person engaged in telework be successful and stave off its potential negative effects? One teleworker who telecommuted from California to Boston offered the following advice for individuals and organizations based on 10 years of personal experience (Gomolski, 2006):

- Self-motivated people will be more productive.
- Telecommuting can improve job satisfaction, but only for those who want to be doing work in this way.
- Organizations should provide mentors to new employees who are telecommuting as a way of socializing them and connecting them to the organization as well as helping them manage the demands of working in this way.

- Organizations should focus on the outcomes produced, not the work styles of the employees, to avoid making them feel "checked up on."

Gomolski's final point hints at another important issue related to communication technology and work, whether traditional or virtual—electronic monitoring. In the last part of this section, we discuss how organizations are using technology to monitor employees' use of communication technology.

Communication Technology and Monitoring Employees

As more work in organizations is being done with the assistance of communication technology, organizations have begun to monitor how employees actually use that technology. Consider the following results from the American Management Association's 2005 Electronic Monitoring and Surveillance Survey:

- 26 percent of organizations have fired employees for misuse of the Internet
- 25 percent have fired employees for misuse of e-mail
- 76 percent monitor employees' web connections
- 50 percent store and review workers' data files (spreadsheets, word processing documents, etc.)
- 55 percent review employees' e-mail messages

It is clear from these data organizations are serious about controlling how their employees use company resources, such as Internet connections and e-mail, but how do they do this? Fairweather (1999) showed that companies use Computer Based Performance Monitoring (CBPM), which includes monitoring keystrokes, the length of phone calls, time away from a desk, time between phone calls, and sending and receiving data through network connections, among other things.

Why do companies monitor their employees in these ways? Three reasons have been put forward in the literature (Fairweather, 1999). First, companies feel that because they own the communication technology systems, they have the right to monitor any and all activity that occurs on them. Second, CBPM allows for another form of quality control. For example, an employee's keystrokes on a computer keyboard can be monitored to determine how much work is actually being conducted during the day, and what that work consists of. Finally, and perhaps most central to monitoring activities is that organizations can track down misuse of the technology. By restricting personal use of e-mail, the Internet, and instant messaging, organizations feel they can increase productivity by decreasing instances of what they consider to be theft of resources.

Let's take as one example a company's monitoring of employee e-mail use. Federal privacy laws that protect other forms of communication may not extend to e-mail. Managers would argue that abuse of e-mail, or using company e-mail for personal reasons, demands that the organization monitor employee use of this organizational technology. "The more one uses e-mail, the more likely one will be to dislike policies that restrain personal choice in usage. The more one sees e-mail as important to one's work, the less favorable a person is toward the idea of policies for e-mail" (Hacker, Goss, Townley & Horton, 1998, p. 446). However, many organizations have developed policies on the use of e-mail in the organization.

Alder and Tompkins (1997) concluded that electronic monitoring can constitute an invasion of worker privacy and result in increased stress and decreased performance. However, they also found that in some cases the proper use of monitoring was beneficial for both workers and the organization. "On the other hand, we have also demonstrated that the proper use of technology to monitor workers may produce benefits for both organizations and their workers" (1997, pp. 283–284). This issue will continue to be the subject of debate.

Applying Organizational Theory to Communication Technology

Much of our discussion in this chapter has been involved in describing the various types of communication technology used in organizations and the associated benefits and challenges of virtual work that they have enabled. Recent research in organizational communication has also applied existing theories to interpret how technology affects and is affected by organizational structure and organizational relationships. Most every organizational theory covered in this book can be applied to the relationship between communication technology and communication in organizations. For example, Weber's Theory of Bureaucracy could show that communication technology establishes rules for behavior in organizations (e.g., you must type x number of words per minute or only view certain types of websites) that serve to control workers' actions and make them predictable. An organizational culture perspective on communication technology could demonstrate how instant messaging and e-mail are modern versions of the "grapevine" in organizations and serve to be a primary means of communicating norms, values, stories, and gossip that define (or counter) the organization's culture. A systems theory perspective could be used to show how the different subsystems in an organization are connected, or not connected, by tracing the network connections among them. Recent communication scholarship has made the most use of two theories covered earlier in this book—structuration theory and critical theory.

A Structuration Perspective on Communication Technology

Giddens' theory of structuration has many facets, but central to the theory is the notion of duality of structure. As discussed in Chapter 6, *duality of structure* implies that organizational structure is both the medium and outcome of human interaction. Structure is produced and reproduced as organizational members interact on a daily basis. In approaching communication technology from a structuration perspective, we see how the relationship between technology and structure can be viewed in the same way: "The articulation of technology and organization recognizes that neither is fixed but that both are changing in relation to each other, and that technological users play active roles in shaping the design of that articulation" (Fulk & DeSanctis, 1995, p. 338). In this quotation you can begin to see a structuration perspective—neither communication technology nor organizational structure are stable entities; both are understandable in relation to the people who are using the technology.

Orlikowski (1992), in applying structuration theory to communication technology, adapted Giddens' concept of duality of structure and renamed it *duality of technology*, explaining the new concept as follows:

> Technology is the product of human action, while it also assumes structural properties. That is, technology is physically constructed by actors working in a given social context, and technology is socially constructed by actors through the different meanings they attach to it and the various features they emphasize and use. However, it is also the case that once developed and deployed, technology tends to become reified and institutionalized, losing its connection with human agents that constructed it or gave it meaning, and appears to be part of the objective, structural properties of the organization. (p. 406)

By using structuration theory, Orlikowski was adeptly able to show how we, as organizational members, through our own actions, serve to construct a perspective on technology that makes it feel as if we are its prisoners. The notion of duality of technology demonstrates that individuals have a choice in how they adopt, integrate, program, use, and do not use various communication technologies. As a result, they create structures that serve to enable and constrain their behavior. This is a liberating perspective in a way; many people feel that we are merely pawns being moved and used by the technology that surrounds us. The structuration perspective acknowledges these structures, but shows how we can and do contribute to their existence and persistence.

A Critical Approach to Communication Technology

At the heart of critical theory, as you will recall from Chapter 5, is a concern with the organization as a site of domination and how power is used and abused in the organizational setting. The role that communication technology plays in supporting management interests over workers' interests and how technology can be used in the maintenance of hegemony are prime concerns of critical organizational theorists. Perhaps because communication technology has been purported to flatten organizational structures and increase worker empowerment, critical theorists have been particularly attentive to how workers may actually be

oppressed by management because of it. As with other organizational phenomena, a critical theorist would argue that communication technology is rarely
"interest free" and its use(s) should be scrutinized for instances of oppression.

For example, although computer information systems have disbursed
power across organizations due to increased access to information and the
removal of hierarchical communication barriers, an alternate reading from a critical perspective shows a less positive side. Gephart (2002) provides us with an initial critical reading of this situation:

> [C]omputerization of the workplace has complex influences on structure and pri-
> marily reinforces *status quo* organizational structure, whether it is decentralized or
> centralized. Implementation and operational strategies for CISs typically are
> decided by power elites and these strategies influence structure more than tech-
> nology itself.

In other words, the technology used in an organization is decided upon by management, and they will only allow the development and implementation of technology that does not interrupt their power base. In this way, the management's
interests are promoted and workers' interests are restricted.

Another application of critical theory to communication technology in
organizations is how the technology the organization provides for the workers
affects workers' professional and personal lives. For example, some companies
provide employees with wireless communication devices (such as Blackberries)
that the workers are encouraged to use for both professional and personal purposes. These devices allow workers to be more flexible with regard to when and
where they do their work, which to some people seems like employee empowerment. However, a critical theory perspective on this situation would question
whose interests are being served and how workers are being oppressed. By providing employees with a Blackberry, organizations may be broadening their scope
of control by expecting that workers should be available around the clock. Workers may actually be oppressed in this situation because the organization can now
reach into their lives 24 hours a day and expect that the worker respond. What
may first appear as empowerment and liberation may actually be an instrument
of hegemony as workers answer e-mail in the middle of the night or revise a doc-
ument during the middle of their child's soccer tournament.

Summary

Communication technology greatly affects life in the organization. On the one
hand, it can ease workers' lives by (1) speeding the sending of information,
(2) improving interpersonal communication, (3) increasing participation in organizational processes, and (4) assisting organizational members with balancing work
and family needs. On the other hand, it can (1) be easily misused by employees for

personal agendas, (2) serve as a poor substitute for face-to-face communication, and (3) serve the interests of management over the interests of workers.

Communication technology will continue to change the very nature of work in the organization. It mediates messages in ways many are often not aware of. Even with in-depth explanations and use of symbols to represent nonvocal communication, it is difficult for recipients to determine the underlying message of an e-mail that may sound critical or comical.

Using communication technologies carefully and following up with a variety of forms of communication will ensure better communication among all participants. We can only guess what the future of communication technology will bring. It is certain, though, that communication technology will continue to influence the way people interact in organizations and the structure of organizational life.

BIBLIOGRAPHY

Ackers, J. (1999). Hierarchies, job, bodies: A theory of gendered organizations. *Gender & Society, 4*(2), 139–158.

Adkins, M., & Brashers, D. E. (1995). The power of language in computer-mediated groups. *Management Communication Quarterly, 8*(3), 289–322.

Aktouf, O. (1992). Management and theories of organizations in the 1990s: Toward a critical radical humanism? *Academy of Management Review, 17*(3), 407–431.

Albrecht, T. L., & Hall, B. J. (1991). Facilitating talk about new ideas: The role of personal relationships in organizational innovation. *Communication Monographs, 58,* 273–288.

Alder, G. S., & Tompkins, P. K. (1997). Electronic performance monitoring: An organizational justice and concertive control perspective. *Management Communication Quarterly, 10*(3), 259–288.

Allen, B. J. (1995). "Diversity" and organizational communication. *Journal of Applied Communication Research, 23,* 143–155.

Allen, M. W., & Brady, R. M. (1997). Total quality management, organizational commitment, perceived organizational support, and intraorganizational communication. *Management Communication Quarterly, 10*(3), 316–341.

Allen, T. D., & Russell, J. E. (1999). Parental leave of absence: Some not-so-family friendly implications. *Journal of Applied Social Psychology, 29,* 166–191.

Almaney, A. (1974). Communication and the systems theory of organization. *Journal of Business Communication, 12*(1), 35–43.

Alvesson, M. (2002). *Understanding organizational culture.* London: Sage.

Alvesson, M., & Deetz, S. (1996). Critical theory and postmodernism approaches to organizational studies. In S. R. Clegg, C. Hardy, & W. R. Nord, (Eds.), *Handbook of organization studies* (pp. 191–217). Thousand Oaks, CA: Sage.

Amason, A. C. (1996). Distinguishing the effects of functional and dysfunctional conflict on strategic decision making: Resolving a paradox for top management teams. *Academy of Management Journal, 39,* 123–148.

American Society for Training and Development. (1998a). Digital Equipment Corp.: Worldwide on-site workbench training program. In S. Cheney (Ed.), *Excellence in practice 2* (pp. 1–10). Alexandria, VA: American Society for Training and Development.

American Society for Training and Development. (1998b). GTE: The culture initiative. In S. Cheney (Ed.), *Excellence in practice 2* (pp. 11–21). Alexandria, VA: American Society for Training and Development.

Amy, A. H. (2005). Leaders as facilitators of organizational learning. Unpublished Doctoral Dissertation. Regent University.

Argyris, C. (1999). *On organizational learning* (2nd ed.). Oxford, UK: Blackwell.

Ashcraft, K. L. (2000). Empowering "professional" relationships: Organizational Communication Meets Feminist Practice. *Management Communication Quarterly, 13*(3), 347–392.

Ashford, S. J., & Tsui, A. S. (1991). Self-regulation for managerial effectiveness: The role of active feedback seeking. *Academy of Management Journal, 34*(2), 251–280.

Ashforth, B. E., & Humphrey, R. H. (1993). Emotional labor in service roles: The influence of identity. *Academy of Management Review, 18,* 88–115.

Ashforth, B. E., Kreiner, G. E., & Fugate, M. (2000). All in a day's work: Boundaries and micro-role transitions. *Academy of Management Review, 25*(3), 472–491.

ASTD state of the industry report (2000). www.astd.org. Accessed July 21, 2006.

Aubert, B. A., & Kelsey, B. L. (2003). Further understanding of trust and performance in virtual teams. *Small Group Research, 34*(5), 575–618.

Austin, J. L. (1962). *How to do things with words.* Cambridge, MA: Harvard University Press.

Avolio, B. J., & Gibbons, T. C. (1988). Developing transformation leaders: A life-span approach. In J. A. Conger & N. Kanungo (Eds.), *Charismatic leadership: The elusive factor in organizational effectiveness* (pp. 277–308). San Francisco: Jossey-Bass.

Babcock, P. (2003). Spotting lies. *SHRM Online.* www.shrm.org/hrmagazine/articles/1003/1003babcock.asp. Accessed July 21, 2006.

Bachler, C. J. (1995). Resume fraud: Lies, omissions, and exaggerations. *Personnel Journal, 74*(6), 50–60.

Bachrach, P., & Baratz, M. (1970). *Power and poverty.* London: Oxford University Press.

Bailey, D. E., & Kurland, N. B. (2002). A review of telework research: Findings, new directions, and lessons for the study of modern work. *Journal of Organizational Behavior, 23,* 383–400.

Bailyn, L., & Fletcher, J. K., & Kolb, D. (1997). Unexpected connections: Considering employees' personal lives can revitalize your business. *Sloan Management Review, 38,* 11–19.

Barevik, P. (1998, April 19). Manager's maxim. *The Guardian*, p. 1.

Barge, J. K., & Little, M. (2002). Dialogical wisdom, communicative practice, and organizational life. *Communication Theory, 12*(4), 375–397.

Barker, J. R. (1998). Tightening the iron cage: Concertive control in self-managing teams. In J. Van Maanen (Ed.), *Qualitative studies of organizations* (pp. 126–158). Thousand Oaks, CA: Sage.

Barker, J. R., & Tompkins, P. K. (1994). Identification in the self-managing organization: Characteristics of target and tenure. *Human Communication Research, 21*(2), 223–240.

Barley, S. R. (1983). Semiotics and the study of occupational and organizational cultures. *Administrative Science Quarterly, 28*, 393–413.

Barnard, C. I. (1938). *The functions of the executive*. Cambridge, MA: Harvard University Press.

Barnett, G. A. (1997). Organizational communication systems: The traditional perspective. In G. A. Barnett and L. Thayer (Eds.), *Organization-communication: Emerging perspectives V: The renaissance of systems thinking* (pp. 1–46). Greenwich, CT: Ablex Publishing Company.

Baron, R. A. (1996). "La vie en rose" revisited: Contrasting perceptions of informal upward feedback among managers and subordinates. *Management Communication Quarterly, 9*(3), 338–348.

Baron, R. A. (1997). Positive effects of conflict: Insights from social cognition. In C. K. W. DeDreu & E. Van De Vliert (Eds.), *Using conflict in organizations* (pp. 177–191). London: Sage.

Bass, B. M. (1985). *Leadership and performance beyond expectations*. New York: Free Press.

Bass, B. M. (1990). *Bass & Stogdill's handbook of leadership: Theory, research & managerial applications*. New York: Free Press.

Barry, D. (1995). Managing the bossless team: Lessons in distributed leadership. In *Self-managed teams: A special report from Organizational Dynamics* (pp. 53–69). New York: American Management Association.

Bass, B. M., & Avolio, B. J. (1994). Potential biases in leadership measures: How prototypes, leniency, and general satisfaction relate to ratings and rankings of transformational and transactional leadership constructs. *Educational and Psychological Measurement, 49*, 509–527.

Bass, B. M., Avolio, B. J. & Atwater, L. (1996). The transformational and transactional leadership of men and women. *Applied Psychology: An International Review, 45*, 5–34.

Bauer, T. A., & Green, S. G. (1996). Development of leader-member exchange: A longitudinal test. *Academy of Management Journal, 39*(6), 1538–1567.

Baxter, L. A. (1988). A dialectical perspective on communication strategies in relationship development. In S. Duck (Ed.), *Handbook of personal relationships* (pp. 257–273). New York: John Wiley and Sons.

Becker, C. B. (1997). The analysis of organizational culture as a thermodynamic process. In G. Barnett & L. Thayer (Eds.), *A turn of the wheel: The case for a renewal of systems inquiry in organizational communication research* (pp. 121–139). Greenwich, CT: Ablex Publishing Company.

Bennis, W. (2001). Postlude: An intellectual memoir. In W. Bennis, G. M. Spreitzer, & T. G. Cummings (Eds.), *The future of leadership* (pp. 254–280). San Francisco: Jossey-Bass.

Bennis, W., & Nanus, B. (1985). *Leaders: The strategies for taking charge*. New York: AMACOM.

Bennis, W., Spreitzer, G. M., & Cummings, T. G. (Eds.). (2001). *The future of leadership*. San Francisco: Jossey-Bass.

Beranek, P. M., & Martz, B. (2005). Making virtual teams more effective: Improving relational links. *Team Performance Management, 11*(5/6), 200–213.

Berlin-Ray, E. (1993). When links become chains: Considering dysfunctions of supportive communication in the workplace. *Communication Monographs, 60*(1), 106–111.

Bird, J. B. (2003). Herb Kelleher: An entrepreneur for all seasons. *The McCombs School of Business Magazine*, www.mccombs.utexas.edu/news/magazine/03s/Kelleher/asp. Accessed July 21, 2006.

Blake, R., & McCanse, A. A. (1991). *Leadership dilemmas: Grid solutions*. Houston, TX: Gulf Publishing.

Blake, R., & Mouton, J. S. (1964). *The managerial grid*. Houston, TX: Gulf Publishing.

Blake, R., & Mouton, J. S. (1978). *The new managerial grid*. Houston, TX: Gulf Publishing.

Blank, R., & Slipp, S. (2000). *From the outside in: Seven strategies for success when you're not a member of the dominant group in your workplace*. New York: AMACOM.

Blanton, K. (2005, February 18). Above glass ceiling the footing is fragile. *The Boston Globe*, p. D1.

Bleecker, S. E. (1998). The virtual organization. In G. Robinson Hickman (Ed.), *Leading organizations* (pp. 44–49). Thousand Oaks, CA: Sage.

Boden, D. (1994). *The business of talk: Organization in action*. Cambridge, MA: Polity Press.

Boje, D. M. (1991). The storytelling organization: A study of story performance in an office-supply firm. *Administrative Science Quarterly, 36*(1), 106–126.

Bouwman, H. van den Hooff, B., van de Wijngaert, L., & van Dijk, J. (2005). *Information and communication technology in organizations*. Thousand Oaks, CA: Sage.

Brotheridge, C. M., & Grandey, A. A. (2002). Emotional labor and burnout: Comparing two perspectives of "people work." *Journal of Vocational Behavior, 60*, 17–39.

Brown, R. (2000, April 15). Personal communication.

Brown, R. H. (2000). *Corporate Leadership*. Athens, OH: Ohio University Press.

Bryman, A. (1996). Leadership in organizations. In S. R. Clegg, C. Hardy, & W. R. Nord (Eds.), *Handbook of organization studies* (pp. 276–292). Thousand Oaks, CA: Sage.

Bryne, J. A. (1993). The horizontal corporation: It's about managing across, not up and down. *BusinessWeek*, 76–81.

Bulkeley, W. M. (1992, March 10). The videophone era may finally be near, bringing big changes. *Wall Street Journal*, p. 1.

Bullis, C. (1993). Organizational socialization research: Enabling, constraining, and shifting perspectives. *Communication Monographs*, 60(1), 10–17.

Bullis, C. (1999). Mad or bad: A response to Kramer and Miller. *Communication Monographs*, 66(4), 368–373.

Bullis, C. (2005). From productivity servant to foundation to connection. *Management Communication Quarterly*, 18(4), 595–603.

Bullis, C., & Bach, B. (1989). Socialization turning points: An examination of change in organizational identification. *Western Journal of Speech Communication*, 53, 273–293.

Bullis, C., & Stout, K. R. (2000). Organizational socialization: A feminist standpoint approach. In P. M. Buzzanell (Ed.), *Rethinking organizational and managerial communication from feminist perspectives* (pp. 47–75). Thousand Oaks, CA: Sage.

Bullock, H. E., & Morales Waugh, I. (2004). Caregiving around the clock: How women in nursing manage career and family demands. *The Society for the Psychological Study of Social Issues*, 60(4), 767–786.

Burke, K. (1950). *A rhetoric oB Palatino Boldf motives*. Upper Saddle River, NJ: Prentice Hall.

Burns, J. M. (1978). *Leadership*. New York: Harper and Row.

Burns, T., & Stalker, G. M. (1968). *The management of innovation*. London: Tavistock Publications.

Burrell, N. A., Buzzanell, P. M., & McMillan, J. J. (1992). *Management Communication Quarterly*, 6, 115–149.

Buzzanell, P. M. (1994). Gaining a voice: Feminist organizational communication theorizing. *Management Communication Quarterly*, 7(4), 339–383.

Buzzanell, P. M., & Burrell, N. A. (1997). Family and workplace conflict: Examining metaphorical conflict schemas and expressions across context and sex. *Human Communication Research*, 24(1), 109–146.

Cahn, M. M. (1971). Theory Y is no bed of roses. *Training and Development Journal*, August, 21–23.

Calas, M. B., & Smircich, L. (1996). From "the woman's" point of view: Feminist approaches to organization studies. In S. R. Clegg, C. Hardy,

and W. R. Nord (Eds.), *Handbook of organization studies* (pp. 218–257). Thousand Oaks, CA: Sage.

Cangelosi, V. E., & Dill, W. R. (1965). Organizational learning: Observations toward a theory. *Administrative Science Quarterly*, 10(1), 175–203.

Carey, A. (1967). The Hawthorne studies: A radical criticism. *American Sociological Review*, 32(3), 403–416.

Chaleff, A. (2003). *The courageous follower: Standing up to and for our leaders*. San Francisco: Berrett-Koehler.

Chansler, P. A., Swamidass, P. M., & Cammann, C. (2003). Self-managing work teams: An empirical study of group cohesiveness in "natural work groups" at a Harley-Davidson Motor Company plant. *Small Group Research*, 34(1), 101–120.

Chapman, R. L., Kennedy, J. L, Newell, A., & Biel, W. C. (1959). The systems research laboratory's Air Defense experiments. *Management Science*, 5(3), 250–269.

Cheney, G. (1983). On various and changing meanings of organizational membership: A field study of organizational identification. *Communication Monographs*, 50, 342–362.

Cheney, G. (1995). Democracy in the workplace: Theory and practice from the perspective of communication. *Journal of Applied Communication Research*, 23, 167–200.

Cheney, G., & Tompkins, P. K. (1987). Coming to terms with organizational identification and commitment. *Central States Speech Journal*, 38, 1–15.

Chinowsky, P. S., & Rojas, E. M. (2003). Virtual teams: Guide to successful implementation. *Journal of Management in Engineering*, July, 98–108.

Cohen, S. G., & Bailey, D. E. (1997). What makes teams work: Group effectiveness research from the shop floor to the executive suite. *Journal of Management*, 23(3), 239–290.

Cohen, C. F., Birkin, S. J., Cohen, M. E., Garfield, M. J., & Webb, H. W. (2006). Managing conflict during an organizational acquisition. *Conflict Resolution Quarterly*, 12(3), 317–331.

Collins, D. (1998). *Organizational change: Sociological perspectives*. New York: Routledge.

Collins, J. (1996, December 1). The classics. www.inc.com/magazine/19961201/1896.html. Accessed July 21, 2006.

Conrad, C. (1983). Organizational power: Faces and symbolic forms. In L. Putnam and M. Pacanowsky (Eds.), *Communication and organizations: An interpretive approach* (pp. 173–194). Beverly Hills, CA: Sage.

Conrad, C. (1990). *Strategic organizational communication: An integrated perspective* (2nd ed.). Fort Worth, TX: Holt, Rinehart and Winston.

Conrad, C., & Witte, K. (1994). Is emotional expression repression oppression? Myths of organizational affective regulations. In S. Detz, (Ed.),

Communication Yearbook, 17, (pp. 417–428). Newbury Park, CA: Sage.

Cooper, C. (2006, June 15). Leaders & success; IBD's 10 secrets to success. *Investor's Business Daily,* p. A03.

Cooper, C. D., & Kurland, N. B. (2002). Telecommuting, professional isolation, and employee development in public and private organizations. *Journal of Organizational Behavior, 23,* 511–532.

Cote, S. (2005). A social interaction model of the effects of emotion regulation on work strain. *Academy of Management Review, 30*(3), 509–530.

Crane, T. G. (1998). *The heart of coaching.* San Diego, CA: FTA Press.

Daft, R. L., & Lengel, R. H. (1986). Organizational information requirements, media richness and structural design. *Management Science, 32,* 554–571.

Dahl, R. (1957). The concept of power. *Behavioral Science, 2,* 201–205.

Dansereau, F., Graen, G., & Haga, W. J. (1975). A vertical dyadic linkage approach to leadership within formal organizations. *Organizational Behavior and Human Performance, 13,* 46–78.

Dansereau, F., & Markham, S. E. (1987). Superior–subordinate communication: Multiple levels of analysis. In F. M. Jablin, L. L. Putnam, K. H. Roberts, and L. W. Porter (Eds.), *Handbook of organizational communication.* Newbury Park, CA: Sage.

Darling, J. R., & Brownlee, L. J. (1984). Conflict management in the academic institutions. *Texas Tech Journal of Education, 11,* 243–257.

Davies, C., & Rossner, J. (1986). *Processes of discrimination: A study of women working in the NHS.* London: Department of Health and Social Security.

Deal, T. E., & Kennedy, A. A. (1982). *Corporate cultures: The rites and rituals of corporate life.* Reading, MA: Addison-Wesley.

Deetz, S. A. (1982). Critical interpretive research in organizational communication. *Western Journal of Speech Communication, 46,* 131–149.

Deetz, S. A. (1992). *Democracy in an age of corporate colonization.* Albany, NY: State University of New York Press.

Devine, D. J., Clayton, L. D., Philips, J. L., Dunford, P. B., & Melner, S. B. (1999). Teams in organizations: Prevalence, characteristics, and effectiveness. *Small Group Research, 30*(6), 678–711.

DeWine, S. (1994). *The consultant's craft: Improving organizational communication.* New York: St. Martin's Press.

DeWine, S., Gibson, M. K., & Smith, M. J. (2000). *Exploring human communication.* Los Angeles: Roxbury.

Disabled population not a full employment. www.vault.com/nr/printable.jsp?cch_id=402&article_id=51338. Accessed January 8, 2007.

Dixon, N. M. (1998). The responsibilities of members in an organization that is learning. *The Learning Organization, 5*(4), 161–167.

Do your virtual teams deliver only virtual performance? (2005, June 1). *Trainingmag.com.* Accessed July 13, 2006.

Dockery, T. M., & Steiner, D. D. (1990). The role of the initial interaction in leader-member exchange. *Group and Organizational Studies, 15*(4), 395–413.

Donabedian, B., McKinnon, S. M., & Burns, W. J. (1998). Task characteristics, managerial socialization, and media selection. *Management Communication Quarterly, 11*(3), 372–400.

Donaldson, T. (2000, November 13). Survey—mastering management: Adding corporate ethics to the bottom line. *Financial Times (London),* p. 6.

Donkin, R. (1996, May 15). Recruitment: Bringing out the best in Joe DiMaggio. *Financial Times,* p. 30.

Dooney, J. (2006, January). SHRM® human capital measure of the month: New hire quality. www.mittonmedia.com/new%20Hire%20Quality-%20SHRM%Feb%20'06.pdf. Accessed January 7, 2006.

Downs, C. W. (1994). Communication satisfaction questionnaire. In R. B. Rubin, P. Palmgreen, and H. E. Sypher (Eds.), *Communication research measures: A sourcebook.* New York: Guilford Press.

Downs, C. W., Clampitt, P., & Pfeiffer, A. (1988). Communication and organization outcomes. In G. G. G. Barnett (Ed.), *Handbook of organizational communication* (pp. 171–212). Norwood, NJ: Ablex Publishing Co.

Downs, C. W., & Hazen, M. (1977). A factor analytic study of communication satisfaction. *Journal of Business Communication, 14,* 63–73.

Dryden, G., & Vos, J. (1997). *The learning revolution.* Auckland: The Learning Web.

Duarte, D. L., & Tennant Snyder, N. (2006). *Mastering virtual teams* (3rd ed.). San Francisco: Jossey-Bass.

Duncan, W. J., Smeltzer, L. R., & Leap, T. L. (1990). Humor and work: Applications of joking behavior to management. *Journal of Management, 16*(2), 255–278.

Duxbury, L., Higgins, C., & Neufeld, D. (1998). Telework and the balance between work and family: Is telework part of the problem or part of the solution? In M. Igbaria & M. Tan (Eds.), *The virtual workplace* (pp. 218–255). Hershey, PA: Idea Group Publishing.

Eisenberg, E. M. (1984). Ambiguity as a strategy in organizational communication. *Communication Monographs, 51,* 227–242.

Eisenberg, E. M., & Riley, P. (2001). Organizational culture. In F. M. Jablin and L. L. Putnam (Eds.), *The new handbook of organizational communication* (pp. 291–322). Thousand Oaks, CA: Sage.

Ellis, C. (2003). The flattening corporation. *Sloan Management Review,* summer, 5.

Elsass, P. M., & Graves, L. M. (1997). Demographic diversity in decision-making groups: The experiences of women and people of color. *Academy of Management Review, 22*(4), 946–973.

Employment characteristics of families summary

(2006, April 27). www.bls.gov.new.rrelese.famee.nr0.htm. Accessed January 8, 2007.

Ethics Resource Center website. www.ethics.org/nbes/nbes2005/release.html. Accessed May 14, 2006.

Fairhurst, G. T. (1993). The leader-member exchange patterns of women leaders in industry: A discourse analysis. *Communication Monographs, 60*(4), 321–351.

Fairhurst, G. T. (2001). Dualisms in leadership research. In F. M. Jablin and L. L. Putnam (Eds.), *The new handbook of organizational communication* (pp. 379–439). Thousand Oaks, CA: Sage.

Fairhurst, G. T., & Chandler, T. A. (1989). Social structure in leader-member interaction. *Communication Monographs, 56*(3), 215–239.

Fairweather, N. B. (1999). Surveillance in employment: The case of teleworking. *Journal of Business Ethics, 22,* 39–49.

Fayol, H. (1949). *General and industrial management.* London: Sir Isaac Pitman and Sons.

Felstiner, W. L. F., Abel, R. L., & Sarat, A. (1980–81). The emergence and transformation of disputes: Naming, blaming, and changing. *Law & Society Review, 15,* 631–654.

Ferguson, K. (1984). *The feminist case against bureaucracy.* Philadelphia: Temple University Press.

Few U.S. workers who could telecommute do so. (2006, July 12). *PC Magazine,* www.pcmag.com. Accessed July 21, 2006.

Fisher, R. (1994). In theory deter, compel, or negotiate? *Negotiation Journal, 10,* 17–32.

Fine, M. G., & Buzzanell, P. M. (2000). Walking the high wire. In P. Buzzanell (Ed.), *Rethinking organizational and managerial communication from a feminist perspective* (pp. 128–156). Thousand Oaks, CA: Sage.

Fineman, S. (Ed.) (1993). *Emotion in organizations.* London: Sage.

Fiol, C. M. (1994). Consensus, diversity and learning organizations. *Organization Science, 5,* 403–420.

Flanagin, A. J., & Waldeck, J. H. (2004). Technology use and organizational newcomer socialization. *Journal of Business Communication, 41*(2), 137–165.

Ford, L., & Kondrasuk, J. (2002). The quest for productivity: A look at 'the new organization.' www.shrm.org/hrresources/whitepapers_published/CMS_000269.asp. Accessed July 21, 2006.

Foss, S. K., Foss, K. A., & Trapp, R. (1985). *Contemporary perspectives on rhetoric.* Prospect Heights, IL: Waveland Press.

Foss, S. K., & Griffin, C. L. (1995). Beyond persuasion: A proposal for an invitational rhetoric. *Communication Monographs, 62*(1), 2–18.

Franz, C. R., & Jin, K. G. (1995). The structure of group conflict in a collaborative work group during information systems development. *Journal of Applied Communication Research, 23,* 108–127.

Friedman, R. A. (1989). Interaction norms as carriers of organizational culture: A study of labor negotiations at International Harvester. *Journal of Contemporary Ethnography, 18*(1), 3–29.

Frost, P. J. (1987). Power, politics, and influence. In F. M. Jablin, L. L. Putnam, K. H. Roberts, and L. W. Porter (Eds.), *Handbook of organizational communication: An interdisciplinary perspective* (pp. 503–548). Newbury Park, CA: Sage.

Fulk, J., & DeSanctis, G. (1995). Electronic communication and changing organizational forms. *Organizational Science, 6*(4), 337–351.

Gale, E. A. M. (2004). The Hawthorne studies—A fable for our times? *QJM: Monthly Journal of the Association of Physicians, 97*(7), 439–449.

Gannon, M. J. (2001). *Working across cultures.* Thousand Oaks, CA: Sage.

Gardner, W. L. (2003). Perceptions of leader charisma, effectiveness, and integrity. *Management Communication Quarterly, 16*(4), 502–507.

Gardner, W. L., & Cleavenger, D. (1998). The impression management strategies associated with transformational leadership at the world-class level. *Management Communication Quarterly, 12*(1), 3–41.

Garavan, T. (1997). The learning organization: A review and evaluation. *The Learning Organization, 4*(1), 18–29.

Garko, M. G. (1992). Persuading subordinates who communicate in attractive and unattractive styles. *Management Communication Quarterly, 5*(3), 289–315.

Geddes, D. (1993). Examining the dimensionality of performance feedback messages: Source and recipient perceptions of influence attempts. *Communication Studies, 44*(3/4), 200–215.

Geddes, D., & Linnehan, F. (1996). Exploring the dimensionality of positive and negative performance feedback. *Communication Quarterly, 44*(3), 326–344.

Gephart, R. P., Jr. (2002). Introduction to the brave new workplace: Organizational behavior in the electronic age. *Journal of Organizational Behavior, 23,* 327–344.

Gibbons, T. C. (1986). *Revisiting the question of born vs. made: Toward a theory of development of transformational leaders.* Unpublished doctoral dissertation. Fielding Institute.

Gibson, M. K. (1998). The mud, blood, and beer guys: A structurational analysis of organizational power, ideology and discourse in a blue collar work community. Paper presented at the National Communication Association, New York.

Gibson, M. K., & Papa, M. J. (2000). The mud, the blood, and the beer guys: Organizational osmosis in blue-collar work groups. *Journal of Applied Communication Research, 28*(1), 68–88.

Giddens, A. (1979). *Central problems in social theory.* Berkeley, CA: University of California Press.

Gladstein Ancona, D. (1990). Outward bound: Strategies for team survival in an organization. *Academy of Management Journal, 33*(2), 334–365.

Gomolski, B. (2006, February 27). Confessions of a full-time telecommuter. www.computerworld.com. Accessed July 21, 2006.

Goodier, B. C., & Eisenberg, E. M. (2006). Seeking the spirit: Communication and the (re)development of a 'spiritual' organization. *Communication Studies. 57*(1), 47–65.

Gossett, L. M. (2002). Kept at arm's length: Questioning the organizational desirability of member identification. *Communication Monographs, 69*(4), 385–404.

Gouran, D. S., & Hirokawa, R. Y. (1983). The role of communication in decision-making groups: A functional perspective. In M. S. Mander (Ed.), *Communication in transition* (pp. 168–185). New York: Praeger.

Grandey, A. A., & Brauburger, A. L. (2002). The emotion regulation behind the customer service smile. In R. G. Lord, R. J. Klimoski, & R. Kanfer (Eds.), *Emotions in the workplace* (pp. 260–294). San Francisco: Jossey-Bass.

Gray, J., & Laidlaw, H. (2004). Improving the measurement of communication satisfaction. *Management Communication Quarterly, 17*(3), 425–448.

Greengrad, C. (1996). Policy matters. *Personnel Journal, 75*, 78.

Greenhaus, J. H., & Powell, G. N. (2005). When work and family are allies: A theory of work-family enrichment. *Academy of Management Review, 31*(1), 72–92.

Griffeth, R. W., & Hom, P. W. (2001). *Retaining valued employees*. Thousand Oaks, CA: Sage.

Gross, G. (2006, June 19). Government managers resist telecommuting plans. www.computerworld.com. Accessed July 21, 2006.

Gross, J. (1999). Emotion and emotion regulation. In L. A. Pervin & O. P. John (Eds.), *Handbook of personality: Theory and research* (2nd ed.). (pp. 525–552). New York: Guilford Press.

Grossman, H., & Chester, N. (1990). *The experience and meaning of work in women's lives*. Hillsdale, NJ: Erlbaum.

Guzley, R. M. (1992). Organizational climate and communication climate. *Management Communication Quarterly, 5*(4), 379–402.

Hackman, J. R., (Ed.), (1990). *Groups that work (and those that don't)*. San Francisco: Jossey-Bass.

Hafen, S. (2004). Organizational gossip: A revolving door of regulation and resistance. *Southern Communication Journal, 69*(3), 223–240.

Handy, C. (2001). The world of fleas and elephants. In W. Bennis, G. M. Spreitzer, & T. G. Cummings (Eds.), *The future of leadership* (pp. 29–40). San Francisco: Jossey-Bass.

Hatch, M. J. (1997). Irony and the social construction of contradiction in the humor of a management team. *Organization Science, 8*, 275–288.

Heilman, M. E., Block, C. J., & Stathatos, P. (1997). The affirmative action stigma of incompetence: Effects of performance information ambiguity. *Academy of Management Journal, 40*(3), 603–625.

Helgesen, S. (1990). *The female advantage: Women's ways of leadership*. New York: Doubleday.

Hersey, P., & Blanchard, K. H. (1988). *Management of organizational behavior: Utilizing human resources* (5th ed.). Upper Saddle River, NJ: Prentice Hall.

Hickson, D., Astley, W., Butler, R., & Wilson, D. (1981). Organization as power. In L. Cummings and B. Staw (Eds.), *Research in organizational behavior* (pp. 151–196). Greenwich, CT: Aigai Press.

Hill, E. J., Ferris, M., & Martinson, V. (2003). Does it matter where you work? *Journal of Vocational Behavior, 63*, 220–241.

Hinds, P., & Kiesler, S. (1995). Communication across boundaries: Work, structure, and use of communication technologies in a large organization. *Organization Science, 6*(4), 373–395.

Hirokawa, R. Y., Kodama, R. A., & Harper, N. L. (1990). Impact of managerial power on persuasive strategy selection by female and male managers. *Management Communication Quarterly, 4*(1), 30–50.

Hobman, E. V., Bordia, P., & Gallois, C. (2003). Consequences of feeling dissimilar from others in a work team. *Journal of Business and Psychology, 17*(3), 301–307.

Hochschild, A. R. (1989). *The second shift*. New York: Avon Books.

Hochschild, A. R. (1983). *The managed heart*. Berkeley: University of California Press.

Hoffman, M. F. (2002). "Do all things with counsel": Benedictine women and organizational democracy. *Communication Studies, 53*(3), 203–218.

House, R. J. (1977). A 1976 theory of charismatic leadership. In J. G. Hunt & L. L. Larson (Eds.), *Leadership: The cutting edge* (pp. 189–207). Carbondale: Southern Illinois University Press.

House, R. J., & Baetz, M. L. (1979). Leadership: Some empirical generalizations and new research directions. *Research in Organizational Behavior, 1*, 341–423.

Hovick, S. R. A., Meyers, R. A., & Timmerman, C. E. (2003). E-mail communication in workplace romantic relationships. *Communication Studies. 54*(4), 468–482.

HRMS Newsletter (2006, February 15). Many employees have had an office romance. www.hrms.netassets.net/templates/template/asp?articleid=1598&zoneid=15. Accessed July 21, 2006.

Hylmo, A. (2006). Telecommuting and the contestability of choice: Employee strategies to legitimize personal decisions to work in a preferred location. *Management Communication Quarterly, 19*(4), 541–569.

Infante, D. A., & Gorden, W. I. (1987). Superior and subordinate communication profiles: Implications for independent-mindedness and upward effectiveness. *Central States Speech Journal, 38*(2), 73–80.

Infante, D. A., & Gorden, W. I. (1991). How employees see the boss: Test of an argumentative and affirming model of supervisors' communication behaviors. *Western Journal of Speech Communication, 55,* 294–304.

Jablin, F. M. (1979). Superior–subordinate communication: The state of the art. *Psychological Bulletin, 86*(6), 1201–1222.

Jablin, F. M. (1982). Organizational communication: An assimilation approach. In M. E. Roloff and C. R. Berger (Eds.), *Social cognition and communication* (pp. 255–286). Newbury Park, CA: Sage.

Jablin, F. M. (1984). Assimilating new members into organizations. In R. N. Bostrom (Ed.), *Communication Yearbook,* 8. Beverly Hills, CA: Sage.

Jablin, F. M. (1987). Organizational entry, assimilation, and exit. In M. F. Jablin, L. L. Putnam, K. H. Roberts, & L. W. Porter (Eds.), *Handbook of Organizational Communication: An Interdisciplinary perspective* (pp. 679–740). Beverly Hills, CA: Sage.

Jablin, F. M. (1990a). Organizational communication. In G. W. C. G. L. Dahnke (Ed.), *Human communication: Theory and research* (pp. 156–182). Belmont, CA: Wadsworth.

Jablin, F. M. (1990b). Task/work relationships: A life-span perspective. In S. R. Corman, S. P. Banks, C. R. Bantz, and M. E. Mayer (Eds.), *Foundations of organizational communication: A reader* (pp. 171–196). New York: Longman.

Jablin, F. M. (2001). Organizational entry, assimilation, and disengagement/exit. In F. M. Jablin and L. L. Putnam (Eds.), *The new handbook of organizational communication* (pp. 732–818). Thousand Oaks, CA: Sage.

Jacobson, C. M. (1981). *The development and evaluation of a self-report instrument to measure leader effectiveness.* Unpublished Doctoral Dissertation, Ohio University, Athens, Ohio.

Janis, I. (1972). *Victims of groupthink.* Boston: Houghton Mifflin.

Jayson, S. (2006, February 9). Workplace romance no longer gets the kiss-off. *USA Today.* p. 9D

Jehn, K. A. (1995). A multimethod examination of the benefits and detriments of intragroup conflict. *Administrative Science Quarterly, 40*(2), 256–282.

Jehn, K. A. (1997). A qualitative analysis of conflict types and dimensions of organizational groups. *Administrative Science Quarterly, 42,* 530–557.

Jobs more flexible, data show (2006, May 5). *Los Angeles Times,* Part C, p. 3.

Johannesen, R. L. (1996). *Ethics in human communication* (4th ed). Prospect Heights, IL: Waveland Press.

Johnson, C. (1994). Gender, legitimate authority, and leader–subordinate conversations. *American Sociological Review, 59,* 122–135.

Johnson, G. M. (1992). Subordinate perceptions of superior's communication competence and task

attraction related to superior's use of compliance-gaining tactics. *Western Journal of Communication, 56,* 54–67.

Jones, R. G. (2006, July 8). Trenton showdown ended, but shutdown lingers on. *The New York Times,* p. 4.

Jones, S. R. G. (1990). Worker interdependence and output: The Hawthorne Studies reevaluated. *American Sociological Review, 55*(2), 176–190.

Kanter, R. (1977). *Men and Women of the Corporation.* New York: Basic Books.

Kanter, R. M. (1997). *Frontiers of management.* Boston, MA: Harvard Business School Press.

Kark, R., & Gan, R. (2004). The transformational leader: Who is (s)he? A feminist perspective. *Journal of Organizational Change, 17*(2), 160–176.

Karl, K. A., & Sutton, C. L. (2000). An examination of the perceived fairness of workplace romance policies. *Journal of Business and Psychology, 14*(3), 429–438.

Katz, D., & Kahn, R. L. (1978). *The social psychology of organizations* (2nd ed.). New York: John Wiley and Sons.

Katzenbach, J. R., & Smith, D. K. (1993). *The wisdom of teams.* Boston, MA: Harvard Business School Press.

Kauffeld, S. (2006). Self-directed work group and team competence. *Journal of Occupational and Organizational Psychology, 79,* 1–21.

Keyton, J. (1999). Analyzing interaction patterns in dysfunctional teams. *Small Group Research, 30*(4). 364–392.

Keyton, J. (2000). The relationship side of groups—Introduction. *Small Group Research, 31*(4), 387–396.

Keyton, J. (2005). *Communication and organizational culture.* Thousand Oaks, CA: Sage.

Kim, S. (1998). Toward understanding family leave policy in public organizations: Family leave use and conceptual framework for the family leave implementation process. *Public Productivity and Management Review, 22,* 71–87.

Kim, Y. Y., & Miller, K. (1990). The effects of attributions and feedback goals on the generation of supervisory feedback message strategies. *Management Communication Quarterly, 4*(1), 6–29.

Kirby, E. L., Golden, A. G., Medved, C. E., Jorgenson, J., & Buzzanell, P. M. (2003). An organizational communication challenge to the discourse of work and family research: From problematics to empowerment. *Communication Yearbook (27),* 1–43.

Kirby, E. L., & Krone, K. J. (2000). "The policy exists but you can't really use it": Communication and the Structuration of Work-Family Policies. *Journal of Applied Communication Research, 30*(1), 50–77.

Knott, K. B., & Natalle, E. J. (1997). Sex differences, organizational level, and supervisors' evaluation of managerial leadership. *Management Communication Quarterly, 10*(4), 523–540.

Koermer, C., Goldstein, M., & Fortson, D. (1993). How supervisors communicatively convey immediacy to subordinates: An exploratory qualitative investigation. *Communication Quarterly, 41*(3), 269–281.

Kotter, J. P. (1982). *The general managers.* NY: Free Press.

Kouzes, J. M., & Posner, B. Z. (2001). Bringing leadership lessons from the past into the future. In W. Bennis, G. M. Spreitzer, & T. G. Cummings (Eds.), *The future of leadership* (pp. 81–96). San Francisco: Jossey-Bass.

Kram, K. E., & Isabella, L. A. (1985). Mentoring alternatives: The role of peer relationships in career development. *Academy of Management Journal, 28*(1), 110–132.

Kramer, M. W., & Berman, J. E. (2001). Making sense of a university's culture: An examination of undergraduate students' stories. *Southern Communication Journal, 66*(4), 297–311.

Kramer, M. W., & Hess, J. A. (2002). Communication rules for the display of emotions in organizational settings. *Management Communication Quarterly, 16*(1), 66–80.

Kramer, M. W., & Miller, V. D. (1999). A response to criticisms of organizational socialization research: In support of contemporary conceptualizations of organizational assimilation. *Communication Monographs, 64*(4), 358–367.

Kreps, G. L. (1990). *Organizational communication,* (2nd ed.) New York: Longman.

Kroman Myers, K., & Oetzel, J. G. (2003). Exploring the dimensions of organizational assimilation: Creating and validating a measure. *Communication Quarterly, 51*(4), 438–457.

Krone, K. J. (1991). Effects of leader-member exchange on subordinates' upward influence attempts. *Communication Research Reports, 8,* 9–18.

Krone, K. J. (1994). Structuring constraints on perceptions of upward influence and supervisory relationships. *Southern Communication Journal, 59*(3), 215–226.

Kunigis, A. (1997). Ten steps for communicators to boost diversity. *Communication World,* April–May, 11–12.

Kusztal, I. L. (2002). Discourses in the use and emergence of organizational conflict. *Conflict Resolution Quarterly, 20* (2), 231–247.

The labor movement to war. Workforce Management (2001, January). www.workforce.com/section /00/feature/23/10/75/231169.html. Accessed July 21, 2006.

Lack of a clear policy can be messy (2006, April 1). *USA Today Magazine.* www.usatodaymagazine .net. Accessed July 21, 2006.

Lamude, K. G., & Daniels, T. D. (1990). Mutual evaluations of communication competence in superior-subordinate relationships: Sex role incongruency and pro-male bias. *Women's Studies in Communication, 13*(2), 39–56.

Lamude, K. G., Daniels, T. D., & Graham, E. E. (1988). The paradoxical influence of sex on communication rules co-orientation and communication satisfaction in superior–subordinate relationships. *Western Journal of Speech Communication, 52,* 122–134.

Lamude, K. G., Scudder, J., Simmons, D., & Torres, P. (2004). Organizational newcomers: Temporary and regular employees, same-sex and mixed-sex superior–subordinate dyads, supervisor influence techniques, subordinates' communication satisfaction, and leader-member exchange. *Communication Research Reports, 21*(1), 60–67.

Landsberger, H. A. (1958). *Hawthorne revisited.* Ithaca, NY: Cornell University Press.

Landmark disability survey finds pervasive disadvantages (2004, June 24). www.necfoundation .org/pressreleases/oressreleses_show.htm?doc_i d=230504. Accessed January 7, 2007.

Lane, N. (2000). The management implications of women's employment disadvantage in a female-dominated profession: a study of NHS nursing. *Journal of Management Studies, 37,* 705–731.

Larson, G. S., & Tompkins, P. K. (2005). Ambivalence and resistance: A study of management in a concertive control system. *Communication Monographs, 72*(1), 1–21.

Lawler, E. E., Mohrman, S. B., & Ledford, G. E. (1995). *Creating high performance organizations.* San Francisco: Jossey-Bass.

Lawrence, P. R., & Lorsch, J. W. (1969). *Developing organizations: Diagnosis and action.* Reading, MA: Addison-Wesley.

Lee, J., & Jablin, F. M. (1995). Maintenance communication in superior–subordinate work relationships. *Human Communication Research, 22*(2), 220–257.

Lengel, R. H., & Daft, R. L. (1988). The selection of communication media as an executive skill. *Academy of Management Executive. 2*(3), 225–232.

Leonard, D. A., Brands, P. A., Edmondson, A., & Fenwick, J. (1998). Virtual teams: Using communication technology to manage geographically dispersed development groups. In S. P. Bradley & B. L. Nolan (Eds.), *Sense & Respond* (pp. 285–298). Boston, MA: Harvard Business School Press.

Lien, M. (2004). Workforce diversity: Opportunities in the melting pot. *Occupational Outlook Quarterly, 48*(2), 28–37.

Likert, R. (1961). *New patterns of management.* New York: McGraw-Hill.

Likert, R. (1967). *The human organization.* New York: McGraw-Hill.

Lincoln, J. R., & Miller, J. (1979). Work and friendship ties in organizations: A comparative analysis of relational networks. *Administrative Science Quarterly, 24,* 181–199.

Lipman-Blumen, J. (2001). Why do we tolerate bad leaders? Magnificent uncertitde, anxiety, and meaning. In W. Bennis, G. M. Spreitzer, & T. G.

Cummings (Eds.), *The future of leadership*, (pp. 125–138). San Francisco: Jossey-Bass.

Lipnack, J., & Stamps, J. (1997). *Virtual teams: Reaching across space, time, and organizations with technology*. New York: John Wiley & Sons.

Locke, E. A. (1976). The nature and causes of job satisfaction. In M. D. Dunnette (Ed.), *Handbook of industrial and organizational psychology* (pp. 1297–1346). Chicago: Rand McNally.

Louis, M. R. (1980). Surprise and sense making: What newcomers experience in entering unfamiliar organizational settings. *Administrative Science Quarterly, 25*, 226–251.

Lukes, S. (1974). *Power: A radical view*. London: MacMillan Press.

Lundberg, C. C., & Brownell, J. (1993). The implications of organizational learning for organizational communication: A review and reformulation. *The International Journal of Organizational Analysis, 1*(1), 29–53.

Luthans, F., Rosenkrantz, S. A., & Hennesslely, H. W. (1985). What do successful managers really do? An observation study of managerial activity. *Journal of Applied Behavioral Science, 21*, 255–270.

Manz, C. C., & Sims, H. P., Jr. (1987). Leading workers to lead themselves: The external leadership of self-managing work teams. *Administrative Science Quarterly, 32*, 106–128.

Marshak, R. J. (1998). A discourse on discourse: Redeeming the meaning of talk. In D. Grant, T. Keenoy, and C. Oswick (Eds.), *Discourse and organization* (pp. 15–30). Thousand Oaks, CA: Sage.

Martin, J. (1992). *Cultures in organizations: Three perspectives*. Oxford: Oxford University Press.

Martin, J. (2000). Hidden gendered assumptions in mainstream organizational theory and research. *Journal of Management Inquiry, 9*(2), 207–216.

Martin, J. (2002). *Organizational culture: Mapping the terrain*. Thousand Oaks, CA: Sage.

Martin, D. M., Rich, C. O., & Gayle, B. M. (2004). Humor works: Communication style and humor functions in manager/subordinate relationships. *Southern Communication Journal, 69*(3), 206–222.

Mattson, M., & Buzzanell, P. M. (1999). Traditional and feminist organizational communication ethical analyses of messages and issues surrounding an actual job loss case. *Journal of Applied Communication Research, 27*, 49–72.

Mayer, A. M. (1995). *Feminism-in-practice: Implications for feminist theory*. Paper presented at the annual conference of the International Communication Association in Albuquerque, New Mexico.

McGregor, D. ([1960] 1985). *The human side of enterprise* (2nd ed.). Boston: McGraw-Hill.

McGregor, D. (2002). Theory X and Theory Y. *Workforce, 81*(1), 32.

McKinney, E. H., Jr., Barker, J. R., Davis, K. J., & Smith, D. (2005). How swift-starting action teams get off the ground. *Management Communication Quarterly, 19*(2), 198–237.

McMillan, J. J., & Northern, N. A. (1995). Organizational codependency: The creation and maintenance of closed systems. *Management Communication Quarterly, 9*(1), 6–45.

McMurrer, D. P., Van Buren, M. E., & Woodwell, W. H. (2000). *The 2000 ASTD state of the industry report*. Alexandria, VA: American Society for Training and Development.

McPhee, R. D. (2004). Clegg and Giddens on power and (post)modernity. Management *Communication Quarterly, 18*(1), 129–145.

Meiners, E. B. (2004). Time pressure: An unexamined issue in organizational newcomers' role development. *Communication Research Reports, 21*(3), 243–251.

Merging cultures (1999, August 11). *Journal of Commerce*, p. 5.

Meyer, M. H., & DeTore, A. (1999). Product development for services. *Academy of Management Executive, 13*(3), 64–76.

Meyerson, D. E., & Fletcher, J. K. (2000). A modest manifesto for shattering the glass ceiling. *Harvard Business Review*, 127–136.

Michener, J. (1978). *Chesapeake*. New York: Random House.

Miles, R. E. (1965). Human relations or human resources? *Harvard Business Review, 43*, 148–163.

Miller, V. D. (1996). An experimental study of newcomers' information seeking behaviors during organizational entry. *Communication Studies, 47* (spring–summer), 1–24.

Miller, V. D., & Jablin, F. M. (1991). Newcomers' information-seeking behaviors during organizational entry: Influence, tactics, and a model of the process. *Academy of Management Review, 16*, 92–120.

Misconceptions about hiring workers with disabilities linger among nation's employers—demonstrating need for policies to promote understand, opportunity. (2002, March 27). Press release. www.heidrich.rutgers.edu. Accessed January 8, 2007.

Modaff, J., & Hopper, R. (1984). Why speech is "basic." *Communication Education, 33*, 37–42.

Montgomery, B. M., & Baxter, L. A. (1998). *Dialectical approaches to studying personal relationships*. Mahwah, NJ: Lawrence Erlbaum Associates.

Morgan, G. (1997). *Images of organization* (2nd ed.). Newbury Park, CA: Sage

Morgan, J. M., Reynolds, C. M., Nelson, T. J., Johanningmeier, A. R., Griffin, M., & Andrade, P. (2004). Tales from the fields: Sources of employee identification in agribusiness. *Management Communication Quarterly, 17*(3), 360–395.

Morgan, B. B., Jr., & Bowers, C. A. (1995). Teamwork stress: Implications for team decision making. In R. A. Guzzo, E. Salas, and Associates (Eds.), *Team effectiveness and decision making in organizations* (pp. 262–290). San Francisco: Jossey-Bass.

Morgan, S. (1994). Personalizing personnel decisions

in feminist organizational theory and practice. *Human Relations, 47*, 665–684.

Morrill, C., & Thomas, C. K. (1992). Organizational conflict management as disputing process: The problem of social escalation. *Human Communication Research, 18*(3), 400–428.

Morris, J. A., & Feldman, D. C. (1996). The dimensions, antecedents, and consequences of emotional labor. *Academy of Management Review, 21*(4), 986–1010.

Mumby, D. K. (1988). *Communication and power in organizations: Discourse, ideology, and domination.* Norwood, NJ: Ablex Publishing Co.

Mumby, D. K. (2000). Common ground from the critical perspective: Overcoming binary oppositions. In S. Corman & M. Poole (Eds.), *Perspectives on organizational communication* (pp. 68–86). New York: Guilford Press.

Mumby, D., & Stohl, C. (1996a). Disciplining organizational communication studies. *Management Communication Quarterly, 10*(4), 50–73.

Mumby, D., & Stohl, C. (1996b). Organizational communication. *Management Communication Quarterly, 10*(1).

Myths and facts about workers with disabilities. www.doleta.gov/disabilaity/htmldocs .myths.cfm. Accessed January 8, 2007.

Natalle, E. J., Papa, M. J., & Graham, E. E. (1994). Feminist philosophy and the transformation of organizational communication. In B. Kovacic (Ed.), *New approaches to organizational communication.* Albany: State University of New York Press.

Navarro, M. (2005, July 24). Love the Job? What about your boss? *New York Times*, p. 1.

Neuhauser, D. C., Bender, R., & Stromberg, K. L. (2000). *Culture.com.* New York: John Wiley & Sons.

Nicotera, A. M. (1994). The use of multiple approaches to conflict: A study of sequences. *Communication Research, 20*(4), 592–621.

Nilles, J. M. (1998). *Managing telework.* New York: John Wiley and Sons.

Noe, J. M. (1995). *A communication rules perspective of emotional expression: An ethnography of impression management in an emergency medical services facility.* Unpublished doctoral dissertation, University of Kansas, Lawrence.

Northouse, P. G. (2001). *Leadership: Theory and practice* (2nd ed.). Thousand Oaks, CA: Sage.

Norton, R. (1983). *Communicator style: Theory, applications, and measures.* Beverly Hills, CA: Sage.

O'Kane, P., Hargie, O., & Tourish, D. (2004). Communication without frontiers: The impact of technology upon organizations. In D. Tourish & O. Hargie (Eds.), *Key issues in organizational communication* (pp. 74–95). New York: Routledge.

Orlikowski, W. J. (1992). The duality of technology: Rethinking the concept of technology in organizations. *Organization Science, 3*(3), 398–427.

Orsburn, J. D., & Moran, L. (2000). *The new self-directed work teams* (2nd ed.). New York: McGraw-Hill.

Orton, J. D., & Weick, K. E. (1990). Loosely coupled systems: A reconceptualization. *Academy of Management Review, 15*(2), 203–223.

Owens, J. (1992). A reappraisal of leadership theory and training. In K. L. Hutchinson (Ed.), *Readings in organizational communication* (pp. 252–265). Dubuque, IA: William C. Brown.

Pacanowsky, M. E., & O'Donnell-Trujillo, N. (1990). Communication and organizational cultures. In S. R. Corman, S. P. Banks, C. R. Bantz, & M. E. Mayer (Eds.), *Foundations of organizational communication: A reader* (pp. 142–153). New York: Longman.

Paine, L. S. (1994). Managing for organizational integrity. *Harvard Business Review*, March–April, 106–117.

Papa, M. J., Auwal, M. A., & Singhal, A. (1997). Organizing for social change within concertive control systems: Member identification, empowerment, and the masking of discipline. *Communication Monographs, 64*(3), 219–249.

Parker, P. S. (2003). Learning leadership: Communication, resistance, and African-American women's executive leadership development. Unpublished doctoral dissertation. University of Texas, Austin.

Pelz, D. (1952). Influence: A key to effective leadership. *Personnel, 29*, 209–217.

Pepper, G. L., & Larson, G. S. (2006). Cultural identity tensions in a post-acquisition organization. *Journal of Applied Communication Research, 34*(1), 49–71.

Peters, T. J., Waterman, R. H., Jr. (1982). *In search of excellence: Lessons from America's best-run companies.* New York: Warner Books.

Peterson, D. R. (1983). Conflict. In H. H. Kelley, (Ed.), *Close relationships,* (pp. 366–367). New York: W. H. Freeman.

Pettigrew, A. M. (1979). On studying organizational cultures. *Administrative Science Quarterly, 24*, 570–581.

Phillips, J. M. (1998). Effects of realistic job previews on multiple organizational outcomes: A meta-analysis. *Academy of Management Journal, 41*(6), 673–690.

Pincus, J. D. (1986). Communication satisfaction, job satisfaction, and job performance. *Human Communication Research, 12*(3), 395–419.

Pinnington, A. (2004). Organizational culture: Liberation or entrapment? In D. Tourish & O. Hargie (Eds.), *Key issues in organizational communication* (pp. 205–219). New York: Routledge.

Pizer, M. K., & Härtel, C. E. (2005). For better or for worse: Organizational culture and emotions. In C. Härtel, W. Zerbe, & N. Ashkanasy (Eds.), *Emotions in organizational behavior* (pp. 335–354). Mahwah, NJ: Lawrence Earlbaum.

Poole, M. S. (1997). A turn of the wheel: The case for a

renewal of systems inquiry in organizational communication research. In G. A. Barnett and L. Thayer (Eds.), *Organization-communication: Emerging perspectives V: The renaissance of systems thinking* (pp. 47–63). Greenwich, CT: Ablex Publishing Co.

Preliminary findings: 2004 national sample survey of registered nurses. www.bhpr.hrsa.gov/heath workforce/reports/rnpopulation/preliminary findings.htm. Accessed January 8, 2007.

Pugh, S. D. (2002). Emotional regulation in individuals and dyads: Causes, costs, and consequences. In R. G. Lord, R. J. Klimoski, & R. Kanfer (Eds.), *Emotions in the workplace* (pp. 147–182). San Francisco: Jossey-Bass.

Putnam, L. L. (1986). Contradictions and paradoxes in organization. In L. Thayer (Ed.), *Organizational communication: Emerging perspectives* (pp. 151–167). Norwood, NJ: Ablex.

Putnam, L. L. (1992). Rethinking the nature of groups in organizations. In R. S. C. L. A. Samovar, (Ed.), *Small group communication: A reader* (6th ed.) (pp. 57–66). Dubuque, IA: William C. Brown.

Putnam, L. L., & Cheney, G. (1992). Organizational communication: Historical developments and future directions. In K. L. Hutchinson (Ed.), *Readings in organizational communication* (pp. 70–89). Dubuque, IA: William. C. Brown.

Putnam, L. L., Phillips, N., & Chapman, P. (1996). Metaphors of communication and organization. In C. H. S. Clegg and W. Nord (Eds.), *Handbook of organizational studies* (pp. 375–408). Thousand Oaks, CA: Sage.

Putnam, L. L., & Poole, M. S. (1987). Conflict and negotiation. In M. F, Jablin, L. L. Putnam, K. H. Roberts, and L. W. Porter (Eds.), *Handbook of organizational communication: An interdisciplinary perspective* (pp. 549–599). Beverly Hills, CA: Sage.

Raelin, J. A. (2003). *Creating leaderful organizations: How to bring out leadership in everyone.* San Francisco: Berrett-Koehler.

Rafaeli, A., & Sutton, R. I. (1989). The expression of emotion in organizational life. *Research in Organizational Behavior, 11*, 1–42.

Rahim, M. A. (2001). Managing organizational conflict: Challenges for organization development and change. In R. T. Golembiewski (Ed.), *Handbook of Organizational Behavior* (2nd ed.). (pp. 365–387). New York: Marcel Dekker.

Rahim, M. A., Garrett, J. E., & Buntzman, G. F. (1992). Ethics of managing interpersonal conflict in organizations. *Journal of Business Ethics, 11*, 87–96.

Rawlins, W. K. (1993). *Friendship matters: Communication, dialectics, and the life course.* New York: Aldine de Gruyter.

Reardon, K. K., & Reardon, K. J. (1999). "All that we can be": Leading the U.S. Army's gender integration effort. *Management Communication Quarterly, 12*(4), 600–617.

Redding, W. C. (1978). *Communication within the organization.* New York: Industrial Communication Council.

Redding, W. C. (1984). Professionalism in training: Guidelines for a code of ethics. Paper presented at the Speech Communication Association, Chicago.

Redding, W. C., & Tompkins, P. K. (1988). Organizational communication: Past and present tenses. In G. M. Goldhaber and G. A. Barnett (Eds.), *Handbook of organizational communication* (pp. 5–33). Norwood, NJ: Ablex Publishing Co.

Redefining management in the knowledge era. *Financial Times Information* (2005, September 27). www.lexis-nexus.com. Accessed July 21, 2006.

Regian, J. W., Shebilske, W. L., & Monk, J. M. (1992). Virtual reality: An instructional medium for visual-spatial tasks. *Journal of Communication, 42*(4), 136–149.

Rice, R. E. (1987). Computer-mediated communication and organizational innovation. *Journal of Communication, 37*(4), 65–94.

Rice, R. E., Chang, S., & Torobin, J. (1992). Communicator style, media use, organizational level, and use and evaluation of electronic messaging. *Management Communication Quarterly, 6*(1), 3–33.

Rice, R. E., & Gattiker, U. E. (2001). New media and organizational structuring. In F. M. Jablin & L. L. Putnam (Eds.), *The new handbook of organizational communication* (pp. 544–581). Thousand Oaks, CA: Sage.

Rice, R. W., Frone, M. R., & McFarlin, D. B. (1992). Work–nonwork conflict and the perceived quality of life. *Journal of Organizational Behavior, 13*, 155–168.

Richards, I. A. (1936). *The philosophy of rhetoric.* London: Oxford University Press.

Richmond, V. P., & McCroskey, J. C. (2000). The impact of supervisor and subordinate immediacy on relational and organizational outcomes. *Communication Monographs, 67*(1), 85–95.

Richtel, M. (2000, February 6). Online revolutions latest twist: Job interviews with a computer. *The New York Times,* p. 1.

Rizzo, B. J., Wanzer, M. B., & Booth-Butterfield, M. (1999). Individual differences in managers' use of humor: Subordinate perceptions of managers' humor. *Communication Research Reports, 16*(4), 360–369.

Roethlisberger, F. J., & Dickson, W. J. (1939). *Management and the worker.* Cambridge, MA: Harvard University Press.

Ross, R., & DeWine, S. (1988). Assessing the Ross–DeWine conflict management message style. *Management Communication Quarterly, 1*(3), 389–413.

Ross-Smith, A. & Kornberger, M. (2004). Gendered rationality? A genealogical exploration of the philosophical and sociological conceptions of rationality, masculinity, and organization. *Gender, Work, and Organization, 11*(3), 280–305.

Russell, R. (1997). Workplace democracy and organizational communication. *Communication Studies, 48*(4), 279–284.

Sackmann, S. (1991). *Cultural knowledge in organizations: Exploring the collective mind*. Newbury Park, CA: Sage.

Saks, A. M., & Ashforth, B. E. (1997). Organizational socialization: Making sense of the past and present as a prologue for the future. *Journal of Vocational Behavior, 51*, 234–279.

Sample, S. B. (2002). *The contrarian's guide to leadership*. San Francisco: Jossey-Bass.

Sandberg, J. C. (1999). The effects of family obligations and workplace resources on men's and women's use of family leaves. In T. L. Parcel (Ed.), *Research in the sociology of work: Work and family*. Stamford, CT: JAI Press.

Sanders, K., & Nauta, A. (2004). Social cohesiveness and absenteeism: The relationship between characteristics of employees and short-term absenteeism within an organization. *Small Group Research, 35*(6), 724–741.

Sashkin, M., & Sashkin, M. G. (2003). *Leadership that matters*. San Francisco: Berrett-Koehler.

Sathe, V. (1983). Implications of corporate culture: A manager's guide to action. *Organizational Dynamics, autumn*, 5–23.

Schein, E. (1985). *Organizational culture and leadership*. San Francisco: Jossey-Bass.

Schein, E. H. (1990). Organizational culture. *American Psychologist, 45*(2), 109–119.

Scholosser, F. K. (2002). So, how do people really use their handheld devices? An interactive study of wireless technology use. *Journal of Organizational Behavior, 23*, 401–423.

Schnake, M. E., Dumler, M. P., Cochran, D. S., & Barnett, T. R. (1990). Effects of differences in superior and subordinate perceptions of supervisors' communication practices. *Journal of Business Communication, 27*(1), 37–50.

Schutz, W. C. (1966). *The interpersonal underworld: A three dimensional theory of interpersonal behavior*. Palo Alto, CA: Science and Behavior Books.

Schwartz, H., & Davis, S. M. (1981). Matching corporate culture and business strategy. *Organizational Dynamics, summer*, 30–48.

Schweiger, D., Sandberg, W., & Ragan, J. W. (1986). Group approaches for improving strategic decision making: A comparative analysis of dialectical inquiry, devil's advocacy, and consensus approaches to strategic decision making. *Academy of Management Journal, 19*, 51–71.

Scott, C. R., Corman, S. R., & Cheney, G. (1998). Development of a structurational model of identification in the organization. *Communication Theory, 8*(3), 298–336.

Scott, C., & Myers, K. K. (2005). The socialization of emotion: Learning emotion management at the fire station. *Journal of Applied Communication, 33*(1), 67–92.

Seminiero, M. (1999, August 11). E-mail firings: A sign of the times? http://news.zdnet.com/2100-9595_22-515388.html. Accessed January 16, 2007.

Senge, P. M. (1990). *The fifth discipline: The art and practice of the learning organization*. New York: Doubleday.

Senge, P. M. (1998). The leader's new work: Building learning organizations. In G. R. Hickman (Ed.), *Leading organizations: Perspectives for a new era* (pp. 439–457). Thousand Oaks, CA: Sage.

Senge, P., Kleiner, A., Roberts, C., Ross, R., Roth, G., & Smith, B. (1999). *The dance of change: The challenges to sustaining momentum in learning organizations*. New York: Doubleday.

Shell, R. L. (2003). *Management of professionals* (2nd ed.). New York: Marcel Dekker, Inc.

Sherriton, J., & Stern, J. L. (1997). *Corporate culture/team culture*. New York: AMACOM.

Shonk, J. H. (1992). *Team-based organizations*. Homewood, IL: Business One Irwin.

SHRM human capital benchmarking study (2005, June 7). www.shrm.org/research/benchmarks/execsumm.asp. Accessed July 21, 2006.

Shuler, S., & Sypher, B. D. (2000). Seeking emotional labor: When managing the heart enhances the work experience. *Management Communication Quarterly, 14*, 751–789.

Shuter, R., & Turner, L. H. (1997). African American and European American women in the workplace. *Western Journal of Speech Communication, 47*(2), 138–156.

Sias, P. M. (2005). Workplace relationship quality and employee information experiences. *Communication Studies, 56*(4), 375–395.

Sias, P. M., & Cahill, D. J. (1998). From coworkers to friends: The development of peer friendships in the workplace. *Western Journal of Communication, 62*(3), 273–299.

Sias, P. M., Heath, R. G., Perry, T., Silva, D., & Fix, B. (2004). Narratives of workplace friendship deterioration. *Journal of Social and Personal Relationships, 21*(3), 321–340.

Sias, P. M., & Jablin, F. M. (1995). Differential superior–subordinate relations, perceptions of fairness, and coworker communication. *Human Communication Research, 22*(1), 5–38.

Silverstein, S. (1999, November 21). Down to a science: Management has evolved from bossing people around to an enlightened approach. *Los Angeles Times*, p. 22.

Smircich, L. (1983). Concepts of culture and organizational analysis. *Administrative Science Quarterly, 28*, 339–358.

Smith, R. C., & Eisenberg, E. (1987). Conflict at Disneyland: A root-metaphor analysis. *Communication Monographs, 54*, 367–380.

Soloman, D. H., & Williams, M. L. M. (1997). Perceptions of social-sexual communication at work: The effects of message, situation, and observer characteristics on judgments of sexual harassment. *Journal of Applied Communication, 25,* 196–216.

Sonnenfeld, J. (1983). Academic learning, worker learning, and the Hawthorne Studies. *Social Forces, 61*(3), 904–909.

Sorenson, P. S., Hawkins, K., & Sorenson, R. (1995). Gender, psychological type and conflict style preference. *Management Communication Quarterly, 9*(1), 115–126.

Sosik, J. J., & Jung, D. I. (2003). Impression management strategies and performance in informational technology consulting. *Management Communication Quarterly, 17*(2), 233–268.

Soule, E. (2002). Managerial moral strategies—In search of a few good principles. *Academy of Management Review, 27*(1), 114–124.

Spreizer, G. M., & Cummings, T. G. (2001). The leadership challenges of the next generation. In W. Bennis, G. M. Spreitzer, & T. G. Cummings (Eds.), *The future of leadership* (pp. 241–253). San Francisco: Jossey-Bass.

Stanford Business School study finds virtual teammates fear their own obsolescence (2004, July 19). www.businesswire.com. Accessed July 17, 2006.

Staw, B. M., Sutton R. I., & Pelled, L. H. (1994). Employee positive emotion and favorable outcomes at the workplace. *Organizational Science, 5,* 51–71.

Steiner, I. (1972). *Group process and productivity.* New York: Academic Press.

Steinfield, C. (1992). Computer-mediated communications in organizational settings: Emerging conceptual frameworks and directions for research. *Management Communication Quarterly, 5*(3), 348–365.

Stewart, T. A. (2001). Trust me on this: Organizational support for trust in a world without hierarchies. In W. Bennis, G. M. Spreitzer, & T. G. Cummings (Eds.), *The future of leadership* (pp. 67–80). San Francisco: Jossey-Bass.

Stogdill, R. M. (1974). *Handbook of leadership: A survey of theory and research.* New York: The Free Press.

Stohl, C. (1995). *Organizational communication: Connectedness in action.* Thousand Oaks, CA: Sage.

Stohl, C., & Redding, W. C. (1987). Messages and message exchange processes. In F. E. Jablin, L. L. Putnam, K. H. Roberts, and L. W. Porter (Eds.), *Handbook of organizational communication: An interdisciplinary perspective* (pp. 451–502). Newbury Park, CA: Sage.

Stohl, C., & Schell, S. E. (1991). A communication-based model of a small-group dysfunction. *Management Communication Quarterly, 5,* 90–110.

Sutton, R. I. (1991). Maintaining norms about expressed emotions: The case of bill collectors. *Administrative Science Quarterly, 36,* 245–268.

Tannen, D. (1990). *You just don't understand: Men and women in conversation.* New York: William Morrow.

Tapping human potential to enhance performance. (1996). *Inc., December,* p. 55.

Taylor, F. W. ([1911] 1998). *The principles of scientific management.* Minneola, NY: Dover Publications.

Taylor, J. (1998). *A survival guide for project managers.* New York: AMACOM.

Taylor, J. R. (1995). Shifting from a heteronomous to an autonomous worldview of organizational communication: Communication theory on the cusp. *Communication Theory, 5*(1), 1–35.

Taylor, J. R. (2001). The "rational" organization reconsidered: An exploration of some of the implications of self-organizing. *Communication Theory, 11*(2), 137–177.

Taylor, P., & Bain, P. (1999). 'An assembly line in the head': Work and employee relations in the call centre. *Industrial Relations Journal, 30*(2), 101–117.

Terkel, S. (1997). *Working: People talk about what they do all day and how they feel about what they do.* New York: New Press.

Teven, J. J., McCroskey, J. C., & Richmond, V. P. (2006). Communication correlates of perceived Machiavellianism of supervisor: Communication orientations and outcomes. *Communication Quarterly, 54*(2), 127–142.

Thomas, P., Pinto, J. K., Parente, D. H., & Urch Druskat, V. (2002). Adaptation to self-managing work teams. *Small Group Research, 33*(1), 3–31.

Tjosvold, D., Dann, V., & Wong, C. (1992). Managing conflict between departments to serve customers. *Human Relations, 45*(10), 325–337.

Tompkins, P. K., & Cheney, G. (1985). Communication and unobtrusive control in contemporary organizations. In R. D. McPhee & P. K. Tompkins (Eds.), *Organizational communication: Traditional themes and new directions* (pp. 179–210). Newbury Park, CA: Sage.

Tortoriello, T. R., Blatt, S. J., & DeWine, S. (1978). *Communication in the organization: An applied approach.* New York: McGraw-Hill.

Toossi, M. (2002, May). A century of change: The U.S. labor force, 1950–2050. *Monthly Labor Review, 125,* 15–28.

Tracy, S. J. (2000). Becoming a character for commerce: Emotion labor, self-subordination, and discursive construction of identity in a total institution. *Management Communication Quarterly, 14,* 90–128.

Trethewey, A. (1999). Isn't it ironic: Using irony to explore the contradictions of organizational life. *Western Journal of Communication, 63,* 140–167.

Trice, H. M., & Beyer, J. M. (1984). Studying organizational cultures through rites and rituals. *Academy of Management Review, 9*(4), 653–669.

Turner, P. K. (1999). What if you don't? A response to Kramer and Miller. *Communication Monographs, 66*(4), 382–389.

2000 electronic monitoring & surveillance survey (2005, May 18). www.amanet.org/PRESS/amanews/ems-5.htm. Accessed Janaury17, 2007.

Urwick, L., & Brech, E. F. L. (1949). *The making of scientific management*. London: Management Publications Trust.

Vangelisti, A. L. (1988). Adolescent socialization into the workplace: A synthesis and critique of current literature. *Youth and Society, 19*(4), 460–484.

Van Maanen, J., & Kunda, G. (1989). Real feelings: Emotional Expression and organizational culture. In L. L. Cummings & B. M. Staw (Eds.), *Research in organizational behavior* (pp. 388–416). Greenwich, CT: JAI Press.

Van Maanen, J. V., & Schein, E. H. (1979). Toward a theory of organizational socialization. *Research in Organizational Behavior, 1*, 209–264.

Van Slyke, E. J. (1999). *Listening to conflict: Finding constructive solutions to workplace disputes*. New York: AMACOM.

Vardi, Y. (2001). The effects of organizational and ethical climates on misconduct at work. *Journal of Business Ethics, 29*(4), 325–337.

von Bertalanffy, L. (1968). *General system theory: Foundations, developments, applications*. New York: George Braziller.

Wageman, R. (1997). Critical success factors for creating superb self-managing teams. *Organizational Dynamics, summer*, 49–60.

Wagoner, R., & Waldron, V. R. (1999). How supervisors convey routine bad news: Facework at UPS. *Southern Communication Journal, 64*(3), 193–210.

Waldeck, J. H., Seibold, D. R., & Flanagin, A. J. (2004). Organizational assimilation and communication technology use. *Communication Monographs, 71*(2), 161–183.

Waldron, V. R. (1991). Achieving communication goals in superior–subordinate relationships: The multifunctionality of upward maintenance tactics. *Communication Monographs, 58*(3), 289–306.

Waldron, V. R. (2000). Relational experiences and emotion at work. In S. Fineman (Ed.), *Emotions in organizations* (2nd ed.) (pp. 64–82). Thousand Oaks, CA: Sage.

Wall, J. A., Jr., & Nolan, L. L. (1986). Perceptions of inequity, satisfaction, and conflict in task in task-oriented groups. *Human Relations, 39*, 1033–1052.

Walton, R. E., & McKersie, R. B. (1965). *A behavioral theory of labor negotiations: An analysis of a social interaction system*. New York: McGraw-Hill.

Wanous, J. P. (1973). Effects of a realistic job preview on job acceptance, job attitudes, and job survival. *Journal of Applied Psychology, 58*, 327–332.

Wanous, J. P. (1992). *Organizational entry: Recruitment, selection, orientation, and socialization of newcomers* (2nd ed.). Reading, MA: Addison-Wesley.

Warters, W. C. (2000). *Mediation in the campus community: Designing and managing effective programs*. San Francisco: Jossey-Bass.

Watzlawick, P., Beavin, J., & Jackson, D. D. (1967). *Pragmatics of human communication*. New York: W. W. Norton.

Weaver, G. R., Trevino, L. K., & Cochran, P. L. (1999). Corporate ethics programs as control systems: Influences of executive commitment and environmental factors. *Academy of Management Journal, 42*(1), 41–57.

Weber, M. (1947). *The theory of social and economic organization*. Translated by A. M. Henderson and T. Parsons, T. Parsons (Ed.), New York: Free Press.

Weick, K. E. (1976). Educational organizations as loosely coupled systems. *Administrative Science Quarterly, 21*, 1–19.

Weick, K. E. (1979). *The social psychology of organizing* (2nd ed). Reading, MA: Addison-Wesley.

Weick, K. E. (1987). Theorizing about organizational communication. In F. M. Jablin, L. L. Putnam, K. H. Roberts, and L. W. Porter (Eds.), *Handbook of organizational communication: An interdisciplinary perspective* (pp. 97–122). Newbury Park, CA: Sage.

Weick, K. E. (2001). Leadership as the legitimization of doubt. In W. Bennis, G. M. Spreitzer, & T. G. Cummings (Eds.), *The future of leadership* (pp. 81–96). San Francisco: Jossey-Bass.

Weick, K. E., & Ashford, S. J. (2001). Learning in organizations. In F. M. Jablin and L. L. Putnam (Eds.), *The new handbook of organizational communication* (pp. 704–731). Thousand Oaks, CA: Sage.

Weitz, J. (1956). Job expectancy and survival. *Journal of Applied Psychology, 40*, 245–247.

Wharton, A. (1999). The psychosocial consequences of emotional labor. *Annals of the American Academy of Political and Social Science, 561*, 158–176.

Wharton, A. (1993). The affective consequences of service work: Managing emotions on the job. *Work and Occupation, 20*, 205–232.

Wheatley, M. J. (1994). *Leadership and the new science: Learning about organization from an orderly universe*. San Francisco: Berrett-Koehler.

White, L. P., & Lam, L. W. (2000). A proposed infrastructural model for the establishment of organizational ethical systems. *Journal of Business Ethics, 28*, 35–42.

Whitener, E. M., Brodt, S. E., Korsgaard, M. A., & Werner, J. M. (1998). Managers as initiators of trust: An exchange relationship framework for understanding managerial trustworthy behavior. *Academy of Management Review, 23*(3), 513–530.

Whitteman, H. (1992). Analyzing interpersonal conflict: Nature of awareness, type of initiating event, situational perceptions, and management styles. *Western Journal of Communication, 58* (summer), 248–280.

Wiener, N. (1954). *The human use of human beings: Cybernetics and society*. Garden City, NY: Doubleday Anchor.

Wiener, Y. (1988). Forms of value systems: A focus on organizational effectiveness and cultural changes and maintenance. *Academy of Management Review, 13,* 534–545.

Wiesenfeld, B. M., Raghuram, S., & Garud, R. (1999). Communication patterns as determinants of organizational identification in virtual organizations. *Organizational Science, 10*(6), 777–790.

Wiseman, V., & Poitras, J. (2002). Mediation within a hierarchical structure: How can it be done successfully. *Conflict Resolution Quarterly, 20*(1), 51–65.

Witherspoon, P. D., & Wohlert, K. L. (1996). An approach to developing communication strategies for enhancing diversity. *Journal of Business Communication, 33,* 375–399.

Witmer, D. F. (1997). Communication and recovery: Structuration as an ontological approach to organizational culture. *Communication Monographs, 64*(4), 324–349.

Wood, J. T. (1998). *But I thought you meant . . . : Misunderstandings in human communication.* Mountain View, CA: Mayfield.

Wooden, J. (2005). *Wooden on leadership.* New York: McGraw-Hill.

Woodward, J. (1965). *Industrial organization: Theory and practice.* London: Oxford University Press.

Wright, B. M., & Barker, J. R. (2000). Assessing concertive control in the team environment. *Journal of Occupational and Organizational Psychology, 73,* 345–361.

INDEX

Action-over-talk, 115–116
Active listening, 128
Adaptive (single-loop) learning, 84
Adaptive subsystems, 78
Administrative theory (Fayol's), 25, 31–37
    elements of, 34–35
    in modern workplace, 35–37
    principles of, 31–34
    Scalar Chain and, 32–33, 35
    versus Taylorism, 35
Advanced communication and information technologies (ACITs), 157
Affective conflict, 179–180
Affirmative action, 12–13
African Americans, 10, 11–12
Americans with Disabilities Act, 10, 293
Anticipatory socialization, 155–156
Antisocial communication techniques, 205
Applicants, misrepresentation of skills by, 134, 135–137
Arbitration, 191–192
Artifacts, 100–101
Asians, 10, 11
Assimilation, 154–160
    anticipatory socialization, 155–156
    criticisms of, 160
    encounter (entry) phase, 156–158
    metamorphosis phase, 158–159
    socialization vs., 155, 160
Asynchronous communication, 283
Attributed charisma, 267
Authority, 31, 51–52
Authority-compliance management style, 64

Bank Wiring Room Observation Study, 47, 48
Bargaining, 190
Barnard, Charles, 49–53, 122
Behavioral flexibility, 129
Benchmarking, 30
Benevolent authoritative management system, 61
Blake, Robert, 63–66
Boundary spanners, 77
Boundary, system, 73, 79
Bounded emotionality, 111
Bureaucracy, Weber's theory of, 37–40

Call centers, 29–30
Cell phones, 283
Centralization, administrative theory and, 32
Centralized organizational structure, 82
Charisma, 266
Charismatic leadership, 265–266
Classical theories of organizations, 23–40
    Fayol's administrative theory, 25, 31–37
    goals of, 24–25
    machine metaphor and, 24
    Taylor's theory of scientific management, 25, 26–30
    Weber's theory of bureaucracy, 25, 37–40
Closed systems, 72, 79–80
CO model. See Communicative organization (CO) model
Coaching, 8–9
Codependency, 80, 228
Codes of ethics, 16
Cohesiveness, team, 242–243
Collective socialization processes, 164–165
Collegial peer relationships, 223
Communication satisfaction, 20–21
Communication technology, 281–299
    accessibility of, 291
    critical theory and, 298–299
    e-mail, 285, 286–287
    employee monitoring, 296–297
    extranets, 285
    information and communication technology (ICT), 282–283
    instant messaging, 285, 287
    Internet, 285
    intranets, 285
    media richness of, 290
    most appropriate for situation, 289–292
    social presence and, 289–290
    structuration theory and, 297–298
    transformation of messages by, 282–283
    videoconferencing, 285, 287–288
    virtual reality, 285, 288–289
    virtual work and, 292–296
    voice mail, 284–285
Communicative construction, 95

Communicative organization (CO) model, 114–133
    action-over-talk and, 115–116
    anticipating misunderstandings, 122–127
    assumptions behind, 114–115
    learning organization and, 114
    Marshak's typology of language and, 115–116
    realistic recruitment and, 146–147
    social interactions and, 127–129
    socialization of new employees and, 153–154
    strategic communication planning and, 129–133
    structuration theory and, 117–121
Competition, 9
Complexity, organizational learning and, 85
Compliance-gaining techniques, 212–213, 216
Computer Based Performance Monitoring (CBPM), 296
Concertive control, 107–108
Conflict. See Organizational conflict
Conflict management, 188–190
    arbitration, 191–192
    bargaining, 190
    individual-level strategies for, 192–193
    mediation, 191–192
    negotiation, 190–191
    organization-level strategies for, 193–194
    strengthening work relationships through, 235
Conflict resolution, 188
Congruency, socialization and, 161–163
Consultative management system, 61–62
Contingency theory, 81–82, 292
Contingent rewards, 266
Cooperation, 49
Cost-per-hire, 140
Countercultures, organizational, 95, 96
Country club management style, 64–65
Coworker relationships. See Workplace relationships
Creative tension, 85
Critical-mass theory, 292
Critical theory, 103–112

communication and, 108–109
communication technology and, 297–298
concertive control and, 107–108
feminist organizational theory and, 110–112
goal of humane workplace, 109–110
hegemony and, 106–107
organizations as site of domination, 103–104
power and, 104–106
Criticisms, conflict and, 180–181
Cultural lens, 89–90
Cultural networks, 93
Culture, 89. *See also* Organizational culture
organizational conflict and, 187–188
strong organizational, 93
subcultures, 11, 91, 95–96
workplace diversity and, 11
Cumulative annoyances, conflict and, 180

Deep acting, 169–170
Democratic workplace, 109–110
Dialectical tensions, 129
Dickson, William, 44
Disabilities, workers with, 10
Discipline, administrative theory and, 31
Discomfort stress, 83
Discursive consciousness, 118
Disjunctive socialization processes, 167
Disjunctive stress, 83
Dispute resolution
arbitrators, 191–192
bargaining, 190
conflict management, 188–190
conflict resolution, 188
individual-level strategies for, 192–193
mediation, 191–192
negotiation, 190–191
organization-level strategies for, 193–194
Distributive bargaining, 190
Diversity
cultural differences and conflict styles, 187–188
increasing in the workplace, 9–11
team composition and, 243–244
workplace discrimination and, 12–13
Divestiture socialization processes, 167
Domination, critical theory and, 103–104

Dynamic homeostasis, systems theory and, 76

E-mail, 283, 285, 286–287
monitoring of employee, 296–297
social presence and, 289
Emotion regulation, 169–170
Emotional dissonance, 171, 173
Emotional labor, 171–174
Emotions, 169–174
amplification of, 170
emotional dissonance, 171
emotional labor and, 171–174
professional vs. unprofessional, 170
regulation of, 169–170
suppression of, 170
Employee monitoring, 296–297
Employees
providing feedback to, 209–211
relationships between. *See* Peer relationships
seeking of feedback by, 211–212
superior-subordinate communication and. *See* Superior-subordinate communication
Empowerment, 9
Encounter phase, assimilation and, 156–158
Entropy, 73
Environment, connecting team to, 248–249
Environmental uncertainty, contingency theory and, 82
Equifinality, 73
Equivocality, 76–77
Ethics
leadership and, 277–279
organizational communication and, 13–18
Ethics programs, 15–16
Ethnicity, workplace diversity and, 10
Exchange assessment, 128–129
Executive leadership development, 268
Exemplification, 271
Exploitative authoritarian management system, 60–61
External rewards, 244
Extranets, 286

Fayol, Henri, 25, 31–37
Fayol's bridge, 32–33
Feedback, 209–212
immediacy of, 208
negative, 210–211
providing to subordinate, 209–211
seeking of by subordinate, 211–212

strengthening work relationships through, 234–235
systems theory and, 75–76
timely, 128
Feminist leadership theory, 268–270
Feminist organizational theory, 110–112
Fixed socialization processes, 166
Formal organizations, 49
Formal socialization processes, 165
Frame-talk, 116, 117
Frankfurt School, 103
Friendships, workplace. *See also* Peer relationships
deterioration of, 233–234
development of, 223–226
negative consequences of, 228
positive consequences of, 226–227

Gender
conflict style and, 187–188
feminist leadership theory, 268–270
feminist organizational theory, 110–112
glass ceiling and, 174, 215
percentage of women in U.S. workforce, 10
superior-subordinate communication and, 215–216
General system theory. *See* Systems theory
Generative (double-loop) learning, 84
Glass ceiling, 174, 215
Global positioning systems (GPS), 283

Hawthorne Effect, 47
Hawthorne Studies, 44–48
Bank Wiring Room Observation Study, 47, 48
criticisms of, 48
Illumination Study, 44–45, 47
implications of for management theory, 47–48
Interviewing Program, 46–47, 48
Relay Assembly Test Room Study, 45–46, 47, 48
Hegemony, 106–107
Heroes, 92–93
Hispanics, 10, 11
Human relations theory, 42–53
Barnard's Function of the Executive, 49–53
failures of, 57–60
focus on individual workers by, 43–44

Human relations theory, *continued*
Hawthorne Studies and, 44–48
human resources theory vs., 59
Human resources theory, 59–66
Blake and Mouton's Managerial
Grid, 63–66
human relations theory vs., 59
Likert's four systems of manage-
ment, 59–63
Humane workplace, 109–110
Humanistic theories of organiza-
tions, 42–66
human relations theory, 42–53,
58–59
human resources theory, 59–66
McGregor's Theory X, 53–54
McGregor's Theory Y, 53, 55–57
Humor, 213–214

Ideal speech situation, 108–109
Idealized influence, 267
Ideology, critical theory and,
106–107
Illegitimate demands, conflict and,
180
Illumination Study, 44–45, 47
Immediacy, 127–128, 208
Impoverished management style,
65
Impression management, leadership and, 270–271
In-group (LMX) relationships,
203–206
Individual conflict styles, 184–188
Individual socialization processes,
165
Individualized consideration, 267
Individual's interest, subordination
of, 31
Informal organizations, 49–50
Informal socialization processes,
166
Information
flow of and contingency theory,
82
lack of and misunderstandings,
125–127
Information and communication
technology (ICT), 282–283
consequences of use of, 283–284
drivers of adoption, 283
transformation of messages by,
282–283
Information-peer relationships, 223
Information technology, 282. *See
also* Communication technology
Informing leadership strategy, 249
Inputs, systems theory and, 75

Inspirational motivation, 267
Instant messaging, 285, 287
Integrative bargaining, 190
Integrative negotiation, 190–191
Intellectual stimulation, 267
Interdepartmental conflict, 180
Intergroup conflict, 180
Internal conflicts, organizational
learning and, 85
Internal rewards, 244
Internet, 285–286
Interpersonal conflict, 180
Interpersonal needs, 221–222
Interpersonal relationships
interpersonal needs and, 221–222
nature of in organization,
218–223
organizational, 219
personal, 219
proxemics and, 220
relational balance and, 221
relational control and, 222–223
Interrelated systems, 72
Interviewing Program, 46–47, 48
Intimidation, 271
Intradepartmental conflict, 180
Intranets, 286
Investiture socialization processes,
167

Job satisfaction, 20

Laissez-faire leader, 262
Language, Marshak's typology of,
116–117
Leader-member exchange (LMX)
relationships, 203–206
Leader-Member Exchange (LMX)
theory, 203–206, 214–215
Leaderful organization, 267–268
Leadership, 258–280
communicator style and, 271–273
impression management and,
270–271
overview of, 259–261
passion and, 279–280
power and ethics and, 277–279
responsibilities of, 274–277
situational approach to, 262–265
teams and, 239–240
trait approach to, 261–262
trust-building and, 273–274
Leadership as serving, 269
Leadership (Managerial) Grid,
63–66
Leadership strategies
for connecting team with environment, 249
informing strategy, 249

parading strategy, 249
probing strategy, 249
Leadership theories, 261–270
charismatic leadership, 265–266
executive leadership development, 268
feminist perspectives on, 268–
270
situational approach to, 262–265
trait approach to leadership,
261–262
transactional and transformational leadership, 266–268
Learning organization, 82–86, 1
14
Liberal feminists, 110–111
Likert, Rensis, 59–63, 74
Linguistic boundaries, systems theory and, 79
LMX Theory. *See* Leader-Member
Exchange (LMX) theory
Loyalty-congruency socialization
process, 161–163

Machiavellianism, 207
Machines, organizations as, 24
Maintenance communication,
204–205
Maintenance inputs, systems the-
ory and, 75
Maintenance subsystems, systems
theory and, 78
Management
Fayol's elements of, 34–35
Fayol's principles of, 31–34
Taylorism and, 27
Management teams, 248
Managerial Grid, Blake and Mou-
ton's, 63–66
Managerial subsystems, 78
Marx, Karl, 103
Materialist feminists, 111
Mayo, Elton, 44
McGregor, Douglas, 53–57
Mechanistic systems, 81
Media richness, 290
Mediation, 191–192
Messages, 3
Metacommunication, 235
Metamorphosis, assimilation and,
158–159
Middle-group relationships,
203–206
Misunderstandings
classical theorists attempts to
minimize, 24–25
communicative organization
(CO) model and, 122–127
from conflicting values, 124–125

human relations theory and, 43–44, 58–59
from lack of information, 125–127
organizational communication and, 115
organizational culture and, 90–91
organizational teams and, 255–257
prevalence of in organizations, 5–7
strategic, 127
superior-subordinate communication and, 199–203
systems theory view of, 68–70
Mommy track, 174
Mouton, Jane, 63–66
Movable offices, 224–225
Mythopoetic talk, 116

Negative entropy, 73
Negative feedback, 76, 210–211, 212
Negotiation, 190–191
New organization members
socialization of. *See* Socialization
superior-subordinate communication and, 199
Nonsummativity, 73
Norms, team, 241–242

Open-system theory, 72–74
boundaries and, 79
characteristics of organizations as systems, 74–80
equivocality and, 76
feedback and, 75–76
homeostasis and, 76
input-throughput-output, 75
principles of, 72–74
requisite variety and, 77
role of communication, 77
subsystems and, 77–79
supersystems and, 78
Open systems, 72
Organic systems, 81
"Organism" metaphor, 70–71
Organizational anticipatory socialization, 156
Organizational assimilation, 154–160
anticipatory socialization, 155–156
criticisms of, 160
encounter (entry) phase, 156–158
metamorphosis phase, 158–159
Organizational communication
assumptions and features of, 3
Barnard's *Function of the Executive* and, 49–51
centrality of to organization, 115

communication satisfaction and, 20–21
critical theory and, 108–109
defining study and practice of, 2–3
ethics and, 13–18
Fayol's Scalar Chain model of, 32–34
human relations theory and, 43–44
ideal speech situation and, 108–109
job satisfaction and, 20
misunderstandings and, 5–7, 115
organizational identification and, 18–20
research activities, 4–5
systems theory and, 77
Organizational conflict, 177–194
affective, 179–180
cultural differences and, 187–188
definitions of, 179–180
events resulting in, 180–182
factors increasing likelihood of, 181–182
factors influencing outcome of, 189–190
individual conflict styles and, 184–188
individual-level strategies for, 192–193
interpersonal, 180
intradepartmental, 180
intragroup, 180
negative consequences of, 182–183
organization-level strategies for, 193–194
organizational responses to, 188–192
positive consequences of, 184
resolution or management of, 188–190
substantive, 179–180
Organizational culture theory, 88–103
countercultures, 95, 96
culture as lens for viewing organization, 89–90
culture-as-root metaphor perspective, 93–97
culture-as-variable perspective, 91–93
definitions of organizational culture, 97–100
as lens for viewing organization, 89–90

misunderstandings and, 90–91
Schein's model of organizational culture, 100–103
subcultures, 91, 95–96
Organizational ethics, 13–18
Organizational identification, 18–20
Organizational interpersonal relationships, 219. *See also* Workplace relationships
Organizational socialization, 160–169
factors affecting, 161–163
socialization processes, 163–169
Organizational teams. *See* Teams
Organizational theories
communicative organization (CO) model. *See* Communicative organization (CO) model
critical theory, 103–112
Fayol's administrative theory, 31–37
feminist organizational theory, 110–112
human relations theory, 42–57
human resources theory, 57–66
Leader-Member Exchange (LMX) theory, 203–206, 214–215
learning organization, 82–86
Likert's four systems of management, 59–63
machine metaphor and, 24
Manergial Grid, Blake and Mouton's, 63–66
organizational culture theory, 88–103
systems theory and, 68–86
Taylor's theory of scientific management, 26–30
Theory X, 53–54
Theory Y, 54–57
Weber's theory of bureaucracy, 37–40
Organizations
changing nature of, 8–9
characteristics of as systems, 74–80
classical theories of, 23–40
flat, 8
hierarchical, 8
humanistic theories of, 42–66
misrepresentation of positions by, 134, 137–138
span of control and, 8
Out-group (SX) relationships, LMX theory and, 203–206
Output, system, 75

Parading leadership strategy, 249
Parallel teams, 248

Participative decision making (PDM), 8
Participative management system, 62–63
Passion, leadership and, 279–280
Peer relationships
 deterioration of, 233–234
 development of in workplace, 223–226
 nature of interpersonal relationships and, 218–223
 negative consequences of, 228
 positive consequences of, 226–227
 romantic relationships, 228–233
 strengthening of, 234–237
Pelz effect, 214
Perceptual congruence, 200
Perceptual incongruence, 199–200
Performance stress, 83
Personal digital assistants (PDAs), 283
Personal relationships, 219. *See also* Workplace relationships
Physical boundaries, 79
Piecework system of remuneration, 26
Positive feedback, 75–76, 234–235
Power
 critical theory and, 104–106
 leadership and, 277–279
Practical consciousness, 118
Primary provoker, 240
Probing leadership strategy, 249
Production inputs, systems theory and, 75
Production (technical) subsystems, 78
Professionalism, emotion regulation and, 170
Project teams, 248. *See also* Teams
Prosocial communication techniques, 205
Proxemics, 220
Psychological boundaries, 79
Psychological immediacy, 127–128

Radical feminism, 111, 269
Random socialization processes, 166
Realistic job previews (RJPs), 141–146
 medium used for, 142–146, 147
 time of administration of, 146
Realistic recruitment, 135, 141–147
Rebuffs, conflict and, 180
Recruitment, 134–147
 applicants' misrepresentation of cultural preferences, 137

applicants' misrepresentation of skills, 134, 135–137
 cost-per-hire, 140
 costs of methods resulting in high turnover, 138–141
 organizations' misrepresentation of position, 134, 137–138
 realistic, 135, 141–147
 realistic job previews (RJPs), 141–146
 traditional, 135, 137–138
Relational balance, 221
Relational communication, 220–221
Relational control, 222–223
Relative openness, 73
Relay Assembly Test Room Study, 45–46, 47, 48
Relevant environment, 72
Remuneration
 Fayol's administrative theory and, 31, 31–32
 Taylorism and, 27, 30
Requisite variety, systems theory and, 77
Resume fraud, 136
Rich media, 290
Richards, I. A., 122–123
Rites and rituals, 93
RJP. *See* Realistic job previews (RJPs)
Roethlisberger, F. J., 44
Role boundary, 164
Romances, workplace, 228–233
Rule-of-thumb training methods, 26, 27
Rules, Weber's theory of bureaucracy and, 39–40

Scalar Chain, 32–33, 35, 36
Scanlon Plan, 55–56
Second principle of thermodynamics, 73
Secondary provoker, 240
Self-directed work teams. *See* Self-managed work teams (SMWTs)
Self-managed work teams (SMWTs), 250–252
 benefits of, 250
 inappropriate situations for, 250–251
 leadership roles in, 251
 success factors, 251–252
 versus traditional teams, 250
Self-promotion, 271
Semantic-information distance, 199–200
Sequential socialization processes, 166

Serial socialization processes, 166–167
Serving, leadership as, 269
Sexual harassment, 229, 232
Situational approach to leadership, 262–265
SMWTs. *See* Self-managed work teams (SMWTs)
Social interactions, CO model and, 127–129
Social presence, 289–290
Socialization, 149–176
 accurate cultural and task information, 150–155
 assimilation vs., 155, 160
 "buying in" vs. "selling out," 152–153
 emotions and, 169–174
 organizational assimilation, 154–160
 organizational socialization and, 160–169
 work-family challenges, 174–176
Socialization processes, 163–169
 collective, 164–165
 disjunctive, 167
 divestiture, 167
 fixed, 166
 formal, 165
 individual, 165
 informal, 166
 investiture, 167
 random, 166
 sequential, 166
 serial, 166–167
 variable, 166
Special peer relationships, 223
Strategic ambiguity, 201–203
Strategic communication planning, 129–133
 components of, 130–131
 construct new interpretation of problem, 130–131
 containment of problem, 130
 as a continuum, 130
 coping with problem, 130
 goal of, 131–133
Strategic misunderstandings, 127
Stress, 83, 245–246
Strong cultures, 92–93
Structuration theory, 117–121, 297–298
Subcultures, 11, 91, 95–96
Substantive conflict, 179–180
Subsystems, 72, 77–79
Superior-subordinate communication, 196–216
 compliance-gaining, 212–213, 216

coworker relationships and, 225–226
defined, 198
feedback, giving and receiving, 209–212
forms of, 198–199
gender and, 215–216
humor and, 213–214
immediacy and, 208
importance of acceptable, 199
Leader-Member Exchange (LMX) theory and, 203–206, 214–215
misunderstandings and, 199–203
semantic-information distance and, 199–200
strategic ambiguity and, 201–203
trust and, 206–207, 273–274
upward distortion and, 200–201
upward influence by subordinates, 214–215
workplace relationships and, 230–231
workplace romances, 230–231
Supersystems, 77, 78
Supervisor-subordinate communication. *See* Superior-subordinate communication
Supervisory exchange (SX) relationships, 203–206
Supplication, 271
Supportive subsystems, 78
Surface acting, 170
Synchronous communication, 283
Synergy, 73
Systematic soldiering, 26
Systems
  characteristics of organizations as, 74–80
  closed, 72, 79–80
  defined, 72, 77
  mechanistic, 81
  open, 72, 74–79
  organic, 81
Systems theory, 68–86
  characteristics of organizations as systems, 74–80
  closed systems, 79–80
  contingency theory and, 81–82
  insight into communication offered by, 71
  the learning organization and, 82–86
  open-systems theory principles, 72–74
  "organism" metaphor, 70–71, 72
  study of misunderstandings through, 68–70

Talk as action thesis, 116–117
Taylor, Frederick, 25, 26–30
Taylorism, 25, 26–30
Team-based organizations, 247–248
Team-building, 274–276
Team management style, 65–66
Teams, 238–257
  acceptance of common goals, 256–257
  benefits of, 238
  characteristics of effective, 254–255
  cohesiveness of, 242–243
  connecting with environment, 248–249
  decision-making process, 241
  definitions of, 238–239, 255
  diversity and, 243–244
  dysfunctional, 240–241, 254
  increased use of by organizations, 246–247
  interdependence and, 256
  management teams, 248
  misunderstandings and, 255–257
  norms of, 241–242
  parallel teams, 248
  project teams, 248
  relational communication in, 239–241
  rewards for accomplishments of, 244–245
  self-managed work teams (SMWTs), 250–252
  size of, 239, 255–256
  stress and, 245–246
  stuckness and, 246
  team-based organizations and, 247–248
  team member's satisfaction with work of, 244–245
  virtual, 252–254
  work teams, 248
Technical (production) subsystems, 78
Technology. *See* Communication technology
Telecommunications, 282. *See also* Communication technology
Telecommuting, 224, 293–296
Telework, 224, 293–296
Theory of bureaucracy (Weber's), 25, 37–40
  in modern workplace, 39–40
  tenets of bureaucracy, 38–39
  types of legitimate authority, 37–38
Theory of scientific management (Taylor's), 25, 26–30
  elements of, 27–28

versus Fayol's administrative theory, 35
in modern workplace, 29–30
systematic soldiering and, 26
Theory of structuration. *See* Structuration theory
Theory X, 53–54
Theory Y, 53, 55–57
Throughput, system, 75
Time and motion studies, 27
Tool-talk, 116–117
Total Quality Management (TQM), 236
Traditional recruitment, 135, 137–138
  evaluation of based on ethical principles, 139–140
  financial costs from high turnover due to, 140–141
  human costs from high turnover due to, 138–140
  organizations' misrepresentation of position, 134, 137–138
  potential ramifications of, 138
Trait approach to leadership, 261–262
Traits, leadership, 261–262
Transactional leadership, 266
Transformation model, 75
Transformational leadership, 266–268
Trust, 206–207, 273–274
Turnover
  financial costs from high, 140–141
  human costs from high, 138–140

Unity of command, 31
Unity of direction, 31
Upward distortion, 200–201
Upward influence, 214–215

Values
  communicative organization (CO) model and, 124–125
  Schein's model of organizational culture and, 101–102
  strong organizational culture and, 92
Variable socialization processes, 166
VDL Theory. *See* Leader-Member Exchange (LMX) theory
Verbal realistic job previews (RJPs), 145–146, 147
Vertical Dyadic Linkage (VDL) Theory. *See* Leader-Member Exchange (LMX) theory
Video, realistic job previews (RJPs), 143–144

Videoconferencing, 283, 285, 287–288
Videostreaming, 285, 288
Vigilant interaction theory, 241
Virtual reality, 285, 288–289
Virtual teams, 252–254
Virtual work, 292–296
Vocational anticipatory socialization, 155
Voice, 215
Voice mail, 284–285
von Bertalanffy, Ludwig, 70–74

Weber, Max, 25, 37–40
Women
    feminist leadership theory and, 268–270
    feminist organizational theory and, 110–112

glass ceiling and, 174, 215
percentage of U.S. workforce, 10
superior-subordinate communication and, 215–216
Work-family balance, 174–176, 294–296
Work teams, 248
Workaholism, 295
Workplace democracy, 109–110
Workplace relationships
    collegial peer relationships, 223
    deterioration of, 233–234
    development of, 223–226
    information-peer relationships, 223
    nature of interpersonal relationships and, 218–223

negative consequences of, 228
positive consequences of, 226–227
romantic relationships, 228–233
special peer relationships, 223
strengthening of, 234–237
superior-subordinate communication and, 225–226
Workplace romances, 228–233
organizational policies on, 231–233
between superior-subordinate, 230–231
Written realistic job previews (RJPs), 144–145

Zone of indifference, 52–53